An All-C P9-DUB-728

GARY CROSS

An All-Consuming Century

Why Commercialism Won in Modern America

COLUMBIA UNIVERSITY PRESS   NEW YORK

COLUMBIA UNIVERSITY PRESS
Publishers Since 1893
New York   Chichester, West Sussex
Copyright © 2000 Columbia University Press
All rights reserved
Library of Congress Cataloging-in-Publication Data

Frontispiece: This car of 1939 promised everything new, from an automatic transmission and a plastic dashboard to streamlining at its best, "airflow styling" (*Collier's,* Oct. 22, 1938, p. 30).

Cross, Gary S.
   An all-consuming century : why commercialism won in modern America / Gary Cross.
       p.   cm.
   Includes index.
   ISBN 0–231–11312–9 (cloth)
   ISBN 0–231–11313–7 (paper)
       1. Consumer protection — United States.   2. Consumers — United States.   I. Title.
HC110.C6 C76 2000
306.3'0973'0904 — dc21   99–087282

♾

Columbia University Press books are printed on permanent and durable acid-free paper.
Printed in the United States of America
Designed by Lisa Hamm
c 10 9 8 7 6 5 4 3
p 10 9 8 7 6 5 4 3

CONTENTS

Preface

To write a book about consumer goods in the twentieth-century United States is to write about a lot. Inevitably, this book has a personal perspective that focuses an otherwise immense topic. It probably reflects more than I might wish of my lifestyle as a male professional with a family living in a small college town far from the coasts. I certainly come to this topic as a historian who has devoted most of his professional life to the study of the first half of that century and whose personal life has straddled the second half. I have long believed that an understanding of the twentieth century must include, but go beyond, the world wars and their impact. In years ahead, we may conclude that one of the most important facts of the century is the astonishing creation of private, yet relatively widely distributed, wealth in the Western world. Past ages have built monuments to empire and the fortuitous blessings of nature, serving mostly tiny elites and surviving today as pyramids, forums, cathedrals, and palaces. The twentieth century in the United States has produced very different things in quantities and varieties never before seen. This has been an age of "auto-mobility," dispersed family houses with electronic access to the world, and rapid-changing fashion in clothing, entertainment, and much else. This private, widespread, and ephemeral commodity culture has changed nearly everything in everyday life, especially how people relate to nature and to one another. Its transformations have been so frequent and common that we find this world of fleeting things natural. We think that this particular mode of affluence is inevitable. And yet we have hardly begun to understand its impact on human personality and society. A history of that consumer culture can help us all understand what a new and challenging world we have created for ourselves and our descendants.

My interest in consumption is rooted in a fascination with the concrete interrelationships between people and things. That means not only how technology and business organization have affected society and culture but also how family, ethnicity, and class have shaped material life. Like most historians, I have mostly embedded my "theory" in the concrete story of why and when, for example, cars became fashion statements and candy bars replaced ethnic foods for many immigrants. Still, I have been influenced by those sociologists and anthropologists who understand goods and their uses as means of creating personal identity and social participation. I am thinking of a wide range of writers, from the early twentieth-century German social theorist Georg Simmel to the 1970s American cultural anthropologist Mary Douglas. I have come to accept that the act of consumption is far more interesting and important than once commonly assumed by intellectual critics of consumer culture. It cannot be reduced to economic manipulation or social emulation. Economists and business pundits who see consuming as merely the personal inclination and desire of shoppers also miss the point. Modern people, and especially Americans, communicate to others and to themselves through their goods. The consumer society has not necessarily produced passive people alienated from their true selves, as regularly assumed by traditional critics. Indeed, a central thesis of this book is that consumerism — the understanding of self in society through goods — has provided, on balance, a more dynamic and popular, while less destructive, ideology of public life than most political belief systems in the twentieth century.

Yet unlike others who have abandoned or rejected the traditional critique, I still find consumer culture problematic. My earlier work drifted toward its ragged edge, in explorations of alternatives to consumerism (reduced work time) and the ambiguous impact of goods on personal relationships (especially toys on parents and children). This approach reflects my age and personal response to having been a teenager and youth in the 1960s and 1970s. When I was about fifteen years old, I found on my mother's bookshelf copies of Vance Packard's *The Status Seekers* and *The Waste Makers*, which resonated with my frustration at the conformity and materialism that seemed to engulf the early 1960s. Five years later, I pored over the dense prose of Herbert Marcuse's *One-Dimensional Man* and, judging from my nearly indecipherable comments in the margins, found this critique of consumer culture meaningful. And like many from my generation, I read Huxley's *Brave New World* and other futuristic indictments of a manipulated, passive society of consumption. Only later did I learn to appreciate the classics of the environmental and consumer-rights movements. Despite the collapse of the counterculture and the ebbing influence of the environmental movement in the 1970s, I retained an emotional and intellectual attachment to this critical tradition. Yet it was impossible to live through the 1980s and 1990s and not see both the failure of the jeremiad tradition and the real appeal of consumption among millions of seemingly rational Americans.

In part, this book is an attempt to sort through and reassess why that tradition failed and what, if anything, can or should be salvaged from it. At the beginning of the new century the problem remains: how to sort out the promises and problems of consumer culture. This approach is not the only approach. It reflects the age and experience of one author. Readers of a different age and experience will, I hope, find something of their world and memory in it.

An All-Consuming Century

CHAPTER 1

The Irony of the Century

The beginning of a new century is a good time to reflect on the preceding hundred years. We need such spans to help us make sense of our past and to force us to think about our future. The twentieth century was an especially ironic time. Despite clashes of ideologies, two devastating world wars, and a forty-five-year cold war that ultimately made the United States the leading global power, the century did not culminate in the victory of American political ideas. Rather, the real winner of the century was consumerism. Visions of a political community of stable, shared values and active citizenship have given way to a dynamic but seemingly passive society of consumption in America, and increasingly across the globe.

The very idea of the primacy of political life has receded, despite the vast expansion of government. Instead, a very different concept of society has emerged — a consuming public, defined and developed by individual acquisition and use of mass-produced goods. Consumerism, the belief that goods give meaning to individuals and their roles in society, was victorious even though it had no formal philosophy, no parties, and no obvious leaders. Consumerism was the "ism" that won — despite repeated attacks on it as a threat to folk and high culture, to "true" community and individuality, and to the environment. Groups as diverse as the traditionalist Arts and Crafts movement of the early twentieth century, the modernist literati of the interwar years, and the environmentalists of the 1960s all fought it with vigor. Even though thinkers, politicians, and social organizers struggled against it, none produced effective alternatives.

Why Consumerism Won

Consumerism succeeded where other ideologies failed because it *concretely* expressed the cardinal political ideals of the century — liberty and democracy — and with relatively little self-destructive behavior or personal humiliation. Consumer goods allowed Americans to free themselves from their old, relatively secure but closed communities and enter the expressive individualism of a dynamic "mass" society. Commodities gave people a sense of freedom, sometimes serving as a substitute for the independence of the shop, craft, or farm that was disappearing as Americans joined the industrial work world. "Passive" consumption may have been an essential element in the emerging mass society of the twentieth century. Still, consumer goods gave people the means to establish new personal identities and to break with old ones without necessarily abandoning family, friends, and the common culture. For example, children of immigrants used amusement parks, new foods, and fashionable clothing to distance themselves from their parents without breaking with them. Even more important, consumer goods became a language, defining, redefining, and easing relationships between friends, family members, lovers, and strangers. Cars and clothes gave identity to young and old, female and male, ethnic majority and minority, telling others who they were and how they expected to be treated. Cosmetics and candy expressed both rebellion and authority, thus providing people with an understanding of themselves in an otherwise indifferent and sometimes unfriendly world. Moreover, goods redefined concepts of the past and future and gave a cadence to the rhythms of daily life when people purchased antiques and novelties and when Christmas became a shopping "season." The taste, feel, and comfort of manufactured objects, designed to maximize physical satisfaction and to intensify pleasure and excitement, created new understandings of personal freedom.[1]

Consumerism redefined democracy, creating social solidarities and opportunities for participation that transcended suffrage rights or political ideologies. A vision of a world of goods available to American citizens in large part replaced the old ideal of a republic of producers and challenged class, religion, and ethnicity as principles of political solidarity. In particular, the promise of a democracy of consumers co-opted class identity. Consumerism was far more than a political smoke screen. It reflected real social needs and, ironically, often fulfilled those needs with less conflict than did other, more substantial forms of social solidarity. Communities, formed around ownership of suburban homes, country club memberships, and college diplomas, excluded and humiliated outsiders and the poor. But religious, political, and other social groups were at least as discriminatory, and these groups often caused even more resentment and hostility, especially if they made absolute claims. Social or faith groups may actually be less flexible than markets in adjusting to change because of their democratic participatory ethic. When voluntary leisure groups, for example, are dominated by their members, they often unintentionally exclude others or become fractionalized. It has been much easier for commercial companies like Walt Disney or Leisure World, who stand outside the markets they organize, to get people to join. There was less risk of humiliation in disclosing oneself as a "member" of a society of Porsche owners than in joining a group that demanded personal interaction. It was relatively easy to "buy" one's way into a community of shoppers, and there were so many from which to choose. Consumerism repeatedly and dynamically reinforced democratic principles of participation and equality when new and exciting goods entered the market. The American Way was affirmed as Americans moved from basic Model T Fords to stylish choices in cars in the 1920s and from the radio to the TV in the 1950s.[2]

In the context of consumerism, liberty is not an abstract right to participate in public discourse or free speech. It means expressing oneself and realizing personal pleasure in and through goods. Democracy does not mean equal rights under the law or common access to the political process but, more concretely, sharing with others in personal ownership and use of particular commodities. Consumerism was realized in daily experiences, always changing, improving, and being redefined to meet the needs of individual Americans in their ordinary but still (to them) special lives as children and parents, wives and husbands, and in thousands of other roles.

In other ways, however, consumerism has been a threat to the kind of individual responsibilities and social solidarities that made political democracy work in the past. The fixation on personal goods has denied the necessity of sacrifice beyond the family. It has allowed little space for social conscience and confined aspiration to the personal realm. Consumerism had no interest in linking the present to the past and future (at least, beyond nostalgia and fantasy). Rear-guard defenders of the simple or cultivated life have had little impact. Indeed, their values have often been commercialized. Only the family, a most fragile institution, had the potential to pull the individual from self-gratification and break up the consuming crowd. Unfortunately, the family has hardly been a constraint on consumption — the home long ago was conquered by the market with mass circulation magazines, radio, TV, and other outlets for advertising domestic goods. And the family lacks stability and critical distance, reduced as it often is to a purchasing unit in a dynamic consumer society. Consumerism has produced a powerful but profoundly ambiguous legacy.

Americans have led the way toward a consumer society (and for this reason, at least, the twentieth century is the American century), but they are by no means solely responsible for it. Consumerism is not American Character incarnate, as European and American critics alike are accustomed to believe. Nor is it merely the extreme end of modernity expressed fully in the New World where, unlike in Europe, the fetters of tradition have always been weak or even powerless.[3] Other cultures have created different mixes of consumerism. Accidents of history, geography, and economics have allowed Europeans to produce a greater share of public goods and services than the United States. European nations have been slower to abandon small-scale, class-segmented shops for discount/department store shopping. They have often spent more on cuisine and long-distance vacations than have Americans. After all, by the mid-1990s Britons and Germans worked merely 43.3 and 41.4 weeks per year on average, compared to the 49.2 work weeks of Americans.[4] In contrast, the United States has led the way in private consumption of relatively large homes and cars. To be sure, the globalization of consumer and media industries has erased some of these differences. The declining power of nation-states and regional cultures has meant greater uniformity in consumption styles.[5]

Still, differences remain, and America in the century of consumption has followed its own path. The predominance of markets over other social and cultural institutions in American history is particularly important. Many factors contributed to this. The absence of an established national church, a weak central bureaucracy, the regional division of the elite, the lack of a distinct national "high culture," the fragmentation of folk cultures due to slavery and diverse immigration, and finally the social and psychological impact of unprecedented mobility all meant that market values encountered relatively few checks. Americans have had a strong tendency to define themselves and their relationships with others through the exchange and use of goods. Americans were hardly unique in this, and important checks on U.S. market culture lasted into the twentieth century, but this tendency made goods especially central to American society.

Modern consumerism is a product of broad transformations of industrial society experienced worldwide. In some ways, it is the wedding of technology to the pursuit of happiness. Desire for comfort, variety, and satisfaction are hardly new to the twentieth century. However, in the past humankind was limited in its weak capacity to harness energy, to accelerate and direct chemical processes, and to mold, assemble, and deliver labor-saving machines, shelter, clothing, and nourishment. People were unable to defeat, even briefly, the terrors of nature. Preachers of constraint made sense when the unlimited desire of the rich and powerful led to the exploitation of the many and the horrors of war and conquest. By contrast, in the twentieth century the industrial West learned to release large portions of humanity from many of these natural fetters. The mass production of consumer goods was the magical key. Thus modern technology seems to have freed modern Americans from the need to restrain desire.

Consumer society also emerged when the ancient dual economy of mass subsistence and elite luxury gave way to an economy capable of delivering vast and diverse stores of goods to the general population. The introduction of Henry Ford's automobile assembly line in 1913 promised a dramatic new possibility — that industrial output could swamp demand for goods. Advertising and appealing shopping centers helped to create wants to match the growing supply of products. The "philosophy" of consumerism was embedded in the words and images of the ad agency and display designer, who welded human physical needs, impulses, and fantasies to packaged goods.

The twentieth-century United States and the culture of consumption have become so closely intertwined that it is difficult for Americans to see consumerism as an ideology or to consider any serious alternatives or modifications to it. Participation in the consumer culture requires wage work, time, and effort, often given without enthusiasm or interest. But this trade-off seems natural today, an inevitable compromise between freedom and necessity. Maintaining a reciprocal relationship between consumption and work keeps the economic system running and orders daily life. This society of goods is not merely the inevitable consequence of mass production or the manipulation of merchandisers. It is a choice, never consciously made, to define self and community through the ownership of goods.

Failed Dreams of Public Life

Given the success of consumerism in 2000, it is ironic that few politically active Americans in 1900 expected that their new century would be one of consumption. The Left longed for popular control over political institutions and workplaces. Populists challenged political elites and radical trade unionists took on the power of railroad, mine, and steel mill owners. The Right defended authority with appeals to racial and social Darwinian ideas. The Center, in the form of Progressivism, labored for efficient and responsible institutions capable of translating American democratic and enlightenment traditions into the industrial era. All three groups thought in terms of citizenship and explained individuals and their relationship to society in political terms. However, over the course of the twentieth century, the self in society came to be defined by consumption.[6]

At the end of the century, religious cults, nationalist violence, and political scandals still got the headlines. But such news was really on the fringes of modern American life, interesting as a sideshow. Identification with class, nation, and even high-minded social reform has declined sharply in the second half of the twentieth century. Religious communities, with their spiritual challenge to consumerist materialism, have gained influence since the 1970s, but their calls for prayer in schools and the banning of abortion hardly challenged the profound hold of goods on American life. In sum, there seemed to be no moral equivalent to the world of consumption.

These are bold remarks. We are not accustomed to understanding consumption as the winner over the ideological "isms" in defining public life. After all, consumerism is about private decisions, not political authority and community. Political ideas and power, most historians assume, drive history; consumption is what takes place when people are free of war, instability, and "abnormal" ideological controls and pressures. Fascism, communism, and other totalitarian "isms" stood in the way of this normalcy. The real victor in the twentieth century, according to this common view, was not consumerism but liberalism in its classic meaning of individual rights, self-directed institutions, political pluralism, unrestricted markets, and limited states.

A conventional view of the twentieth century has been repeated again and again in Western Civilization textbooks and articulated recently by Francis Fukuyama. It is the story of the rise and fall of totalitarianisms of the Left and Right. Arising out of World War I, these deviations from the logic of the market and the efficacy and justice of representative democracy were unhappy historical accidents. Totalitarian victories between 1917 (the Bolshevik Revolution) and 1975 (the communist unification of Vietnam) were, the story goes, the consequences of temporary crises in capitalist development, holdovers of absolutist and aristocratic traditions in a few un-lucky countries, and the unfortunate influence of utopian intellectuals. These ill-fated deviations, expressed in Nazism and communism, took advantage of the upheaval of World War I and its aftermath, economic depression, and later, in the case of communism, of World War II and decolonization. The forces of liberalism, led by the United States, courageously strove to overcome the destructive results of totalitarianism through an Age of Dictators, World War II, and the Cold War. While the fascist aberration was crushed in 1945, it took another forty-five years to eliminate the other deviation, communism. The rules of rational society have finally been fully enshrined and "history" as an epochal striving has come to an end. The result has been the victory of democratic capitalism.[7]

According to this common view, the consumer society today is merely the arena in which people have gotten on with life. The market is a natural setting of exciting change and constant adjustment. It is also where rational, disciplined, and imaginative individuals can compete, play, and win, free from coercion or unreasonable constraint. Without the "artificial" interference of big and "ideological" government, the inefficiencies of big business, big media, and big everything else melt away. From this perspective, consumerism is not so much a victor over the other "isms" as a natural world freed from utopian ideologies, pushed onward by the dynamics of technology and personal liberty.[8]

To be sure, market liberalism and democratic capitalism seem to have won with universal acclaim. Centralized management of society has few proponents today. Russia, the birthplace of communism, abandoned its Marxist heritage, following closely on the heels of its erstwhile satellites. Even where communist parties still reign, like in China and Vietnam, markets have replaced dreams of collectivism.

There are, however, problems with this tale of the victory of democratic capitalism. First, the collapse of communism did not mean the triumph of a civic or open society. One reason is simply that the abandonment of communism had relatively little to do with the desire for political democracy and civil freedoms. Communism's failure was more economic than political; it did not come close to meeting the ultimate goal: "from each according to their ability, to each according to their need." For all of its claims of producing full employment and meeting everyone's basic requirements for health, education, food, and other necessities, the Marxist system was unable either to increase productivity or to meet the widening horizons of desire. The lack of incentives for hard work created a society in permanent slow motion that could never satisfy the demand for consumer goods. In the West, the linkage of discipline (at work) with freedom (in consumption) was able to do both. Employment brought income roughly commensurate with effort, and money bought an endless array of appealing items. Under modern capitalism, people accepted displays of wealth as tokens of achievement and as things for those who had "not yet" arrived to strive for. By contrast, the communist elite could not serve as a model of consumerist emulation without appearing to be "privileged." Communist regimes, based on economic planning and cultural isolation from the "decadent" West, could not make their people work harder or contain their desire for more goods. The communists were unable to create social solidarity and instead relied upon power.[9] For East Europeans, the promise of mass consumption was preferable to the nightmare of solidarity even if it meant also the dominance of money and the private control of wealth. In reality, the fall of communism had more to do with the appeals of capitalist consumerism than political democracy.

It is no surprise that the seeming victory of liberal capitalism has not led to an unambiguous restoration of free institutions. In fact, the opposite appears to be the case in both East and West. Not only did the collapse of European communism in 1989 fail to revive civil society,[10] but democratic values and institutions appeared to be in decline in the West as well. In the United States, the end of the external threat of communism created an "enemy crisis" and probably contributed to the "culture wars" between the secularists and religious absolutists that have helped create a stalemated political climate. Despite efforts of many to find identity in ethnicity, religion, or even gender, there seems to be "no golden past to recover."[11] While sociologist Amitai Etzioni complained that Americans were unwilling to compromise between their longings for order and autonomy to create a more civil society,[12] William Greider lamented the hollowing out of the democratic process in American political life. By the 1990s, participation in presidential elections had declined by 20 percent since 1960 and members of Congress were elected by as little as 15 or 20 percent of their constituents, despite escalating spending for electoral campaigns. More broadly, Robert Putnam noted the decline of American participation in the civic and social organizations essential for democracy.[13]

At the end of the century, the decline of democratic political and social institutions was evident everywhere in the industrial world. Opinion makers agreed that the market alone could measure the will of the people through the billions of votes cast daily at cash registers. Politicians were sold like soft drinks in election campaigns. Even the growth of a new conservatism in the 1980s was not really a mass political movement. It was a sophisticated and largely successful sales effort promoting unfettered markets. It took advantage of the decline of communities and organizations that had once encouraged popular political participation and government devoted to meeting social needs. The 1990s changed little. The 1996 American political conventions featured promises to help or free families to make their own spending decisions. The conclusion is obvious: consumerism, not political democracy, won the century. Regimes based on mobilizing people around ideas of social solidarity seem to end up demonic, or at least bureaucratic and corrupt. And even the relatively open and undemanding goals of liberal democracy for public life have failed to compete with consumerism.

Our Ambivalence Toward Consumerism

In fact, consumer society has partially replaced civil society. This has not necessarily been a bad thing. Communities of shoppers have served as effective counters to the political and cultural solidarities that produced Nazism and contemporary ethnic or religious bigotry. Consumerism has created emotional and social outlets that ideological groups formerly harnessed for demonic, or at least authoritarian, purposes. As C. B. McPherson notes, "possessive individualism," that seventeenth-century "vice" of personal acquisition, was a substitute for the more disruptive passions of vengeance, glory, and domination.[14] Similarly, modern consumerism has saved affluent countries since 1945 from many far more destabilizing and manifestly more destructive forms of behavior like ethnic feuds, racial bigotry, and militarism.

Mass consumption wonderfully combines hedonism with work, fantasy with hard-nosed realism, often maximizing extremes in a flurry of numbing activity. It surely has produced a harried society.[15] But who would voluntarily abandon this way of life for the confining worlds of our ancestors or the stagnant and hypocritical existences of the former communist East? The consumer culture may be for cowards and the lazy, people who cannot find themselves or relate to others without the crutch of goods. But who among us does not fit this definition in some way? How many of us are really outside that culture? We have survived the twentieth century with consumerism. Could we have done so without it? Would we not have destroyed ourselves in ideological fratricide or succumbed to a coercive, corrupt, and stagnant society without the thrills and securities of material possessions?

Consumer culture may be the fate of modern democracies unable or unwilling to provide their members with deeper and more direct means of expressing individuality and sociability. But in another sense consumer culture is democracy's highest achievement, giving meaning and dignity to people when workplace participation, ethnic solidarity, and even representative democracy have failed. Of course, consumerism has done this without challenging manipulative power and inherited money. Indeed, the American Way of Life in the twentieth century, based on popular access to consumer goods, has replaced the older American Dream of property and independence. It has provided meaning while magnifying the power and wealth of American elites. It is easy to see why some might view this as a perfect world.

Still, most of us, no matter our politics, are repulsed by the absolute identity of society with the market and individual choice with shopping. After all, we support laws that restrict consumption at the margins at least, by prohibiting the free market in most addictive drugs and by regulating children's access to dangerous substances like tobacco and pornography that we otherwise tolerate on store shelves. When intellectuals point out that the personal desire for goods is sometimes irrational — shaped by frustrating efforts to compete with neighbors or even an elusive quest for happiness, youth, sexuality, or power — we, at least, find this true in *other* people. Despite the ads that identify our aspirations with material status, in our "serious" moments, most of us still claim to strive for more spiritual, rational, or sensitive selves.

We still long for a circle of friends and seek the fellowship of communities. And we do so in a thousand ways, from the playful exuberance of football games to the sober joys of worship. Americans still dream of a public life structured by government, education, and church. We desire a society sustained by shared traditions, collective sacrifices, and personal interactions. We lament how affluence — the ownership, care, and longing for goods — gets in the way of relationships and takes time and attention away from "real life." Many would even agree that the commercial bias, under which everything has a price and everything can be possessed and "used up" without regard to the living, dead, or yet to live, has frustrated what we really want for ourselves and our posterity.[16] We complain that our society of shoppers has produced social relations that are more impersonal, ephemeral, and certainly less community-minded than we wish. Many lament the corruption and aimlessness at the center of political life; the various addictions afflicting families; the shallowness of our lives; and the irresponsibility of our culture toward both our grandparents and our grandchildren. Many people still feel that individuality and community experienced only through commodities is insufficient. Consumerism seems to stand in the way of greater happiness and friendship.[17] Couldn't we do better with all of the material and technological advantages that the twentieth century has brought us?

It is possible that these sentiments are mere platitudes, subjects of Sunday morning sermons and the "expected" answers to survey questions — largely irrelevant to our actual behavior, impulses, and dreams. They may be no more than the tired refrain from the overplayed song of the old jeremiad against consumer culture. Throughout the century, writers as diverse as José Ortega y Gasset, Sinclair Lewis, Lewis Mumford, Theodor Adorno, and Jane Jacobs have attacked the commercialization of American culture and society. Their efforts were often insightful. Nevertheless, modern cultural Jeremiahs never understood why and how the consumer culture worked in the lives of ordinary Americans. They saw the consuming "masses," not the system of consumption itself, as the threat. They retreated into the idea of an "authentic" personality and often ended up promoting an individualism that simply created new forms of consumerism.[18] Underlying their responses were the social interests and educational traditions of the intellectual elite, alien to the experiences of ordinary people. This negative reaction to mass consumer society had little chance of winning a popular following and often degenerated into "handwringing." Its echo can still be heard today in intellectuals' doubts about consumerism. As an effective critique or alternative to consumer culture, however, it has lost its power.[19]

Many opinion leaders in the press and popular culture daily celebrate consumerism. Economists often insist that individual liberty is identical with the subjective desires of consumers. Stanley Lebergott, for example, mocks the jeremiad against consumerism as arbitrary or hostile to progress: who complains of the comforts of consumption, "housewives or specialists in American Studies?" Human needs are endless and irrepressible and to deny them is to deny our humanity and freedom. There is no disputing taste.[20] Despite their homilies on patriotism and civic virtue, politicians commonly act as if the main point of government is to facilitate consumer choice by lowering taxes.

By the late 1970s, even a few academics in the humanities were getting into the act, claiming that goods were the main way that people communicated with each other. Mary Douglas and Baron Isherwood's *The World of Goods: Towards an Anthropology of Consumption* (1979) led the way. It became fashionable to say that there are no "false needs," there is no language outside the market. These thinkers found futile, imperialistic, or even demonic any effort to get at a truth beyond the ephemeral consumer culture. Political and social ideas that projected holistic alternatives to current society were labeled "utopian" and illusory because no one could escape the market culture. These affirmative intellectuals attempted to reconcile art and thought with an eclectic popular commercial culture. They argued that architecture should learn from the glitter of Las Vegas and that youths made their own meanings and uses of clothes and commercial popular music.[21]

At one level this rejection of the jeremiad tradition is a realistic acceptance of the victory of the commercial language of "adcult" over high culture and a positive rejection of the elitism of the artistic and philosophical canon. Relatively few Americans watch the "uplifting" fare on public television, despite gallant efforts to make it entertaining and to keep it free from annoying ads. Parks are relatively empty while malls are full. Celebrants of consumerism note that there certainly are no physical or even economic impediments to life beyond the market. Yet Americans have chosen consumer culture, and it is about time intellectual elites ceased their unwanted and presumptuous preaching.[22]

Still, Americans have lingering doubts that consumerism will satisfy and work indefinitely. Neither the hard-nosed economist nor the pandering politician nor the cynical intellectual may ultimately have grasped the complexity of popular will and desire. Americans still want more than more shopping and more stuff. They often choose consumption because "real" community and "true" individuality are difficult, frustrating, and thus boring. Americans know that goods are about more than "meanings." Commodities are objects of individual desires that, even in an affluent age, must still be managed. Consumerism also means making choices between personal wants and public needs and among different uses of time and qualities of social and personal life. Buying more things and earning the money to obtain them takes time that otherwise would be free from work and the market. The fact that Americans work more than Europeans is no accident. It is related to the greater American emphasis upon consumption, and Americans are not entirely happy about the consequences. The unambiguous celebration of consumerism either ignores or is disdainful of these very real longings for a culture beyond consumption. Even more important, the affirmative school has largely forgotten that the culture of constraint has shaped and channeled consumerism in the past. In their energetic denial of the jeremiad tradition, they ignore the fact that this culture of constraint has largely been eclipsed in recent years. Reading a celebrant like James Twitchell would make one think that the jeremiad tradition was dominant at the end of the century. Far from it. Since the 1960s, advocates of personal and collective limits on consumer desire have lost influence in culture, society, and politics. The fact is that consumerism remains problematic even if the problem was never really understood by the Jeremiahs.

The dilemma appears to be that the American system, so successful at mobilizing resources to produce goods and services that individuals really want, also frustrates their hopes for themselves and their relationships with others. Individual striving and satisfaction are too often confined to objects and services while social interaction is reduced to "reading" each other through our possessions and by sharing goods and aspirations for them. Affluent America is more content than poorer countries, but only up to a point.[23] Consumerism has costs beyond the spiritual and aesthetic, so long emphasized by cultural critics. The quest for meaning through possession obliges Americans to work more than they want doing jobs they often do not like. By focusing on individualistic wants, the market system undermines willingness to pay for public goods like parks, environmental protection, and community centers.[24]

A Need for Perspective

We are right not to be comfortable with the future of consumer society, but we still need to know why consumerism won. We must acknowledge the failure of critics of consumer culture while recognizing the cultural and social costs of this victory. To do so we must understand the history of twentieth-century consumerism. Neither the jeremiad against consumerism nor the celebration of it will take us very far in understanding why it won the twentieth century and what that victory may mean for the twenty-first century.

A deeper and more mature understanding of the history of consumerism can take us beyond the simplistic, naive, and futile struggle between the handwringer and the cheerleader. In fact, that history will show a far more subtle and interesting world of the shopper than either side ever depicted. While the traditional jeremiad never explained how the consumer culture worked for Americans, the modern celebrant cannot see why it might not work in the future. The critic attempted to impose a culture of constraint that was undemocratic; the proponent tends to rationalize a consumer culture without constraints. Huxley's *Brave New World* and Orwell's *1984* anticipated a world of manipulated and mechanized hedonism that never happened, but today's faith in an endless horizon of freely chosen "meanings" in goods is no more likely to come true.

This book explores why and how consumerism won the twentieth century by meeting American needs, and why it may not be able to fulfill those needs in the next century. It is divided into two pairs of chapters, the first covering the years 1900 to 1960 and the second 1960 to 2000, with a transitional chapter in between. In part, this is a story of new technologies, new businesses, and new economic realities. In part, it is an analysis of how and why Americans responded to the consumer goods that they encountered. The first pair of chapters show how a distinct consumer society emerged in the United States between 1900 and 1930 and how it was consolidated during the economic and social upheavals of the 1930s and 1940s and the seemingly placid 1950s. It was during these years that Americans encountered a dramatic new world of clothing, cosmetics, candy bars, and cars. These goods gave people ways of identifying themselves in groups when the old associations of family and neighborhood no longer worked. Consumers extended their personalities in the physical sensations of taste, speed, mood enhancement, control, and comfort. The complex appeals of new products prevailed over the apparent failure of capitalism in the 1930s, laying the groundwork for a full-scale ideology of consumers' democracy after World War II. The tone of this story is largely positive, explaining how and why consumer culture prevailed.

The next (transitional) chapter shows that this consumer culture has never been without its critics. Indeed, the United States has been the home of both the least restrained materialism and the most aggressive and often thoughtful criticism of consumption. This reflects more than hypocrisy, for these two value systems have complemented each other. Thus during the 1920s, when desire was released in an orgy of spending, Americans also outlawed alcohol, regulated the media, and preached a culture of personal simplicity. Regulation justified an expanding horizon of consumption by the very fact that it set boundaries. More positively, a culture of constraint tried also to provide a common language of limits and choices. Yet over the long run, this critical tradition floundered in binding or providing alternatives to consumerism. An explanation of why and how it failed provides a backdrop to the very different and far less positive story of the rest of the century.

The next two chapters tell of the rise and ultimate fall of movements to rationalize and constrain consumption. The 1960s and later 1980s produced opposing movements of the Left and Right that removed remaining limits to the consumer culture. The anticonsumerism of the "radical" sixties offered environmental and egalitarian critiques of a waste-making and ad-drenched culture, but these critiques did not impede the growth of that culture. Instead, the countercultural challenge to the conformist spending of the 1950s opened new channels of desire by breaking with the constraints of the postwar generation. The conservative upsurge of the 1980s and 1990s indulged in its own brand of self-aggrandizement by promoting unrestricted markets. The result was a consumerism that thrived without serious checks and turned in subtly but distinctly antisocial directions.

The book concludes with this dilemma: As the twentieth century ended, consumerism faced no practical limits, though it is arguable that it never needed them more. The failure of the culture of limits and the unwillingness of the culture of celebration to deal seriously with the need for constraint left the market nearly unfettered. As Americans faced a new century, the cultural divisions between Left and Right made any practical assessment and reform very difficult. Yet the history of our all-consuming century still suggests possibilities for new thinking and action — an appreciation for the meaning of goods in people's lives with, at the margins, an awareness of the need to reform and revive the still valid portion of the culture of constraint.

While the exhaustion of alternatives to the market is evident everywhere today, the fact that consumerism has won does not mean that it is either the destiny of humankind or sustainable in its present form in the twenty-first century. The past hundred years have been full of surprises. The good news is that we have made it through those turbulent times. The bad news may be the way we did it. The triumph of consumption in the past century is not a certain model for the next. It is one thing to note that the consumer culture may well have helped us survive the century by displacing the aggression and hatred that surely could have destroyed humanity in the arms race; it is another to argue that humanity can survive another century with six billion people and counting who increasingly define their existence by their consumption of manufactured goods. We need to understand the triumph of consumerism and how it has shaped our lives. And we need to go beyond this understanding to find ways of preventing it from absorbing human life.

CHAPTER 2

Setting the Course, 1900–1930

No century began with as much promise for change as the twentieth. The automobile and airplane, motion pictures and radio, the electric light and appliances, bottled soft drinks and canned soups, all so prosaic and common at the end of the century, were the new wonders of 1900. While these were hardly all American inventions, the United States was poised to take advantage of them on a massive scale. This young nation had just completed a century of unprecedented progress, conquering and unifying an "empty" continent of extraordinary fertility (compare with Australia). This was hardly a painless process: native cultures were crushed, traditional ways of life were cast aside for the machine age and the modern market, and far more dreams of riches were dashed than were fulfilled. But in 1900, the United States was already the richest country in human history — and well situated to create far more wealth. And despite the legacy of slavery, property and opportunity were sufficiently well distributed to produce an extraordinarily broad and high standard of living. According to German sociologist Werner Sombart, plenty of "roast beef and apple pie" saved the United States from the extremes of class war that plagued Europe at this time.[1] American consumer society rose on the solid base of increasing purchasing power. Discretionary spending (beyond that for the necessities of housing, clothing, and food) increased from 20 percent to almost 35 percent in the first three decades of the century. To consume took on whole new meanings.[2] American prosperity gave quite ordinary citizens cars, electric gadgets, telephones, and ready-to-wear fashions for which European masses would have to wait until mid-century. On top of this, Americans had more free time in which to enjoy these goods: work weeks decreased by almost 10 hours between 1900 and 1926, to 50.6 hours.[3]

Affluence was about far more than rising personal income or even rising standards in housing, transportation, nutrition, clothing, education, and health care. New consumer goods brought more than physical comforts, pleasure, and mobility. They introduced new styles of life, especially fresh ways of accommodating the societal changes that gripped turn-of-the-century Americans. New products helped Americans adjust to a changing world of work. Commodities gave immigrants tools for coping with an alien culture and offered new meanings of democracy during a time when politics was becoming ever more remote to average citizens. Consumer goods became innovative and often creative building blocks for the construction of different identities and new communities when the old ones were in decline. Prosperity meant a shift from purely utilitarian to symbolic goods.[4] Fashionable furnishings, packaged products, domestic appliances, and cars expressed new versions of self and community, new understandings of past and future. Through their packaging, display, and advertising, consumer goods came to embody a distinct and eventually dominant alternative to political and even religious visions of American life.

Shopping and Social Change

The surge in free time, personal income, and new products made possible a new consumer society. In turn, new spending opportunities helped Americans adapt to profound social change. Nineteenth-century Americans had tried to define themselves through possession of land, job skills, and businesses, but those markers of self-worth were in rapid decline by 1900. The percentage of the workforce on farms dropped from nearly 53 percent in 1870 to 37.5 percent in 1900 and 21.4 percent by 1930. The broad pattern is clear: Americans took industrial and service jobs in which incomes were often higher but autonomy was lost. Because of a wave of mergers in the 1890s, businesses became larger and more concentrated, reducing everyone, from machine tender to accountant to factory manager, to economic subjects of the corporation. While independent storekeepers and farmers dwindled, sales, marketing, and finance jobs grew as big business tried to distribute the goods of an increasingly productive economy. Indeed, white-collar employment rose from 17.6 percent of the workforce in 1900 to 29.4 percent in 1930.[5] While these often low-level professionals, salespeople, and managers thought of themselves as middle class, their jobs were no longer independent and often offered little mobility. Instead, new white-collar employees increasingly won status and a sense of betterment through their consumption and leisure activities rather than their work.

The same was at least as true for the relatively well-paid skilled industrial worker. Behind the image of general American affluence was a sharply segmented income scale, especially in industry. A comparison of real wages between Birmingham, England and Pittsburgh at the turn of the century shows that *unskilled* English workers enjoyed a higher standard than did their American counterparts. What distinguished the American labor force was not so much high wages, but the fact that the salaries of well-paid skilled workers (often native) often put them at the same lifestyle level as the presumably "higher" class white-collar workers. This phenomenon contributed to a divided working class and relatively weak class consciousness. However, it led also to a strong consumer consciousness built on individual aspiration. High-wage workers could afford the same housing and luxuries as many white-collar employees. Moreover, less skilled Pittsburghers saved and worked long hours in order to move up the wage scale. They looked up to the higher-paid skilled workers and hoped to gain access to status-enhancing goods.[6]

A strategy of substituting consumer aspirations for producer dreams extended beyond the ranks of the native Caucasian blue-collar worker. It appealed also to the immigrant or uprooted American, for whom new consumer goods offered a relatively quick way of assimilating in a city or suburb. Between 1880 and 1930, the United States received 27 million immigrants. African American migration from the southern states into northern cities also began at this time. The black population of Chicago, for example, rose from 14,852 in 1890 to 109,458 in 1920. The Italian peasant or country black could avoid some humiliation and establish an identity with a new suit of fashionable clothes and new products as easy to find as canned soups or the movies. Indeed, these cheap goods and experiences promised symbolic entry into an American world that many immigrants could only dream about. By the 1920s, the movies, with their palacelike settings and glamorous images onscreen, allowed millions of working-class Americans of all races and ethnicities to live vicariously through the stars in a world of affluence.[7]

Twentieth-century Americans discarded frontier values — Lincoln's old idea of the democracy of labor and property — and often replaced them with the new dream of display and consumption: the "democratization of desire," self-satisfaction in the attainment of more and more things. This trend was hardly a total rejection of the values of the nineteenth century. Rather, the consumer society perpetuated the pioneers' faith that prosperity would be the reward for hard work and discomfort on the isolated homestead or ranch. Now redemption was from the loneliness of the city and the business rat race. Consumption relieved the pain of increasingly meaningless labor. While new urban "luxuries" tore many from the rigors of pioneer life, the frontier survived in the acquisitive and individualistic personality of the modern American.[8]

While the new culture of spending gave identity to individuals, it also redefined the meaning of democracy in a nation where political involvement was in sharp retreat. Voting in national elections had declined from 80 percent in the 1890s to less than 50 percent by the 1920s. The defeat of a farmer-labor coalition in the general election of 1896 was the beginning of this trend. Simultaneously, the increased rigidity of segregation in the South under Democratic Party leadership[9] and the split of immigrant and native voters between the two parties in the North blocked any successful coalition for social reform.[10] Progressivists and trade unionists largely failed to win economic regulation and collective bargaining in the years 1900 to 1920. Protective labor legislation (e.g., reducing working hours or limiting children's labor) was confined mostly to the state level. Antitrust legislation was used more against unions than big corporations. Even the 1913 constitutional amendment allowing income taxes had little effect on wealth distribution because the rates were so low. And in the wake of the conservative upsurge after the 1920 election of Warren Harding and concerted efforts of employers to prevent collective bargaining (known as the American Plan), trade unions suffered a heavy decline.[11]

There was, however, an alternative to extending democracy through unions or protective or welfare legislation. It was to form a productionist-consumer democracy that would retain managerial control over work and output while promising personal (rather than class) access to the material fruits of productivity. For example, Frederick W. Taylor's scientific management movement claimed to overcome workplace conflict by using individual wage incentives and managerial innovation to increase the share of the economic pie for both capital and labor. By 1912, Taylor had articulated a social compromise. His solution rejected regulation and unions for an implicit bargain: labor would cede its claims over the workplace to management in exchange for high personally disposable income and shorter hours. A good expression of this "bargain" was Henry Ford's assembly line, which maintained rigorous managerial control over production in exchange for the exceptionally generous offer of a five-dollar/eight-hour day for production workers (1913 – 14).[12] American output per worker hour increased by 60 percent from the 1870s to 1900. It rose again another 69 percent in the next twenty years.[13] That productivity, more than legal reforms, became the base for the consumers' democracy. The decline of a political vision of social equality made a culture of mass consumption seem a natural and inevitable alternative. Increasingly more fragmented, mobile, and unorganized, Americans joined "consumption communities" that did not require an active citizenry but were comprised, according to historian Daniel Boorstin, of "people who have a feeling of shared well-being, shared risks, common interests and common concerns that come from consuming the same kinds of objects." Americans defined their status and dismissed boredom and anxiety by joining the crowd who bought Life Savers . . . or Lincolns.[14]

This is a compelling analysis of the politics of consumption in the early twentieth-century United States. However, it only tells part of the story. It would be unfair to say that the eclipse of active and collective politics led to a passive and individualistic consumer society. The personal and social use of goods was complex and often quite expressive and participatory. In the generation after 1900, consumption had became a substitute for conversation in a society where rituals of communication were already weak and growing weaker. Americans before modern consumerism surely were no expert communicators, and cars, fashion fads, or record collections certainly did not destroy people's capacity to relate to one another or to their history. The truth instead is that modern consumption helped individuals contend with social conflict and ambiguity, evade clear-cut choices, and even hold contradictory desires.

As important, consumer goods were liberating in ways that other expressions of self and society were not. Unlike racial or even class characteristics, cars and foods as well as hats and clothes could be put on and taken off, depending on social and psychological circumstances. Up-to-date products could be acquired by anyone with the money to buy them and could be discarded or sold almost as easily. Of course, fashionable clothes, cars, and vacations intimidated those too poor to keep up or too inexperienced to know how to use them. Still, a fundamental change had occurred since the days of court aristocracies and sumptuary laws: in 1900, almost any labor, service, or property, no matter how low in status, could be converted into money to purchase the latest dress or flashy suit. Social

21

status and birth were no longer relevant in this ultimate democracy of spending. Symbolic goods also helped ordinary shy people avoid self-disclosure. They aided immigrants, the young, the newly urbanized, or the simply insecure to avoid the humiliation of being nobodies and the anxiety of facing a world of strangers. As a nation of newcomers, Americans had special needs for hats, shoes, foods, and cars to help them "place themselves advantageously and to get on briskly."[15]

There was, of course, a dark side to modern consumerism. If consumer culture leveled social differences and gave individuals the freedom to define themselves, it also reflected an American society divided by class and burdened by its "hidden injuries."[16] Shopping sometimes was a defensive reaction to insults from the class above or an offensive response to the intrusion of the classes below. Houses and their furnishings allowed some people to join the group while giving others a way to exclude the "unworthy." Consumption became a means of waging class war — but at a personal level and with a minimum of overt violence. Even "aggressive" social gestures (as many understood private luxury cars when they first appeared about 1900) could be disguised by the claim that the individual was merely asserting personal freedom. And most of the time, the goods that asserted status also had nonsocial meanings and appeals — control over nature, freedom from the past, or simply individual pleasure in feel, taste, appearance, and comfort. The secret success of consumerism was that these messages to self and others were so layered, complex, and hidden.

American consumption society had links to the fashion system of the European court. Rich Americans aspired to that aristocratic standard when they raided European castles for furnishings that symbolized heritage and exclusivity to decorate their San Simeons or Biltmore Estates. But these were more or less ludicrous gestures in a country where hereditary social position was regularly challenged. Few ordinary Americans accepted the corollary to this upper-class pretense — that they were mere tradespeople or peasants, fixed eternally in low status. Although it is easy to exaggerate the point, American society was not based on the myth of fixed stations but rather on the myth of mobility (at least for whites). The decline of ethnic and neighborhood loyalties in this century reinforced an individualism long based on market values.[17]

Again, this hardly meant an egalitarian or classless society. American consumer society fed on distinction, but differences were fluid and continually interrelating. Thorstein Veblen's famous *Theory of the Leisure Class,* published in 1899, looked back to the conspicuous spending of the *nou-*

veaux riches of America's Gilded Age. He found an elite displaying its money power with ostentatious time killers (like golf) and vicarious consumption (which hard-working entrepreneurs enjoyed through their wives' luxuries). Such spending allowed this "leisure class" to make invidious comparisons with those incapable of keeping up. Nevertheless, this aristocracy of spending shaped the meaning of goods further down the social scale: "Members of each stratum accept as their ideal of decency the scheme of life in vogue in the next higher stratum," Veblen observed. Mass consumption did not lead to an egalitarian community of affluent and secure citizens. Rather, competition for status goods divided and often frustrated spenders.[18]

In fact, early twentieth-century America, with all of its mobility and change, spread the spirit of emulation. Robert and Helen Lynd observed in their classic study of Muncie, Indiana (Middletown) a dramatic change: while in 1890, "Middletown appears to have lived on a series of plateaus as regards standards of living . . . Today [the mid-1920s] the edges of the plateaus have been shaved off, and everyone lives on the slope from any point of which desirable things belonging to people all the way up to the top are in view."[19] This change intensified the frustrating effort to join those above and gain distance from those below. The expression, "Keeping up with the Joneses" (from a 1910 comic strip) meant less emulation of the rich than not falling behind one's own crowd. This, however, was hardly reassuring to the faint of heart. In an economy that made luxuries like cars available to a majority (but not all), keeping up was not seeking status but simply trying to be among the majority.[20]

The myth of mobility often was more humiliating to the relatively poor American than permanent low status would have been to a member of a caste society. Low income and a dead-end job was clearly "the penalty for and the proof of personal failure."[21] In the United States, individual laborers had comparatively little pride in tools or their ancestral farms to shelter them from the disdain of the rich or powerful. The American system worked because it assumed and often created material progress. Americans endured the humiliation of poverty only because it was supposed to be temporary and to spur the individual on to achievement and a seat nearer the head of the table.[22]

Many Americans never reached the "American standard of living." In 1930, only half of households had flush toilets and a third still had no electricity; scarcely one in three manual wage earners owned a car, even though a used automobile could be bought for $60. Consumerism was a middle-class phenomenon early in the century, even in the United States. In the 1920s, Chicago wage earners continued to shop in neighborhood shops and attend local theaters; they avoided the commercialized chain and department stores. Downtown movie palaces, which catered to the business and professional classes, scared them away.[23]

Nevertheless, we need perspective on these facts and figures. Europeans saw the United States as the land of high wages, a place where common laborers could own the cars they helped to make, whereas European craftsmen could hardly afford bicycles. In the period 1925–29, real wages were about 60 percent higher in the United States than in Britain and had roughly two and a half times the purchasing power of French workers' income. It is hardly surprising that a French trade unionist in the 1920s might believe that American consumer capitalism was moving "toward some form of socialism."[24] The point was not that the United States experienced universal prosperity, but that high productivity made cheap manufactured goods quickly available down the social scale.

Many Americans lamented the decline of civil society and political democracy in the early twentieth century. Goods that offered the thrill of novelty also made people anxious about losing neighborhood shops and traditional skills to the department store and mechanized production. Advertisers and marketers countered these fears by associating the new with the old and by linking mass-production efficiency with personal needs. This new culture accommodated flux, but it also protected and reassured Americans against the insecurities caused by change. The growth of the consumer society coincided with the decline of self-sufficiency, neighborliness, and family interactions. It replaced traditional social roles and identities with those purchased in the market. The point is not that Americans had more goods and were happy with a system that delivered them; rather, the key point is that through goods and services, Americans found a way to understand themselves, others, the past, and the future. They might well have preferred an alternative if it had been available. For good or ill, the consumerist system created meaning for Americans far more effectively than politics and civil society.

New Goods, New Desires

Modern American consumer society was founded on dramatically new products that became available to the masses only in the 1900s. The car was clearly the bellwether commodity, and its Americanization powerfully illustrates the possibilities of a "democratic" luxury. The 1885 German invention of the internal combustion engine made possible the first American automobile in 1892. At that time, the car in the United States was a handcrafted luxury just as it was in Europe. In 1905, when the mean annual income was $450, a typical car cost from $600 to $7,500. It was the "rich man's toy," used for show by the likes of William Vanderbilt, who kept a 100-car garage on Long Island. For the filthy rich, cars were like prized horses or yachts displayed and enjoyed in "season"; they were sometimes decorated with flowers and paraded at parties. Of course, there were cars for the herd, but they were not well made. In 1910, the life expectancy of a cheap car was less than 10,000 miles, and even farmers drove scarcely 1,800 miles a year because their vehicles were roofless and thus could be used only in the dry and warm months.[25]

The Model T Ford changed all that. In 1908, its first year of production, Henry Ford sold the Tin Lizzie for the moderate price of $950, reasonable for the solid middle class. Ford succeeded in extending ownership

The first recorded traffic jam in New York City, in 1916, was made possible by the mass production of the Model T Ford.   (Library of Congress)

25

to a far wider market by gradually reducing the price to only $290 for a much improved, enclosed model by 1924. When Ford introduced the assembly line in 1913, he may have ushered in the era of intense, repetitious, and unskilled factory work; but he also compensated his workers with additional leisure and income (in the unheard-of eight-hour work day that earned up to $5). These wages made car ownership a real possibility for auto workers. The Model T was utilitarian, from 1914, painted only in black; it was boxy and obviously mass produced. Still, Ford had kept his promise to "build a motor car for the great multitude . . . after the simplest designs that modern engineering can devise . . . so low in price that no man making a good salary will be unable to own one." In fact, 15.5 million Model Ts were sold in its 19 years of production. The car was durable as well as cheap, a practical time saver and thus a money saver, reducing travel hours to town for farmers and making self-directed pleasure trips a possibility, especially appreciated in a nation of small towns and isolated farms spread across a vast land. In 1910 only 180,000 cars were made in the United States; by 1924, manufacturers produced 4 million. In 1927, the United States built 85 percent of the world's automobiles, and by 1929 there was one car for every five Americans (better than one for every three in California). These figures are fantastic, especially when compared with Europe: there was only one car for every 43 Britons and one for every 335 Italians.[26] The automobile, a private vehicle of extraordinary speed available to a broad swath of the public, became a symbol of a new American way of life.

The same innovative spirit and high per capita income that brought mass-produced cars made possible a plethora of other mass-produced goods and experiences. Just as internal combustion revolutionized travel, electricity transformed the street and the home. Improvements in electric power (especially alternating current) led to the modern electric motor in 1888 and to an amazing array of new contraptions — electric trollies to take city folk to the great "white ways" of brightly lit amusement and theater districts; electric wires that brought power to new domestic gadgets. The electric fan appeared by 1890, and the electric iron and kettle followed in 1893. Electric toasters, hotplates, and waffle irons also were sold shortly after 1900, and the Hoover vacuum cleaner hit consumer markets in 1908. Improvements in the incandescent light bulb and the telephone made them available as ordinary household devices in the 1900s. Nevertheless, only after American homes were refitted for electricity (only about half had it in 1920) and the two-pronged plug was adapted in 1917 did electric appliances become common. The first electric washing machine for home use appeared in 1914, and one third of electrified houses included one by 1930. This device became much more useful with the development of the automatic washer in 1935 — although few households had them until the 1950s. While the early electric stove had to compete with gas, improvements in the 1930s gradually resulted in a shift to electric ranges. The refrigerator was the last of the major household appliances to be electrified. The introduction of freon and improved motors and thermostats in 1930 led to half of electrified homes having electric refrigerators by 1937. Finally, the radio appeared first as a "wireless telegraph" in 1896, but twenty years after the invention of the vacuum tube in 1906, the modern appliance filled living rooms with music, news, comedy, drama, and ads. Within a decade after radios first appeared widely in stores in 1922, 55 percent of American homes contained them. Americans embraced electric appliances quickly, a generation ahead of most Europeans.[27]

Technological change radically transformed the consuming experience. The invention of roll photographic film and the Kodak camera in 1888 and the movie camera in 1892 gave the masses the personal snapshot and a little later the motion picture theater, whose stars and stories were shared simultaneously by millions. New ways of packaging and preparing everything from food and drink to clothes and furniture made possible astonishing changes in life — more goods obtained more often and with greater convenience.[28] Inventions, from the pressure cooker for canning (1874) and machines for folding cardboard boxes (1879) to metal tubes for toothpaste (1892) and cellophane (1927), made it possible to package products in conveniently portable portions. Sales of canned goods rose from 34.5 million to almost 200 million cases in the thirty years after 1904.

As economic historian Stanley Lebergott notes, consumers used electric lighting, cars, prepared foods, and even medicines and health care to extend the greatest scarcity in life — free time. Moreover, the decline of family size between 1900 to 1930 in America (from 3.6 to 2.5 children) freed parents from time devoted to child rearing and created new possibilities for leisure.[29] While factories became more efficient, Americans spent increasing portions of their income on what Victorians would have called luxuries. Between 1900 and 1929, there was a 161 percent increase in spending for clothing (largely a necessity), but a 199 percent rise in personal care products (mostly a luxury). Similarly, 168 percent more was spent on housing as compared to 322 percent for transportation (mostly for cars), and 164 percent additional spending on medical care was dwarfed by a 285 percent rise in spending on recreation.[30]

American consumer culture was built on much more than new products. At least as important were innovations in selling — new approaches to retailing, buying on credit, packaging, and advertising. What Ford did for manufacturing, Richard Sears did for retailing. Indeed, both men were born the same year, 1863. Sears, whose career began with a modest mail-order business in 1886, registered nearly $41 million in sales by 1908. His company appealed to the ordinary farmer and wage earner, winning customers (as did Ford) with low prices. In 1897, Sears offered a sewing machine for $15.55 at a time when name-brand equivalents cost three to six times as much. The secret was high-volume sales and eliminating middlemen. The company was not alone: by 1900, nearly 1,200 catalogs brought variety and fashion to the most isolated, backward towns in the United States. Sears led the way by distributing 3.8 million catalogs in 1908. Sears, Roebuck and Company was quick to recognize the next phase. With the shift of population from small towns and farms to the suburbs by the mid-1920s, Sears built stores on the fringes of cities. By 1930, the company's 338 stores outfitted families, their houses, and their cars with up-to-date but practical goods. F. W. Woolworth's chain variety stores brought cheap versions of main street department store merchandise to 600 small towns and urban neighborhoods by 1912. Products of all kinds became available to most Americans and were seen by practically everyone. Paralleling the availability of cheap manufactured goods was the decline of the price of entertainment: Americans left out of relatively expensive theaters and music halls could attend the movies for a nickel in many cities by 1905 and by the mid-1920s could listen to the radio nearly everywhere for "free."[31] These trends extended the consumer culture downward socially and outward from the cities into rural America.

In 1900, not only were goods accessible and cheap, but there were incentives for buying more and more. Indeed, retailers had long before developed the art of rapid selling. In the 1860s, department stores had learned how to encourage spending by allowing anyone to enter their retail floors and even to handle merchandise, offered at fixed prices. These practices not only reduced the need for skilled staff (formerly necessary for bartering), but lessened time-consuming and often embarrassing exchanges between customers and staff. By 1909, progressive department stores, beginning with Filene's of Boston, cycled merchandise rapidly and efficiency through their stores. Staff marked down the prices of goods that did not sell after a determined period and dispatched slow-moving merchandise to bargain basements. This practice freed up capital and display space for new goods and habituated customers to expect bargains and novelty.[32]

Even more important in accelerating American spending was the installment plan. American purchases of cars, pianos, and other big-ticket items nearly doubled over the 1898–1916 period (reaching 7.6 percent of household income) because of credit. By 1924, almost three quarters of new cars were bought on time. And in 1925, 70 percent of furniture, 75 percent of radios, 80 percent of phonographs, 80 percent of appliances, and 90 percent of pianos were purchased on the installment plan. Buying on time certainly reduced the distance between what the rich and the merely middle class could possess. It also encouraged a faith that nothing was beyond reach of the family with a steady paycheck (excluding many wage earners). This did not mean that Americans became spendthrifts. Rather, installment buying encouraged consumers to reduce impulsive spending on ephemeral luxuries and plan purchases of durable luxuries. It taught them to set aside enough each month to make the payments, and this meant steadiness in work and play.[33]

It was not the sheer quantity of goods or even their utility that enabled consumerism to win the century. As important were the social and psychological meanings of commodities, created by the magic of modern retailing environments, packaging, and promotion. The department store, as it evolved in the second half of the nineteenth century, combined the appeal of accessible goods with the promise of luxury and taste. Window displays, marble columns and floors, and services like child care, concerts, and personalized tailoring made customers feel special and excited their imaginations. These stores took on the aura of churches. They created a link between the spiritual and the commercial in the minds of the retailing giant John Wanamaker and his customers. As historian William Leach shows, the turn-of-the-century department store and its elegant and colorful displays democratized desire, encouraging a taste for luxury and tempting consumers to buy finer goods.[34]

Packaged goods also assumed new symbolic meanings. The generic cracker in the barrel and the potato by the pound were gradually replaced by the products of a vast and diverse processing industry: Campbell and Heinz offered precooked soups, condiments, and vegetables in quantities for single-family meals; C. W. Post and W. K. Kellogg provided boxed cereals in lieu of fat- and protein-saturated meat and egg breakfasts; and Colgate and Gillette sold toothpaste and safety razors designed for daily, in-

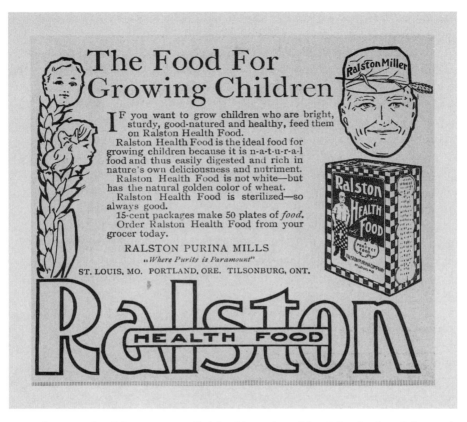

An example of the attempt to link health, packaged breakfast food, and the needs of children with a brand name. (*Collier's*, April 25, 1908, p. 33)

expensive, and convenient hygiene. Among the many packaged sweets that appeared were Life Savers (1913), a safe, "fresh," impulse confection to hide telltale breath, sold in saloons and tobacco shops. Soon after 1900, the cigarette became the "fast food" of the tobacco industry, providing a quick and convenient jolt yet advertised to sooth frazzled nerves and aid digestion.[35] Despite their diversity, these packaged goods offered Americans similar new personal freedoms. They were hygienic, freeing individuals from other people's germs; portable and self-administered, liberating people from the barber or communal stew pot; and, of course, convenient — easily acquired, used, and discarded.

The packaging of goods had still more advantages. It helped manufacturers and retailers sell mass-produced products on a mass scale while also satisfying customers' psychological and social longings. As business historian Richard Tedlow notes, the first three decades of the twentieth century was the golden age of national name brands. Improvements in transportation, advertising, packaging machinery, and corporate growth and coordination made it possible for a few manufacturers in almost every product line to dominate. Trademarks — from the stereotyped black cook on Aunt Jemima pancake mix to the simple white and red Campbell's Soup label design — persuaded customers to demand branded products from retailers. Packages seduced shoppers with the subliminal appeal of their color and shape and made them loyal consumers with the predictable flavor and feel of their contents.

Name brands did more than create dominant companies. They also served also to democratize American life at a time when social differences were extreme. Relatively homogenous products were sold everywhere and to everyone no matter their ethnicity or job: "Purchasing consumer goods came to be an important attribute shared by . . . diverse peoples."[36] The best example of the power of the name brand is Coca-Cola. This soft drink was invented in 1886 by the Atlanta druggist John Pemberton, but it became the refreshment of choice across the land soon after Asa Candler bought controlling shares in 1891. Using massive advertising, wide-ranging distribution, and a simple but striking trademarked label and bottle shape, Candler transformed Coca-Cola into a national soft drink. Indeed, Coke came to symbolize American consumerism. As early as 1929, it was sold in 66 countries. Candler created a mystique about the drink's "secret" formula. More important, his company's successful legal battles with trademark infringers in the 1910s and commitment to a single, uniform product made Coke the unchallenged leader in the soft drink industry until the rise of Pepsi-Cola in the late 1930s.[37]

Packaging provided still more subtle opportunities for manufacturers to sell and for consumers to feel good about buying products that could help them adapt to change. When women bought Quaker Oats (beginning in 1886), they purchased more than a wholesome cereal — they bought an image of a seventeenth-century figure of rectitude and tradition. As historian Thomas Hine notes, "the way to spur the consumption of material goods was to dematerialize them. A food was not just something for breakfast, but rather something to inspire confidence, an indication that you were doing a good job as a mother." The personality on the label was a bridge from manufacturer to customer, replacing the old personal relationship between storekeeper and shopper. In an increasingly mobile society, customers were more likely to know "Sunny Jim" or "Betty Crocker" than the clerk behind the counter. These were symbols of reliability and security in a society where people could no longer count on personal trust in the retailer.[38]

The principles of uniform packaging transformed the retail store. As early as 1907, A & P food stores offered only packaged goods. In 1916, Piggly Wiggly opened the first self-service grocery store, relying on packaging to sell from open shelves and thus eliminating the need for a clerk to fetch foodstuffs from behind a counter. The new system depersonalized and speeded up the buying experience. It also tempted the impulse buyer to fill the new shopping basket. Name-brand shopping eliminated the embarrassment of talking to a sales clerk. Retailers found that customers bought more without staff advice or intimidation. Self-service stores were open and airy and gave the feeling of abundance that encouraged free spending.[39]

It was inevitable that eating places became name-brand products in themselves. White Castle, a restaurant chain created in 1921 by Billy Ingram, assumed the form of a package — a box with reliable contents. Soon other fast food, gas station, and motel chains copied this principle. "When you sit in a White Castle" (said a 1932 brochure) "Remember that you are one of thousands; you are sitting on the same kind of stool; you are being served on the same kind of counter; the coffee you drink is made in accordance with a certain formula." This meant a predictable and inevitably bland hamburger, but also a sandwich that was no better or worse than anyone else's[40] — further evidence of consumers' democracy as well as their manipulation by retailers.

While department stores imparted an aura of luxury to shopping and name-brand packaging evoked emotional attachment, advertising gave Americans a vocabulary for "conversing" through goods. Much advertising was one-sided, selling goods with sophisticated and manipulative appeals. But ads also gave meaning to consumption, showing how products could be used to shape personal identity and social relationships.

The main stage for such dramatic speaking was the popular magazine. The leading name in popular periodicals was Cyrus Curtis. His publications (including the *Saturday Evening Post* and *Ladies' Home Journal*) won a large readership through low annual subscriptions. With huge circulation, he earned vast profits from mass-market advertising. Subscriptions of all magazines rose from 18 to 64 million between 1890 and 1905. These magazines served as vehicles for promoting new products of all

An early example of tie-in marketing was the Campbell Kids image, created first to promote the popular canned soup in 1905 and then in 1910 as a popular children's doll. (Library of Congress)

kinds — from bicycles and cars to soft drinks and chewing gum. Advertising revenues rose from $542 million in 1900 to $2.94 billion in 1920, reaching almost $3.43 billion by 1929. Ads, displaying fashion, cosmetics, and household goods, became the main purpose of women's magazines. As one advertising executive admitted in 1907, "a magazine is simply a device to induce people to read advertising." By 1931, advertising constituted 50 – 65 percent of the contents of general and women's magazines. It is understandable why many saw the advertiser as a threat to the moral and aesthetic authority of the clergy, teachers, and serious writers.[41]

Given the close association between advertising and the mass market, both friends and foes of commercial copy believed that ads created economic demand to absorb the increased supply of goods produced in mechanized factories.[42] Also, since products had become standardized, ads seemed necessary to teach shoppers to distinguish between name brands like Del Monte and generic canned peas. The advertiser's job went beyond announcing products and prices to persuade consumers of the nutritional value of canned soup and the hygienic virtues of tooth brushing (with a specific kind of toothpaste).[43]

Clearing vast warehouses required more than brand-name exposure or even selling innovation. It demanded that ads focus on consumers' needs and feelings. Increasingly the product itself took second place. Beginning about 1905, advertising innovators like Ernest Calkins advocated that modern psychology be used to link products with the desires and insecurities of consumers, thus creating a longing for particular items. Through the powerful forces of association, ad copy writers peddled personal adequacy, romance, sexual potency, and preventatives of aging and death. In the 1920s, merchandisers accepted the sociologist's claim that patriarchy, based on the family as producer, was in decline. The new family was a unit of consumption. The father provided the money, but the mother was in charge of the family's real purpose — spending. Business consultant Christine Frederick advised advertisers to appeal directly to women who, she noted, had become the purchasers of 80 percent of American goods. "Mrs. Consumer" was a "new kind of aristocracy living in luxury and leisure upon the labors of man, — the commoner." She would civilize man with well-considered purchases. The merchandiser had to understand her personality, aspirations, and anxieties. Advertising also increasingly focused on a distinctive youth market with copy suggesting the incompetence of adults, especially fathers.[44]

Magazine ads seldom addressed the needs of laborers, blacks, or ethnic minorities. Advertisers freely admitted that they directed their messages to only the richer two thirds or even half of the population. Advertised goods were often emblems of status, representing the values of bourgeois possessiveness or aristocratic snobbery that had trickled down, through ads, to the insecure and aspiring.[45]

Both advertisers and their critics agreed that consumers (especially women) were passive and that the function of ads was to manipulate rather than to inform. By the 1920s, ads followed the model of the personal confession, a storytelling formula found in tabloids and *True Story* magazine. The insecure reader learned what happened to the businessman or housewife who did not use mouthwash or disinfectant. One advertiser insisted that his typical reader had the "mind of a child of ten."[46] This approach presumed that women and children were susceptible to emotional appeals and to manipulation. Sociologist Robert Lynd argued that manufacturers were "compelled to create 'acceptance' to keep ahead of the production curve." Advertisers, he claimed, took advantage of the contradictions besetting the individual consumer who, in response to the frustrations of social change, found comfort in consumption.[47]

But ads were more than manipulations of anxiety. Unfortunately, analysis of advertising by both contemporaries and historians has focused too narrowly on how ads have impeded rational choice and undermined "citizenship" by replacing civil and political debate with one-way commercial appeals. Typically, Robert Lynd believed that advertising encouraged an escape from responsibility. In this way, American consumer culture was likened to political totalitarianism: "Modern merchandising manipulates our hunger for a way out, a fresh start, by selling us a new car, an Easter bonnet, or an electric razor as a momentary splurge into authoritative certainty."[48]

While ads were controlling and copy writers self-consciously set themselves above their audience, these messages were more than cynical appeals to status consciousness or insecurity. They were scripts of social dramas that helped people cope with modern life by giving goods meaning and making them into props that said who consumers were or aspired to be. As historian Roland Marchand notes, advertising was "integrative propaganda" that portrayed the American dream and its frustrations. Attached to goods, this propaganda gave Americans a language for conversing with each other and themselves. Naturally, these ads appealed to "externals" — in dress, grooming, and scent — and often reinforced the idea that "impressions" counted for everything: "Let your face reflect confidence —

not worry" declared an ad for Williams Shaving Cream. Such messages capitalized "on an increasing public uncertainty that true ability and character would always win out in the scramble for success [and] stressed the narrowness of the line that separated those who succeeded from those who failed." Listerine mouthwash became a necessity in the bathrooms of millions of Americans when, in the 1920s, ads warned the insecure that "halitosis" (offensive breath) unbeknownst to them could ruin their careers, love lives, and friendships unless prevented with daily use of Listerine.[49] The *Book of Etiquette* was sold with a similar pitch: "Are you conscious of your crudities? Do you make friends easily? How would you take celery — asparagus — radishes? Unless you are absolutely sure of yourself, you will be embarrassed. And embarrassment *cannot be concealed*." The *Book of Etiquette* offered security with the essentials of authoritative social ritual. Such ads may have made people more superficial in their judgments of others and themselves, but these appeals were also rational and advantageous. In an increasingly mobile society, such reliance on "externals" was a sensible way of communicating because many people important to Americans "really" did not know them (their families, personalities, or characters). Doubtless many Americans would have agreed with the explanation by a "leading citizen" of Lynd's Middletown of why people judged others by their houses and cars: "It's perfectly natural. You see, they know money, and they don't know you."[50]

These dramas in advertising assuaged social anxieties. More positively, they also promised Americans membership in an exciting community of consumers, no matter how rich or ordinary their lives might actually have been. The Majestic kitchen stove claimed to be "most satisfactory for the palatial residence or modest home." Pond's mass-produced beauty cream was endorsed by "the distinguished in the society of five nations [who] . . . trust their beauty to the same sure care" (including Mrs. Cornelius Vanderbilt Jr., Lady Louis Montbatten, and the Duquesa de Alba). Ads in the 1920s declared that anyone could have the luxury of a vacuum cleaner or a radio, no matter if they lived in a bungalow or a gabled mansion. Consumer goods were supposed to end class envy by giving the common American access to the world of luxury. An ad for a 1924 Chevrolet called "The Psychology of the Automobile" makes this point very clear. The once poor laborer and mechanic, the ad copy notes, now

> drives to the building operation or construction job in his own car. He is now a capitalist — the owner of a taxable asset. . . . Evenings and

Sundays, he takes his family into the country or to the now near town fifty to one hundred miles away. He has become somebody, has a broader and more tolerant view of the one-time cartoon hayseed and the fat-cigared plutocrat. How can Bolshevism flourish in a motorized country having a standard of living and thinking too high to permit the existence of an ignorant, narrow, peasant majority? Is not the automobile entitled to the major credit in this elevation of our standard of citizenship?[51]

These appeals may have depoliticized the masses by implying that there was no reason to envy the rich or to identify with the poor tenement dweller. But they also asserted the right of all to participate in a common material culture without necessarily giving up "who you really are," be it a Jew, an Appalachian farmer, or a midwestern storekeeper. In the United States, cheap advertised goods gradually "eliminated the visual distinction of class . . . [so that] nine-tenths of the men are well dressed in clothing of such uniform appearance that bank clerk and bank president appear the same."[52]

Ads also tended to incorporate opposites. In a seemingly confused collage of images, commercial messages could appeal to a nostalgia for the familiarity of bygone villages but also evoke the excitement of modern urban skylines. As Marchand notes, "people wanted to enjoy the benefits of modern technology without relinquishing any of the emotional satisfactions of a simpler life." Ads pointed to a popular ambiguity about modernity and thus reconciled the past and the future, the social and the private. Intellectuals may have sought consistency and clarity or choice between the "restoration" of the old and pursuit of "progress" in the new, but most people wanted both. Like religion, consumer culture reconciled different impulses.[53]

Finally, ads personalized goods. Instead of simply gluing mixed emotional metaphors onto soap, cars, and clothes, copy writers associated these feelings with admired characters. Powerful companies also adopted nostalgic themes and colorful personalities in ads to win a friendly image: wizened grandmothers sold coffee or shortening and cute Kewpie figures peddled Jell-O desserts. General Mills offered insecure homemakers, who might lack a trusted relative's guidance in modern cooking, the authority of Betty Crocker, an image of the ideal homemaker/home economist. This icon of domestic modernity changed in dress and face over the decades to reflect the times. She appeared not only on cake mix packages but also in pamphlets and on radio programs, dispensing practical advice about the modern kitchen. Toy shops offered boys eager for a masculine hero and friend A. C. Gilbert, the maker of the erector set, who understood their longings for playful freedom. Gilbert embellished his ads and his products with his image and exciting stories of manly success in college sports, business, and engineering.[54] Products increasingly embodied what people in a "mass" society wanted, a reassuring and inspiring friend. Ads were far more than manipulations, "forcing" people into performing their passive duty of spending to keep the mass-production economy humming. Ads linked material goods to immaterial longings, blending social, psychological, and physical needs indivisibly.

Generations, Gender, and Goods

Commercial goods, when introduced, displayed, packaged, and advertised, facilitated the often confused journey into the twentieth century. Americans experienced a loss of communal culture with its personal but fixed roles and witnessed the birth of a mass society in which relations were more impersonal and ephemeral but also more individualistic and even expressive. Products gave Americans ways of identifying themselves in groups when the old associations of family and neighborhood no longer worked.

This was often a painful, ambiguous transition. Many older immigrants, upon settling in American cities, were anguished by the loss of culture, religious faith, family ties, and friendships. Boston Brahmins saw urban immigrants as uncivilized, and Western populists viewed them as untested by the character-building rigors of the frontier. The foreign-born, however, often tried to preserve ethnic and religious traditions against the threat or temptation of American materialism. Immigrant parents sometimes were intimidated by their children's education and demanded their offsprings' pay packets for family needs. In response, the second generation often criticized parents for their ignorance of good English and flaunted their Americanness with new clothes and entertainments.[55]

Nevertheless, consumption often ameliorated tensions. Jewish immigrants, who had little desire or opportunity to return to the ghettos and persecution that they had known in Europe, were often committed to forging a new American identity. An obvious way of doing this was through modern consumer goods. "The vacation in the mountains or by the sea," notes historian Andrew Heinze, "embodied the Jewish vision of an earthly paradise, a haven from persecution; the well-furnished parlor, crowned with a piano, supported American democratic ideals by upholding the inherent dignity of the ordinary family."[56] Purchasing these goods did not necessarily mean abandoning religious tradition or ethnic heritage. The superficiality of consumer goods suggested that deeper values could survive.

At the same time, new arenas of spending helped children of immigrants establish their own identities. By visiting amusement parks, penny arcades, baseball parks, and dance halls and by wearing new clothes and adopting new foods, second-generation immigrants distanced themselves from their parents while participating in American society. New pleasure spots, emerging as urban institutions in the 1890s and 1900s, fit their needs. These commercial venues were easily accessible, via streetcars and other public transportation, to work sites and residential areas. At the same time, they were free from association with any ethnic group or neighborhood. While reformers hoped that schools, playgrounds, and settlement house activities would make immigrants into Americans, the foreign-born usually found commercial entertainment centers more attractive ways of settling in the new land.[57] The secret was that commercial amusement centers simultaneously broke from folk culture and appealed to youthful freedom. They offered an escape from ethnic neighborhoods and the judging eyes of relatives. This was a kind of Americanization that the apolitical young could relate to.

A good example were the amusement parks that sprung up on the outskirts of most American cities in the 1890s and 1900s. New York's Coney Island, once a den for gamblers, drunks, and prostitutes, had become by the 1890s a unique and tantalizing mix of concert and dance halls and thrilling amusement rides for respectable members of both sexes. It was a public place of shared experience and individual expression. Three self-contained amusement parks dominated Coney Island by 1900: Steeplechase Park (with fun houses, rides, shows, and blow holes that lifted skirts), Luna Park (with romance at the Canals of Venice as well as the excitement of roller coasters), and Dreamland (with thrilling rides featuring biblical themes). Coney Island was not a rejection of self-control and respectability. Instead, it was a place where people could find temporary relief from the constraints of family and ethnic values in a playful and provocative, yet controlled and even vaguely uplifting, environment. It was a modern festival, not confined to a special time like Mardi Gras but to a special place, accessible almost at will.[58]

Youths of all backgrounds reached for the commercial pleasures that liberated them from family and routine. Consumer culture redefined youth, transforming it from mostly a period of growth and transition to family and work responsibilities into a time of membership in a distinct consumption community. Dance halls, far from residential areas and accommodating 500 to 3,000 fun seekers, appeared in American cities around 1900. These places provided a dramatic change from the boredom of wage work. In contrast to traditional neighborhood picnic grounds or social clubs, dance halls gave the opportunity to experiment with "tough dancing" that encouraged heterosexual contact and even simulated intercourse. Young wage-earning women invested in clothing and cosmetics in hope of gaining attention and "treats" of refreshment and gifts from the men they danced and flirted with. Movies also offered a setting for heterosexual encounters beyond parental supervision, especially after 1905 when nickelodeons appeared along streetcar lines. By 1910, women were already 40 percent of the audience in New York, and many observers believed that the movie houses drew men away from male saloons for outings with women. The new rituals of dating accompanied this commercial culture of fun.[59]

Between 1900 and 1930, many young people extended their schooling beyond the eighth grade and a relatively large number went to college. The effect was not only a better educated citizenry, but an "extracurriculum" that became a peer culture of consumption.[60] As historian Paula Fass notes, the student generation after World War I often rejected the formality of Victorian society and insisted on their "right to self-expression, self-determination, and personal satisfaction."[61] Despite the demands of studying and long lists of college regulations, student life was organized around a peer culture. One midwestern university observer noted, "failure in studies is not as important to college students as failure in social adjustment." The "real work" of American collegians in the 1920s was responding positively to fads in dress, speech, music, and dance. While such a recreational culture placed a premium on superficiality, it also taught the useful skills of adjusting rapidly to change and of conforming to group norms. This commercialized peer culture provided a transition to an adulthood of companionate marriage, corporate-business "getting-on," and status-conscious consumption.[62]

The opportunity for "automobility" with the family car added another dimension to the liberation of middle-class youths. Now these young people could use the parental house as a dormitory. In one 1920s survey, only 16 percent of families ate three meals together each day, and a mere 38 per-

Dreamland at Coney Island in the 1900s was a magical place combining the exotic and the ultramodern as an escape from the dreariness of everyday work and family.
(Library of Congress)

cent gathered regularly for one. The teenage couple escaped the front parlor for the privacy of the automobile, movie theater, or dance hall.[63]

Fashion and cosmetics also gave young women fresh identities and distance from family. As Jane Addams, a leading social worker from Chicago observed, "The working girl, whose family lives in a tenement . . . who has little social standing and has to make her own place, knows full well how much habit and style of dress has to do with her position. . . . Her clothes are her background, and from them she is largely judged." In the 1920s, above-the-knee hemlines and rolled stockings let the young discard their elders' full-length skirts. Clothes and cosmetics helped immigrant women define themselves as "American" and enabled them to compete in the dating game. Similarly, African American cosmetics (especially skin whiteners and hair straighteners) were advertised as "glorifying our womanhood," giving dignity of sorts to women stereotyped with racial and rural images. Cosmetics allowed females of all races and backgrounds to "put on" a personality. These young women rejected the nineteenth cen-

41

tury's pejorative distinction between depth of character and deceptive appearance. Make-up allowed the "new woman" to assume innovative, diverse, and multiple images: a young mother by day could transform herself into a belle of the ball by night. Is it any surprise then that per capital output of cosmetics rose almost threefold in the 1920s and that there was an eightfold increase in the number of beauty shops in that decade?[64]

These forms of consumption sparked fears among white middle-class parents that their children were being corrupted by working-class and black culture. "The public dance hall and the cheap theater . . . and finally the contagious love of diversion and excitement," opined a report to a Minneapolis Vice Commission, "seemingly possess all elements of society in our cities."[65] Solutions to this threat ranged from revitalizing middle-class home life (especially with the flight to the suburbs) and regulating dance halls and movies to creating alternative, but uplifting, enjoyments for youths and the poor. Reformers did not realize that consumer culture could cross class, race, or age boundaries without corrupting the "innocent."

By the end of the nineteenth century, however, many middle-class families were leaving their homes for popular theaters, dancing academies, and even amusement parks.[66] The key to making these public pleasures acceptable was to disassociate them from the "dangerous" working classes and minorities and to identify them with the vitality and spontaneity of youth and childhood. This process paralleled growing toleration of youthful exuberance and sexuality (as seen in the declining role of chaperons at dances). Adults began to embrace a "cleaned up" version of working-class commercial leisure, increasingly deemed vital and modern rather than dangerous. In 1913, famed performers Irene and Vernon Castle legitimized "tough" dance steps like the "bunny hug" with origins in brothels and popular in working-class dance halls by transforming them into ballroom standards like the fox trot. Irene Castle represented not the working-class "charity girl" but an "elegantly youthful and girlish image" with her bobbed hair. In the early 1920s, the *Saturday Evening Post* printed stories about youthful females who smoked and drank, appealing to a flapper audience. Youthfulness became the sought-after standard in women's magazines. Ads for face cream invited the middle-class mother to get back the youthful face of her daughter. "Better than jewels," declared an ad for Palmolive Soap, was "that school girl complexion." Cosmetics lost much of their association with "painted women" and became a way for respectable ladies to regain a bit of youthful vitality.[67] The culture of consumption that often divided classes and ages could also bring them together.

This focus on youth helped resolve a growing family tension. Early twentieth-century parents were frustrated at how childhood had changed since they were young. Teenagers no longer made an obvious transition to the worlds of family and work responsibility under the watchful eyes of parents or paternalistic employers. Child labor at home or in outside jobs had become far less common, especially in the middle classes. Instead, youth had become increasingly a time of play and spending that adults did not fully control. Still, parents found opportunities for influencing their offspring by making compromises with the new culture of youth.

For example, shopping for teenage girls' clothes gave parents a chance to negotiate with their children. An article from *Parents' Magazine* entitled "If I Were That Girl's Mother" was typical of the advice offered to mothers confused about how to introduce their daughters to the troubling world of consumption. Rather than fight every purchase her daughter desired, the mother should offer an allowance that provided "a small margin for the very personal treasures dear to every child's heart." Mother should sympathize with the girl's anxieties about fitting into her peer culture. Parents needed to acknowledge that fashions had changed, that each generation had a right to its own style. A short dress today did not mean the same thing as it did when the mother was a child. At the same time, an weekly allowance would teach the child to recognize the limits of the family's resources. The parent should insist that the daughter earn some of the money she wanted to spend on herself. All this was a very subtle game. This article rejected old standards and methods of asserting parental authority for a policy of indirect control: "While we may still cling to our fundamentals, we are ready to change the outer form of their expression." In "discussions" over what the daughter could buy, the mother was to balance her authority against the child's new rights. And spending became the arena for this complex negotiation.[68]

In many ways, adults used new consumer goods to express their increasing acceptance of children's freedom from work and their support for a more sheltered but also more democratic family. The association of spending and the indulgent parent was, of course, not new to the early twentieth century. Progressively, in late Victorian America (at least in the middle class), the sheltered child embodied the adult's longing for an emotional life apart from the impersonal market. In their Christmas gifts to children, parents expected no economic "return" on their "investment." Santa Claus with his bottomless sack of toys perfectly expressed both a new sentimentality toward the innocence and vitality of childhood and the

"What you see, you get"

Priceless motion pictures of your dear ones
... as they are today

Kodak home movie cameras may have been only for the rich in the 1920s, but they captured a common longing — preserving family memories with an easy-to-use technology. (*Vanity Fair*, Nov. 1927, p. 11)

modern celebration of abundance in a new consumer culture. Santa removed the ambivalence parents felt about the connection between the "spiritual" home and the "materialist" market by disguising the commercial origins of Christmas toys. Gifts from Santa's sack preserved the innocence and wonder of childhood and thus the sanctity of the home as a refuge from calculation and routine work.[69]

Egalitarian family values were expressed in spending on playrooms, protected sandboxes, and swing sets for the backyard. In the 1920s, experts insisted that play areas be equipped with bare, easily cleaned floors, cheerful colors, and ample shelving for toys, books, and musical instruments. Children with such play spaces and lots of good toys would not want to play in the street or to stray from a happy future of suburban living. The piano, according to an ad, was a purchase that would nurture "your children's appreciation of music." Another ad lectured: "Music is born in the child — but parents must bring it out" with a piano. Similarly, as early as 1928, Kodak's home movie camera was sold with the idea that parents could preserve their children just "as they are today" on film.[70] Through the new consumption, the powerful ideals of childhood innocence and vitality, with their promise of bringing the family together, were given full expression.

By 1910, children were more than beneficiaries of joyful spending by adults. They had become serious consumers in their own right. While child-rearing experts like Sidonie Gruenberg told parents that children needed allowances to learn how to be cultivated consumers, toymakers discovered that children were enthusiastic shoppers: "an advertisement to a child had no barriers to climb, no scruples to overcome," noted a cynical trade magazine.[71] Children were the future, and this meant that they had the right to make their own consumer choices. Advertisers had discovered the youthful "spendthrift," but parents also had begun to equate children's spending with their "right" to youthful autonomy and self-expression. Ads encouraged boys to long for air rifles, bicycles, and electric trains and insisted that the child knew best in choosing the right toy. Still, Lionel invited the boy to "Take your dad into partnership. . . . Make him your pal" with an electric train. Such purchases both affirmed the boy's autonomy and renewed ties with the older generation. Ads in magazines like *American Boy* insisted that erector sets or other construction and "scientific" toys were more than playthings. They taught boys how to be successful men in a world of technology and business. Just as consumer goods both linked (and broke) the generations, they also affirmed that fun and the work ethic were no longer enemies.[72]

Parents got their way, while indulging the child, when they bought the right stuff. Adults persuaded kids to do what was necessary (drink milk, wash their hands, or eat dinner) by favoring them with Thompson's Malted Milk, Lifebuoy soap "wash-up charts," or a Squibb Chocolate Vitavose food additive. The Playskool (originally a home desk equipped with craft and educational toys) would "keep [children] happily busy indoors" when they wanted to play outside on rainy days. "And, Mother, they'll not take up your time either for with PLAYSKOOL you don't have to be the teacher. PLAYSKOOL is a Home Kindergarten, Teacher and Companion, all in one."[73] Consumer goods repeatedly affirmed the seemingly contradictory — parental authority and children's freedom. They could even substitute for the parent's control.

The introduction of innovative home appliances also resolved apparently conflicting tensions during a period of confusion about the future roles of married women. Ads for new kitchen and cleaning appliances claimed that they liberated women from traditional drudgery. At the same time, these goods reaffirmed homebound duties. Vacuum cleaners and refrigerators were portrayed as "mechanical servants," giving their owners freedom from unreliable or demanding human maids but also suggesting

45

that affluent women do their own housework. In 1912, Thomas Edison echoed this idea: "The housewife of the future will be neither a slave to servants nor herself a drudge. She will give less attention to the home, because the home will need less; she will be rather a domestic engineer than a domestic laborer, with the greatest of all handmaidens, electricity, at her service."[74]

The message was quite subtle. On the one hand, modern appliances freed time for leisure and service activities outside the home. On the other hand, housework, aided by modern appliances, was not really work and the middle-class homemaker could do it herself without loss of status. This second theme was gradually reinforced when home appliances began to lose their look as machines and turn into *objets d'art*. The Victorian ideal of the parlor as a fine art museum was extended into the kitchen. The smooth surfaces and streamlining of the Coldspot refrigerator of 1935 hid the critical motor, while toasters took on the look of silver sets appropriate for display on the breakfast table. The new domestic machine extended the middle-class wife's traditional role as an impresario of family parties: "Make entertaining a simple, joyous job" with the GE refrigerator, read an ad in 1928. Cooking with a new gas range eliminated toil, but the stove also became, according to advertisers, a device that encouraged traditional "crafts" and allowed women to "return" to artistry in cooking. Appliances were supposed to bring convenience — note the rise in the 1920s of the compact and gradually multiple bathroom located near bedrooms. At the same time, appliances were supposed to be consistent with traditional Victorian values. The American Radiator was sold not merely to provide the comfort and ease of central heating, but because it supposedly enhanced family togetherness, much as had the piano and parlor of the nineteenth century: "People who are comfortable are courteous; they grow heated only when they are cold." By demanding central heating, wives and mothers created a congenial physical environment necessary to avoid the "many domestic tragedies" that "start at the breakfast table." Once again, consumer goods accommodated rapidly changing American family life by allowing American women to embrace both modern and traditional roles.[75]

Time and Consumption

Just as consumption relieved social tension by helping Americans get into or away from the crowd or family, it shaped meanings of time in an epoch when change was particularly frustrating and confusing. Consumables reconciled ambiguous attitudes toward the past and future and reduced anxiety about change. Framed reproductions of village scenes, mantel knickknacks, and archaic housing styles all appealed to sentimentalized memory and the desire to combat change. In the 1920s, the American middle class shared with the Du Ponts at Wintertur and the Rockefellers at Williamsburg a fascination with American crafts and the restoration of old houses.[76] East Coast buyers sought pseudocolonial exteriors even if they also wanted modern floor plans in their suburban homes. With affluence came a taste for still earlier housing styles — "stockbroker Tudor," for example.[77] When newlyweds bought complete rooms of furniture, they marked the beginning of a distinctly personal world and created "symbols of security" against change. Souvenirs from cherished vacations or prized gewgaws of departed relatives brought the past into the present.[78]

Living rooms remained private museums, much as they had been in Victorian times. However, what had been a mark of bourgeois respectability in the nineteenth century gradually extended down the social ladder into the white collar and even the skilled working class. The Victorian home and its interior were supposed to evoke and reflect decorous and courteous behavior among family members. Furnishings were props in a "comfortable theater for middle-class self-presentation." Manufactured fabric, cabinetry, and upholstery in rich and complex patterns blended imperceptibly with handmade lace and needlepoint in parlor displays. This ideal survived into the twentieth century despite the trend toward convenience and informal comfort. The all-purpose living room replaced the formal front parlor, and families shifted resources from "permanent" furnishings to that symbol of change and mobility, the automobile. Still, as historian Katherine Grier notes, "displays of mementos on the desk or mantel and the 'art group' of ceramics and glass atop the center table remained."[79]

The back and forth between ideas of progress and tradition can be seen in that most Victorian of domestic furnishings, the piano. More than a musical instrument, it was essentially a marker of tradition and respectability in the late nineteenth century. Thanks to modern manufacturing, the piano found its way into surprisingly modest Victorian parlors. However, after 1900, it gave way to the innovative "player" variety (which made up half of piano sales by the early 1920s). Ironically, the modern appeal of convenience and authoritative musicality with the piano rolls that featured famous virtuosi paved the way for the radio and the eclipse of the player piano by the late 1920s. The traditional piano then regained its role as a symbol of stability, experiencing an extraordinary comeback in the 1930s. Amateur piano playing expressed traditional home and family life, was a form of personal creativity in a mechanistic age, and promised moral uplift against "crude" popular culture. The piano joined the package of middle-class domestic "refinements" in the battle against uncontrolled change.[80]

Other goods were unambiguous tokens of modernity and anticipations of the future. As sociologist Herbert Blumer notes, fashion has provided an "orderly preparation for the immediate future," leading consumers through time.[81] Changing hemlines or lapels reflected not simply rejection of the past but measured and usually modest adjustments to the future. And ironically, as fashion became more democratic, available at Macy's or even Sears, the celebrity of the screen, stage, or fan magazine became essential for alerting ordinary people about where fashion was going.[82]

Women's fashions are an excellent example. The flapper style of dress and grooming was a point-by-point refutation of the Gibson Girl (short bobbed vs. long hair; simple above-knee skirt and rolled-down socks vs. long skirt with draping). More active dances like the Tango of 1911, the introduction of women to sports, and the need for more "practical" garments for motoring all contributed to the shedding of cloth and corsets. Ready-to-wear clothing, modeled after the haute couture of Paris, became widespread in the 1920s. Artificial silk (known as rayon after 1936) also made stylish dresses and underwear affordable for ordinary women. In the United States, the large population made long production lines of fashionable clothing efficient. John Wanamaker's mail-order catalog of 1919 promised certainty for the insecure fashion seeker: "Can you be sure of *correct and newest fashions?* You couldn't be *more* sure than at Wanamaker's. Our home is in the fashion center of New York and we are in constant touch with our Paris office."[83]

Fads and novelties were hardly invented in the early twentieth century, but there were certainly a lot of them in this period: ping pong appeared in 1903, the diabolo toy in 1908, the card game Rook in 1910, Ouija boards in 1918, pogo sticks in 1921, mah-jongg in 1922, and crossword puzzles in 1924 — just to mention a few prominent crazes. Many were associated with children's play (teddy bears in 1906, Billiken dolls in 1908, and Kewpie dolls in 1912).[84] Card and board games also often celebrated contemporary events and modern trends. From the 1880s, Parker Brothers used cheap color lithography to create a series of novelty board games (Around the World with Nellie Bly, The World's Fair Game, Motor Carriage Game, and Sherlock Holmes Game).[85] Parents shared gifts of "up-to-dateness" with their children in toys that celebrated the new, and more important, that prepared the young for change. Because parents often saw their offspring as vehicles of progress, they bought toys that seemed to anticipate future roles of sons and daughters. Electric trains (introduced widely in 1910) and construction toys like the erector set of 1913 were designed to prepare boys for an optimistic world of mechanical gadgetry and business success. By contrast, girls in this period learned about their future roles by making their dolls into actors in domestic dramas of modern care giving, conviviality, and consumption. They had permission to retreat into childhood but were also cajoled into being good future mothers and homemakers.[86]

Goods not only anticipated the future; their acquisition suggested personal progress. Americans learned from exhibitions and world's fairs (Philadelphia in 1876, Chicago in 1893, Buffalo in 1901, and St. Louis in 1904) that the future meant new, exciting consumer goods that would solve all problems. Chicago's "Century of Progress" (1933–34) and New York's "World of Tomorrow" (1938–39) reinforced this faith in the consumption fix. Progress came to mean not merely liberating technology but rising from one standard of living to the next. While the rich or the young might form the avant garde, all classes and ages would eventually join the march upward and onward. A principle function of ads and the magazine articles that accompanied them was to identify the "next stage" and why Americans should welcome and aspire to that promised future.[87]

A good example of this pattern is the way the automobile was promoted. The car changed annually in the 1900s, often with substantial improvements. The horseless carriage of 1899 was unmechanical in appearance and so short that it looked "as though a horse were to be attached at any time." By 1905, the automobile was very different — longer, lower, with an engine in front (not under the seat) with prominent exposed mechanical parts. It practically shouted: "I am a machine and I am beautiful." The auto became associated in the public mind with fashion, changing regularly and identified by the year it was produced. "'Last year's car' has come to be as much a phrase of reproach as 'last year's hat'," noted one writer in 1914.[88]

As we have seen, between 1908 and the early 1920s, Ford's Model T was the standard in auto-mobility. By the 1920s, however, it was surpassed by the more stylish, comfortable, and prestigious cars of General Motors (GM). When Ford fell behind in defining the American Way of Life, so did its market share (from 55 percent in 1921 to only 25 percent in 1927). Even though GM's Chevrolet of 1923 sold for $860 compared to the Ford, a bargain at $290, it offered innovations in style as well as small technical changes. In the mid-1920s, master designer Harley Earl's La Salle Cadillac pioneered a new look with a unified body shape, flashy colors, a lowered silhouette, and rounded corners.[89] But the lowly Chevrolet was not far behind. A 1927 ad trumpeted that its

> handsome, modish colors . . . emphasize the symmetry of the body lines and enhance the individuality of the various models. Beautiful upholstery fabrics, patterned to harmonize with the body colors, give to closed car interiors the comfort and charm of a drawing room — while full-crown, one-piece fenders and bullet-type head lamps lend an air of custom elegance.[90]

Even Henry Ford had to advertise and adapt to new styling. Despite regular cuts in price, stagnant sales of his Model T forced Ford to take out magazine ads in 1924 and to abandon his Tin Lizzie for the more up-to-date Model A in 1927.[91]

The trend toward timely style helped overcome market saturation. After all, 55 percent of American families owned cars by 1927, and the possibilities of selling to the lower half were slight. The Big Three of Ford, GM, and Chrysler already had 72 percent of car sales by the mid-1920s, so there was little incentive to compete through lower prices. Instead, manufacturers favored distinct styles and images rather than mechanical improvements. Consumers demanded cars that imparted an image of progress in life that their jobs often did not provide. Cars were increasingly fashion products, like clothes, ways of defining the new.[92]

A related GM innovation was the development of a full range of cars. Beginning with the Chevrolet and rising on a steady slope to the Pontiac, Oldsmobile, Buick, and Cadillac, GM designed automobiles for every price range. In contrast to Ford's practical, mass-market Model T, GM under Alfred P. Sloan offered a dream of gaining status with a car that instantly marked the owner as having "arrived." Trade-in allowances for used cars and installment buying encouraged buyers to "move up" from a Chevrolet to a Pontiac or even a Buick. Cars had always been ways of symbolizing status, but beginning in the 1920s, Sloan made status climbing into a way of marking personal progress.[93]

The future through consumption meant more than bigger and better or greater social status. It also suggested faster and faster change. Robert and Helen Lynd noted that "each new thrilling invention" raised the "psy-

50 *Body Styles and Types*
500 *Color Combinations*
Standard — *Fisher Custom Built* — *Fleetwood Custom Built*

The Cadillac led the way in GM's styling revolution, promising "individualized luxury" with an extraordinary range of color and body combinations.

(*Vanity Fair*, Sept. 1926, p. 47)

chological standard of living," increasing the "desirability of making money, and lots of it." Americans seemed to forget their old goal of rising up the ladder of professional success for the more attainable objective of "buying a living" and the expectation of material progress without end.[94] Mass-production engineering and design improvement allowed the retooling and surface changes necessary for products to be introduced and transformed more quickly. As Simon Patten noted, "It is not the increase of goods for consumption that raises the standard of life . . . [but] the rapidity with which [the consumer] tires of any one pleasure. To have a high standard of life means to enjoy a pleasure intensely and to tire of it quickly."[95]

While the new and improved gave Americans the thrill of novelty, goods also helped people "control" time. This was the appeal of the Gillette safety razor: "The Gillette is a builder of regular habits. Own a Gillette — be master of your time — shave in three minutes." No longer would men have to wait for a barber or use time-consuming straight razors. Cosmetics helped control time in the most human dimension — aging. In a 1911 ad, Palmolive soap claimed that it borrowed special palm and olive oils from the mysterious Orient but, aided by modern science, Palmolive did what the oils "by themselves cannot do" — "Bring life and health to skin." Another ad claimed: "Halting birthdays in their tracks is a job for the anti-birthday specialist, Marie Earle," producer of a line of make-up products. And men were not left out. Ads for Colgate Shaving Cream insisted that with daily use a man at forty could still have a youthful and healthy face (in stark contrast to the ancient look of his bewhiskered dad at the same age a generation earlier) — and win in the game of business. As Jackson Lears notes, merchandisers taught Americans eager to learn that they could control their physical and even psychological lives.[96]

Finally, consumer culture shaped time by appropriating and creating holidays. The religious calendar had traditionally marked seasonal transitions and annual renewals of faith and family. Even before the twentieth century, these sacred days had been commercialized, but in the 1900s, Christmas displays became majestic. The Grand Court of Wanamaker's department store in Philadelphia was decorated like a cathedral and featured concerts of carols.[97] In Victorian America, Easter had been appropriated by florists, the card and novelty industries, and women's fashion. The Easter Parade, once a religious promenade, had become a fashion show. By the 1890s, lesser holidays like St. Valentine's Day had become times for buying candy, and new holidays like Mother's Day and Father's Day had close, if not always welcomed, associations with the floral, candy, and other "gift" industries practically from their inceptions (1908 and 1910 respectively).[98] Yet, as historian Leigh Eric Schmidt notes, the commercialization of these holidays was not simply a hostile takeover. The sentimentality of celebrations in churches and homes carried over into the card and novelty industry. The commercialization of the festival calendar was in fact a smooth transition from the Victorians' romantic and aesthetic understanding of religious, moral, and even patriotic holidays.[99] Goods may have always marked the special occasion. Nevertheless, by the twentieth century, shopping for them had become the central means of marking holiday time.

The Sensuality of Shopping

Not all acts of consumption between 1900 and 1930 could be reduced to social meanings or markers of time. Some goods brought comfort and ease, sensations of power and speed, or those many joys of the five senses. Cars and appliances promised personal power and immediate gratification. When the electric starter replaced the hand crank in cars after 1913, the individual's ability to command the machine rose while effort expended decreased. The Chrysler "70" (1926) pledged "70 miles and more, per hour. . . . 5 to 25 miles [per hour] in 6" seconds." The Franklin car gave drivers the sensation of "riding the crest of a new era of fast travel with an airplane-type engine." Henry Adams captured this appeal when he wrote in 1904 that "At the rate of progress since 1800, every American who lived into the year 2000 would know how to control unlimited power."[100] New technologies made individuals into masters of nature, space, and time. Dreams of controlling one's job or rising to entrepreneurial independence might have faded or been dashed, but Americans could gain power over their immediate environment with the help of personal machines.

When cars were equipped with more cylinders and horsepower, their increased speed annihilated space. While an average day's car trip covered only 125 miles in 1916, a day's journey of 400 miles was common by 1936. Speed intensified experience by packing more of it into a minute, hour, or day. It promised more life per life. Fast cars guaranteed not immortality or peace of mind, but a secular salvation: intense experience in the moment. The car also revolutionized leisure by liberating the pleasure-seeker from the constraints of streetcar or train timetables and fixed routes. The auto also meant freedom from forced encounters with strangers in those railed "voyage tubes." As a result, streetcar rides dropped from 15.7 billion in 1923 to merely 8.3 billion by 1940. Time and space were freed for individual choice. Improvements in roads in the 1920s let thousands of easterners tour picturesque New England towns in the summers and journey to the Florida seashore in winter.[101] This may have been an apolitical freedom, but for many Americans it was satisfactory, even superior.

Another kind of potency was available in the phonograph. In a well-known ad of 1913, the Victor-Victrola company showed its phonograph surrounded by miniature images of opera and theatrical figures of the day. The implication was that this machine put the world's artistic elite at the disposal of the family in the privacy of their parlor. The National Phonograph Company of Thomas Edison promised that all could dance when their recordings were played. No one needed to labor at the piano, and novices didn't have to suffer the embarrassment of learning new dance steps in public. The phonograph gave the individual immediate gratification and full enjoyment of the world's best dance music in the privacy of the home.[102]

Victor Exclusive Talent

The best friends you can have—who cheer you with their music and song, who unfold to you all the beauties of the compositions of the great masters, who through their superb art touch your very heart strings and become to you a wellspring of inspiration.

Painting adapted from the
Chicago Tribune cartoon of John T. McCutcheon

Copyright 1913 by
Victor Talking Machine Co., Camden, N. J.

Victor-Victrola

The phonograph promised to bring the concert hall's greatest stars into the privacy of the parlor. (*Collier's*, April 11, 1913, back cover)

These images of personal, private, and immediate control of the world's most romantic moments were easily transferred to the still more potent radio. Millions were attracted to the device in the early 1920s because they could reel in messages and music from thousands of miles away. "Two fingers and one lever — that is all you need to tune the Thompson Minuet," trumpeted an ad in 1925. RCA's Radiola battery radio promised that "you can take your entertainment with you everywhere," and to prove it, showed a picture of a young couple carrying their radio along on a picnic.[103] The individual controlled it all.

Still, consumer goods were about more than power. Another important benefit was new taste sensations — candy, soft drinks, and cigarettes, all uniquely engineered and packaged pleasures of flavor and stimulation. Milton Hershey's milk chocolate bar, manufactured first in 1894, offered a velvety combination of a sugar jolt and a calming sensation. From Peru, early Coca-Cola ads claimed, came the coca leaf with its "invigorating properties" and from Africa, the cola nut with its "sustaining properties." Even though Coke makers soon found that they could sell the drink as a tasty thirst quencher, a substitute for plain water and alcoholic beverages, Coke remained a magical mixture.[104] Frank Mars's Snickers candy bar (1930) offered an even more complex taste profile: the crunch of peanuts, the smooth sweetness of caramel, and the doughy feel of nougat, all subtly enveloped in milk chocolate. These sweets improved on nature, packing more sugar and fat than any mere fruit or nut could offer. Note the extravagant sensuousness of this ad for Life Savers in 1922:

> I want something — don't know just why — to turn over and twist around on my tongue. The answer is Life Savers, so snappy so comforting, so smooth and cool, they keep my throat moist and flexible and each one sort of wears down slowly giving off that spicy honey-fed aromatic piquant flavor until it's just a thin brittle delicious rim of sweetness; and it breaks and is gone, like a pleasant dream, but I can dream it all over again whenever I like.[105]

Food engineering stimulated physical desire and often created dependencies. The combination of tasty tar and addictive nicotine in cigarettes and the distinct taste but also caffeine (and briefly even cocaine) of Coca-Cola created a new sensual world. These manufactured sensations partly replaced the glutton's indulgence in sheer quantity of carbohydrates, protein, and animal fat. Technology could surpass the sensuous joys of nature's Garden of Eden with foods synthesized to taste, smell, and look "supernatural." The new packaged pleasures of the palate were subtle, bringing a kind of epicure's refinement to the taste buds of the masses and with it a succession of enticements that led imperceptibly into dependency. There were differences between the chocoholic and the alcoholic. But there were also similarities.[106]

The cigarette is perhaps the best example of these new engineered sensations. While it was made cheap with James Bonsack's rolling machine of 1881, this did not guarantee consumer acceptance. Reformers like Lucy Gaston referred to cigarettes as "coffin nails" in the 1890s and cigarette sales trailed off, in part, from negative publicity. Government attacks on American Tobacco as a monopoly in 1907 led to its breakup in 1911. However, in 1914 a successor company, Reynolds Tobacco, reversed the industry's fortunes when it heavily advertised its new brand, Camels, at a dime a pack. American Tobacco responded with Lucky Strikes, and Liggett & Meyers with Chesterfields. These new cigarettes were not only cheap but also consisted of relatively mild and sweet blends of tobacco that appealed to a new and broad smoking public. The U.S. military helped to popularize the habit with men by providing cigarettes to nervous soldiers during World War I. Advertising to "new," presumably more independent, women in the 1920s extended sales still further, especially when cigarettes were sold as a weight-control aid. The cigarette became a quick and relatively nonintrusive, nondisruptive part of the daily routine. It was as addictive as more "dangerous" drugs, but compared to smelly cigars, messy pipes, or vulgar chewing tobacco, cigarettes were less noticed by respectable people. Cigarettes were advertised as mood enhancers and alternatively as relaxing. They also gave the smoker a slight, "winning" edge that could be "kept up" all day long. The object of the cigarette manufacturer was to balance sensations and to avoid satiation, no matter how many cigarettes were smoked. Camels promised that "the blend is so mellow and smooth that there is never a tired taste, no matter how many you may choose to light." If the dose was not quite right, Phillips Milk of Magnesia claimed that it could reduce the alkaline excess so "you minimize any after-effects from smoking. Feel fine all the time." It is no surprise then that annual cigarette consumption per capita rose from 51 in 1900 to 998 by 1929.[107]

Although these packaged pleasures often offered extranatural combinations of taste and stimulation (as well as the burdens of addiction, tooth decay, unwanted weight, and life-threatening diseases), they also met social needs. Candy bars and carbonated sugar water were signs of Americanization, a fast and portable liberation from the constraints of the ethnic and/or family dinner table. Children could sneak a sweet on their way home from school without parents knowing. The convenience of candy bars and their energy-packed potency made them meal substitutes for individuals "on the go." Coca-Cola was often advertised as simply an enhancer of whatever the drinker did — going to baseball games or playing bridge. "Things go better with Coke." Women smoked because this practice separated them from the past and brought them into "the group of the new, young, and liberated."[108] Consumption associated the sensual with the social world. Everything came easier and with more intensity.

Blending Consumer Cultures

It was with a powerful mix of meanings, messages, and sensations that consumer goods did their therapeutic work. Perhaps most subtly, these products blended the anarchic pleasures of the plebeian crowd with the aspirations and self-constraint of the genteel individual.[109] In 1900, Americans were not a passive faceless throng, but individual people participating in a dynamic culture of consumption. Relatively few got lost in suggestible crowds or in self-destructive consumption. The group on the street or in the theater or bar became relatively less important in the twentieth century. The consumer culture largely destroyed the Victorian distinction between the ephemeral crowd and the cultivated individual.[110] The throngs dispersed into the private settings of home and car, even though the consumer culture became more general by breaking down ethnic and regional divisions. The result was the irony of Americans experiencing common goods, entertainment, and fantasies in private.

The blending of mass and private experiences in consumption took many forms. For example, American entertainment industries combined the "low" crowd with "high" character, as when American world's fairs mixed the titillation of the sideshow carnival with self-improving educational exhibits. While the Centennial Exhibition in Philadelphia (1876) banished amusements outside the gates, Chicago's fair of 1893 offered a midway that featured the exotic belly dancing of "Little Egypt" and the thrill of the new Ferris Wheel along with the stately architecture of the Court of Honor and sober displays of scientific achievement in the White City. The world's fair in St. Louis (1904) dropped the pretense, putting the midway at the center, and attracted ten million visitors. The genius of American commercial culture has been its success in blending the anarchic sensuousness and emotional release of plebeian play with the respectable and improving ideals of individual and family "rational recreation." The nineteenth-century impresario, P. T. Barnum, had followed this principle well in a succession of entertainment enterprises (beginning with his dime museum, which featured both tightrope walkers and "educational" depictions of biblical events). From the 1860s, the American vaudeville industry won respectable family audiences by prohibiting drinking in the stalls and by controlling prostitution. Impresarios offered something for everybody — from sentimental songs about motherhood and the Old Country and exciting displays of sharpshooting to "gold brick" performances of opera singers.[111]

The film industry also learned how to blend the low and the high, the plebeian crowd and the bourgeois individualist. The first exhibitions of motion pictures in the 1890s were largely directed at busy workingmen who enjoyed the instant thrill of a boxing match or a burlesque scene by peering into a peephole at a penny arcade. Peep shows, along with fortune-telling machines, coin-operated phonographs, and candy dispensers, offered quick doses of pleasure in brief visits as the men hurried to and from work. When the nickelodeon brought projected films to audiences in 1905, movies still appealed to the needs and tastes of working people rather than the affluent (as the films were shown in uncomfortable and often dingy storefronts). The nickelodeons featured thrill-packed comedy and adventure in ten-minute segments. When women and children attended, middle-class reformers worried about the corruption of their morals. Yet a small group of distributors (especially Adolph Zukor, Marcus Loew, and William Fox) turned the film industry upscale by adapting the theater, rather than the penny arcade, as the model. These innovators offered feature-length European films (like the *Life of Moses*) that projected celebrated actors onto a stage-size screen in front of decorous audiences. A middle-class clientele was attracted not only to theatrical films but also to the clean, comfortable, and orderly exhibition halls or "movie palaces" built in the 1910s. Soon Zukor and the others moved into production, displacing the cheap, low-class programs common in the nickelodeons. This new breed of film offered powerful cultural fusions: theatrical stories that drew middle-class patrons were combined with intimate close-ups and fast-paced action that still reached working-class audiences; love interest attracted women while female sexuality allured men. "Stars" were elevated above the crowd with their wealth, fashion, and their aristocratic circles of friends, while their social background and the roles that they played still resonated with ordinary people.[112]

Here, as with the dance hall, a working-class entertainment "trickled up" the social ladder. Both became not only more respectable but also part of a new cross-class social ritual — the modern courtship practice of dating. Going to a movie in a clean, well-managed theater became a socially acceptable alternative to meeting in the parental parlor. The movie date was also a relatively unintimidating way for insecure and inexperienced youths to be with one another without sacrificing decency. Respectability no longer required education, Anglo-Saxon roots, or even a comfortable income. It meant "appearance, dress, and deportment" in public places that increasingly were "integrated" socially.[113]

The only barrier that the purchase of a ticket, service, or product could not overcome was race. In the opening years of the twentieth century, commercial culture, it seemed, could be a "mass" culture only if looked "white" by excluding the visibly "black." Americans of African descent were segregated in theaters even in the North and excluded from white sports teams. Even more revealing, they were increasingly parodied in comedy at the very moment when discrimination and satire directed toward European ethnic groups was disappearing.[114]

With this important exception, early twentieth-century consumer culture blurred ethnic and class divisions. And thus vaudeville, the movies, amusement parks, and dance halls became "mass" commodities. Genteel self-restraint survived, of course, in concert halls and college English classes. But fun, fashion, and fantasy goods gradually ceased to be frivolous and vain to the respectable bourgeoisie. Instead, they became a release from boredom, a form of youthful vitality, a means of self-expression and freedom from stuffy tradition. Not only had the crowd become more "civilized," but a new morality of fun made joining it acceptable.[115]

Yet even as middle-class Americans began to "take in" movies and let their daughters go to them with the boy down the street, the consuming crowd was breaking up. That throng, as a gathering of mingling, interacting individuals, was being silenced, separated, and increasingly brought together only by the projections of voices and images distributed from centralized "dream factories" in New York and Hollywood. The change was far more complex and interesting than suggested by the image of the passive pack. Only in limited, extraordinary situations (sporting events and amusement parks, for example) did Americans join the crowd. Instead, they adopted the privacy of the car, learned the decorum of silence in the movie theater, and chose the radio at home over a night on the town.

Once again the automobile showed the contradictory meaning of consumption. The individualized mobility of the car transformed the space of pleasure — privatizing while extending and homogenizing it. As Ford said, his Model T was "large enough for the family, but small enough for the individual to run and care for . . . and enjoy with his family the blessings of hours of pleasure in God's great open spaces."[116] The automobile was supposed to isolate and unify the family, empower its owner, and free its occupants from the crush of urban life. Beginning in the 1920s, Coney Island, tied as it was to the streetcar, began to give way to suburban venues like Playland at Rye Beach, reached mostly by auto. The car culture produced a plethora of new privatized pleasures, enjoyed by millions. The drive-in restaurant appeared in Dallas in 1921 with Royce Hailey's Pig Stand, and the suburban shopping center was introduced in 1923 with Kansas City's Country Club Plaza. From the mid-1920s, New York City department stores built branches in suburban locations to accommodate car owners unable to find center city parking. The forced mixing with other people during train travel that led to still more crowds at railroad-owned terminal hotels and resorts gave way to a new kind of tourism. The car freed the family from the peering eyes of strangers, and at the end of the day, a motel room facing the parking lot was as private as the car.[117] The crowd may have reappeared in the traffic jam, but Americans were at least no longer touching and smelling one another.

The suburban home itself was increasingly a packaged good that combined isolation from others with additional living space. In the 1920s, housing lots in automobile suburbs averaged about 5,000 square feet while lots in districts served by urban streetcars averaged only 3,000. Along with the car, housing expanded well beyond the reach of public rail lines, especially for the middle class. Los Angeles alone opened 3,200 subdivisions to Anglo-Saxon midwesterners seeking a promised land of sunshine, spacious lawns, and freedom from cities crowded with immigrants.[118]

However, unlike in Europe, home ownership and its promise of privacy was not restricted to the middle class. Despite required down payments of 50 percent with only five to seven years to pay the balance, 40 percent of immigrant families were homeowners by the late 1920s. Privacy and its symbolism were of central importance even before many of the working class could afford to suburbanize: "The front door bell and the bay window have been a boon to the social conditions of the tenement dweller," noted a government official in 1901. "Everything also has to be in keeping with that bay window — better furnishings and belongings of all types." While the live-in boarder was common in the American working-class household before World War I, soon the need for extra money gave way to the desire for a private married and family life. It is not surprising that this outsider had nearly disappeared by 1930.[119]

The idea that the home could remain like a moated castle in an age of high-rise corporate offices and massive factories survived in that strange male ritual, the "do-it-yourself" movement. Affluent men, who had no economic need for doing their own home repair or gardening, threw themselves into installing workshops in basements and buying lawn mowers after 1900. By building pine-paneled recreation rooms in the house and vine-covered trellises in the backyard, men who otherwise were thoroughly enmeshed in the modern world of machines or corporate decision making proved that they still could do something creative by and for themselves. Magazines and tool makers promoted home improvement projects for the sake of family togetherness. Stanley Tools, declared one ad, made "father and son partners!" As witnessed one father: "We started with a few simple repairs about the house. Then we made our own work bench; after that a table. Now we have just started on our most ambitious effort — a model of an old galleon" — all with the help of tools provided by Stanley.[120]

Still, the suburban home, even with these personal gestures, increasingly functioned less as a refuge from society than a launching pad into it. In the 1920s, the formal parlor, which had served in the Victorian bourgeois home as a buffer between the public and the family, was eliminated from new houses. This rather elaborate use of space became less necessary because formal entertaining became less common. A more relaxed setting, the informal "living room," emerged, designed for daily use by the family. Another change was at least as important — the decline in the size and even existence of the front porch, formerly used to view and greet neighbors. In effect, the attached garage replaced it. As the century rolled on, that garage grew while the home lost its function as a platform for neighborly encounters. The house became an extension of the automobile and a point of access to as much as a refuge from public life.[121]

The car became a threat to the home because it provided such an obvious escape from family life. While Robert and Helen Lynd found families in the 1920s who spent most of their free money on the car because "it keeps the family together," another rather more affluent "Middletowner" observed the opposite: "Our [teenage] daughters don't use our car much because they are always with somebody else in their car when we go out motoring." The automobile produced a most ambiguous effect: it made possible the private detached suburban home, yet it undermined the very family "togetherness" that the suburban home was supposed to provide. This caused only occasional consternation because Americans wanted both privacy and participation, and the consumer culture of cars and suburbs provided them. The long succession of new and improved goods in and around the American home has continuously replayed this story of tension between the quest for privacy and the longing for access to the wider world.[122]

Like the car, the mass media offered both private and public experience. Although movie going remained a crowd activity, it tended to discourage face-to-face contact and interaction. In particular, the addition of sound to the movies by 1927 created a new, more passive audience. During the era before sound movies, audiences tolerated talking and even "talking back" to the screen. With sound, moviegoers insisted on silence so that the screen could speak. Once again, this did not mean that viewers simply sat in passive awe of the stars. When actors could finally talk and sing, individual viewers identified with them as unique individuals. Bing Crosby and Greta Garbo gained an "aura" and were revered when seen on thousands of screens across the country, even as millions of individuals felt that these stars were also their "personal friends."[123]

Even more, the radio met Americans' need for a personal experience of mass culture. In the privacy of their own homes, listeners heard voices and music that were simultaneously shared by millions nationwide. Like the film, radio was a product of a centralized technology. A consortium of American manufacturers formed the Radio Corporation of America (RCA) in 1920 and subsequently, the National Broadcasting Company (NBC) in 1926. Within a year, NBC was competing with the Columbia Broadcasting System. Together, these networks created an oligopoly dispensing entertainment to people across the country. With telephone line linkages between transmitters, network broadcasting from concert halls and sports events was possible. As a result, radio rapidly became a national culture. There were only a few scattered radio stations in 1920, but 600 stations broadcast programs by 1930. By then, despite the price of roughly $100, 40 percent of American households contained a radio.[124] Radio remained an outlet for ethnic and local culture, especially in its first decade, but the national reach of the networks meant the erosion of diversity. More positively, the networks contributed to a national culture by bringing the

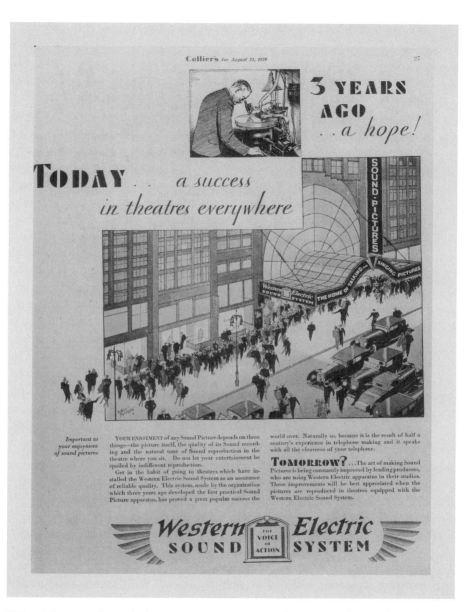

This celebration of sound pictures captured an extraordinary optimism in the ability of American corporations to deliver technologies of pleasure to Americans in the 1920s. (*Collier's*, Aug. 21, 1929, p. 27)

isolated farmer and the ethnic factory worker into the blend of American life.

The radio also created a unique home experience. As early as 1924, the device ceased being a technological mystery enjoyed only by initiated males in the garage or attic. Instead, it was relocated to the living room and wrapped in a stylish cabinet that matched the coffee table. The radio was transformed from a laboratory apparatus into a piece of furniture. This most modern of contraptions blended into the traditional parlor and emitted a glow from the mysterious radio tubes, suggesting the aura of the hearth. By the mid-1920s, radio operation required no more skill than turning tuning and volume knobs. Loudspeakers had replaced awkward headphones. Radio became a family pastime. It meant listening, not transmitting; consuming, not creating. Radio functioned as one of the male's domestic accoutrements, like slippers and cigars, and as a friendly voice in a lonely house during the day for homemakers. It was unlike the telephone that brought personal exchange or the phonograph that delivered an impersonal performance; it transmitted a voice of a celebrity "friend" through the "ether," magically "commanded" to be in the living room as a "guest."[125] The family "used to scatter in the evening" noted one Middletown mother, "but now we all sit around and listen to radio."[126] The radio was (and remains) well adapted to household activities. It relieved the isolation of homemakers at a time when the number of relatives and children at home all day was declining. It offered privacy, mobility, choice, and a plethora of sounds and information at a twist of the dial. Most of all, the radio wonderfully reconciled privacy with longings for a community of shared information and entertainment.[127]

For many American intellectuals of the early twentieth century, consumerism in all its forms reflected the poverty of desire, the substitution of titillation, conformity, and display for true joy, social solidarity, and individual fulfillment. Still, consumerism was also a response to desire, providing not only instant but multiple gratifications that religion, politics, and learning separately had not be able to deliver. With commodities, early twentieth-century Americans received the social and the private, the timely and the timeless, a combination plate of sensations. Consumer culture was and is, as James Twitchell notes, the "return to the puerile, the raw and uncontrolled," a rebellion against the "civilizing process" imposed by church, classroom, and the etiquette of the dinner table and a release into fashion, amusement, and junk food. But it would have been less powerful and easier for critics to combat had it been merely a return to "preindustrial culture"[128] rather than also the complete opposite — a dash into the future. This struggle for fun in all of its vulgarity was blended with traditional order, improvement, and privacy. Perhaps most important, consumer goods defined and eased the initiation, maintenance, and dissolution of social relationships, allowing individuals to protest and to define boundaries with others. To own was to be in society. Americans shared the same symbolic world through advertising, radio, and movies — media that painted goods with meaning.[129] Without these products to define their personalities, people would have been "naked" to the crowd, faced with the humiliation of revealing who they "really" were and with uncertainty about how to act and what to say. American society was experiencing a decline in the social ties of ethnicity and neighborhood, yet divisions of work and heritage still made communicating difficult. Consumerism may have been a poor conversation, lacking depth, honest self-disclosure, or solid connections with the world, past or future. But people embraced it, and we must try to understand why.

CHAPTER 3

Promises of More, 1930–1960

N othing speaks more to the power of consumerism than its hold on the American psyche during the Depression and World War II. Despite joblessness and wartime austerity, ordinary Americans held tight to old consuming habits and dreams. They clung to their "luxuries" or longed for their return. Even though economic collapse in the 1930s and diversion of commodities to the war effort in the 1940s dramatically reduced personal spending, American business continued to seek new ways and new things to sell consumers. In spite of challenges to the social order, most Americans continued to define themselves and their relationships with others through consumer goods. After the war, Americans did not simply pick up where they left off before the Depression. They fulfilled the dreams that the years of hardship had nourished. The postwar period was an era of unprecedented prosperity, built on an extraordinary, fortuitous confluence of economic and social opportunities. In the generation after 1945, Americans celebrated that prosperity with exuberant spending on cars, houses, and appliances. This consumerism reflected often confused hopes and fears: desires for both innovation and tradition, participation and privacy. Most of all, it confirmed a form of domestic consumption that today we associate with the 1950s, but that in fact had roots in the longings of the 1930s. Through the ups and downs of the years between 1930 and 1960, consumption remained at the center of the American experience.

In many ways, this is ironic. The economic and military crises of this period produced profound political upheaval. The election of Franklin D.

Roosevelt in 1932 led to a flood of government programs designed to stimulate the moribund economy. The 1930s also saw the rise of trade unions, and the 1940s saw the beginnings of the civil rights movement. The war years brought dramatic increases in income tax rates and the creation of a permanent arms economy. Yet despite these political changes, consumerism followed its own trajectory, creating an ever more individualistic culture — a consensus around a democracy of goods that by the 1950s seemed to suppress ideological conflict.

Surprising Continuities and Consuming Compensations

The Great Depression ended an era of economic expansion. The families of the jobless had to drop out of the shopping spree. The ranks of the unemployed rose from 1.5 million (or 3.2 percent of the workforce) in 1929 to 12.8 million (almost 25 percent) when Roosevelt came to office in 1933. Despite slow improvement thereafter, the unemployment rate never dropped below 7.7 million (14.3 percent) during the 1930s. Meanwhile, national income tumbled from $81 billion in 1929 to $41 billion in 1932. Even when price decreases were taken into account, per capita income fell from $681 at the apex in 1929 to only $495 in 1933.[1] In hindsight, economists found that the Depression resulted from a combination of bad breaks and bad decisions. A downturn in the business cycle coincided with an unfortunate point in economic evolution — when old industries and businesses (like coal, steel, agriculture, and small retailing) had not yet given ground to a dynamic new cluster of manufacturing and business enterprises that would dominate the consumer economy later in the century. Wiser public policy (especially lowering interest rates and expanding the money supply) would have eased the catastrophic effects of deflation and layoffs.[2]

No one at the time understood much of this. To many Americans living in the early Depression, the 1920s symbolized excess, a vain and irresponsible decade for which the Depression was a punishment. The display of wealth and glorification of greed that had been common in the 1920s now seemed un-American. Miserly wealth was a millstone around the neck of a nation seeking to climb out of the economic abyss. Even movie stars went for modesty in dress and ceased marrying aristocrats. They had themselves pictured in magazines as regular guys and gals with families and hearths. Some people, like the sociologist Jesse Steiner, even saw an opportunity for a cultural revolution — an abandonment of emulative consumption for a new democratic leisure society built on cost-free home recreational activity. This frugal sentiment took many forms, from condemnation of "immorality" in the movies, critiques of "waste" in manufacturing, and an attack on excessive consumer credit to support for open-air participation in sports, patronage of public libraries, and cultivation of other uplifting and noncommercial leisure activities.[3]

There were signs of downscaling. Sales of men's suits dropped sharply and males abandoned stiff collars, garters, undershirts, and bathing suit tops as increased informality paralleled cost cutting. Even women, who were far less willing to forego new clothes than men, gave up expensive materials and wore simpler frocks. The craft of sewing even returned. Not the Vanderbilts, but popularly elevated stars like Norma Shearer and Greta Garbo served as models for fashionable hair styles, clothes, and make-up. The 1920s dream of "my blue heaven," the privacy of the bungalow, was lost for many when house-building rates tumbled and young couples were sometimes forced to double up with parents. Thin wallets led to record sales of glass jars for home canning. The "live-at-home movement" meant foregoing the night on the town and instead listening to the radio, playing cards with relatives, or, if they could afford it, fretting over jigsaw puzzles. Roosevelt's own philatelic enthusiasms helped to create a fad in stamp collecting. Meanwhile, pricey golf country clubs lost a million members in the first four years of the Depression, and sporting event gate and amusement sales dropped by almost half.[4]

As common as cutting back, however, was a very different response — a refusal to retrench. Many Depression-era Americans were unwilling to abandon the "luxuries" of the 1920s. Cigarette smokers could not give up their habit. Sales dropped merely 6 percent by 1933 and rose 22 percent over 1929 levels by 1936. Perhaps addiction and the hope that smoking would soothe frazzled nerves explain the hold of tobacco. Americans were loath to abandon other luxuries. Although sales of new cars dropped by 70 percent between 1929 and 1932, Americans held on to their old Model Ts, and gasoline sales actually rose 16 percent between 1929 and 1935. The car had become a necessity, required to find or keep a job. Even more, it provided a sense of well-being. For the American worker, noted the Lynds in 1937, an automobile "gives the status which his job increasingly denies, and, more than any other possession or facility to which he has access, it symbolizes living, having a good time, the thing that keeps you working."[5]

Americans did not let the Depression stop their growing habit of auto vacations. Thirty-five million took to the road in the summer of 1935 alone.

Visitors to national parks kept rising too — from 174,000 to 209,300 between 1929 and 1935. The trailer, a motoring fad that appeared first in 1929, had attracted 56,000 new buyers by 1936. Trailer parks cropped up to accommodate middle-aged and retired vacationers, especially in Florida and California. The trailer presented mixed possibilities: it was cheap housing for the jobless and an inexpensive way to travel, but also a permanent vacation dwelling for the retired and a luxury mobile home for the former camper.[6]

The Depression-spawned car trailer made possible the Florida trailer park that catered to retirees fleeing from the winters of the North, as in this image from 1941.
(Library of Congress)

Despite the Depression, Americans bought new electrical appliances, especially refrigerators. While sales of the domestic gadgetry introduced after World War I (e.g., stoves and washing machines) declined, Americans flocked to buy the new and improved refrigerator. Sales rose more than sevenfold between 1929 and 1935. Some people gave up their telephones and others did not order them, but many bought radios. By 1940, 28 million homes containing 86 percent of Americans had at least one radio, up from 12 million in 1929. Perhaps this was an economical investment. While Americans spent 150 million hours per week in the 1930s at the movies, they expended almost one billion hours listening to "free" radio. In any case, 40 percent of households on a typical winter evening in 1938 had the radio turned on.[7]

In many ways, the consumer culture of the 1930s had hardly changed. Luxuries of a decade earlier had become necessities; established expectations were not easily reversed — even by bankruptcy and joblessness. Relatively few consumers defaulted on installment payments. Still, more than inertia was at work in the consumerism of the Depression era. The impact of the crash was uneven and relative. American jobless rates varied enormously by occupation and region. By 1932, while the purchasing power of hourly wage earners was half of the 1929 rate, more regularly employed salaried workers saw their earnings drop only a quarter. Because prices often declined further than did hourly wages, those with steady, full-time jobs could get bargains. More important still, because of support from family members and a bare-bones welfare system, few of the jobless experienced health-threatening misery. Instead, unemployment meant social and psychological deprivation.[8]

Many of the Depression's victims were in daily contact with the more affluent, a humiliation that doubtless deepened the desire to rejoin the party that for others had never ended. Moreover, as American sociologist Glen Elder notes, "Comparisons with past gratifications and standards only served to intensify discontent in deprived families. . . . The higher the climb before the Depression, the greater the investment in the way things were at that time, and the more intense the frustration of downward mobility."[9] The result was that many Americans associated status and even adulthood with goods. The Depression led to a frustrated consumerism more than a rejection of the capitalist system.[10]

The humiliation of downsizing took many forms and produced many responses, all leading to a greater commitment to a consumption society. One reaction that may be particularly hard to understand was to gamble.

Why waste scarce funds on the very poor odds of a bet, especially the Irish Sweepstakes and other foreign or illegal lotteries? American middle-class magazine readers were lectured on the virtues of thrift (and the benefits of home canning) in those lean times, and many "respectable people" expected the poor to cut back on frills and wasteful habits like gambling. However, few working people had either the domestic equipment or the will to make much use of such self-help advice. Instead, gambling provided a psychological release that thrift never could have given the economically insecure.[11]

Gambling was not new, of course. It had played an important economic and cultural role in the United States from its colonial beginnings. Making wagers was an almost natural complement of American enterprise culture — the dream of gain with minimum labor made possible by risk taking. Nevertheless, gambling, like other "vices," had been marginalized and restricted in the late nineteenth century. Significantly, however, it gained a new lease on life at the depth of the Depression in 1931 when wide-open casino gambling was legalized in Las Vegas. At first, the casinos drew workers building the Boulder Dam, but soon the desert Sodom attracted bettors from southern California. Promoters advertised Las Vegas as the "last frontier," a playful museum of Old West culture. For investors, it was a sure-fire money-making opportunity in a region where mining and the railroad economy had suffered enormously.[12]

Las Vegas was only one choice in an astonishing array of gambling sites available in cities and many towns. Hotels and stores, which before the 1930s would not think of allowing gambling devices on their property, now offered pinball games, punchboards, and jar games. These were mostly very low-stakes operations. Punchboards were merely cardboard sheets fitted with up to 1000 tickets which, for a nickel, could be "punched" with a very slight chance of revealing a payoff of up to $2.50. African Americans from south Chicago patronized some 500 Policy Stations, which provided an illegal lottery. In 1936, an estimated one billion dollars was "invested" in foreign lotteries and sweepstakes. Net receipts from American pari-mutuel betting at the track rose from $7 million to $55 million in the 1930s. Many states also relaxed rules on racetrack betting. Similarly, chain letters, church Bingo, and the board game Monopoly of Charles Darrow drew on the same spirit of speculation. In 1938, 29 percent of people surveyed admitted to betting in churches.[13]

Noted psychologist Paul Lazarsfeld believed that gambling was a way of escaping from economic insecurity and its humiliations. Jobless gamblers regressed to the childlike belief that because they wanted to win, they would. Even if this theory is unfair, we cannot entirely discount the psychological effects of poverty. The impact of reduced income on people who expected expanded access to goods "must have made the pinch of hard times seem intolerable," noted the American sociologist Jesse Steiner. For many working people, especially because the cost was nominal, gambling appeared to be a wise investment. "Why not me?" they asked. Losses were soon forgotten and winnings were cherished memories. This was certainly fatalistic, but it was also optimistic. The future would take care of itself and it might also bring "pennies from heaven."[14]

The Depression made Americans more materialistic in other ways. While the high-minded might condemn the greed behind street gambling, the family and the home became just as important venues for a frustrated consumerism. In response to the trauma of austerity, families tried to keep up with old spending routines, especially on luxuries. As economic historian Winifred Wandersee notes, "To many families a radio, the latest movie, a package of cigarettes, or the daily newspaper were as necessary to the family well-being as food, clothing, and shelter."[15] Some American families tried to maintain consumption routines through deficit spending. Installment buying, which had become common in the 1920s, continued in the Depression decade. In 1932, about 60 percent of furniture, autos, and household appliances were bought on time. Sales on credit comprised nearly 15 percent of consumption. In the late 1930s, department stores like Wanamaker's began to offer revolving charge plans to ease spending on fashionable clothes and modern furniture.[16] Between 1933 and 1939, consumer loans for household durables more than doubled. Spending for goods formed a basis for family cohesion. The absence of the income required not only reduced the status of the provider but also threatened the unity of the family.[17]

Social pressures to spend also led Americans to withdraw from neighborhoods and social clubs, accelerating a long-term trend toward family privacy. A major cause of distress was the inability of the jobless to keep up social obligations in spending. A couple without work complained:

> you can't even have a card game without serving sandwiches and coffee . . . but all that costs something. We had some people with whom we kept up our contacts, and by common agreement we decided that we wouldn't serve refreshments. Somehow it wasn't much fun any longer and very soon we broke up.

In one urban survey, participation at neighborhood parties declined from 20 percent to 3 percent. This humiliation particularly obsessed men. Some abandoned old hobbies like photography and quit their shutterbug clubs, embarrassed at having to look at the pictures taken by others. Despite the growth of trade unions during the Depression, these institutions of class solidarity only temporarily reversed the logic of individualism. Free time became more domesticated and isolated. Money increasingly became the mark of personal and family status.[18]

The obsession with the home was not hard to understand. By 1933, half of American mortgages were in default. Political leaders had long believed that government encouragement of home ownership would create "good citizenship." That was Herbert Hoover's motto in his 1928 presidential campaign leading to his 1931 Commission on Home Building and Home Ownership. His rival and successor, Franklin Roosevelt, agreed. In June 1933, Congress created the Home Owners Loan Corporation to refinance loans and save families from foreclosure. The Federal Housing Administration of 1934 was even more important. It guaranteed private loans and established the standard 30-year loan with a 10 percent down payment. Roosevelt also supported highway construction that laid the foundation of modern suburban sprawl. In 1939, he signed legislation that offered tax deductions on mortgage interest, further encouraging home ownership. Not surprisingly, housing starts rose from a low of 93,000 in 1932 to nearly 600,000 in 1941.[19]

Further encouraging domesticity was the increased access to cheap radios. The daily round of prime-time situation comedies (beginning with *Amos 'n' Andy* in late 1929), variety shows (featuring vaudevillians like Eddy Cantor), and detective shows like *The Shadow* almost coincided with the Depression. Radio was far more than a substitute for a night out on the town. It eased family members through the day: morning quiz and talk shows were followed by afternoon soap operas and after-school children's adventure shows. Why risk or trouble yourself with the actual world that might humiliate, bore, or anger when you could reel a "star" in to the comfortable confines of your home and just as quickly get rid of her with a twist of a dial?[20]

Most important, the Depression reinforced a personal commitment to traditional work and sex roles. Numerous studies discovered that male workers were not forming a militant jobless class but were frustrated by free time without the money to consume. None of the unemployed family men whom sociologist Mirra Komarovsky studied in the 1930s found freedom from the lifelong routine of labor satisfying.[21] Husbands longed for work and the provider role that accompanied it, and wives hoped soon to become once again active consumers for the family and home. Even the Social Security Act of 1935 treated wives as dependents within a conventional male-breadwinning family.[22] It was only a question of opportunity, which came with the postwar economic boom, for traditional sex roles to return in full force. Suburban dads commuting to work to earn the wherewithall for moms to be modern homemakers may have been a myth for many Americans, but this was still the dominant dream that sustained consumerism.[23] After World War II, millions of working-class Americans tried to join the middle class in sampling the things that advertisers and their more fortunate neighbors had continuously displayed during the lean years. These reveries of spending did not subvert the rectitudes of family and home (as gambling did). Rather, consumerism reinforced that stable, private world — even as it continued the gradual American disengagement from neighborhood and community.

Despite the shock of the Depression and its tenacity, few Americans saw the economic slump as anything but temporary. A Gallup poll conducted in 1939 found that 88 percent of Americans still believed that they were in the middle class (even though 31 percent admitted that they had only a "lower" class income). To be middle class meant to have the material aspiration for a modern home and the character necessary for earning it. The Depression had frustrated, but certainly not destroyed, that vision of self.[24]

Selling Depressed America

While consumers longed for the good old days, manufacturers did not simply wait for the recovery. The Depression was an opportunity for new, more aggressive marketing, tapping ever deeper into the American buyer's desires. The most obvious impact was merchandisers' efforts to meet the immediate needs of downscale customers: prices fell and sellers looked for new buyers. Luxury car sales dropped from 150,000 in 1929 to 10,000 in 1937. The surviving manufacturers, like Lincoln, Packard, and Cadillac, decreased prices and offered economy models. Those that did not follow this strategy (including Pierce-Arrow and Stutz) disappeared. Low-priced cars increased from 52 percent of sales in 1926 to 73 percent in 1933. This did not mean that new cars were of lower quality. Rather, again to attract scarce customers, manufacturers raised the standard of the "middle range."

Henry Ford abandoned his Model A in 1932 for a far more powerful and stylish car with a V-8 engine.[25] Other nonessentials also got cheaper. Cigarette prices dropped back to 10 cents a pack. Decca reduced the price of a phonograph record to 35 cents (compared to the competition's 75-cent disc) — forcing artists to take a cut in royalties with the promise of higher volume. If Kodak's home movie camera or Schick's new "dry" electric razor cost too much for most, they could still be purchased on the installment plan for as little as 25 cents per week. By 1933, small tabletop radios sold for $10, down from the $133 average for a radio in 1929. The Depression forced other concessions to consumers: professional baseball, long resistant to change, finally succumbed to popular pressure for occasional night games. When weekly movie attendance dropped from 90 million in 1929 to 60 million by 1932, exhibitors began offering double features.[26]

Retailers joined the trend by offering bargains and convenient shopping. By 1930, Chicago Loop stores stayed open Saturday nights to lure commuters back into the city on the weekend. Macy's of New York kept its doors open until 9:00 P.M. on Thursdays. Discount retailers were even more aggressive. In 1930, Michael Cullen offered a no-frills self-service supermarket to cash-poor New Yorkers. Within two years, he had expanded to eight stores. "King Kullen, the World's Great Price Wrecker" was his motto, and he dazzled shoppers with massive displays of groceries. King Kullen cut costs by shifting the work of shopping to the customer and by taking advantage of distressed wholesalers and bankrupt retailers. He had many imitators: cheap clothing, furniture, and plumbing supply stores sprang up in old hotel garages and bankrupt factories. By the late 1930s, the now outdated A & P neighborhood store could no longer compete and the chain was forced to open fewer, but much larger, supermarkets. Increasingly, price, not service, quality, or status, became the key in American consumerism. Small merchants tried to save neighborhood stores by lobbying for minimum price mark-up laws, but they had no lasting impact. The promise of the most at the lowest price whenever you wanted it lured back American consumers.[27]

During the Depression, sellers also chased buyers with ads and promotions. Magazine advertising continued to feature cars, packaged food, and cosmetics, thus keeping the image of affluence in front of Americans who could only dream and wait for a chance later to buy and participate. Ads succeeded in getting Americans to buy Scott tissue, Chase & Sanborn coffee, and Miracle Whip salad dressing — even if they were more expensive than their generic equivalents. Consumers clung to name-brand products (comprising 48 percent of household and food products sold in 1931). Even before the Depression, the National Retail Furniture Association (1928) built an advertising war chest to "change consumer habits from price to style." Gradually, Americans responded by buying new sofas to fit the fashion just as they did with cars and clothing. Cigarette companies offered new promotions and gimmicks: coupons in packs of Raleighs and menthol in the tobacco of Spuds and Kools. Petty enterprise also thrived. Jobless families with a little money opened motor camps, roadside food stands, and hole-in-the-wall beauty parlors, often with garish signs. Many failed, of course, but from such hardy entrepreneurs emerged McDonald's and other business successes of the postwar era.[28]

Perhaps the best example of this trend was the commercialization of radio. Turning the radio waves into an advertising medium certainly predated the Depression. As early as 1922, ads were sold to pay for broadcasting, and with the coming of the networks, advertising agencies learned the power of radio ads. Lucky Strike cigarette sales rose 47 percent in 1928 after a major radio ad campaign. The Depression greatly encouraged commercialization. By 1931, advertisers demanded that broadcasters give them more freedom to peddle goods to cash-strapped Americans. *Fortune* noted that before the Depression "radio was polite. Radio was genteel. Radio was the guest in the home, not the salesman on the doorstep. . . . But some 18 months of further Depression have changed all that." Network revenue from radio commercials rose 316 percent between 1928 and 1934. Advertising was truly a Depression-proof industry. Hard-sell ads became brazen: Detroit's WJR aired 30 commercials in one 45-minute period. Attention-getting gongs or pistol shots announced many commercials. Also common were "personal" ads from famous pitchmen like crooner Rudy Vallee and comedian Jack Benny. A government survey during the week of March 6, 1938 found a third of broadcast hours devoted to advertising. By 1942, A. C. Nielsen's sampling of radio listenership began to take the guesswork out of buying and selling radio audiences. According to CBS's William Paley, commercial radio was "a new force for the distribution of goods as well as in the dissemination of ideas."[29]

The Depression also had a dramatic impact on another venue of the consumer culture — the general magazine. "Free" radio and economic hardship slowed the growth of circulation. Far more serious was the decline of revenue from advertising (from nearly $200 million in 1929 to less than $100 million by 1931, returning to pre-Depression levels only in 1942). This grim reality closed the doors of respected magazines like *Literary Di-*

Smoking overtime?
Who cares!

Suppose you *do* light 'em pretty fast when the fun flows high. What of it, brother? You'll wake to-morrow with a taste like a dewdrop on a daisy... if you keep to Spuds. They've a secret no one can copy...of taming the firebug in smoke...temper-ing parched tongues with a hint of an April breeze ...giving you unspoiled flavor. *You'll like 'em!*

When you can't be bothered to count smokes,...count on Spuds for mouth-happiness

SPUD
MENTHOL - COOLED
CIGARETTES

CORK TIP or PLAIN

15ᶜ FOR 20
(20c IN CANADA)

THE AXTON-FISHER TOBACCO COMPANY, INCORPORATED, LOUISVILLE, KENTUCKY

"Menthol-cooled" cigarettes promised continuous pleasure no matter how much you smoked.   (*Collier's*, Nov. 13, 1934, p. 3)

gest and *The Century*. Even *Woman's World*, still able to attract a rural readership of 1.5 million with a wholesome diet of patriotic, home, and church features, succumbed in 1940 because advertisers wanted to reach a more upscale audience. The old standard, the *Saturday Evening Post*, just got by. Magazines had to not only reach a large readership, but also sell to the "right" market to survive. As one ad executive insisted, "higher income groups" still had unmet desires. Beginning in the 1920s, *Time* and *The New Yorker* attracted a new class of college-educated professional readers with brief but snappy articles. This audience was eager to keep up with trends but lacked either the time or the desire to explore deeply. Most important, these readers attracted advertisers because they had money and spent it. In the 1930s, *Fortune, Business Week*, and *Newsweek* followed the same formula. These magazines thrived with cheerful stories about the successful and interesting while glossing over the dreariness and dilemmas of the Depression. With *Life*, Henry Luce, publisher of *Time*, perfected the genre, using photographs to attract middle-class readers for advertisers. *Life* set the stage for morning "happy talk" TV shows that displaced the picture magazine in the 1970s.[30]

The Depression years were tough times, and mere advertising or low prices were often not enough to scare up customers. Inevitably, marketing became ever more creative. The 1930s saw the full flowering of the popular licensed image or name stamped on the consumer product. The likeness of Mickey Mouse or Orphan Annie put a "child's friend" on an ordinary sand pail or cereal box. Licensing gave manufacturers leverage over store owners, but it also helped increase retail sales by reducing the need for trained sales staff and in-house promotions.[31] Walt Disney was the master of character licensing in the 1930s.[32] Disney exploited the nation's love affair with Mickey by licensing his image in a doll in 1930, and soon thereafter on everything from toothbrushes and watches to lamp shades. These products in effect advertised for each other and the Disney empire. Disney took this marketing magic a step further in 1937 when he licensed the images of the animated feature film *Snow White and the Seven Dwarves* before the public had even seen them in the movie. By the summer of 1939, Pinocchio toys and dolls were in production for the February 1940 release of the movie. Disney had developed a marketing strategy that would become common after World War II — coordinating the appearance of licensed goods and movie spectaculars and thus creating special seasons of fantasy consumption.[33]

Although product licensing covered a wide assortment of goods, this and other marketing gimmicks were especially directed toward children. While discretionary spending for toys and other kids' stuff was down in the 1930s, merchandisers found a solution: selling cheap, often single-piece, toy figures. Lead soldiers, long packaged in complete sets, appeared in the mid-1930s in cheap rubber, plastic, and metal. Sold individually, they were inexpensive enough for even a nine-year-old boy to buy. The collecting habit, long central to boys' play, had begun to shift from amassing free shells or bottle caps to buying and collecting the constantly expanding number of military figures and bubble gum cards.[34] Radio was another contributor to the growth of the child's consumer culture. The hours after school and before dinner became the children's time to control the radio. Radio advertisers used the heroes of programs in premiums to increase sales. Buck Rogers, Charlie McCarthy, and Little Orphan Annie sold malt drinks, breakfast foods, and coffee when children collected labels and box tops from these products to "earn" compasses and decoder rings with their favorite hero's picture on them.[35] Reaching a slightly older age group was the comic book (appearing first in 1934). By 1940, up to 1.35 million read Superman comic books weekly (and many more kids watched the tie-in movie series and heard the radio program). In the 1930s, a commercialized fantasy world for children emerged where parents had no role except often to pay for it.[36]

Despite the Depression, enterprising entertainers found that high school students with odd jobs and indulgent parents eagerly bought bobby socks and swing records. Ads in youth magazines for everything from candy bars and cosmetics to sports equipment and fashions promised health, beauty, and a vibrant social life. The Depression kept teens in high school longer and thus extended their contact with the consumer peer culture that spontaneously appeared in school halls and cafeterias. Benny Goodman's clarinet attracted thousands of teenagers to his New York concert appearance in the winter of 1937. The next spring, organizers of the Carnival of Swing at New York's Randall's Island got 23,000 jitterbugging youths to dance to the music of 23 swing bands. Although swing was "hot" and young people wore increasingly distinctive clothes, the movies and ads continued to glorify parent-pleasing images of teenagers. Andy Hardy movies, for example, featured a good-natured if exuberant lad who in the end always took Dad's advice. At least in the 1930s, as historian Grace Palladino notes, the "commercial teenage culture . . . had to pass through the purifying filter of the middle-class world before it could be deemed safe for teenage consumption."[37]

The radio relieved stress in the 1930s and 1940s with soothing music or escapist fantasy at a turn of a dial — and it brought family members together in the home to enjoy the world's entertainment.   (Library of Congress)

Beyond trying to find new markets in previously neglected age groups, innovators redoubled their efforts to associate their products with pleasure and progress. From the late 1930s, ads for perfume, soap, stockings, and Jantzen swimwear began to display scandalous amounts of skin on models. Department stores, movie houses, and trains introduced air conditioning in the mid-1930s as another way to attract customers.[38] To entice people back to the showrooms, cars were redesigned to give the air of modernity and progress despite dreary economic conditions. The mid-1930s witnessed a number of minor engineering changes: all-steel bodies, improved shock absorbers, and radios. In 1938, Oldsmobile offered an automatic transmission as an option. More important were styling changes. Streamlining removed the boxy look: "In designing the Airflow Chrysler to slip through the air, Chrysler engineers created a car with perfect aerodynamic contours," bragged an ad.[39] The style changed the look of trains, buses, trailers, and even home appliances. The 1935 Super-Six Coldspot refrigerator, created by Raymond Loewy for Sears, featured rounded corners and hidden motors. Even buildings and furniture adopted the clean and sleek look.[40] Streamlining suggested forward motion even if the economy was stagnant and the future uninviting.

This emphasis upon the future and style was part of corporate America's attempt to find a solution to the Depression through "consumer engineering." Ernest Calkins claimed that unemployment was due to underconsumption. It was the job of the consumption engineer to find new goods to buy. The product designer had to "dig in deeper and anticipate wants and desires not yet realized, but foreshadowed by trends and implicit in the habits and folkways" of the nation. As important, manufacturers needed "to make more goods that are used up" and "to make them markedly new, and encourage new buying, exactly as the fashion designers make skirts longer so you can no longer be happy with your short ones." Especially for products where technological stagnation had set in, new styles and designs alone could bring buyers back and convince Americans that the future was an endless horizon of spending.[41]

This message of progress was reaffirmed in the fairs of Chicago, San Francisco, and especially New York in the 1930s. All three seemed to deliberately deny the economic crisis, emphasizing instead the promise of endless betterment through consumer goods offered by major corporations. Pavilions like Democracity and Futurama at the New York World's Fair of 1939 combined technological utopianism with the appeal of sensual ease. Cars controlled by radio beams and speeding along at up to 100 miles per hour illustrated GM's vision of the United States in 1960. From easy chairs on conveyer belts, visitors to Futurama gazed upon an ultramodern city and an uncluttered countryside, an image of technology without ecological or social costs. The future brought not more smokestacks, alienating machines, and uncertain employment, but "cozy village-like suburban communities." Displays at the fair urged visitors to "modernize their kitchens as business had their offices with comfort and convenience."[42] In 1939, a promised future of variety and comfort was just around the corner. Consumer goods would bring it all to all — and in the privacy of their own homes. But Americans would have to wait for a few more years.

War and Promises Fulfilled

The war years brought personal hardship and a vastly expanded public sector, but this dramatic disruption also set the stage for a new wave of private spending. The federal government lifted the United States out of the

This car of 1939 promised everything new, from an automatic transmission and a plastic dashboard to streamlining at its best, "airflow styling."

(*Collier's*, Oct. 22, 1938, p. 30)

Depression by preparing for and waging World War II. The federal budget rose from about $9 billion in 1939 to $100 billion by 1945, elevating the GNP from $91 to $166 billion. Naturally, much of this money made its way back into the private sector. Home-front workers found their wallets and purses full, many for the first time in a decade. "People are crazy with money," noted one jeweler in an industry that boomed during the war. "They don't care what they buy. They purchase things . . . just for the fun of spending." Dollars poured into entertainment (even racetrack gambling rose 2.5 fold during the war). This made sense because there was little to buy when military needs dried up supplies of nylon stockings, cars, and radios. Housing shortages forced war workers into rented rooms and makeshift trailer camps. The rationing of gasoline and other essentials frustrated many and made them long for the free market. By the end of 1944, savings reached $140 billion. Much of this cash was burning holes in the pockets of millions of Americans just waiting for the day when they could spend it on washing machines, cars, and other long-deferred wants.[43]

These people understandably embraced ad campaigns that identified the American Way with private consumption. Leading ad makers had long resented their image as "hucksters." During the Depression, they attempted to redefine themselves as champions of a dynamic free economy that stood up against elitists and bureaucrats who frustrated the will of the people (see chapter 4). The war, however, was a unique opportunity to refurbish the advertisers' image. Ad agencies gained respect when they produced effective propaganda in support of the war effort. More important, they shaped popular opinion by addressing the critical question: "What are we fighting for?" Their answer was well summarized by one ad: "For years we have fought for a higher standard of living, and now we are fighting to protect it against those who are jealous of our national accomplishments." A Nash-Kelvinator ad showed a paratrooper affirming, "We have so many things, here in America, that belong only to a free people . . . warm, comfortable homes, automobiles and radios by the million." The implication was that the enemy had no comforts and their leaders denied them all freedom to consume. This applied to fascism in World War II and was easily transferred to communism after the war. As historian Frank Fox explains this campaign, "The war was seen as a test, perhaps *the* test, of the American Way of Life. And if the American Way passed this test — it deserved never to be questioned again."[44] All challenges to the fairness or rationality of capitalism were dismissed with the promise of a postwar consumers' democracy.

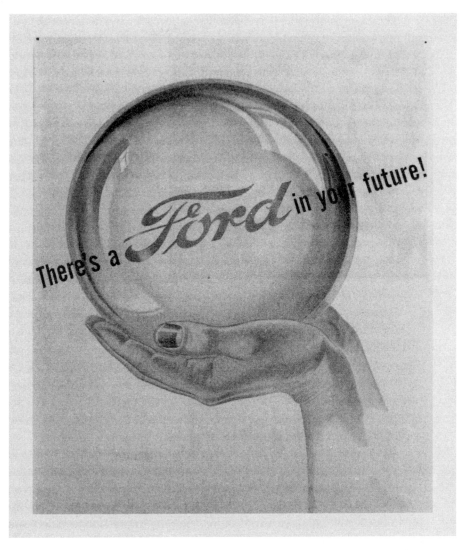

This fortune-teller's crystal ball assured war-weary Americans that the tanks rolling off the assembly line would soon turn into family cars by the millions, after victory.

(*Time*, Dec. 4, 1944, p. 13)

The advertising industry prepared Americans for an era of private consumption after the war. Americans, declared the *Saturday Evening Post*, "are fighting for a glorious future of mass employment, mass production and mass distribution and ownership." Refrigerators would soon replace tanks on the assembly lines. New technologies developed to win the war would make radios better than ever; just a little more wait and sacrifice, and TV would be available to all. Du Pont promised that the nylon that was going into parachutes would soon go on women's legs, and cheaply. The reward for wartime sacrifice was a powerful blend of nostalgic sentiment and materialist progress. Kelvinator promised the postwar woman and her family would "live happily ever after" with

> A bright, sunny house that's a blend of old and new, with a white shuttered door and a picket fence around a world all our own. . . . A garden where you can go while sunshine warms you through and through. . . . And a kitchen . . . that's *full* of magical things. A wonderful new electric range (the kind they're planning now) that starts coffee perking and biscuits browning before we wake up. . . .[45]

American big business had learned how to overcome its Depression-era image as heartless and irresponsible by associating itself with its products rather than its factories. The promise of the postwar era was a resurrection of the consumerist message from the 1920s — an image of seamless harmony, the blending of old and new, the spiritual and material, the private and public. To consume was to be free.

The war and victory created a political climate extremely favorable to the advertisers' vision of the American Way. Leftist advocates of a regulated/corporatist capitalism suffered a string of defeats in 1946 and 1947. Trade union drives in the South failed, as did lobbying for government-guaranteed full employment. Unions became more conservative and parochial after the Taft-Hartley Act of 1947 that restricted union activity. Even the United Automobile Workers' Walter Reuther, the leader of labor's progressive wing, abandoned mass-organization campaigns and social-reform legislation for bargaining in the interests of his relatively high-paid members. A rejuvenated American business community and the rise of anticommunism confined organized labor to bread-and-butter issues. More important, Reuther was responding to the deep-felt commitment of American workers to consumerism. For most wage-earners employed in factories, stores, or offices, work was instrumental — providing the means to enjoy time off the job. Reuther combined anticommunism with a commitment to an expanding "living wage" for union members. His "consumer-oriented Americanism" was not only politically prudent; it was what most working people wanted. The key debate in American politics became which policies brought the greatest purchasing power. The question of wealth, its influence and distribution, largely disappeared.[46]

The politics of purchasing power delivered the goods to many. The percentage of wage earners' family income required for food dropped from 43 percent in 1918 to 32 percent in 1950, falling still further to 20 percent in 1973. Accompanying this decline was a freeing of dollars for consumer goods. By 1973, almost 40 percent of African American families and 70 percent of white wage earners owned their own homes. In that year, 68 percent of black workers and 95 percent of white wage earners possessed a car. Serious economic and social inequality remained, but Americans across the political spectrum embraced the idea that unending, depression-free growth had finally arrived. Consumer society was a positive answer to communism. The ideal was not sacrifice, but personal freedom to chose. This society of consumption, despite all of its potential for excess, still seemed to create stable families. "No man who owns his own house and lot can be a Communist. He has too much to do," boasted housing developer William Levitt.[47]

Despite all the celebration of economic individualism, the government did not simply stay out of the marketplace but helped citizens get into it. In the GI Bill of Rights of 1944, Congress offered veterans low-interest loans for housing. In combination with the earlier FHA mortgages, veterans' loans accounted for nearly 50 percent of new mortgages between 1947 and 1957. These government-backed loans fueled extraordinary growth in suburban America (where home building increased by 43 percent in the seven years after 1946). The 1956 Interstate Highway Act paid for the great freeway network that made possible middle-class flight to the suburbs and their shopping centers.[48]

Advertising also contributed to the boom, creating demand even in the face of fact. Despite widely publicized scientific evidence linking smoking to cancer in the early 1950s, cigarette makers stilled fears with massive ad campaigns for filtered cigarettes. One spread in *Life* in May 1953 made the vague claim that Kent removed "seven times more nicotine and tar," strongly implying that filters actually made cigarettes safe. Tests, however, showed that Winston's filter left as much tar and nicotine as was in the unfiltered Camel. An effective filter would have eliminated the "flavor" and impeded the draw of smoke that smokers expected. In the meantime, between 1957 and 1962, tobacco companies' spending for TV commercials rose from $40 to $115 million,, a very effective smoke screen against the public health message. Billboards showing sexy women and tough men smoking Marlboros and other brands continued to make the habit appealing. TV ads claimed that you could have it all, or at least have both "flavor" and an effective filter. After a brief decrease in smoking in the 1950s, the upward curve resumed. Cigarette sales rose from 332,345 million in 1945 to 506,127 million in 1960. This was a powerful, if negative, tribute to the impact of advertising on postwar spending.[49]

The Postwar Splurge

When the war ended in August 1945, Americans were ready and able to consume. Moralists condemned this mad dash to buy and, even more, the mass appeal of "loud" furniture and even louder music, as well as extravagant cars and fast foods. But for those who had so long done without, this saturnalia of spending was hardly a surprise. In 1946, personal consumption was 20 percent higher than in 1945 and 70 percent higher than in 1941 (21 percent greater in actual goods when inflation is taken into account). Four billion dollars more would have been spent if goods like washing machines had been available. The post-1945 crop of babies created instant markets for everything from toys and layettes to larger cars and new houses. The generation born after World War II was the largest in American history. More than 55.77 million children were under 15 years old by 1960, compared to only 32.97 million in 1940.[50] American postwar prosperity was also built on global economic and political hegemony. While Western Europe and Japan recovered from the ravages of war, the United States faced no serious competition. Cheap domestic oil and expanded energy output allowed for sustained income growth. The wage earner was increasingly characterized not by John Lewis's coal miners who had to fight wage cuts but Walter Reuther's auto workers who won the Cost-of-Living Adjustment in 1948. Even though the price of houses doubled in the 1940s and cars became much more expensive with the introduction of high-compression engines, Americans still bought and bought.[51]

Some worrywarts feared a major slowdown after the postwar spending spree, but they were wrong. Rising incomes meant not sated markets but more expensive and diverse goods. Americans bought more meat (especially steak), more clothes (especially if the family had a teenage daughter), and, of course, more cars. Despite rising consumer debt, in 1952 there was no sign of slower spending. Anxieties about the return of the Depression disappeared quickly, and with them caution. Optimism continued for years. A 1955 study found that the heavy sales years of the early postwar period did not "borrow" from future business. Contrary to common sense, it seemed the more a product was owned, the bigger the market for still more. High-demand goods led to multiple sales per household (for example, radios or phonographs). At base, consumer research confirmed the obvious — that needs were never fully gratified. Americans bought new cars for the latest step-up feature (like automatic transmissions). Analysis merely confirmed what advertisers had realized in the 1930s — that the young and upwardly mobile were better customers than the less affluent.[52]

Experts admitted that the market for new cars was primarily "middle and upper-income families" and that already by the mid-1950s "sales are heavily dependent on people who can afford two cars." Eighty-five percent of new cars were purchased by only 47 percent of America's families. As a result, car makers saw no market for a cheap basic vehicle. The poor bought used cars, and two thirds of the autos sold were pre-owned. Even Chevy buyers were relatively well off — with a median income of $7,100 at a time when the median U.S. household income was $4,700. Merchandisers understood that those "well provided with the standard goods" are the market for new and innovative products. They were the vanguard of consumerism.[53]

If the middle class led this upward march, the working class was hardly excluded. The pace of progress was enormous. In the 14 years between 1940 and 1954, the percentage of households with indoor plumbing rose from 65 to 80. The flush toilet was already part of the "standard" package in 1940. The story was different with other household goods. In 1940, telephones were owned by only 36 percent of American families. By 1954, however, 80 percent of households had a phone. The refrigerator, a key element in the new standard of comfort, rose from 44 percent to 91 percent of households, and, of course, the TV increased from next to no homes to 61 percent over the same period. In 1954, merchandisers were already claiming that garbage disposals and air conditioning would soon become part of the standard package. Even if this prediction was premature, Americans quickly moved from wringer to automatic washers, from clotheslines to electric dryers, and from black-and-white TV to color. The earliest versions of new products may have not been very reliable or efficient (like the first dishwashers), and a number of innovations of the era proved to be

This ultramodern kitchen promised to free time for family even if that meant more work like sewing a dress for an appreciative daughter.

(*Better Homes & Gardens*, Feb. 1950, p. 91)

duds — like TVs implanted in kitchen stoves or garages so large as to double as "recreation" rooms. Nevertheless, the winning theme was bigger and better. This well-entrenched expectation cut even deeper into the American psyche: new goods represented progress and marked the upward march of time.[54]

The joy of the "push button" in everything from automobile transmissions to sewing machines sometimes made little engineering sense, but these devices all proclaimed an age of effortlessness, where everything was automatic and carefree. "With a GE Room Air Conditioner you choose your own weather with the flick of a finger." And Kelvinator's "Automatic cook" range let the family sit "right down to a delicious dinner when you've been out all afternoon." Sometimes, even a button was unnecessary. A 1952 ad featured the "XP-300," a "car of the future," complete with a convertible top that "goes up automatically when the first drop hits the car." Americans lost the race to launch the first space vehicle. The embarrassing blowup of the Vanguard rocket on the pad contrasted with the Soviets' successful launching of the Sputnik satellite in 1957. Still, Nixon declared that the United States won the war for the future in his "kitchen debate" with Khrushchev in 1959. He put down the Soviet leader with his comment, "Isn't it better to talk about the relative merits of washing machines than the relative strength of jets." On that terrain, the United States won hands down. And everybody knew it.[55]

Postwar consumerism fulfilled the dreams of the consumer engineers of the 1930s. Goods increasingly were sold for style and fashion rather than utility. The least likely products took on a space age form: vacuum cleaners that had for decades looked like mechanized carpet sweepers gave way to the Hoover Constellation, shaped like a space satellite. Flying saucer lamps, boomerang-shaped coffee tables, and abstract mobiles à la Calder were mass-produced replicas of the modernist style of the 1920s and 1930s. The old prestige of the permanent and handcrafted gave way to the convenient, stylish, and, most of all, up-to-date. Instant Chip and Dip replaced sandwiches for "drop-by guests." Wood gave way to plastic; wool and cotton succumbed to "wash-and-wear" synthetics. Everything was temporary — house, car, and even the family in some cases. The idea was "moving up," or at least moving on. TV serials like *Route 66* and the Beatnik Bible *On the Road* celebrated restlessness. As popular cultural historian Thomas Hine notes, "Precisely because people did not expect to hold on to possessions for the rest, or even for very much, of their lives, it became all right for these to become fun, fashionable and fantastic."[56]

Everything moved fast. Cars equipped with high-compression engines came with speedometers going up to 120 M.P.H. By the late 1950s, 20 percent of American families were pulling up stakes every year as homes became like cars, objects to be traded in. Already in 1949, retailers reported that the average hit phonograph record was on the charts only three months, and that was before rock 'n' roll! While in 1950, 108 radio shows had been on the air for a decade, few TV shows survived more than a few years. Even Mr. Television, Milton Berle, lasted only eight years and only with several changes of format.[57]

Most Americans participated in some way in this new world of constant change. The trend was most obvious in cars. Since the 1920s, GM's Alfred P. Sloan had envisioned a car of power and fashion that would continuously create demand. His dream finally came true in the 1950s with annual model changes. As Sloan described it, "The changes in the new model should be so novel and attractive as to create demand for the new value and, so to speak, create a certain amount of dissatisfaction with past models as compared with the new one." The dominant fashion of the postwar era was drawn from the powerful and avant garde image of the jet fighter, especially the Lockheed P-38 Lightning. This plane's tail inspired Harley Earl, a long-time GM designer, to introduce the fin in 1948 on the Cadillac.[58]

Although at first an emblem of luxury, the fin spread to plebeian cars like the Chevrolet and Plymouth by 1953. In fact, the price differential between luxury and economy models declined. The 1930 Cadillac cost four times the average price of a car, but by 1955 it was down to 1.7 times. This was a leveling upward: lower-status cars copied the Cadillac by adding glass, ever larger fins and grills, more color and chrome, and more horsepower. With each passing year the standard rose visibly. By 1955, the Chevrolet had a radically new look — long, low, and equipped with a V-8 engine. It even came with an optional air conditioner, and it sold 1.83 million units. This extravagance reached its culmination in 1957 with the "battle of the fins." Even the usually sedate De Soto featured sets of triple taillights that looked like rocket exhausts. The famously ugly Edsel of 1957 hardly was strange at the time, despite its front grill that suggested to some a vagina. Although the Edsel may have been a failure, car sales had gone up dramatically. Car registrations rose from 25.8 million in 1945 to 61.7 million by 1960, with car sales peaking at 7.9 million in 1955 (compared to a prewar high of 4.5 million in 1929). Changes in power, color combinations, and style in the 1955 model brought more customers into the showrooms than even the usually optimistic forecasters had predicted. By 1956, half of lower-priced Chevrolets were sold in their most expensive models (costing $2,500 rather than $2,000). Buying became even easier when banks lengthened the typical car loan from two to three years. No one was supposed to be left out of the good times, and they got better all the time. Even the Left loved to joke, "There is nothing too good for the working class."[59]

Motivational psychologist Ernest Dichter told advertisers that it was their job to teach Americans that it was all right to enjoy themselves while consuming cigarettes and beer. Sweets were not just for holidays, but a regular gift to oneself: "The reward element in candy eating, even in the adult, acts like an antidote to mechanization and industrialization." Dichter argued that people felt both guilt and pleasure in spending and that ads had to offer "absolution." He concluded: "America is experiencing a revolution in self-indulgence. . . . We've learned that one rarely makes one's ultimate goal — so why not enjoy life now?"[60]

This was an era that Thomas Hine has called the Populuxe, popular luxury enjoyed as continuous change. Inevitably such a culture had its caricatures. Las Vegas is perhaps the best example. Its postwar growth was explosive, launched by the gangster Benjamin "Bugsy" Siegel and his Flamingo Hotel. The town once evoked a nostalgia for the Wild West, but after the war, casino developers imported to the desert of southern Nevada the look of luxurious South Florida resorts with suggestions of a Hollywood set. The new Las Vegas gleefully rejected history and even geography and climate in its effort to create an artificial space and time. The New Frontier Hotel of 1955 was "Out of this World," offering a total package of comforts and luxury, including swimming pools, golf courses, riding stables, and headliner shows in an ultramodern, self-contained environment. Casino designers mass-marketed an experience, ultimately the enjoyment of affluence, expressed in willful disregard of prudence and thrift in gambling. Still, Las Vegas and places like it remained Sodoms set on the very edge of civilization, completely separate from, if accessible to, the secure and "decent" world of the suburbs.[61]

Containing Contradictions: Domestic Consumption

Despite the obvious excesses of fads, fins, and gambling dens, postwar consumerism was not a Mardi Gras. It was more about buying and furnishing homes and filling garages. Ads appealed to Americans whose recent memories of fear and loneliness during the war made them long for the securities of home and family life: "My partner deserves the *best* . . . she's going to have a Bendix" washer, said a middle-class man with his arm around his middle-aged wife in a 1945 *Life* ad. Spending was good, not because Americans deserved a party after the long ordeal, but because new products promised to restore family. Personal spending on housing in-

Diamond's Guide to Car Watching
(can you identify them?)*

Here are the southern exposures of nine northbound 57's. Dramatically different as these new cars are, they have one thing in common. On each is some chrome plating that started with DIAMOND Chromic Acid. DIAMOND ALKALI is one of the world's largest producers of chromium chemicals, and DIAMOND research has recently developed a new additive for chrome platers which reduces plating time and cost, gives a harder, brighter finish.

Progress like this helps explain why DIAMOND's "Chemicals you live by" are preferred by so many industries, found in so many places.
DIAMOND ALKALI COMPANY, Cleveland 14, Ohio.

Diamond Chemicals

* 1. CADILLAC   2. CHEVROLET   3. DODGE   4. FORD   5. MERCURY   6. OLDSMOBILE   7. PLYMOUTH   8. RAMBLER   9. STUDEBAKER

The battle of the fins led to an extraordinary range of styles, easily identified by many participants in the "populuxe" culture of the mid-1950s.

(*Newsweek*, April 1, 1957, p. 79)

creased from 10.4 percent in 1946 to 14.2 percent in 1960. Builders constructed only 603,000 homes in 1940, but erected 1.95 million in 1950 and continued at a rate that did not drop below 1.22 million annually throughout the 1950s. The middle-class bungalow culture of the 1920s had become available to a part of the white working class in the 1950s. Most, but hardly all, blacks and other poor people were left out of the suburban rush; they moved into the inner cities abandoned by whites. Still, for better or worse, the suburban consumer culture set the standard.[62]

The cracker-box houses that suddenly appeared in open fields on the outskirts of cities appalled affluent critics because of their cookie-cutter construction. These homes erected by William Levitt and others, however, met the immediate needs of returning veterans facing a major housing shortage. Levitt's homes (available only in ranch or Cape Cod models) had barely 800 square feet of floor space and no basements. Still, they included luxuries such as fireplaces, kitchen appliances, and sometimes even built-in TVs. Most important, the price was right at $7,900 for two bedrooms and $9,500 for three. A veteran could move in with only $58 in down payment. Moreover, these homes were considered "starters," especially by their younger owners, who dreamed of a separate dining room and a second bath. Levittowners put up additions as soon as they could afford them and dressed up the house fronts with siding or porches to give their homes distinction.[63]

The single-story ranch rectangle that dominated the earliest postwar housing developments quickly gave way to the raised ranch or bi-level — with a lower floor divided between living space and a garage. The split-level home, introduced in 1955, provided still more space and interest. Men "finished" basements to make room for older children's play and privacy in recreation rooms. Gradually, as tract housing enlarged, these rooms were moved upstairs into a resurrected back parlor usually called a family room next to the kitchen. This space was a cozy and low-maintenance symbol of family and relaxation. By the early 1960s, new houses averaged 1,240 square feet, 57 percent more than the postwar Levittown homes. The progression was obvious — not only more space per house but with it, more personal room for children and parents.[64]

The domesticity of the 1950s was not a return to the past. The suburb meant the breakup of community and kin networks, usually left behind in the city. The family and home had finally become a center of shared consumer goods — cars, furnishings, and TVs — a dream from the 1930s and

How the Levitts help meet the housing demand

SOME YEARS AGO, builders Levitt & Sons, of Manhasset, Long Island, decided that usual home building methods were disorganized, slow, and costly.

They envisioned a bold plan. First, to assure adequate building supplies at all times, they would stockpile, through a wholly owned subsidiary, everything they needed for hundreds of homes—including whole forests of Pacific timber reserves. They would pre-cut and pre-fit,

Levitt & Sons were ready with the plan in detail, and the organization.

Such an unusual program called for unusual financing. But the Bank of the Manhattan Company recognized the merit of the Levitt building project and provided liberal *commercial* credit.

Today, Levitt is America's largest home builder. Six communities and a veterans' city of 25,000 people owe their existence to the Levitts' new idea. And this year,

Levittown homes may have been starkly simple, but they symbolized new methods of building and bold financing. These "cracker boxes" met the housing needs of new families while also providing jobs and prosperity.   (*Time*, Sept. 20, 1948, p. 96)

1940s fulfilled. The suburbanite was often oblivious to the materialistic nature of home life, however. As historian Elaine Tyler May shows, the conservative backlash of the 1950s was as much against consumerism — of a type — as against communism. Many saw sexual license, a cosmopolitan culture, and the welfare state as a threat to their "belief in upward mobility as the reward for the frugal and virtuous." Against this danger stood the middle-class family as a "psychological fortress that would, presumably, protect [suburbanites] against themselves." It was a site of restraint, or more accurately of narcissism, "contained" within the virtuous walls of marriage and child rearing, and free from the temptations of the crowd. The joy of family and home spending on it was compensation for all of life's disappointments. For men, the domestic nest was expected to be a refuge from and compensation for boring and stressful jobs. For women, whose lack of public recognition for their talents was often a source of unrecognized frustrations, the home was supposed to be an exciting, ever-changing, ever-improving place of appliances and modern decorations. Finally, for children the home and its contents provided a sheltered setting for lives easier and happier than their parents' had been. The house, no matter how ordinary and common, provided "something to show for all your years of living," noted sociologist Herbert Gans. "Happiness came from raising healthy, independent kids, decorating the home to one's own tastes, and sitting back in the evening with other family members and relaxing in front of the new television set." That these pleasures and joys were defined by consumer goods and thus were "materialistic" could be easily forgotten. After all, Americans spent their money on red wagons for children's play on backyard patios, on big living-room TVs for Sunday-night family viewing, and on family vacations to Disneyland (not Coney Island). Las Vegas was far away.[65]

The new suburbanites were glad to be free of the confines of military barracks and of the need to double up with parents, once common because of war and the Depression. Yet suburbia also created rootlessness and at times anxiety. Frequent moves compounded the loss of daily contact with and advice from relatives about child rearing and marriage. William Whyte described 1950s suburban life as a throwaway society where, because so many moved so often, "If one loses some old friends, there will always be comparable ones to replace them." Sociologist David Riesman believed the postwar suburbanite was caught between the "peer-group he has left and another he has not quite achieved." Such Americans sought stability and found solace in religion. Many listened to baby doctor Benjamin Spock and positive-thinking preacher Norman Vincent Peale. Even self-help books by the 1950s were directed as much toward "adjustment" to family and friends as toward obtaining job success. Goods helped to resolve those tensions and create a sense of security.[66]

The common mid-century American home was, as historian Lynn Spigel notes, a "form of theater, a stage on which to play out a set of bourgeois social conventions." Advertisements, magazine articles, and advice books provided the scripts of these dramas and comedies. They presented the home as a "showcase, recommending ways to create glamorous backgrounds on which to enact spectacular scenes." Americans used their houses and the things they put in them to act out often contradictory needs. As motivation research guru Ernest Dichter put it, the 1950s home reflected the "basic conflict between attachment to the old, the accustomed, the confining security-stimulating surroundings and the great liberation of boundless freedom."[67] While Americans continued to be obsessed by the technological future, they also longed for the certainties of an invented past. The clear thinking and self-reliance of the tough frontiersmen and sheriffs on TV westerns in the later 1950s offered a comforting myth about American tradition. Thus suburbanites were drawn to the pioneers' simplicity as expressed in knotty pine furniture — even if their kitchens contained Formica-topped counters and dinettes made of metal and colorful plastic. These complementary themes were well captured in Disney's Tomorrowland and Frontierland. House designs freely mixed the modern and the traditional — a California ranch houses might have cupolas on the garage; a bi-level home might have white pillars framing the front door. These aesthetic contradictions made the modern house "warm."[68]

The 1950s picture window, according to Dichter, "was not only a way of looking out on one's achievement but also a way for neighbors to look in. Often it framed a lamp and other decorative items that were purchased specifically for display there." Readers of Vance Packard's *Status Seekers* delighted in learning about how Italian Americans needed a lot of "goop" in their houses — "shadow boxes, splashes of marble, stucco, and rococo furnishings," while Polish Americans demanded "pink and turquoise" for their decorative touches. The more affluent WASP preferred, Packard insisted, "Early American gestunk," a "white fence and the white clapboard house" with a "rustic-looking lantern" lighting the sidewalk leading to the front door. These diverse and still ethnically based displays of status were only one part of the picture. As Dichter saw it, the home was a way for the newly married to break with the rituals and rules of their parents. It was an opportunity for self-expression: "Today the modern woman begins not only to dress herself to suit her moods, but also to decorate her home accordingly." Consumer goods continued to allow Americans both to join with others and to distinguish themselves.[69]

At the same time, the home was also an interior space in which to stage family life and to create moods. Domestic goods were the props of these public presentations and private dramas. A shiny new car was the provider's "gift" to the family. The new Mixmaster and vacuum cleaner were the homemaker's tools to display her artistry. Betty Crocker's *Picture Cook Book*, notes cultural historian Karal Ann Marling, made the mundane labor of cooking "look both effortless and dramatic." Power tools and lawn equipment gave men a sense of competency in a craft. Grown men spent their weekends assembling models of battleships and building miniature railroads. Others fancied themselves landscape painters (sometimes helped along by paint-by-number sets). Portable power tools for drilling and sawing became widely available in the late 1940s, greatly easing home repairs and expanding the do-it-yourself cult among men. These tools of male domesticity created a $12 billion industry by 1960. Husbands and wives shared in the joys of the Weber grill and patio barbecues.[70]

Some consumer goods were supposed to build bridges between the home and the neighborhood. Tupperware is a good example. In 1951, these "space age" molded plastic containers were the latest in domestic convenience. However, what made them unique was that they were sold only by homemakers to other homemakers in neighborhood events. Tupperware parties combined games and gossip with the obvious expectation that guests would buy at least a few Tupperware products. This was, of course, an exploitation of neighborliness and a sneak attack of crass commerce on the sanctity of the home. Still, these parties were also the occasion for social interaction between people who hardly knew each other in a low-risk situation for buyer and seller alike. As sociologist Alison Clarke puts it, "Rather than adding decoration to products, Tupperware added a ritual, the party, which helped new suburbanites deal with the insecurity and loneliness that was part of their pioneering lives." While the ritual sold goods, it also made it easy for strangers to meet.[71]

Similarly, men had their stuff around which to build neighborly exchanges. Lawn mowing and fertilizing provided an opportunity for "cooperation and competition" with backyard neighbors. Creating and maintaining a carpet of grass became an obsession after the war, aided by new power mowers as well as new herbicides and fertilizers. In 1947, the Scott Company introduced the convenient combination of the two, "Weed and Feed." Power mower sales jumped from 35,000 in 1940 to 1.16 million in 1951. As historian Virginia Jenkins notes, "On the American front lawn men use power machinery and chemicals, the tools of war, to engage in a battle for supremacy with Mother Nature." They competed for crabgrass-free lawns and shunned neighbors who failed to keep out the dandelions.[72]

The TV was easily the most important domestic consumer product in the 1950s. In many ways, it was a dramatic extension of radio. Television was developed largely by the radio industry (primarily NBC-RCA in the United States). The Depression and especially World War II delayed mass purchase of the "box" until after 1945, when there were still fewer than 10,000 TV sets in the country. Even though a TV cost about $700 in 1945, the price of a prewar car, TV sales quickly made up for lost time as prices dropped. In 1950, 9 percent of American homes had a TV, but by 1960, nearly 90 percent of households had the tube and it was watched an average of five hours per day. Americans quickly adapted to their privatized visual entertainment. Between 1946 and 1953, movie audiences had shrunk by half. Despite the inferiority of the black-and-white TV screen (especially when compared to innovations like CinemaScope), movie makers survived only by appealing to youths who wanted to get away from the home. The radio suffered a very similar fate when sponsors quickly shifted to the new medium and network programs disappeared. Radio's remaining advantage was its portability. It combined wonderfully with the car, and again with young people seeking freedom from the family room.[73]

That spot was reserved for the TV. Broadcasters picked up the family format that radio had to abandon — providing a broad array of programs without reaching much beyond the wide girth of the white middle class. Early TV often adapted radio programs to the video screen: situation comedies like *Life of Riley* and variety shows including *Ed Sullivan*, along with adventure, soap opera, quiz, and kids' programs, provided daily diversion for all family members. By the late 1950s, sophisticates lost their live drama (like *Playhouse Ninety*) and serious news programs (for example, Edward R. Murrow's *See It Now*) to westerns, family "sitcoms," and detective shows. In 1959, 32 westerns literally saturated prime-time programming hours. Highbrow critics complained that "bad stuff drives out the good, since it is more easily understood and enjoyed."[74] However, American television

probably homogenized popular culture more than debased it. Programming lowered the taste of the educated and rich while introducing the
working class to middle-class child-rearing and consumer values on *The
Donna Reed Show*. Network educational programming on Sundays (a
quaint holdover of Victorian Sabbatarian sentiments) gave way in 1964 to
the National Football League, which could sell millions of viewers to Bud-
weiser and General Motors. Yet football was hardly a lower-class pleasure.
Since its origins as a diversion of the Ivy League elite, football had always
been a middle-class spectator sport. In a way, TV football replaced the far
more plebeian sport of boxing, which had dominated the TV waves until
1960 when middle-class sensibilities led to the canceling of the Friday Night
Fight. Once again, American consumerism blended class and even ethnic
cultures. The 1950s preserved a cross-class culture beyond TV mythology
in, for example, diners, bowling alleys, and even trailer courts. These con-

Like the radio, this TV by Magnavox promised to bring the family together infor-
mally while making the living room a window on the world.

(*Time*, Dec. 12, 1958, p. 12)

101

sumer settings attracted a wide range of Americans that only in the 1970s would narrow to less affluent families.[75]

This blend of the classes was clearly seen in Disneyland. ABC television (part owners) provided publicity in a Sunday night program that shamelessly promoted the southern California amusement complex that Walt Disney opened in 1955. Coney Island had long been associated with the popular classes, but Disneyland transformed the plebeian amusement park that had been mostly patronized by young singles into a middle-class family rite of passage. Hundreds of scrubbed, crew-cut, smiling youths roamed the grounds, keeping Disneyland spotless and orderly. Parents and children entered the gate onto "Main Street USA," an idealization of a late Victorian small town. A plaza led to amusement rides featuring Walt Disney's images of the American frontier, African adventures, cartoon fantasies, and the space-age future. Disney hoped that the crowds would be edified as well as entertained: the old would recall the past, the young would learn the "American spirit" and the adventure of the future, and families would grow closer in their shared experience.[76]

TV was often an entertaining and idealized projection of the families who watched it. Situation comedies and soap operas regularly presented familiar personalities in a "society that has been in constant transformation through geographic mobility and loss of extended families." *Father Knows Best* and *Leave It to Beaver* portrayed nuclear families led by strong but gentle fathers, subtly submissive but engaged mothers, and "ordinary," good-natured kids with problems easily and entertainingly solved every week. The soaps offered a "stand-in for the moral community," where real personal problems (in mostly middle-class settings) were confronted, affection and advice shared, and family values ultimately affirmed.[77]

Even more than radio in the 1930s, television offered the personal power to experience it all. It was a marriage of omniscience and physical security, bringing the world to viewers without their having to join a crowd. As Lynn Spigel notes, TV let Americans both "conquer and domesticate space." It was a radarlike technology in the shape of furniture, an electronic hearth. It required new family rules over talking, touching the screen, and control of knobs. The TV became a family member — a baby sitter, a welcomed guest, and sometimes even an annoying relative. With TV, Americans had both individual choice and family togetherness. And if three or four channels were not enough, Dumont, an early manufacturer and broadcaster, had a solution. His Duoscope TV had two receivers in the same cabinet, set at right angles. This arrangement allowed couples to watch two shows (with the help of polarized glasses) and to be together at the same time. A more practical solution appeared by the end of the 1950s: cheap portable TV sets that let family members watch favorite shows by themselves.[78]

Perhaps most important, TV was an admakers' pipeline into the home. By 1957, the average viewer saw 420 ads that took up more than five hours per week. One station showed 50 ads in two hours, one morning in 1964.[79] Television became nearly a perfect expression of suburban life: it celebrated domesticity in sitcoms and warned of urban dangers in action-adventure shows, while enticing viewers through commercials to the "miracle miles" of fast-food chains and shopping malls. It reinforced the trend (established by radio) of homebound privacy and a national, even global, entertainment culture.

Beyond the Home

Family consumption in the 1950s centered on the home, but it was also mobile, built around the car. The postwar era became the golden age of the drive-in eatery. In 1937, the McDonald brothers' hot dog stand near the Santa Anita, California racetrack was just another example of Depression-era petty entrepreneurship. The brothers rode the wave of prosperity when they graduated in 1948 to a drive-in restaurant in San Bernardino. Noting that their customers ranged from teenagers to young families on the go, they decided to cultivate families. "Give Mom a Night Off" became the pitch, and the McDonald brothers avoided the jukeboxes and cigarette machines that attracted teenagers. McDonald's was to be clean and wholesome, like Sunday school and the Girl Scouts. At least as important for success was informality and speed of service, even if that meant sacrificing variety in the menu and in quality of service. The brothers introduced fast, cheap, uncomplicated food and replaced carhops, plates, and silverware with a short menu of hamburgers and prepackaged condiments. "Buy'm by the bag," at 15 cents apiece was their slogan. In 1954, the McDonald brothers were joined by Ray Kroc, a salesman of commercial milk shake mixers. In 1960 he bought them out. Kroc franchised and used strict controls over food quality and store appearance to replicate this formula all over the nation. It was an easy sell. The war experience had acclimatized Americans in war factories and at the front to standardized food. McDonald's offered more. Kroc realized that predictable food at familiar sites was essential to winning consumers in a mobile and hurried society. Young parents broke with old neighborhood eateries once patronized by their elders, and their kids learned to salivate at the sight of McDonald's "Golden Arches."[80]

Kemmons Wilson, a Tennessee house builder, followed a similar plan when he founded the Holiday Inn motel chain in 1952. His concept was simple — provide predictable lodging located on main thoroughfares that would attract middle-class travelers, especially families. He introduced a new generation of motels that bypassed the country roads and little towns where the first wave of motels were often located. The old "Daily Rest Inn" run by a sweet elderly couple (or maybe not) who catered to families (or perhaps the "hot pillow trade") could not guarantee a middle-class family standard. It gradually disappeared, especially with the coming of the interstate freeways, and in its place, the reliable if not so inexpensive Holiday Inns beckoned the road-weary with an unmistakable sign that promised uniform service and common decency. By the 1960s, a "heraldry" of corporate emblems could be seen for miles from the freeway, offering predictable food, lodging, and muffler repair to car people.[81]

The privacy and freedom of the car culture complemented the consumerist nest of the home, but it also threatened to make the family house merely a launching pad for individual networking. By 1960, the two-car garage seemed to consume the front of new ranch houses. While socializing across backyard fences may have survived in the American suburb, sidewalk conversation gradually disappeared. In fact, sidewalks became rare in new developments after 1960. As urban historian Kenneth Jackson describes the phenomenon: "There are few places as desolate and lonely as a suburban street on a hot afternoon."[82]

Still, cars and patios were supposed to bring families, if not communities, together when tradition and work no longer did. Once again, the car and consumer culture could just as well be divisive. We have already seen how teenagers used cars to create their own peer culture. As early as the 1920s, when the market for secondhand cars appeared, young Americans bought them and won freedom from their families. Seldom had anything like this ever happened in the history of the family. Prosperity and permissive parenting encouraged a youth consumer culture that seemed to open the floodgates of sexuality and carefree spending, once associated with the teeming crowds of central cities. Now the middle-class parent saw this self-indulgence in the pimple-faced kid across the kitchen table. The teenage consumer culture had become distinct in the late 1930s. During the war, adolescent spending was fueled by income from jobs and the absence of parental controls when dads were at war and moms at work. After 1945, teenagers continued to earn substantial pocket money from part-time jobs. Prosperity and new attitudes meant that far fewer parents demanded that their children hand over their wages to help support the family. By 1948, youths and children influenced some $20 billion in consumer spending. Young people bought 8 million radios, purchased roughly 50 million comic books a month, and consumed 190 million candy bars per week. Teenagers turned used cars (especially the V-8s made in the late 1930s) into hot rods by souping up engines and sloping down the front ends. Prospects of getting relatively good paying jobs in factories encouraged working-class teenage spending.[83]

By the early 1950s, young people had largely taken over movies and radio. They formed a major share of the audience of the 4,000 drive-in theaters that cropped up after the war. Teenagers flocked to the 3-D movies that first appeared in 1951, despite their cheap, poorly developed stories that promised little more than a monster's claws or shapely female forms "coming right at you." The radio became an ideal arena for rock 'n' roll, which emerged in 1954. Cheap table radios and, by the late 1950s, the transistor radio and cheap phonographs (offered at $1 down, $1 a week) brought the latest tunes to nearly every teenager — no matter what Mom and Dad might have thought. Disc jockeys like Alan Freed and Wolfman Jack identified with the youthful listener and were closely associated with the music. In 1948, RCA introduced the inexpensive 45 R.P.M. record. In contrast to the long-playing 33 R.P.M. record (introduced the same year), the "45" turned out to be an ideal product for youth consumption: these small, lightweight discs with the large hole in the center could be rapidly distributed. They were inexpensive and thus easy to collect, and the impatient teenager could play or reject them in an instant.[84]

Radio broadcasters were not the first to see the potential of a teenage consumer culture. *Seventeen Magazine* (introduced in 1944) developed a new marketing formula. Articles reduced teenage anxieties about grooming, fashion, diets, dating, and friendship by introducing young women to clothing, cosmetics, and fashion accessories that promised solutions. *Seventeen*'s staff advised clothing manufacturers on how to market teen fashions and convinced department stores to introduce special teenage clothing lines. By 1948, *Seventeen* reached a million teenage girls. Department stores learned to fit young bodies with more stylish and popular clothing.

Managers told salesclerks to talk to the teenager, even if a parent were present. One store even set up "soundproof rooms where parents are barred and the youngsters can freely take down their hair." More common was Neiman-Marcus's strategy for expanded sales — setting off the youth department from the rest of the store and providing a special entrance.[85]

Merchandisers certainly exploited this new market, but they were only prying open a bud ready to burst. Since the 1920s, the idea of youth as a gateway to change had crept into magazine articles and advertising. When *middle-class* youths cut loose with a new dance or fashion, it was innocent vitality, not working-class anarchy. Parents had learned to associate spending with a measure of youthful freedom, even if that autonomy meant a moratorium on planning for adulthood and instead led to conformity with a materialist peer culture. Ads continuously drummed home this beat: Coca-Cola adds its own life and sparkle to the "natural gaiety of youth." Although parents would continue to fret that swooning over Frank Sinatra or Frankie Avalon did not prepare teenage girls for work and family, they unconsciously recognized that childhood was increasingly a period of training in consumption rather than preparation for work. And they began to see their relationship with their offspring as one of indulgence rather than obedience — as long as things did not get out of hand. As sociologist David Riesman noted in 1950, "Middle-class children have allowances of their own at four or five. The allowances are expected to be spent, whereas in the earlier era they were often used as cudgels of thrift." Baby-boom children learned how to be consumers through their toys. Doll and toy makers joined with beauty and household goods companies to make miniature home permanents, play-sized linen closets full of tiny boxes of household supplies, and toy dish and pan sets for little girls' play. The child had become a "consumer trainee" and would eventually be a "consumer tutor" for Mom and Dad.[86]

This all seemed harmless enough, but there was an underside to youth consumerism that frightened parents. During the war, zoot-suited Hispanic teens in California excited moral outrage among Anglos. In the late 1940s, hot-rodders antagonized adults with illegal drag racing on the streets of Queens and Los Angeles. Moralists demanded action when they saw the lurid comic books that children were reading in the early 1950s. Adults found it difficult to distinguish between youth and delinquent culture. Teenagers inevitably distanced themselves from parental control. They gravitated to peer groups that sometimes drifted into criminality in street-corner lounging, cruising by car, or congregating at drive-in restaurants. The title of the best-selling *The Shook Up Generation: Teen-Age Terror in Slum and Suburb*, by noted writer Harrison Salisbury, sums up the adult attitude. At the heart of this anxiety was the fear that working-class values were polluting the middle-class teenager.[87]

Rock music, and especially Elvis Presley, became the focal point for these fears in the mid-1950s. Elvis, the teenager who majored in shop in high school and had no musical training, became a new kind of folk hero to teens. He designed a winning look with shoe lifts, shirt collar up in back, a swagger, and a wild wave in his hair. His music was a composite of black rhythm and blues with white country and western. Elvis was a youth singing only to youths. How different from Bing Crosby or even Frank Sinatra! Yet he was also an artifice, designed and shaped to fit his market by his handlers. Most important, he was a "cover" for forbidden black music to a white audience.[88] Reluctantly Ed Sullivan, "unofficial Minister of Culture in America," gave in to pressure to book Elvis in 1956 on his Sunday-night variety show. Elvis still frightened parents with his gyrating hips, defiant sneer, and "black" sound. But within months a rival, more appealing to respectable adults, appeared. Pat Boone, a college student, married, and father of three, did "covers" of lively black tunes ("Tutti Fruitti" and "Ain't That a Shame"). Soon even Elvis became respectable when he willingly went off to the army after he was drafted in 1957. Rock continued to be associated with rebellion — fostering the independence of youth and challenging parental authority and values. Yet its association with big business and the oft-repeated transformation of rock rebels to respectable crooners when they succeeded and their fans aged made this commercial folk music far from revolutionary. After all, Elvis ended up producing bland beach-blanket movies and singing at casinos in Las Vegas.[89]

By 1960, the "moral panic" over teenage consumption had abated. Advertising moguls like Eugene Gilbert gushed about the profitability of youth markets to adults who otherwise might have fretted about them. By the end of the 1950s, he wrote popular magazine columns seeking to assuage adult anxieties regarding the crazes of their offspring. So relaxed had the climate become that when the Twist was introduced in 1961, adults embraced the dance almost as fast as did young people. The fear of the working-class "greaser" infecting middle-class youths proved to be unfounded. When middle-class teens embraced the relatively tame folk song and the "loveable moppets," the early Beatles, anxious American parents were relieved.[90] The "boundlessness" of youth consumption could be contained to the rock record heard in the family's basement rec room.

The cheap phonograph record became the center of a teenage consumer culture in the 1950s and 1960s. (Library of Congress)

Despite the political and economic upheavals of the years 1930 to 1960, American consumer culture stayed on its course, along the tracks well furrowed in the thirty years before. In many ways, this is astonishing. After all, the crises of economic collapse and war encouraged notions of leisure and community that challenged the commercialization of the 1920s. Public recreation programs, begun in the Depression, were alternatives to commercial entertainment; and organizations devoted to the collective rights of labor and consumers challenged the individualism of the shopper and the passivity of the consuming crowd. During the war, patriots called for collective sacrifice and attacked those who cheated on their ration stamps. Some Americans also demanded that those enriched by the war pay extraordinarily high progressive income taxes.

Yet beneath all this was a deeper and stronger current. Many crisis-era Americans were deprived of those material symbols of belonging and sharing that had come to define their place in the wider community and had greased the gears of personal life. They remembered these goods and still saw them in stores and movies. They found it hard to give up their cars, cigarettes, and other stuff — and many of the rich did not. The less fortunate dreamed of getting them back. Inevitably, the postwar era unleashed these deferred desires in extraordinary and even extravagant ways. The new affluence of the 1950s made real Alfred Sloan's decades-old dream of the car as an ever-changing fashion statement. Postwar wealth popularized modern design, integrating it in forward-leaning appliances, cars, and even neon signs in Las Vegas. Affluence added places at the table of plenty for millions who had long awaited their chance to join the party.

Still, for many Americans the shopping binge after 1945 was less a party than a confirmation and celebration of personal and family life. The Depression years had encouraged an already well-developed inwardness, and the public life of the barracks and war years certainly did not reverse the trend. The consuming crowds at America's Coney Islands and Times Squares were always the exceptions. The car and radio had broken up the interacting throng long before 1945. In the postwar years, Americans expanded this culture of consumption — ever widening desire that still was largely confined to their homes and devoted mostly to their families. Television was a step up from radio, creating a private window on the world. In measured ways, Americans connected to each other through a shared TV culture of ads and programs. Goods, ranging from kitchen appliances and cars to lawn mowers and toys, gave family life and family members meanings and roles while also helping them create a public image to present to neighbors and the wider community.

Obviously, postwar consumerism did not work for all — not for the poor, the single-parented, and the minority family confined to the city.[91] But for many, it surmounted the contradictions that few wanted to choose between — change and continuity and private and public. There were emerging signs of new tensions that this system of consumption could not easily resolve — conflicts between familial and individualist values and between middle-class and opposition aspirations and behaviors. Such stresses at times blistered to the surface, especially in parental anxiety about youths. Still, the consumerist "system" largely worked — not because it was the best of all possible worlds, but because it combined aspiration and constraint. For good and bad reasons, that balance satisfied many, and many still lament its passing.

CHAPTER 4

Coping with Abundance

U p to this point, we have seen how Americans have defined themselves and their place in society through goods. Their spending ways have said as much about their desires as their purchases, as much about the meanings of the things they bought as their physical consumption. Still, Americans have not always been pleased with a culture built around such longings. At this midpoint in our journey through the all-consuming century, we need to pause to ask: How in the first half of the century did Americans challenge and restrain this culture of consumption?

Americans have a long history of tension between the pursuit of material pleasure and the quest for simplicity. The extraordinary abundance of America's virgin land, relatively free from the grasp of the privileged few, attracted wave after wave of immigrants and pioneers willing to forego familiarity and relative comfort in the present for the hope of far greater material rewards in the future. Fulfillment was supposed to come to those who worked hard and were faithful to the dream of success. If Max Weber's famous saying that America was born "modern" has any validity, it is in that America was born a market. Yet these same settlers brought with them a rich religious and moral heritage that made a virtue of self-control and of communities protected from vice and corruption. The same country that has been addicted to alcohol, tobacco, and other drugs has also been the home of Prohibition, antidrug "czars," and stringent regulations on smoking. The culture that defined itself by its ever-rising "standard of living" also produced prophets of personal simplicity.

Americans were not merely contradictory. Appeals for restraint were a vital check in a society that seemed to have so few limitations. Boundaries have been necessary in every culture, separating "good" desires from "bad" to prevent cultural chaos. In the early twentieth century, when Americans were breaking traditional rules of frugality and self-control in so many ways, boundaries had to be redrawn to prove that society still had rules. To a degree, the call for constraint justified indulgence by defining the limits of desire. This "Puritan" streak was hypocritical — attacking the consumption of the poor or minorities while ignoring similar indulgence by the rich and white. Yet appeals for self-control have sometimes seriously challenged consumerism by establishing limits and suggesting social and personal meanings beyond goods. The fact that these appeals have been marginalized in recent years does not mean that they were simply nostalgic or petulant holdovers from an aristocratic or religious age when elites imposed their will on the masses.[1] The failure of alternatives and restraint shows more how the market has prevailed over other means of defining self and society.

Setting Limits in a Free Nation

In a country where personal freedom has been so closely identified with the right to buy and sell, it has been difficult to constrain consumption. Justification for abridging market rights has been narrow throughout American history and it became more so in the nineteenth century. Even theoretically, a person's freedom to sell could be restricted only if it impeded the rights of others to the market. The right to buy could be abridged only if the consumer was deceived or too immature to make rational purchases. Americans learned their John Locke very well: government was supposed to be primarily an arbiter of free exchange. This, of course, did not mean a war of all against all in unrestricted competition. The market disciplined participants into making prudent decisions. Self-control had to be practiced to assure success, and virtue went beyond enlightened self-interest. Still, the Founders came close to accepting the notion that the individual could be defined by rational choice in fulfilling personal desires. Complementing this was an evangelical tradition that emphasized personal religious experience over doctrine or ritual. As historian Jackson Lears notes, this sentiment easily slid into the dream of self-transforming spending. The end-all of life was personal satisfaction. Americans found it easy to identify society with the market where individual desires were fulfilled and where people related to each other through exchanging and displaying their goods.[2]

Still, the rationalist/experiential understanding of the individual did not go unchallenged. Both the Puritan and the Catholic traditions found market choice too optimistic, ignoring the power of concupiscence, that inborn susceptibility to self-destructive, obsessive desire. Pleasure could lead to pain if not carefully monitored or actively resisted: a glass of beer drew the drinker down the path to whiskey. Moreover, personal life was supposed to be based on deferred gratification, and cultivation of taste and skill. Community went beyond mutual respect for individual rights in the market: believers had an obligation to strive for a godly society, a fore-shadowing of the Kingdom of God, by protecting the sanctity of home and community from those who would tempt sinners. These religious traditions saw temptations everywhere in a society where unfettered markets produced an inevitable excess. Few individual capitalists ever intended this result, but free competition produced ubiquitous outlets for desire and a tendency for the enterpriser to cross the line between the hard sell and manipulation of the weak or uninformed. Moralists stood ready to define and defend that boundary. This very mixed heritage continued to shape American attitudes toward consumption in the twentieth century.[3]

Inevitably, challenges to consumerism during the first half of this century were defensive, cast quite narrowly. They may be divided into four arenas: 1) protecting "addicts" from themselves; 2) preserving a "simple" personal life; 3) defending the rights of the consumer against the power of the producer; and 4) guarding time and space in society from advertising and commerce. The first two challenged the consumerist understanding of individual desire and fulfillment; the second two, the market definition of community. Each of these approaches addressed serious flaws in the society of consumption, even if none were able to avoid compromise or divert the consumerist trajectory.

Since the early nineteenth century, Americans have recognized that their particular combination of freedom and prosperity allows vice to flourish. Professional gamblers, prostitutes, and "medicine show" charlatans had ample opportunity to prey on the unprotected who had coins in their pockets. Compounding the anonymity of new cities were the freedom and loneliness of the frontier. Both environments lacked the social constraints of the traditional village or the tight-knit family. Establishing new forms of control was a major theme in American history. Thus as "civilization" moved west, so did repression of gambling and other vices. These efforts went beyond eliminating disorder or creating the discipline necessary for honest business and hard-working labor. Vice reform also meant saving "sinners" from the temptations of a rich land. As early as the 1820s, temperance advocates understood the potentially addictive character of alcohol. The real problem was solo drinking, a common practice in a country where social bonds were often weak and alcohol served less to encourage conviviality than to provide an escape from loneliness. A modern American understanding of addiction emerged: the individual "giving in" to a powerful grasping force. Like the devil, drink took over the person who lacked self-control and was unprotected by family and community or their surrogates, the temperance society. More stable social conditions produced a dramatic decline in alcohol use, from 7 gallons of alcohol per capita in 1830 to 2.5 gallons in 1910. Yet demands for legislation by the Anti-Saloon League (founded in 1894) and other groups resulted in about half of the nation living under some form of prohibition by 1913. A clear majority accepted the Eighteenth Amendment of 1919 that outlawed most alcohol use. Among its proponents were the American Medical Association, prominent feminists, and leading industrialists like Henry Ford.[4]

Prohibition was a challenge to the free market (as brewers and distillers correctly protested) and thus a radical measure in capitalist America. While commonly understood today as a peevish attempt by rural conservatives to "restore" morality and industrialists to create a sober and efficient workforce, the Prohibition movement was more than an act of intolerance toward a free-spirited, largely immigrant people. It was an attempt to address a common problem of affluence — eliminating a highly appealing but potentially self-destructive product from the market. Excessive alcohol use undermined family stability. For some, it seemed to demand higher and higher doses to maintain exhilaration. Whether Prohibition was the way to solve this problem is, of course, questionable, but its fourteen-year reign did reduce alcoholism and its related diseases and social problems (even as it created a disregard for the law and enriched organized criminals).[5]

Protecting the compulsive consumer from self-destruction took many other forms. Americans were heavy users of opium and cocaine in patent medicines for decades before the Pure Food and Drug Act of 1906 finally regulated the cure-all industry. More stringent was the response to recreational drug use. In a frustrating effort to stop the international flow of narcotics of all kinds, the Harrison Act of 1914 prohibited cocaine, morphine, and opiates for nonmedical purposes. These drugs had well-known addictive properties (and thus pharmacists and physicians' organizations supported their banning), but they also were associated with minorities and immigrants. Other potentially addictive drugs, including nicotine and caffeine, were left off the list (even though some proposed that they be included). What was the difference? Surely the prohibited drugs were more virulent and perhaps more difficult to regulate. But nicotine (in the form of tobacco products) and caffeine (in the form of coffee and tea) also had, by the 1910s, very strong economic interests behind them. In any case, these drugs became the basis for major consumer industries and managed the moods of many Americans throughout the day. Defining the difference between socially acceptable desire and addiction was essential for caffeine and nicotine habits — and industries — to flourish.[6]

Gambling also became a target of those seeking to monitor the compulsive consumer. Like drinking, gambling is as old as human society. But in modern America it was a particular threat because it mocked the work and production ethic that justified American materialism. Local bannings drove gambling to the margins of the nation (ultimately to the western desert). Eastern states abolished their lotteries in the 1830s, and nearly all regions had ended them by the Civil War. In 1894, New York State forbade off-track betting on horse races, and in 1911 the state closed down the tracks. Again, the object was to protect gamblers from themselves. Illegal gambling persisted, of course, in Miami in the 1920s and in northern cities (with the numbers racket and racetrack wire services). Still, it was driven to the margins of respectable society.[7]

As we have seen, betting restrictions were loosened in the 1930s. Legalization of charitable gambling (e.g., bingo) began in Massachusetts in 1931, and other states legalized pari-mutuel horse race betting in 1933. Popular opinion remained cautious, however. Repeated attempts to revive state lotteries failed in the 1930s, despite the incentive to find an alternative to taxes for increasing scarce public revenues. While half of the adult population admitted to gambling in 1950, a survey the next year found only 38 percent favoring its legalization. This was hypocritical, of course, but the inconsistency pointed to an unstated logic: keeping gambling outside the everyday marketplace limited its temptation and impact on the worlds of work and family.[8]

The call for constraint of obsessive consumption went beyond the obvious addictions. Dieting became a virtue when mass affluence eliminated the well-fed look as the mark of distinction. Weight control became symbolic of a wider effort to self-regulate desire and to recover or sustain youth. Obesity was a sign of both aging and weak will at the table. In the 1920s, the gaunt figure of Rudolph Valentino, rather than the gold watch chain across the gigantic belly, became the male ideal. As early as 1914, weight-reducing salons appeared in Chicago just as the ideal female body shifted from the hourglass to the girlishly straight and thin. In the first two decades of this century, kitchens shrank by half, becoming laboratories of measured nutrition. Between 1880 and 1920, a number of diet fads appeared, including fasting, Fletcherism (ritual hyperchewing of food), calorie counting, thyroid medication, and even surgical fat removal. John Harvey Kellogg's world-famous Sanitarium in Battle Creek, Michigan was a center for food- and health-conscious Americans seeking relief from the evils of meat, spices, tobacco, coffee, and cola. This town became even more renowned as a center for the manufacture of breakfast cereals (as an alternative to meat and eggs) following J. H. Kellogg's popularization of corn flakes. Modern nutrition, as taught in home economics classes, was meant to end centuries of poor meal planning. By 1930, Americans had already begun to shift to fruit and vegetables and away from potatoes, flour, and red meat. Especially dramatic, each American consumed only 55.3 pounds of beef in 1930 compared to 72.4 pounds in 1899.[9] Affluence meant unprecedented temptation and new duties of self-control in the most basic form of consumption.

Finally, Americans restricted another potential area of compulsive consumption — consumer credit. Before World War I, department stores refused to extend credit to any but the wives of "substantial citizens." Even this form of deferred payment was only a courtesy, because full payment was usually expected within thirty days. The very concept of buy now, pay later was an affront to Victorian notions of prudence and character. Although expensive consumer durables like pianos and furniture had long been sold on time, this practice was not advertised until the 1930s. Installment purchasing for cars was the norm by the 1920s, but moralists still attacked it, and Ford was slow to accept the practice. Even house mortgages were of short duration (five or ten years), and down payments were frequently 50 percent of the purchase price.[10] Thrift was more than prudent; it was a barrier to indulgence — pleasure and comfort not paid for ahead of time with hard work.

Creating and preserving personal alternatives to consumer culture represented a second challenge to this democracy of desire. Henry David Thoreau's legacy of simplicity and self-reliance survived in dozens of ways in the twentieth century. The life and writings of Scott Nearing, with his vision of rural communal life, inspired a fringe. By contrast, the French writer, Charles Wagner, won a wide middle-class audience with Rousseauian sermons against "the complexity of life [that] appears in the multiplicity of our material needs." For Wagner and his American followers, simplicity was an attitude more than an actual abandonment of modern comforts: "It may be that the man in the carriage is simple, in spite of his grand position, and is not the slave of his wealth." Still, Wagner's evocation of the "charm of an old easy-chair" appealed to Americans uncomfortable about the clutter and clatter of the new. Ralph Borsodi's *The Ugly Civilization* (1929) was a popular reprise of a common Romantic theme — a lament on how the factory threatened the autonomous individual and a protest against the "fallacy that mankind's comfort is dependent upon an unending increase in production." Industrialism has created an "earn-and-buy economy," causing Americans to "measure men we know by what they earn . . . measure the life we have to spend in terms of money. But 'Time is not money' at all. *Time is life itself.*" Borsodi's solution was utopian: self-reliance and uplifting crafts, worshipfully practiced in the glow of the domestic hearth (though perhaps aided by electricity).[11] The homey virtues of simple living had been extolled in American thought from the Puritans on through the early Republic, Transcendentalism, and the genteel culture and Progressivism of the turn of the century. Even the consummate capitalist accumulator Andrew Carnegie was "a man both driven and repelled by his acquisitive desires," according to historian David Shi.[12]

Underlying this attraction to the self-disciplined, simple life was often a deep distrust of how affluence seemed to have unleashed desire and its frustrations among the uneducated masses. The influential French sociologist Emile Durkheim believed that ordinary people were incapable of sorting through choices and controlling their longings when tempted by the growing array of goods so tantalizingly showcased in stores. The Spanish intellectual José Ortega y Gasset's *Revolt of the Masses* (1932) argued that new shopping and amusement sections of cities amassed crowds of uneducated but no longer impoverished people. Uprooted from their traditional folk cultures and the control of village clergy and gentry, yet unprepared to embrace the high culture of the urban elite, these crowds were supposedly lured onto the street by the promise of immediate pleasure.[13]

These views were hardly confined to defenders of a dying European aristocracy and high culture. Early twentieth-century American reformers were obsessed with the inability of immigrant workers to control their desires. For example, Progressivists counseled immigrant mothers to prepare more economical and presumably more nourishing meals, condemned fathers for wasting family funds on alcohol and gambling, and scolded unmarried women for lusting after fashion when they should have been saving their wages for marriage. Reformers condemned dance halls, amusement parks, and pool halls as contrary to "clean recreation."[14] Richard Edwards's 1910 evaluation of *Popular Amusements* makes the point plainly: the young especially were "being lulled to sleep by the *habit of being amused*. . . . The lust for profit has picked open the bud. It is no cause for wonder that youth wilts under the process."[15]

Thorstein Veblen (1857–1929) took this critique of consumer desire in a very different direction. In his *Theory of the Leisure Class* (1898), he found unrestrained consumption among the rich, not the poor or young. He agreed with conservatives that desire, unleashed from economic necessity, produced strife and unhappiness among all classes. But for Veblen the rich were more tempted by wants than the "masses." Unlike the poor, they did not have to control their longings and thus could indulge themselves in ostentatious and emulative spending. Members of the leisure class could distance themselves from others through conspicuous display of their freedom from work by playing golf and giving extravagant parties. If, according to Veblen, the rich cultivated unproductive desire, common people were hardly immune from such temptations. Because of their precocious affluence, the rich set the standards for those below, who hoped some day to catch up. As society became more mobile and urban, these rounds of spending became increasingly more intense. Fashion passed from the traditional aristocratic court to the modern shopping district. Greater contact between people of different social rank meant increased opportunity for imitation and "invidious comparison." Mass consumption, Veblen suggested, led not to an egalitarian community but to ever more competition for status.[16] In the end, he adopted a quite conventional solution. The only antidote to the frustration and decadence of status seeking was the simple life. Veblen confronted an old American concern — the conflict between the work ethic and the fruits of labor, prosperity. He sided with the work ethic, seeing luxurious spending as a threat to the value of honest labor rather than an incentive to and just reward of effort. Veblen's romantic invocation of crafts and simplicity was an antidote to the excesses of the late nineteenth-century leisure class.[17]

The early twentieth century produced numerous calls for and even occasional efforts at restoring traditional crafts and folkways. Educators encouraged the preservation of games, folk songs, and crafts in schools. Urban planners were nostalgic about the pace of small-town life and even attempted to recapture it in quaint suburban town centers. For the sake of a slower-paced, freer, and less obsessed life, a few joined rural communities or voluntarily chose to do without the goods that others required. The gospel of the simple life proclaimed that pleasure and meaning could be found in quiet, repeated, and simple experiences and in work with ordinary objects, all conforming to the rhythm of nature. This doctrine challenged the ephemeral and emulative in consumer society.[18]

It would be unfair to label this impulse as merely a modern form of asceticism. Far from mortifying the flesh and denouncing conviviality, simple lifers often presumed a positive alternative. They argued that when individuals embraced fads and fashion, they failed to deepen their skills and understanding. Far from denying life beyond work and obligation, these improvers insisted that free time should be more than a compensation for or relief from toil. Instead, free time, not work, was the real purpose of life. Many assumed that the increased productivity made possible by the assembly line would create leisure time, not just more goods. Implicit in this thinking was the belief that basic needs could be satisfied and thus wage earners would opt for more time from work when their needs were met. For example, in 1932 economist Walter Pitkin predicted that a combination of technological improvements (e.g., making cars last for 500,000 miles) and growing boredom with consumer goods would lead to a fundamental shift in human activity. Americans would turn away from the production of material goods and toward education, health, and recreation. Even more striking would be the reduction of work time, which Pitkin believed would drop to 22–27 hours per week by 1967. The new problem would be how to organize and cultivate free time, not how to produce and sell goods.[19]

The cultivation of self and society beyond goods need not be elitist, according to Simon Patten (1852–1922). This American economist argued that affluence would elevate personal desire and create a wider, more democratic culture. Patten drew fresh conclusions from orthodox economic theory. With affluence, the desirability of each additional unit of food and drink would decrease and therefore the demand for newer, "higher" forms of consumption would increase. Put another way, the needs of the flesh would decline and any new surplus of time, energy, and resources could be devoted to refined recreation and the arts. Affluence created a new basis for civilization. It was no longer necessary to gratify oneself with gluttony and intoxication in anticipation of lean times. The new problem in the age of plenty was "adjustment" to changed conditions of abundance — learning not to overindulge and instead to reach for higher satisfactions. For Patten, technology did not unleash chaotic desire but rather freed people from traditional reactions to scarcity. The problem was to learn how to transcend crude desires rooted in a society where wants were unfulfilled, not to restrain new desires with coercive institutions or old-fashioned moralities.[20]

Cultivation took many forms. John Dewey denounced utilitarian education that did not prepare for the creative and intellectual development of the individual in leisure hours. He was one among many in the early century who demanded "education for life," essential because he expected that leisure time would rise sharply. In 1917, the National Education Association adopted the goal of "education for the worthy use of leisure," and later the New York Principals' Association insisted that the humanities could "counteract the influences" of advertising. Few felt the need to justify English or history courses by insisting that they trained students to be good memo writers or flexible business leaders. The point was to learn to be a lifelong lover of arts and learning.[21]

If adults were deficient in formal education, they could catch up by reading the classic foundations of learning at home. The "Five-Foot Shelf of Books," selected by Charles Eliot, once president of Harvard University, provided the essentials of a liberal education. These books were advertised (in 1923) to make the reader an "interesting and responsive companion" and to help avoid "growing mentally fat for lack of exercise." The Book-of-the-Month Club, created in 1926 by Harry Scherman, was intended to keep the busy but still literate middle-class reader abreast of the "best" of current books. Although purists criticized the Club for spoon-feeding culture to the middlebrow, the judges who selected the books upheld genteel moral and aesthetic standards — self-control and antimaterialism. Educational radio was another venue for personal uplift. As early as 1923, there were 72 educational radio stations that featured classical music, dramatic readings, book reviews, and children's educational programs. The networks presented opera from the Metropolitan Opera House and Walter Damrosch's classical music appreciation programs commercial free. These efforts to popularize high culture assumed that an educated minority had the authority to serve as cultural gatekeepers, and also that this elite was committed to communicating effectively with a broad and interested public.[22]

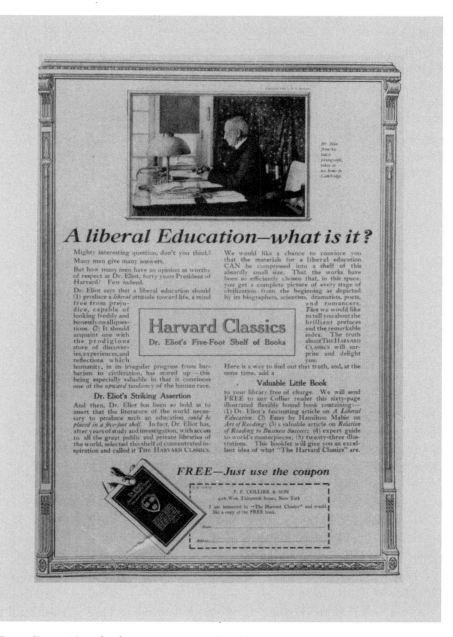

Harvard's president for forty years promised a "liberal attitude toward life" and a sharing in civilization's "upward tendency" for those who bought and read his "Five-Foot Shelf of Books." Learning had yet to become merely a path to economic success. *(Collier's*, Dec. 12, 1916, p. 3)*

A similar earnestness went into early twentieth-century efforts at public recreation. Progressive-era programs focused on the young, especially in building neighborhood playgrounds and pools to divert children from the dangers of the street. Reformers also gained funds for public museums and libraries. In the 1920s, public golf and tennis facilities found support in high places.[23] Even more impressive were New Deal public works projects: by 1937, Roosevelt had spent $1.5 billion building a wide array of playgrounds, parks, tennis courts, swimming pools, and cultural centers.[24] These recreational facilities were designed to challenge commercial amusements that appealed to immediate pleasures rather than cultivated skills. This was a very serious mission. In sociologist William Ogburn's words, recreation was "to give direction to social change itself and to achieve a better social order."[25]

American adult educators, sociologists, librarians, and recreation professionals recognized that they faced a powerful opponent in commercial entertainment and sought to create an alternative public culture. Sociological studies of urban dance halls, saloons, and vice all made a similar point: commercialized play produced maladjusted people.[26] These reports attacked commercial amusements for encouraging spectator passivity, denying creativity and the intimate culture of the neighborhood, and exploiting sex and violence. An assessment by the President's Research Committee on Social Trends (1933) summed up their frustration: "How can the appeals made by churches, libraries, concerts, museums and adult education for a goodly share in our growing leisure be made to compete effectively with the appeals of commercialized recreation?"[27] This vision of cultivated life had its heroes, but all recognized that the foe had the upper hand.

This inequality had long been a problem. Indeed, the idea of making consumers a greater force against business was a third way of challenging market meanings of life. A major theme of Progressivism had been the growing inequality between consumers and producers, an effect of corporate dominance over markets and the resulting price gouging and misinformed consumers. Protecting the consumers' interests was never easy. The failure of the American antitrust movement in the 1890s and 1900s proves the point. It was no easy task determining what was a "safe" product or setting the boundaries of hyperbole in advertising. Even the muckrakers, quick to attack marginal meat packers and outrageous patent medicine panaceas, were tolerant of advertising "exaggeration." Making matters much more difficult, businesses viewed almost any attempt to regulate the contents of foods, drugs, and other products and to restrict advertising as a threat to property. In 1914, the Federal Trade Commission was assigned the modest role of policing deceptive commercial practices and of regulating the labeling of consumer products. By the 1920s, it had become more of an umpire between competing businesses than a defender of consumers' interests. The Pure Food and Drug Act of 1906 did little more than require disclosure of narcotics and alcohol contents on patent medicine labels and prohibit manufacturers from claiming ingredients not present. Advertising and business interests repeatedly evaded regulation. Voluntary schemes such as the "Truth-in-Advertising" campaign of *Printers' Ink* (the main American periodical for the advertising industry) simply called for moderation in ad claims. In 1925, the Better Business Bureau became a kind of private Federal Trade Commission but lacked enforcement powers and any consensus regarding what constituted inappropriate business practices. Despite legislation proposed in 1933 that would have given the consumer-oriented Food and Drug Administration authority in this area, the Wheeler-Lea Act of 1938 bestowed upon the generally pro-business FTC control over deceptive advertising.[28]

Given the difficulties of the regulatory route, advocates of consumer protection were obliged to emphasize consumer education. The frustration of many was expressed by Robert Lynd in 1933 when he complained that there was no coherent policy of consumer rights: "Historically this has its roots in a long tradition of focusing attention upon the productive forces of the nation, of identifying consumer welfare with business prosperity, and of over-dependence upon the rational adequacy of the consumer's unaided choices." Leadership was needed to "give to the spending of the national income the same degree of concern that is at present bestowed upon the earning of that income. Such coherent leadership is needed if schools and other agencies are to educate the individual consumer in the practice of the fine art of spending money."[29]

Candidates for such leadership came from various corners. In 1929, educator John Dewey and economist Paul Douglas founded a new party, the League for Independent Political Action. They hoped that this organization could build a constituency against monopoly and for modern democracy based on consumer rights. Less political but often just as militant were the efforts of home economists to encourage consumer literacy through the public schools. The American Home Economics Association and a number of women's and urban black groups called for stricter food and drug controls and buyers' protests against high prices, especially in the 1930s.[30] World War II produced still one more effort at regulating consumption in the public interest, the Office of Price Administration. Although designed to control hoarding of vital materials and resources for the war effort, it also strove to limit inflation and price gouging the consumer. The OPA was more than a watchdog bureaucracy. Volunteer local committees and boards were filled with consumer rights activists who supported OPA policy.[31]

In the 1930s and 1940s, consumer protection had an intellectual and emotional appeal that today has largely been forgotten. Consumers' Research (CR) was a leading force in shaping that ideal. This product testing and information service was founded in 1929 by Stuart Chase and F. J. Schlink. Their books *Tragedy of Waste* (1925) and *Your Money's Worth* (1927) attacked wasteful consumption that they believed was fostered by deceptive advertising. They called for consumer education and an organization to protect the unsuspecting buyer. By offering the public detailed facts about the quality and features of practical goods, Consumers' Research tried to be a counterforce to commercial propaganda. CR staff saw themselves as an elite teaching an ignorant mass (even though supporters were mostly middle class). Still, the message was democratic: consumer society should not perpetuate class difference based on status fashions or differences in knowledge about goods. CR's object was to make free enterprise work better by creating a better informed and more powerful consumer community. Consumer education was supposed to raise shoppers from the ranks of the patronized and manipulated mass and to make spending a genuinely rational act, appropriate for a democratic community. Consumers' Research saw itself as restoring the ethos of the nineteenth-century town hall in the age of the consumer.[32]

A fourth way of setting limits on the consumer culture was to fence off time and space from commerce. This too had deep roots. The idea of separating the home and family from the market was an essential part of Victorian culture. Indeed, the key to the success of impersonal business and industrial efficiency in the nineteenth century was to take trade and production from the home. In return, this separation freed time and space for the full flowering of an intimate family life. There were many examples of this principle, ranging from so-called blue laws restricting Sunday commerce and prohibitions of door-to-door salespeople to zoning laws protecting residential neighborhoods from business intrusions. Each attempted to preserve the distinction between commercial and domestic space and time, between market work and family life.[33]

Those who longed for home as a haven often also feared what they saw

THE **DOUGH YOU BLOW** —will bring U.S. woe!

1918 What a boom we were handed by World War No. 1! Money came easily—went easily. Everybody was splurging on everything—from silk underwear to diamond sunbursts. Prices went skying. Sugar eventually hit 28¢ a pound!

1921 Bye-bye, boom. Factories closed; men laid off. Prices and wages sinking fast. Wish we'd banked some of that dough we'd blown a few years back! With jobs scarce, that money would have come in mighty handy, then.

1929 Prosperity. Stocks up fifty points in a week. Again everybody was buying everything—yachts, jewelry, stocks, real estate, regardless of cost. Depression? Phooey . . . we thought we'd found a way to lick depression.

1932 Or had we? Bread lines, apple venders. WPA. "Brother, can you spare a dime?" No jobs. Prices dropping. Wages dropping. Everything dropping—except the mortgage on the house. "What goes up must come down."

1944 We're splurging again. Americans have been earning more money. But even today there are fewer goods to spend it on—so naturally prices rise. We must keep them in check. DON'T LET *IT* ALL HAPPEN AGAIN!

4 THINGS TO DO to keep prices down and help avoid another depression

1. Buy only what you really need.

2. When you buy, pay no more than the ceiling prices. Pay your ration points in full.

3. Keep your *own* prices down. Don't take advantage of war conditions to ask for more—for your labor, your services, or the goods you sell.

4. *Save.* Buy and hold all the War Bonds you can afford—to help pay for the war and insure your future. Keep up your insurance.

EVERY WAR BOND YOU BUY WILL HELP **US** KEEP **PRICES DOWN**

A warning from the War Advertising Council that excessive wartime spending would lead to inflation and then depression.   (*Time*, Dec. 25, 1944, p. 83)

as the impulsive consumption of the street crowd. Family life was to be the seat of constraint, sober and uplifting cultivation, and innocence, in sharp contrast to the consumer culture of the suggestible and unpredictable crowd. These beliefs were rooted in the idea of a "natural" realm of the private family and self set against the presumably artificial character of society — a common notion that extended from the Enlightenment through Romanticism. The domestic world of personal relationships, freed from the bustle of the marketplace, was supposed to help the old persevere in their family values and prepare the young to withstand the lures of street pleasures.[34]

Founders of modern home economics, Catharine Beecher (1800–1878) and Ellen Richards (1842–1911), gave the housewife the role of guarding the domestic sanctuary. Her decisions as a wise consumer were to make the home a place of health, beauty, and love.[35] The family dinner table should be sacrosanct because, according to Richards, it "inculcated the virtues of self-control, self-denial, regard for others, good temper, good manners, pleasant speech." Elegance in dining room furnishings and menus was justified as an essential prop of morality against the masses who "take their pleasure in large groups, after the fashion of the primitive communities." This was the point of the flight to the suburbs that began during the early decades of industrialization. The well-appointed suburban house inculcated virtue and protected the family from the vices of the consuming mass. This view justified much hypocrisy, but it also made the home a bulwark against market values.[36]

As important was the innocence of childhood. Indeed, much anticonsumerist rhetoric came out of the cult of the child. By 1900, especially for white middle-class Americans, children had became "priceless," no longer economic assets to be sent to work at an early age to provide parents with income. Rather, offspring became emotional assets for educated and affluent parents, who protected their young from the labor market and valued them as blessed members of a realm of imagination and play from which adults were excluded. It was among these parents that educators and psychologists won audiences for their child development theories. These experts promised bright, happy, and successful offspring if parents properly recognized and cultivated each of the child's developmental stages. This new model of scientific child rearing stood in opposition to the indulgent and promiscuous world of consumerism. Educational toys, from traditional building blocks to innovative craft and construction sets, isolated the child from the crowd's fads and indulgences and provided scientific, step-by-step training for success. In 1900, middle-class children were supposed to be guarded from sex, violence, and alluring pleasures in magazines, movies, amusement parks, and dance halls, and even from legal drugs like alcohol and tobacco. The preservation of the innocence of childhood was and remains the main argument for restricting the sale of pleasure.[37]

Protecting domestic space and child time from the market took many forms. Particularly revealing were attempts to shelter the home from advertising and to shield the young from the consumer market. A striking example was the early reluctance to advertise on radio. Because messages were transmitted over public radio frequencies, broadcasting was subject to government regulation in ways that private telephone wires were not. There was also a general consensus that radio, as a new medium of science, should be a vehicle of cultural and educational uplift. In 1924, for example, Herbert Hoover, then Secretary of Commerce, favored only indirect advertising (short messages of sponsorship similar to public TV underwriting in the 1990s). "If a speech by the President," Hoover worried, "is to be as the meat in a sandwich of two patent medicine advertisements there will be no radio left." And even David Sarnoff, founder of NBC, first proposed that broadcasts be financed not by ads but by a percentage from the sale of radios.[38]

Most important, radio transmissions disturbed the presumed quiet and harmony of the home, so broadcasters had to be wary of breaking this inner sanctum. Even *Printers' Ink* held in 1923 that "the family circle is not a public place, and advertising has no business intruding there unless it is invited." As late as 1931, a prominent commentator on the new medium evoked an image of radio invading the home like a thief: "utilizing the very air we breathe," radio waves entered "the homes of the nation though doors and windows, no matter how tightly barred." Publicity for radio in the early 1920s emphasized the technology's role in reinforcing the cultural function of the Victorian parlor. It was definitely not to be an audio billboard in the home. Even when WEAF of Long Island broke the ice in 1922 and started selling air time to a real estate developer, the station still refused to allow prices to be mentioned or samples offered.[39]

As radio historian Susan Smulyan notes, "General public acceptance of broadcast advertising came only as a result of the radio industry's sustained campaign to promote it." That push began when rising broadcasting costs combined with a dominant laissez-faire political philosophy led to the creation of the commercial networks (NBC and CBS) in 1926 and 1927.[40] Still, the early networks were reluctant to turn the living room into a pit of com-

127

mercial chatter. In the 1930s, despite a great expansion of advertising, the networks banned ads that disparaged competitors or mentioned prices; and they rejected programming that glorified crime, greed, or cruelty even if an advertiser would pay for it. Advertising on daytime programs was rare as late as 1932, in part due to the surviving scruples that these hours should be devoted to commercial-free educational programming. The networks financed "sustained programs" (advertising-free) through the 1930s, featuring classical music like the NBC Symphony, children's literature, and even the news. This concession to public service justified network opposition to a bill in 1934 that would have given 25 percent of the radio frequencies to educational stations. It also reflected a common belief that the airwaves belonged to the public and that division between the home and the marketplace should remain distinct.[41]

Early TV had fewer scruples about the commercial "invasion" of the home and welcomed ads on all types of programs. Yet in 1952, the National Association of Broadcasters still asked members not to "triple spot" ads and to limit commercials to three minutes per half hour of prime-time programming. The public revulsion against ad-driven TV remained strong into the 1960s. Newspaper critics attacked the *Mickey Mouse Club* when it first appeared in 1955 for its excessive and irritating ads. Grayson Kirk, president of Columbia University, condemned ads as a "withering blight" ruining "an important communications medium." Federal Communications Commission Director Newton Minow attacked commercial TV as a "Great Wasteland." Even Allen B. DuMont, a major promoter of early TV, admitted in 1961 that he had helped to create a Frankenstein: "Rather than honored, perhaps I should instead be censured."[42] Only slowly was the bad conscience about the commercialization of the home lost.

Similarly, protecting children from the market was a serious public policy issue in the early twentieth century. Although federal legislation restricting child labor came only in 1938, the number of ten- to fifteen-year-old wage earners decreased from 1.99 million to 667,000 during the 1920s. In that decade, the idea that parents had the right to a child's labor and income disappeared in many sectors of the U.S. population. Ironically, just as it became culturally taboo for parents to send children into the labor market, their offspring were being introduced to a consumer market. Many saw the contradiction. If children were to be protected from the world of work, so too should they be only guardedly introduced to the world of consumption. Both were realms for freely consenting adults. Experts advised that children should be trained to shop wisely through carefully apportioned spending money. Despite the potential advantage of selling directly to children, merchandisers were very careful not to offend parents. Children should not be "lured" through advertising into wanting a toy or sweet. They were vulnerable because they lacked the rational capacity of the adult. Until the 1930s, toymakers mostly appealed to parents, not children, and even in the 1930s, toy and candy companies did not advertise on children's radio programs. Ad agencies were extremely careful not to offend parents with children's radio programming that exploited "blood and thunder" themes.[43]

When moralists tried to control the content of movies, they claimed that they were protecting children. In 1909, American filmmakers forestalled municipal restrictions by policing themselves through their own Board of Censorship. Repeatedly, the film industry imposed self-censorship in response to the public outcry against the poor example presented to the young in films. This impulse culminated in 1934 with industry self-regulation that not only prohibited graphic violence and sexual innuendo but also outlawed racial or radical political themes.[44] These efforts to protect children from the consumer market were sometimes ruses to impose particular moral or religious standards on the public. Still, they did set boundaries in the name of innocence.

Why and How Constraints Failed

A rich America was bound to be a nation of consuming Americans. A country that was largely constructed on the market and that had so few rituals and traditions other than goods through which to form identity and community would have almost inevitably followed a consumerist course. The fences of constraint lined this road and made it twist and turn, but these barriers were always weak and often broke down from the pressure of the flow of commercial traffic.

However, the problem went beyond the overwhelming power of the market. The ethic of constraint was itself riddled with inconsistencies and contradictions. The laudable goal of reducing addictions all too easily slipped into attacks on the character and culture of minorities — "wet" immigrants or city folk, blacks crazed with cocaine, Chinese opium dens. The problem of distinguishing need from obsession and legitimate marketing from "pushing" dependency faced all members of the affluent society. This subtle difference was lost when Prohibitionists identified minorities with addictive behavior.

These distinctions became even more difficult to make after Prohibition had failed. The Eighteenth Amendment had required the civil life of the church parlor. Perhaps inevitably, a sizeable minority in 1919 and a strong majority within a few years rejected this standard. Americans evaded Prohibition in hundreds of ways. They patronized speakeasy bars, talked their doctors into prescribing medicinal alcohol, and even made raisin cake into an illegal drink. Within a decade, repeal won support of the Du Ponts and key Democrats like John Raskob. The well-funded Association Against the Prohibition Amendment argued that Prohibition was a failure as well as a threat to free enterprise and personal freedom — a very potent combination of appeals. Following Roosevelt's inauguration in 1933, repeal won the support of almost 73 percent of state convention delegates. With state option, only eight southern and midwestern states remained "dry." No longer did that once imposing coalition of rural religious conservatives and industrials dominate American politics. Arguably, Prohibition lost support from the most powerful groups in the United States because more relaxed consumer values became more important than production values of thrift and discipline. Drinking became a status symbol during Prohibition when the rich set the standard with their illegal, high-priced booze. Prohibitionists were easily isolated as killjoys and even un-American for denying personal choice and responsibility in drinking.[45]

Prohibition certainly was an extreme and unworkable solution. Still, the politics of repeal marginalized serious discussion about the difference between fun and indulgence or the obligation of society to protect the vulnerable from obsessive desire, be it for drink, drugs, food, or gambling. At the same time, business moved one step closer to the doctrine that there should be no limits on the "free market." Groups like Alcoholics Anonymous emerged in this void, providing compulsive drinkers with therapeutic support for gaining self-control. Their underlying presumption was that addiction was an individual problem and a sign of personal inadequacy. The responsibility of merchandisers for fostering chemical dependency was often pushed aside.[46]

If Americans found it hard to address the complexities of compulsive desire in a consumer culture, they found it just as difficult to create personal alternatives to consumerism. Neither the idea of simplicity nor cultivation had much chance of reaching more than a small audience. These goals were always class bound, primarily appealing to an insecure middle class. Relatively few youths of the streets used the public playgrounds built to raise them out of poverty in the 1910s and 1920s.[47] To many, that culture of improvement seemed elitist and, perhaps worse, didactic and boring. In the 1930s, it was easy for cartoonists to get laughs from moviegoers with caricatures of the long-haired conductor in the "Silly Symphonies" series. Too often, the improving culture emphasized self-control rather than the release and expression of emotions; too often it denied dreams and insisted on the cultivation of skills and habits that made sense to the educated business class but seemed irrelevant to many wage earners with no chance for mobility.

To the general public, the jeremiad against consumer culture appeared to be a confused knot of nagging and arrogance, a condemnation of a mass culture that was fun combined with an insistence on freedom for self-expression that seemed to many to be antisocial. Well-meaning advocates of uplift either separated themselves from the common culture or attempted to impose their values upon a reluctant society — and neither approach seemed very democratic. To many average Americans, consumer critics were easily characterized as Puritans, attempting to create a permanent Lent against a continuous Mardi Gras. And why would anyone choose Lent?[48]

At base, the philosophy of simplicity and uplift lacked any clear and accepted principles that could claim to represent the common culture. This led inevitably to biases that condemned some forms of consumption while indulging others. Judgments were often rooted in class, gender, race, and even age conflicts. Veblen's ethic of utility, simplicity, and individualism ignored the appeal of a culture of novelty and kitsch without any clear justification except taste. It contributed to a new elite style, less obviously privileged and haughty than the ostentatious consumption of the Vanderbilts in 1900 but elite just the same in its celebration of the severely modern and denigration of the "decorative" bric-a-brac of the masses. This style was less formal and perhaps more accessible, but rooted in the market nevertheless. In the long run, top hats were replaced by designer T-shirts.[49]

Those who tried to organize alternatives to consumerism were caught in a dilemma. They had extraordinary difficulties in reaching stated goals — "true" community and individuality without goods and purchased pleasure getting in the way. Ironically, voluntary groups — from amateur singing societies to agate collectors' clubs — have been often less flexible than markets in adjusting to their members' personal needs. The problem has been that they were run by participants. Too often, these groups have appealed to the desires of core membership rather than expanding their vision to bring in new members or to find ways of bridging differences between "ins" and "outs." When groups were dominated by their members, they easily excluded others or became fractionalized. People less skilled at self-expression and less secure in disclosing themselves to others preferred to "join" society through their goods rather than through direct personal interaction. Volunteer organizations often lacked the seemingly magical power of the consumer culture to give individuals a sense of *self* within a chosen *group* of spenders. Advocates of simplicity and cultivation did not see how consumer society accommodated that insecurity by giving people the cloak of goods to hide their nakedness and to tell their stories for them.[50]

High culture has always had its appeal and will continue to do so. Still, it was not really necessary to social and cultural stability in a consumer culture. While Simon Patten hoped that affluence would lead to the cultural uplifting of the masses, he discovered that this improvement might well mean more varied and quality consumer goods instead of museums, concert halls, and libraries. He was unusual among early twentieth-century intellectuals in his toleration of the commercial street culture. He recognized that it offered the "vital excitement" that people no longer experienced in monotonous jobs. Playful spending was compensation for work deprived of independence and skill. Patten also realized that increased desire for goods of all kinds reinforced the work ethic. With higher wages, labor strife and the work-shy individual will disappear because "laborers will feel the spur of expanding wants more keenly after each of their advances, and in order to gratify them they will be forced to accept the discipline of the new industrial regime." At the same time, "the housewife with new flowered and fragile dishes" will become "responsible . . . and her house must mirror forth her virtues" in hours of cleaning and careful meal planning. Affluence led to a new stable equilibrium between spirit-uplifting consumption and disciplined labor. Traditional high culture need not be a part of the equation at all.[51]

Finally, despite often heroic efforts to find alternatives to commercialism, proponents of personal life beyond the market were often caught in the very forces they attacked. The practice of simplicity was riddled with inconsistency and hypocrisy. Because this virtue was personal and "spiritual," it was often confined to a few gestures that occasionally interrupted an otherwise thoroughly materialistic life. Until the Depression, department store magnate Marshall Field had his window displays covered on

Sundays. His colleague John Wanamaker embraced Charles Wagner's ethic of simplicity, spending a good share of his fortune on churches and charity. Wanamaker even built a simple bungalow next to his palatial country home. Asa Candler of Coca-Cola led a similar life in Atlanta. All three men combined personal religion with a goal of unrestrained moneymaking — and never saw any contradiction. Historian William Leach attributes Wanamaker's skill in reconciling opposites to the "personal" character of his religious faith and his "non-judgmental" ethic. His piety was the source of his "simplicity" while his toleration was a rationale for boundless consumption. Various early twentieth-century philosophies and religions, including "mind cure," celebrated positive attitudes and self-fulfillment. They paved the way for a purely secular, feel-good impulse that refused to evaluate desire, materialist or otherwise.[52]

Ironically, the ideal of simplicity and cultivation contributed in many ways to the practice and vocabulary of consumerism. The Arts and Crafts movement of the 1890s, with its glorification of unadorned furnishings and functional interior decoration, became a fashion statement of the rich, at least in their summer "cottages." If "character" and "friendliness" were supposed to be virtues for their own sake, they could be also useful business tools. From the 1910s, the self-help literature of Dale Carnegie and others showed how a pleasing and trustworthy personality could lead to material success. By the 1920s, even Charles Eliot's great books were sold for their practical value in improving the image of the businessman. The cultivated person had became a commodity.[53]

The very foundations of high culture crumbled in the flood of consumerism. The cultural expert funneled academic and high culture to the middle class until the 1960s. Much earlier, however, middlebrow magazines had introduced an opposing idea — faith in the "ready-made capacity for independent judgment" of ordinary middle-class people. The view that a specific body of knowledge was necessary for the superior person gave way to the idea that practical competence in business should be the true mark of accomplishment. Culture, in turn, became a matter of personal choice, not a bulwark against the rush of commercialization but rather a lifestyle unimpeded by the "elitism" of imposed standards. Self-cultivation through the arts and moral constraint was gradually replaced by the notion of personal growth and a fullness of experience that was entirely consistent with "trying on" various consumer fashions and packaged pleasures. By the late 1920s, intellectuals themselves had undermined the genteel code. Character and control were superseded by the values of vitality, spontaneity, and self-realization. This new openness to change was the very lifeblood of a consumer society. Cultural and moral self-improvement succumbed, as historian Joan Rubin put it, to the "endless search for items that would, above all, supply personal gratification and influence over others." Middlebrow culture was a transition into consumer culture.[54]

Attempts to organize consumers into an active political force also largely failed. Despite serious and repeated efforts through the 1930s, no effective consumer rights group emerged to challenge the lobbying of producers. Theoretically, in an age when most goods were purchased on the market and when identity was shaped so much by them, consumer issues should have dominated. But consumers were also producers. They had to have jobs and good wages to be serious spenders. While they bought many and diverse things, they usually produced only one thing. Thus they had a stronger, more focused interest in defending their producer status than their many consumer roles. New Deal officials found it easy to argue that policies encouraging industries to fix prices ultimately benefited the consumer, who in the first instance earned a profit or wage. Very few consumers organized as shoppers. In the 1930s, popular books attacking deceptive marketing and dangerous or worthless products put advertisers and some producers on the defensive. Nevertheless, it was quite easy for business to bounce back.[55]

Advertisers assumed the language of high politics when they claimed to "serve" consumer citizens who, as shoppers, voted with their purchases. In the 1930s, ad people insisted that they were the guardians of the choice that all too often was threatened by government. They redefined freedom to mean not civil liberty or the right to work, but the ability to find identity in the choice of goods to buy. As we have seen, such messages were especially directed to women. Ads defined household goods as liberators from drudgery and as expressions of personal choice.[56] By the mid-1930s, the advertising industry had wrapped itself in the flag of promised prosperity and accused critics of strangling the economy with regulation. Major corporations joined in the fray. GM's "The American Way" ad campaign celebrated American commitment to material progress and promoted corporate freedom to develop new and exciting products. Adman Roy Durstine insisted that his trade introduced innovation and lowered prices by stimulating mass demand. If ads were sometimes irritating, they had to be to "break through our indifference" and teach us to take out insurance or brush our teeth. In Durstine's mind, those who demanded regulation believed "that the United States is finished." Rather than calling for the redistribution of income or work, Durstine demanded that Americans trust innovators at progressive corporations like his client, GE: "In thousands of industrial laboratories American business is preparing the surprises of tomorrow."[57]

In 1939, the Advertising Federation of America went even further, organizing an assault on critics by identifying advertising as "the mouthpiece of free enterprise" and declaring any opponent of their trade as "those who prefer collectivism and regimentation by political force." That same year, the House Committee on Un-American Activities conducted hearings on communist infiltration of the consumer rights movement. This attack was made far easier by the fact that Consumers' Research had been decimated by internal strife, including a strike by staff members in 1936. The conflict led CR founder Schlink to create a rival, the Consumer Union, and denounce his erstwhile colleagues as Marxists. Though the consumer rights movement experienced a temporary resurgence during World War II, not until the 1960s would it regain its influence. What survived were largely product testing services (such as offered by *Consumer Reports*). This narrowing of the scope of consumer rights to the privilege of being informed about the pricing and attributes of goods has tended to reinforce both the individualism and the materialism of American consumption.[58]

After 1945, consumers did not become a political force capable of defending their rational and utilitarian needs against the power of corporations and advertising. Instead, they were assigned a role that was more expedient to business: the job of spending in order that others might work. Consumers were delegated the right and duty to spend without inclusion in the wider realm of economic decision making.

This linkage between spending and full employment became a truism after World War II, but it was still a radically new way of understanding economic growth during the interwar years. As early as the 1920s, some American business leaders recognized their factories produced more than people wanted. They complained about "buyers' strikes" and the apparent diminishing desire for goods. Still, most economists rejected this thinking, insisting on the old orthodox theory that consumption would always absorb production. One innovative solution to the apparent problem of "overproduction" was to reduce work time. This approach would have meant more employment through job sharing and, as important, increased leisure and reduced emphasis upon consumer goods. However, such an approach was far too sharp a break with the past. In fact, it gained only brief support from the labor movement and a few politicians and intellectuals in the early 1930s when the idea of a national thirty-hour work week was unsuccessfully floated.[59]

The more acceptable, although still radical, answer was to find ways of increasing consumer spending. Already in the 1920s, William T. Foster and Waddill Catchings argued that insufficient purchasing power of the masses slowed the flow of money between production and consumption. This guaranteed gluts when consumers lacked the funds to buy what they produced as workers. While economic theory held that this was impossible, Foster and Catchings insisted that the growing concentration of wealth meant that the rich saved too much and consumed too little. High wages and perhaps countercyclic government spending would put money back in the hands of people who would buy and thus prevent underconsumption.[60]

This idea of the right and duty to spend got a big boost in the 1930s with the New Deal. Public works administrators Harold Ickes and Harry Hopkins stressed labor-intensive projects to increase the dollars in the hands of people likely to spend and thus stimulate the economy. According to Hopkins, business declined because "consumer incomes did not increase fast enough to take goods off the market." Moreover, from August 1935, Marriner S. Eccles of the Federal Reserve Board promoted "easy money." His objective was to reemploy the jobless in order to stimulate spending. This was a clear alternative to reducing the standard work week, which in his view "may mean sharing poverty rather than sharing wealth." Eccles agreed with those who argued that taxes on the poor (consumption taxes) should be lowered while income, corporate, and estate taxes on the rich should be raised to redistribute income from wealthy oversavers to those who would spend.[61]

This approach challenged orthodox laissez-faire doctrine — that low wages and prices would create jobs and markets. But it also insisted that spending, rather than reduced work time and increased leisure, was the solution. Maurice Leven and a team from the Brookings Institution insisted in 1934 that "there is not the slightest doubt that, did incomes permit, the demands of the American people for consumptive goods and services would be quickly and vastly increased" and thus "we cannot materially shorten the working day and still produce the quantity of goods and services which the American people aspire to consume." The alternative to a reduction of work and a society less committed to consumerism was an increase in spending. Following the economic slump of 1937, advisers like Hopkins and Beardsely Ruml won FDR over to the principle of government deficit spending to create mass purchasing power. At the very time when the consumer rights movement was being marginalized, the link between full employment and the "duty to spend" was being forged. With the latter came the doctrine that work for its own sake and spending of any kind were of unquestioned value.[62]

By the end of the 1930s, most serious political players had accepted the centrality of the "duty to spend." Still, they had significant differences about how to get increased spending and who was to do it. Leven and company wanted only lower consumer prices. Business and advertising interests proposed more effective commercial propaganda and product innovations. This would presumably get more affluent shoppers to spend rather than to save. More egalitarian political solutions included public works and full employment guarantees or even a far steeper progressive income tax. The latter was proposed by the old advocate of consumer rights, Stuart Chase, in his *Idle Money Idle Men*: "If the government wants to 'soak the rich' to the full extent of their unproductive savings, nothing but good can come of it, provided the taxes so collected are transformed into active purchasing power." In fact, income tax rates rose significantly in the 1930s. They increased from 0.4 percent to 4.4 percent for households earning $10,000 to $15,000 and from 14.5 percent to 71 percent for incomes over $1 million. Far more dramatic were the tax boosts during World War II (rising to an 18.6 percent rate for the $10 – $15,000 income range and to 85 percent for income over million). The rationale for the progressive income tax was shifted from "fairness" to the more ideologically neutral idea of a "tool of economic growth."[63]

While government encouraged consumption, the labor movement treated it as a right. The nineteenth-century idea that working for another person was wage slavery was transformed in the twentieth century to the notion that laborers had the right to a "living wage." In 1898, Samuel Gompers of the American Federation of Labor demanded income "sufficient to maintain an average-sized family in a manner consistent with whatever the contemporary local civilization recognizes as indispensable to physical and mental health, or as required by the rational self-respect of human beings." The claim that working people deserved access to a fair share of the nation's productivity was essentially an egalitarian idea, for wage earners' dignity came from participating in a consumer society. A living wage did not mean joining a status-seeking society or the bourgeoisie. Still, as union official John Mitchell insisted, "no limit should be set to the aspirations of the workingmen, nor to the demands for higher wages." Trade union leaders even justified their call for a shorter work day with claims that more leisure would stimulate spending and thus economic growth.[64]

This idea had long roots. In his *Wealth and Progress* (1887), labor writer George Gunton argued that the increased wants of the highest-paid workers led to better wages for all and mass markets for business. Expanding desire alone made humans "superior to the animals" and allowed them to "rise in the scale of intellectual and moral development." The reduction of work time (to eight hours a day) would stimulate those desires. It would increase workers' "social opportunity" to observe the material culture of the rich and thus to accept a regime of hard and disciplined labor in order to pay for their rising material expectations. His argument provided a rationale for a consumer society that rejected the tradition of workers' virtue in simplicity and skilled labor.[65]

By the end of the 1930s, Gunton's argument linking consumption and work had become orthodox. Spending became a duty, required to make hard workers and ensure national economic growth. As a result, the social order no longer required a corps of cultural improvers. Rather, individuals, wandering through an expanding maze of needs, became "naturally" and without visible coercion willing to accept the discipline of steady labor.[66] During the Depression, Sidney Hillman of the clothing workers' union insisted that high wages meant not only social fairness but a smooth-working consumer economy. As we have seen, even Walter Reuther, the left-wing leader of the United Auto Workers, abandoned his union's commitment to the thirty-hour week in 1945, arguing instead for a "balanced economy of full employment — full production — full consumption."[67]

Government spending and labor union pressure for higher wages remained controversial. Still, after World War II, personal spending became a patriotic duty and private consumption became the bedrock of American democracy. In the words of economist George Katona, American consumer society fulfilled the "dream of unlimited economic opportunities in a classless society." Only the private sector could create the wealth to build more schools and parks. Any systematic transfer of resources to "public goods," as advocated by old-fashioned liberals like John K. Galbraith, only meant stagnation.[68] The OPA and its vision of the "citizen consumer" ended when this agency gave way to uncontrolled retail prices in 1946. As historian Lizabeth Cohen shows, a consensus between government, labor, and business quickly emerged after the war. All factions agreed that a shift from a military to a peace economy required mass consumption. This was more than a matter of avoiding a return to the Depression. It was a policy of using purchasing power for the masses as a tool in the war of ideas against communism. It was also an alternative to deliberate income redistribution (and with it class conflict and government bureaucracy). Consumer sovereignty in the marketplace had replaced consumer rights in political life.[69]

Finally, the restraints on consumer culture were eroded by the inability of Americans to preserve the sanctuaries of childhood and home. This was in large part due to the fact that the home itself had become a nest of consumer goods and that children were excellent consumers. Domesticity was not really a refuge from mass society after all. Simplicity may have been a check on the showy and ephemeral, but the home created its own consumer culture. It became the site for highly commercialized holiday celebrations, for example. A "gospel of contentment" that sacralized home and family also stimulated the sentimental greeting card and knick-knack industry. Early twentieth-century tastemakers like Martha Bruere (1871–1953) have been followed by Martha Stewart in the 1990s in promoting ideals of domestic refinement.[70] The distinction between the fashion plate and the prudent homemaker was cultural and aesthetic, but both were equally consumerist. Edward Bok's moralizing *Ladies' Home Journal* from the 1900s evolved by the 1920s into an advertising vehicle that promoted domestic appliances and "new and improved" soaps, foods, and cosmetics.[71] Few noticed the change or complained that the sanctuary of the home was being threatened by commercial appeals in magazines and catalogs. Comfortable Americans attacked "street" spending while advocating domestic comforts and leisure as expressions of family togetherness and values. Domesticity proved to be no refuge from commercial life, only an escape from a consumer culture of the crowd.

The scruples against "invading" the home with advertising chatter largely disappeared in the 1930s. Radio had proven that people would accept advertising in the home if they liked the program and, as we have seen, during the Depression local stations willingly accepted hard-sell ads to remain profitable. Even though only 31 percent of CBS programs in 1934 were sponsored, those programs "sustained" by the networks were increasingly relegated to Sundays or morning hours when few were listening. This was the fate of many of the music appreciation, home economics, and farm programs. College education stations complained of being relegated to poor, noisy frequencies, and, due to decreased public funding, their numbers declined from 121 in 1925 to only 53 in 1931. The Communications Act of 1934 failed to regulate ads, and the voluntary nature of controls over the number and kind of commercials carried over into the TV age. There was no revolution that overturned the old ethic of the domestic sanctuary. It simply faded into a small shrill voice by the end of the 1950s under the unrelenting pressure of admen, their clients and broadcasters, and a public progressively accustomed to the constant din of the commercial.[72]

Childhood was also a poor bastion against the consumer culture. Parents expressed their love with gifts of toys and amusement that encouraged the child to enjoy that brief period of freedom from the world of work and self-denial. While parents withdrew children from the job market, they introduced them to the consumer market. Children represented change and the future — and thus adults gave them up-to-date and innovative toys and other products. The teddy bear craze of 1906 was perhaps the best early example of a pattern that would be repeated over and over again in the twentieth century — the celebration of the new through the collective fantasy of the commercial fad. By 1900, Christmas had become the child's holiday. It celebrated not only the innocence of children but also their indulgence through Santa, who put consumer novelties under the tree.[73]

The Rousseauian dream of a "natural child," carefully protected from the allures of adult society, was gradually transformed into the uninhibited child for whom the consumer culture was a reprieve from future responsibility and adult impositions. As we have seen, the twentieth-century youth became a major target of manufacturers of novelty, fantasy, and fun. Parents complained, fought back occasionally, and attempted to confine and shape their children's experience with the consuming crowd. Nevertheless, adults also introduced their offspring to that crowd on the boardwalk where they bought Kewpie dolls. New needs eroded barriers. As historian Peter Stearns notes, middle-class parents learned through doll ads and child-rearing manuals that children could more effectively cope with emotions through toys than with real people. Moreover, consumer goods often compensated for limited spontaneity in an orderly home.[74] In subtle ways, the home as refuge gradually became the home as a nest of gadgets. Childhood as a moratorium from the market became a target of the impresarios of fun and fads.

All this is a sad story. The culture of constraint failed to defend itself from the power and appeal of an ever-advancing consumerism. Efforts to monitor and provide consumers with guidance against obsessive desire were fatally confined to the criminalization of "hard drugs" and self-help groups.

Promoters of self-cultivation failed to find moral equivalents to consumerism. The consumer rights movement was reduced to savvy shopping and the duty to spend. The sacred realms of home and childhood became sites of extravagant spending. Advocates for limiting consumerism have almost always been on the margins, listened to more than followed. Some people might chalk this up to "human nature." Others might argue that America has always been more of a market than a community. America's mobility and relatively easy affluence meant that its people almost inevitably defined themselves by and related to others through their things. There is doubtless much truth to both claims.

However, we should not forget that appeals to constraint coexisted with calls for consumption. American "Puritanism" may be so strong precisely because American indulgence continually revives it. Ironically, Puritanical Americans have also reinforced materialism. When defining boundaries and taboos in consumption, they have justified indulgence elsewhere. Prohibition of "hard drugs" meant toleration of "soft drugs." The original Puritans' constraint provided the discipline that made them and their descendants rich. Moreover, the quest for spiritual depth often drifted imperceptibly into the longing for material fulfillment. When reformers attacked ostentatious wealth, they inadvertently embraced a democracy of greed. The consumer rights movement easily slid into the obligation to consume. Sanctifying the family quietly shifted into spending to please individual family members.

Counteracting the excesses of the consumer culture became all the more difficult because of the very diversity of American cultural traditions. The lack of an established religion or national educational system prevented the kind of consensus over the meaning of national civilization that made the BBC work in Britain. The United States had no national high culture, nor, given the diversity of immigration and the impact of slavery, a cohesive national folk tradition. Any effort to establish a high culture appeared foreign or theocratic, as indeed it often was. More important, as we have seen, there was a real alternative in the cross-class, cross-ethnic blending of high and low, private and public, improving and anarchic in a dynamic consumer culture. There was little intellectual and moral space for self-fulfillment or community outside this extraordinary blend of consumer choice and consuming crowds.

This did not mean that those intellectual and moral appeals were unimportant. In the course of the twentieth century, boundaries to consumerism broke down only gradually and only after much resistance. The critique of consumerism was often hypocritical and just as often played into merely new forms of consumption. Nevertheless, we should not forget that this lament served also as the guilty conscience of a consuming society. In the 1950s, it often appeared in the very places where unabashed spending was being promoted. Ads that idealized materialism and status seeking appeared in the same magazines where intellectuals defended the simple life and lashed out at conformity in the tasteless and trackless suburbs. Some articles in *Time* praised the push-button ease of modern appliances and others condemned such conveniences for making Americans soft and mindless. A famous satire on the postwar housing industry, "Mr. Blandings Builds His Castle," first appeared the April 1946 issue of *Fortune*, practically the official organ of capitalism in the United States. William Whyte, also a writer for *Fortune*, could still lament the relative decline of liberal-arts education in the 1950s. And in recognition of this "problem," Bell Telephone dispatched some "promising middle-management men to the University of Pennsylvania for a year of special study in the humanities." As late as 1958, liberal critic John K. Galbraith could claim that businesspeople who read *Business Week* were "lost to fame." For real prestige, they must read Proust.[75]

The critical tradition was more than the rantings of disaffected intellectuals or cultural reactionaries unwilling to embrace the full measure of a democratic age. The essential idea of constraint was at the heart of the early consumer culture. The works of Veblen and his successors like Robert Lynd were influential well beyond the ivory tower or Greenwich Village. Aldous Huxley's satire in *Brave New World* of an Americanized world where consumers purchased doses of "feelies" was popular when it was written in 1928. It became a standard in English and humanities courses in American universities into the 1960s. The culture of constraint affected entrepreneurs whose philanthropy countered their pecuniary obsessions. It may not have produced any successful alternative models to consumerism, but it surely shaped the spending and lifestyle choices of many and created pockets of life relatively free of the market. Commodities provided ways to express individuality, but they still often worked within the language and meanings of family, home, and community. Goods remained vehicles for sharing meaning and life, not merely expressions of individualistic desire and isolation. Finally, a wider culture limited and enveloped commodities. Through the 1970s, important regions of personal and social life remained off-limits to the market.

The unqualified victory of consumerism was not a preordained conclusion. Indeed, in the 1960s and 1970s, some elements of a culture of constraint were revived and even sent in new directions. Defenders of a more simple, less driven culture received another hearing. The rights of consumers against the growing power of advertising were resurrected. Further, the environmental movement put a new face on anticonsumerism. Yet the burdens and failures of the culture of constraint ultimately were not transcended. Americans could not avoid the logic of consumerism — and individualism was progressively reduced to a fashion statement and society to a market.

CHAPTER 5

A New Consumerism, 1960–1980

T he 1960s and 1970s were decades of upheaval, challenging the apparent consensus of the 1950s on many fronts. In particular, Americans questioned the costs of unrestrained consumption: deceptive advertising and merchandising as well as growing pollution and waste. Some raised doubts about the contained and seemingly conformist model of consumption that prevailed in the postwar generation. Critics mocked the superficiality of the "populuxe" culture of the suburbs and its intolerance of individual freedom. Today conservatives like to think that these views were held by a small minority of pampered baby boomer youths and marginal intellectuals, but they were rooted in a far broader anxiety about the costs of consumerism. Without denying notable accomplishments of the consumer rights and environmental movements, it is difficult today to understand the thunder of those decades given the relatively meager results of these challenges to consumerism. The materialism of the 1950s was by no means turned back; rather, consumption became even more ubiquitous. By 1980 there were far more cars, ads, and credit cards and many more ways of expressing oneself through goods than there had been in 1960. Indeed, it would be fair to say that consumerism had become even more individualistic and socially fragmenting than it had been in the 1950s. While liberals often hold Ronald Reagan's presidency responsible for these disturbing trends, the roots of this extreme spending culture lay also in the 1960s critique of consumerism itself. Yet so overwhelming has been the defeat of this critique that it is hard not to see it as the last gasp of an elitist culture embodied briefly in the youthful excess of a pampered generation. But that would do injustice both to the seriousness of the critique and to the profound meaning of the victory of a new consumerism.

Consensus and Critiques of Consumerism at Mid-Century

By the early 1960s, a consensus had emerged around managed growth. Presidential economic advisers James Tobin and Walter Heller openly embraced the Keynesian doctrine that government was obliged to maintain high wages and rising consumer demand. This policy, they believed, should be acceptable even to conservatives because it neither required a redistribution of wealth nor threatened private property.[1] High wages meant high profits when everyone assumed the duty to spend. Classes converged and ideology disappeared, noted sociologist Harold Wilensky, thanks to the mass production/mass consumption machine. Mainstream sociologist Seymour Martin Lipset's declaration sums up this optimistic view: "the fundamental problems of the industrial revolution have been solved." Daniel Bell saw an "end of ideology" where questions of adjustments rather than principles would absorb future policy makers. Even business leaders embraced President Johnson's Great Society social programs as the price for affluence. Government spending oiled a well-constructed economic machine — making it work better by adjusting consumer demand when needed and by bringing the poor into the system through education and a helping hand.[2]

In sharp contrast to the old ideal of a republic of thrift, the continuous expansion of personal desire was the foundation of an apparently frictionless economic democracy. Economist George Katona declared, "It is precisely the wanting and striving for improvements in private living standards that forms the solid basis of American prosperity. Only if the so-called private opulence increases still further can we hope to overcome public poverty."[3] The key was aspiration, not the mere meeting of needs. The driving force was not in leveling but in stimulating wants.[4]

Where there was aspiration, there was advertising. Marketing professor Steuart Britt offered a conventional defense of advertising in 1960. Of course, ads sold stuff Americans did not need. All people really require is a cave and a fire, but advertising informed them of the new and improved. Without it, Americans would still be content with the old and inferior. Britt admitted that consumer choice led to waste and trivia, "but the alternative of government regulation is far worse." In any case, the consumer is "sovereign." More and more goods chased the discretionary dollars of spenders, requiring aggressive advertising to get an audience. And consumers were demanding and fickle. Britt reminded readers that 80 – 90 percent of new product ideas never got to market and that scarcely 4 percent of these survived more than two years. Ads were necessary in a system of self-service shopping and were far cheaper than the old system of pushy sales staff.[5]

These ideas were the stock in trade of advertising and marketing courses in American business schools. Nevertheless, they began to be challenged by the late 1950s. Senator Estes Kefauver proposed a Department of the Consumer in the cabinet, convinced that the market alone could not protect consumers' interests. Politicians saw a better educated and more affluent public demanding safer and higher quality products. They noted also that consumers were frustrated by their difficulty in determining true credit costs or making knowledgeable comparisons between similar products.[6] As Senator Warren Magnuson put it, the self-regulation of business had become inadequate due to the "recent explosion in consumer buying and credit and the changing conditions in technology and marketing." Consumer exploitation had replaced labor exploitation as the central problem of modern society, and consumers needed friends in government.[7]

At the core of this critique was an attack on advertising. Vance Packard's *Hidden Persuaders* revived the idea popularized by F. J. Schlink and Stuart Chase in the 1920s that business manipulated consumers into buying goods they really did not need. Packard exposed a new trend in advertising called motivational research, which used depth psychology to sell goods by appealing to the desire for status and self-indulgence and by preying on feelings of personal inadequacy. Packard's critique was no lament by a marginal intellectual. His book became a major best-seller. Even advertisers were worried about their public image,[8] and with good reason. In 1958, TV quiz-show scandals involving sponsors who fed answers to popular contestants to raise ratings added to a growing discontent with hard-sell TV ads and commercial manipulation.[9]

Reporting on fraud against consumers became a minor industry in the 1960s. For example, Sidney Margolius warned Americans about loan sharks, unnecessary car repairs, home improvement scams, and overpriced insurance. He attacked the food industry for converting "inexpensive ingredients into costly processed foods." Prices for heavily advertised breakfast cereals rose twice as fast as those of other foods, even though they were often of little nutritional value. Ads and labeling were often deceptive.

Honey Comb cereal, for example, had more salt than honey on it. Lack of standards in packaging made comparisons of volume and prices impossible, Margolius complained. Advertising efforts to make meaningless distinctions between different brands of detergents and toothpaste only drove up prices.[10] Even the sacred cow of 1950s consumerism, the car, was under attack. From 1957, declining sales told auto makers that the planned obsolescence of the annual model change and the resulting excesses of fins and chrome were no longer working. The car industry had obviously favored fashion over utilitarian improvements. That certainly was Ralph Nader's point in *Unsafe at Any Speed: The Designed-in Dangers in the American Automobile* (1965). The young consumer advocate argued that rising numbers of car injuries resulted not from more collisions per se but from lack of seat belts, cushioning, and other safety devices in American cars.[11]

Many consumer advocates like Margolius took a distinctly patronizing tone when they warned that the poor were wasting their welfare payments on overpriced food and clothing. At the same time, the middle class kept up an artificial standard of living only with "moonlighting husbands, working wives and some remarkable and often lifelong juggling of debts." The consumer, hoodwinked by clever cheats and too vain and insecure to stand up to the flimflam, needed the advice of experts and the protection of government.[12]

Other critics went beyond this notion of the "benighted consumer." Ralph Nader argued that corporate influence over regulatory agencies and monopolistic pricing were as important as deceptive merchandising. Only in a freely competitive economy would producers be forced to respond to consumers. At the same time, Nader favored public-supported legal assistance to the poor so that they could defend their interests against finance companies, landlords, and car dealers. Consumers needed protection from the industry that had not yet been "toilet trained" and continued to dump dangerous chemicals into the water supply and the air.[13]

Nader's advocacy of consumer rights dovetailed with a wide-ranging critique of unrestrained growth and its impact on the environment. Awareness of the problem had been growing for years. As early as 1943, the boom town of Los Angeles experienced its first bout with "smog," dust mixed with industrial and automobile emissions. Other new byproducts of postwar consumption included pollution from DDT (used first as a pesticide in 1939), detergents (which began replacing soap in 1946), and plastics. In 1965, power outages in New York brought home how dependent Americans

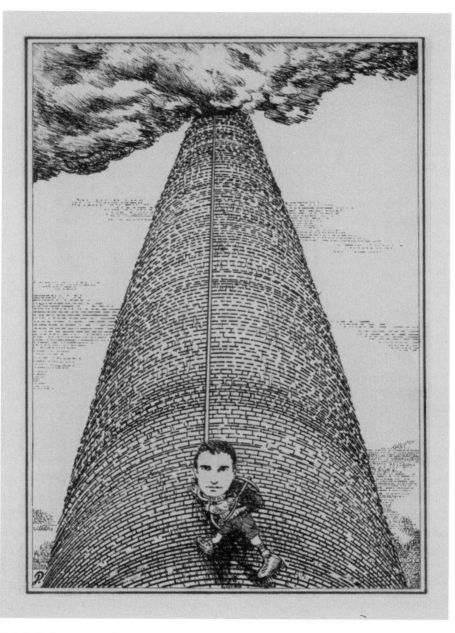

Ralph Nader as crusader against industrial pollution.

(1972 drawing by Dennis Hermanson, Library of Congress)

had become on a complex and imperfect energy/power system. Ground-water contamination from storage tanks, hazardous waste sites, and land-fills was becoming a major problem by the 1960s.[14]

In response, a new kind of environmentalism emerged that went beyond advocating resource and wilderness management — thinking that had dominated the conservationism of the Progressive era. The new environmentalists proposed a systematic critique of economic growth. Setting the tone of this analysis were Fairfield Osborn's *Our Plundered Planet* (1948) and *The Limits of the Earth* (1953). In these books, Osborn attacked the common view that modern technology had eliminated the need to preserve resources and nature's equilibrium. He insisted that Americans had to abandon the comforting faith that growth could overcome all human problems: "the goal of humanitarianism is not the quantity but the quality of living. If we evade the choice, the inevitable looms ahead of us — even sterner forces will make the decision for us. We cannot delay or evade. For now, as we look, we can see the limits of the earth."[15]

Rachel Carson's *Silent Spring* (1962) shared this urgency in its indictment of the indiscriminate use of pesticides: "Future historians may well be amazed by our distorted sense of proportion. How could intelligent beings seek to control a few unwanted species by a method that contaminated the entire environment and brought the threat of disease and death even to their own kind?" Chemicals that polluted air and water supplies affected the entire food chain — and all for the sake of "perfect" vegetables and the suburban demand "that crabgrass must go at whatever cost."[16] Carson's program was modest (she advocated using natural pests rather than chemicals), but she also raised questions about the ecological costs of the consumer culture.

Others went much further. Paul Ehrlich's *The Population Bomb* (1968) was a hard-hitting attack on population growth, another critical component of prosperity. The "economics of the 1960s are dead," he insisted. Affluence was a party that has come to an end. "In the 1970s the world will undergo famines," and the United States, the greatest consumer, could not stand in isolation. In an apocalyptic tone common for the era, Ehrlich insisted that Americans must reduce family size immediately. The central problem was easy to see: "too many cars, too many factories, too much detergent . . . all can be traced easily to *too many people*." While some environmentalists questioned his emphasis on population (over pollution) controls, Ehrlich's prescription surely was a frontal attack on the growth ethic. He wanted a tax policy to discourage large families (even proposing a tax on diaper services) and he suggested that enlightened people mock and openly condemn couples with three or more children as foolish and selfish.[17]

Still more germane to this growing concern about the effect of growth was the attack on excessive use of scarce resources. Vance Packard's *The Waste Makers* (1960) complained that American's economic miracle in the 1950s was based on the "throwaway spirit" and planned obsolescence. He argued that manufacturers designed cars and appliances to have ever shorter life expectancies and to become undesirable long before they were worn out. By 1956, cars were scrapped three years earlier than they were in the late 1940s. Moreover, the car and furniture industries copied that old trick of the women's fashion business by using changes in color, style, and material to make products indispensable one season and anathema the next. According to Packard, manufacturers facing stagnant markets used these tactics to create an "artificial demand." The long-term cost was the exhaustion of scarce resources.[18]

An even more powerful warning of resource shortages was the Club of Rome's *The Limits to Growth* (1972). This manifesto boldly claimed that "The basic behavior mode of the world system is exponential growth of population and capital, followed by collapse." Using mathematical calculations to predict population change and resource use, this book anticipated global shortages in essential raw materials, pollution, and starvation by 2100 unless zero population and limited growth were achieved.[19] E. F. Schumacher's *Small Is Beautiful* (1973) did not engage in such dire predictions, but flatly rejected the social costs of growth: "The cultivation and expansion of needs is the antithesis of wisdom. It is also the antithesis of freedom and peace." Unlimited development of consumer markets not only destroyed "non-renewable goods" but also devastated communities and meaningful work by encouraging centralized production over local crafts. People must take precedence over goods, insisted Schumacher, even cheap and plentiful goods.[20]

The consumer rights and environmental movements had a similar response to the consumerism of the 1950s, an appeal to fairness and prudence. With important exceptions, their solutions tended to be pragmatic, requiring legislative reform or specific, if voluntary, behavioral changes. A different kind of critique came from a disenchantment with the culture of the 1950s and its containment of individual expression.

This revolt against the conformity and "materialism" of the suburban populuxe was associated with the Bohemian or beatnik, but it was hardly invented by these social outcasts. In the late 1950s, the threat of mass consumer society to individual creativity was an oft-repeated refrain in the pages of *Life*, *Time*, and even *Readers' Digest*. Affluence had produced feelings of guilt. Americans brought up in the Depression were disquieted by signs that creature comforts had made the young soft (and they did not refrain from lecturing their offspring on this theme). The push-button age had made children lazy and flabby, perhaps too decadent to prevail against the Red Hordes. And the success of the Russian Sputnik over the American space program in 1957 seemed to prove the point. Americans brought up on the virtues of thrift and making do resisted the blandishments of hucksters and motivational research's pleas to spend freely. Many also began to question the price of the populuxe — jobs that male providers often secretly hated and expectations that female homemakers find fulfillment in shiny kitchen floors and well-equipped children.[21]

Especially troubling was how merchandisers seemed to threaten vaunted values of individual sufficiency. Again Packard's best-selling books struck a nerve. In *Status Seekers* and *Hidden Persuaders*, he lamented how Americans were taking their clues from the advertising and entertainment media rather than from themselves. The new affluence did not create a classless society. Instead, it produced a mass of insecure individuals each trying to define and display themselves through their goods. Packard despaired at how the modern home with its pseudocolonial decor appealed to status rather than practicality or the "real" lives of its owners. His solutions were ascetic, prudent, and most of all individualistic. Abandoning the status game and being true to oneself alone would bring "self-respect, serenity, and individual fulfillment."[22] In many ways, Packard was only updating the turn-of-the-century ideas of Thorstein Veblen, but with a twist: he attacked not the filthy rich "leisure class" but the aspiring working and lower middle classes. His views echoed the popular song "Little Boxes," which mocked the tract houses of postwar wage earners that were constructed of "ticky tacky" and made their inhabitants "all come out the same." This was as much a put-down of the populuxe culture of the wage earner as an attack upon consumer conformity.

A common assumption in this critique of consumerism was that wage earners were no longer exploited by their employers and economic inequality. Rather, in the words of the influential German emigré, Herbert Marcuse, many workers had become "happy slaves" duped by the belief "that the system delivers the goods." The true exploitation for Marcuse was in confining gratifications to the consumer culture, "which, in satisfy ing [the consumer's] needs, perpetuates his servitude." Workers' longing for speed boats and flashy cars enslaved them to meaningless jobs. By the late 1960s, Marcuse found hope for liberation only among the "young middle-class intelligentsia, and among the ghetto black populations," who either had discovered the emptiness of affluence or were excluded from, and thus not duped by, the commodity system.[23]

Few Americans had read or understood this German philosopher. Still, he gave abstract expression to ideas that gained wide currency. As early as 1957, Norman Mailer argued for resistance to "slow death by conformity." In a classic "Beat" manifesto, Mailer put the issue simply, "one is Hip or one is Square." And to be the "white Negro," apart from the oppressive world of middle-class respectability, was the only way to be free. In his 1961 essay, "The Bomb in the Brooks Brothers Suit," David McReynolds saw an emerging middle-class rebellion against the confining life of the consumer culture. The revolutionaries were no longer from the working class ("Old Sam Gompers' dinner pail is full"). Rather, the modern rebel was the educated, if insecure, white-collar employee who could see from experience the madness of Madison Avenue.[24] This understanding of "revolution" was at the heart of the counterculture when it was adopted by middle-class youths in the 1960s.

It is not entirely fair to interpret the counterculture of the late 1960s and early 1970s as the logical outgrowth of these critiques of consumer culture. Certainly Packard did not see the connection (given his commitment to a self-denying individualism), and even Marcuse was critical of the ease by which notions of personal liberation were "co-opted" by money makers who peddled drug accessories and hard rock music. But that culture of youth did draw upon the critique of conformity and the idealization of the authentic self.

Charles Reich's countercultural manifesto, *The Greening of America*, faithfully reflected that youth movement by indicting the "system" without repeating the older call for simplicity. The socioeconomic order destroyed individuality, not by naked economic or physical oppression but by enslaving wage earners while satisfying their false wants as consumers. Reich's solution was not to resurrect a rugged frontier individualism (as Packard suggested) or to cultivate the arts (as some conservative critics and even Marcuse advised). Rather, his answer came from the contradictions of the consumer culture itself: "In trying to sell more and more commodities by the use of [real] needs, advertising cannot help but raise the intensity of the needs themselves." Ads, for example, appealed to the desire for status and thus made people want dignity. This made revolutionaries out of the "satisfied" middle class (at least the young), whose vision was expanded by the ultimate inability of affluence to deliver on its promises. This required no radical break with a culture of expanding desires. On the contrary, affluence led to "Consciousness III," a new willingness to experience adventure, sex, nature, physical activity, and an inner life that had been contained by the domestic consumerism of the 1950s.[25]

As many have noted, the hippies' free love and drug culture of the mid-1960s was a "democratic" version of the Beats' Bohemian tradition of the late 1950s. Not only had many of the hippies grown up with such classical critiques of middle-class culture as Paul Goodman's *Growing Up Absurd*, J. D. Salinger's *Catcher in the Rye*, and even *Mad Magazine*, but some had even read Beat primers like Jack Kerouac's *On the Road* and Allen Ginsberg's *Howl*.[26] Still, in January 1967, the hippies took a new path when they rejected the Beats' coffeehouse and personal odyssey for the mass "Human Be-In," a free-flowing event in San Francisco involving thousands in rock music, poetry, and theatrical happenings in the open air. As self-appointed countercultural leader Jerry Rubin recalled, "all the tribes [were] getting together doing their own thing." Rubin saw this event as a beginning of a new community, free from the old hierarchies and hypocrisies of the 1950s. The Beats' austere individualism disappeared, but the critique of conformity did not.[27]

The new youth culture repudiated the "happy slave's" trade-off of repressive and meaningless work for the right to join the consumer society. A 1966 *Newsweek* survey of college seniors found only 31 percent were seriously considering careers in business, while 74 percent felt business was a "dog eat dog" world. A *Fortune* study found that money making appealed to few students, and many criticized the conformity and lack of personal fulfillment in business.[28] The basis of this attack on the consumer culture was a quest for self-expression. The "trip," be it with drugs, politics, or whatever, was a personal adventure — a protest against the confinement of affluence. As Reich insisted, a "Consciousness III person will not study law to help society, if law is not what he wants to do with his life." Or as Rubin put it, "Our message: Don't grow up. Growing up means giving up your dreams."[29] All this may have been irresponsible, a denial of duty to family, community, and country, possible only in a rich country where youths could afford to forget that they would soon have obligations. Nevertheless, it was also an extraordinary rejection of a culture that identified "de-

livering the goods" to the masses with freedom. Even more, it was a refusal to confine desire within the circle of work and the home.

Together, the consumer rights, environmental, and countercultural
movements offered a serious critique of the consumerist consensus of
the 1950s. This led to wide-ranging attacks on unrestrained markets, attempts to reduce controls, and even challenges to cultural norms. Yet by
the end of the 1970s, not only were political challenges to the consumer
market largely marginalized, but the cultural attack on consumerism had
proven to be ephemeral and even a boon to a new kind of individualistic
consumerism.

Achievements and Failures

From the vantage of 2000, the achievements of the consumer rights movement in the 1960s and early 1970s are breathtaking. Public concerns about
product safety resulted in the Hazardous Substances Labeling Act of 1960
that required warnings on dangerous household products. The Child Protection Act (1966) banned toys and other articles containing hazardous
substances. The Consumer Product Safety Commission of 1972 provided
for a continuous review of consumer goods for risks. Growing evidence
that tobacco caused cancer led the Federal Trade Commission in 1964 to
require warnings on cigarette packages. TV and radio commercials for tobacco were finally outlawed in 1971. Concerns about the rising mayhem on
the highways led to the Automobile Safety Act (1966) that required seat
belts and other safety measures on new cars. Growing public frustration at
deceptive sales practices contributed to the Truth in Packaging Act (1966),
obliging weight and content information on product labels and thus en-
abling consumers to comparison shop. Finally, the Truth in Lending Act
(1968) demanded that lenders inform debtors of annual interest rates and
limited the practice of garnishing wages.

From one perspective, these laws were necessary to secure the confidence of buyers and borrowers in an ever more complex and impersonal
market. From another standpoint, they expressed the newfound power of
consumer groups. Working with reform-minded members of Congress
and recently energized regulatory agencies, these groups took on some of
the most powerful industries in the country.[30] Only in 1967 had the Consumer Federation combined 147 organizations into an effective lobby. This

and other public interest groups worked closely with prominent liberal senators (especially Abraham Ribicoff, Paul Douglas, Philip Hart, and Warren Magnuson) to defeat business interests. Along a wide front, they manipulated often receptive media and successfully appealed to citizens' growing distrust of big business.[31]

Regulatory agencies, long in slumber, showed renewed life after 1960. Newton Minow, newly appointed chair of the Federal Communications Commission, attacked network television programming as a lost opportunity to uplift American culture and inform the public, and he promised no more automatic renewals of broadcasting licenses. In 1963, he won from Congress a rule requiring new TVs to be equipped with VHF channels, essential for the development of non-network and especially public broadcasting. And in 1967, Congress established the Corporation for Public Broadcasting to provide an alternative to the ad machines of network TV.[32]

The Federal Trade Commission (FTC) greatly stepped up its traditional role in regulating TV advertising, challenging the ad claims of products as common as Wonder bread and Listerine. In 1962, advertisers attempted to preempt regulation by adopting an ethics code that banned false statements, unfair comparisons, and appeals to indecency. Still, the FTC did not let up. Aided by legislation in 1974 that allowed it to issue rules applicable to a whole industry, the agency became even more aggressive.[33]

Given traditional concerns about protecting the "innocence" of the young, lobbyists and the FTC turned their guns on ads pitched to children. By the early 1970s, admen were sending $200 million worth of messages per year to kids, pushing toys, sugared cereals, and candy. In 1968, Peggy Charren and Evelyn Sarson formed Action for Childrens' Television (ACT) to force the networks to offer programming that had a higher purpose than gathering kids around the set to see commercials. In 1971, ACT called for the elimination of kid-oriented ads altogether by claiming that commercials interfered with parental rights to educate their own children. The logic of this demand was that children under 12 were incapable of making consumer choices. The point was the need to protect the innocent, a traditional counter to the advertiser's claim that commercials were sacrosanct forms of free speech. "Would any mother let in a man at the front door who says he wants to show some new toys to her three-year-old?" asked Sarson. In order to avoid government control, the Association of National Advertisers developed voluntary guidelines in 1972 that eliminated ads showing disdain for adults or exploiting children's anxiety about being accepted by peer groups. At the same time, the National Association of Broadcasters recommended that stations reduce advertising from 16 to 12 minutes per hour of children's programming on weekdays and condemned "host" advertising (Captain Kangaroo selling toys on his own program, for example), and "program-length commercials" (shows that featuring toys in the story lines).[34]

The pressure on advertising to children, however, did not let up. Concerns over the propaganda for sugared cereals led to full-scale investigations of the impact of Sugar Pops and other high-cost, low-nutrition foods on children's diets.[35] In 1977, President Carter's appointment to the FTC chair, Michael Pertschuk, decided to focus on ad exploitation of kids. Pertschuk later noted that by attacking commercials directed at children, he had framed "the issue as an inescapable and conservative extension of the common law's historic strictures against the commercial exploitation of minors." Did not parents have rights against commercials that turned their offspring into "programmed pleaders of advertised products"? By their very nature as appeals to the innocent young, these ads could be deemed "unfair" and thus subject to regulation. Pertschuk saw an opportunity to draw a boundary that limited "market speech" at a moment when consumers were concerned about both ads and their impact on children.[36]

In February 1978, the FTC agreed to open an inquiry into prohibiting childrens' TV advertising. Although consumer groups had originally targeted sugared cereal and candy advertisements, the FTC extended the scope of the potential ban to include all advertising to children. In a published report, young staffers at the FTC argued that commercials aimed at kids under 8 years old were inherently deceptive because children did not understand their purpose. The report noted that children saw 20,000 commercials a year and that infants were attracted to the advertisements long before they noticed programming. To ban them was not a violation of First Amendment rights because such commercials fit the legal definition of an "attractive nuisance." In any case, the "state has a legitimate interest in curtailing speech that interferes with the paramount parental interest in the child rearing process."[37] This was an extraordinary attack on a growing belief of American business — that children, like adults, were consumers to be marketed to. It was a defense of parental rights in an arena where those rights were being increasingly ignored.

A related development was the Civil Rights Act of 1964, legislation that guaranteed consumer choice rather than protecting consumers from producers. This law provided for "full and equal enjoyment of the goods, services, facilities, privileges, advantages, and accommodations of any place of public accommodation." Directed toward the desegregation of consumption, it was the culmination of black boycotts against racial discrimination on buses, at lunch counters, and in other retail establishments that had begun in Montgomery, Alabama, in 1955. For those who had been humiliated by segregated facilities and denied access to consumer choice, this act was more important than other consumer rights laws. It began a new phase in American marketing — corporate interest in African American consumers and how to win them.[38]

By the end of the 1970s, however, the brief ascendancy of the consumer rights movement had ended. The eclipse of business interests was very short indeed. By 1976, they had begun to learn how to lobby a more decentralized Congress and to use Public Action Committee funds and grassroots pressure groups to regain dominance. Ironically, the best years of the consumer rights movement may have been under the conservative Nixon rather than the liberal Carter administration. The determining factor was the degree of business influence in Congress, not the party in power in either the executive or the legislative branch.[39]

The advertising industry won a critical point in 1976 when the Supreme Court recognized that ads could be protected speech. A coalition of farm, grocery, and other independent businesses defeated a proposal in 1978 for a federal consumer protection agency. Admakers attacked any interference in the "right" of children to have information about the products they bought and enjoyed.[40] Even *The Washington Post* in 1978 mocked the FTC for its attack on kid ads, accusing the agency of becoming a "National Nanny" by trying "to protect children from the weaknesses of their parents." In effect, this editorial denied to the consumer rights movement its most powerful theme — the defense of the family. Instead, as Pertschuk later complained, it was the FTC "that allegedly threatened to undermine the moral fiber and authority of the family by seeking to substitute government-imposed censorship for parental discipline." The possibility that the cereal, candy, and toy industries' pipeline to American youth would be closed drove these businesses to concerted lobbying in Congress. In the spring of 1980, Congress prohibited the FTC from banning "unfair" ads (rather than openly deceptive ones), in effect derailing the agency's attack on the inherent "unfairness" of ads directed toward children. Admitting defeat, the FTC dropped its initiative, a turning point in the decline of the consumer rights movement.[41]

Why was this movement not more successful? The simple and obvious answer is that business interests regained their influence over the political process. The consumer rights movement had success only when those powerful interests were in abeyance. The ideology of the unfettered market dominated American political discourse for most of its history. Under normal circumstances, consumers had little collective interest in any particular product, while manufacturers had a very strong incentive to organize and lobby to keep their costs down or prices up. Thus consumer activists were easily isolated. Given a narrow range of legal or regulatory options, they were prone to seemingly petty concerns — determining whether, for example, a TV advertiser deceived viewers by using marbles in a soup commercial to make the meat in the bowl rise and look better. By the late 1970s, free enterprisers had no difficulty in portraying regulators as tyrants and hair-splitting legalists who caused inflation. Indeed, "big government" has never recovered from this characterization.

In several ways all this is ironic. Consumer rights advocates were hardly the sworn enemies of the free market. Indeed, most assumed the basic principle of capitalism — the "rational consumer" who tried to maximize personal utility. Regulation was intended to facilitate reasoned choice or to protect the unreasoning young from manipulation. Yet, as we have seen again and again, consumption was often not rational or utilitarian. While Ralph Nader and others adopted a wider vision of consumer rights, many saw no farther than the product ratings in *Consumer Reports*. The opportunity to develop a social view of consumption, help people cope with the psychological needs met by goods, or explore alternatives to the acquisition of things in the market was all too often lost.[42]

The environmental movement saw a similar rise and stall. From 1969 to 1972, pollution was practically a national obsession. When oil spills fouled California beaches in 1967 and 250 million gallons of crude oil polluted the beautiful coastline along the Santa Barbara Channel in 1969, the cry rose against offshore petroleum drilling. In 1969, the Cuyahoga River that flowed through Cleveland burst into flame because of pollution. The first Earth Day on April 22, 1970 drew national media attention to the problem of imprudent consumption. In this context, legislative reform was inevitable. The Water Quality Act (1965) began an extraordinary string of environmental laws. The Air Quality Act (1967) required states to submit plans to Washington to control air pollution. The National Environmental Policy Act (1970) demanded environmental impact studies from federally funded projects. Soon, the President established the Environmental

Protection Agency (EPA). Most important, the revised and toughened Clean Air Act (1970) authorized the EPA to establish national air-quality standards. It even required states to make plans for reducing pollution emissions by 90 percent in five years, even though science at that time did not have the means to make this possible. The law was supposed to force the development of new technology. In 1972, the pesticide DDT was finally banned. The Water Pollution Control Act (1972) promised to make major waterways fishable and swimmable by 1983. Local authorities took up the call for recycling paper and glass and, by requiring consumers to sort their trash, returned in small ways to an older tradition of salvaging waste. These laws were wide ranging but broadly successful.[43]

It would not last. The boycott of the Organization of Petroleum Exporting Countries (OPEC) during the winter of 1973–74 rocked a nation long used to limitless and cheap supplies of oil and tested the country's commitment to constraint. By 1969, oil already contributed 43 percent of U.S. energy consumption. Meanwhile, America's need for foreign oil rose from 8 percent of total national demand in 1950 to 40 percent by 1974. De-

Los Angeles skyline in 1954. Already smog covered the freeways.

(Library of Congress)

spite this growing dependency, the real price of fossil fuels on the eve of the crisis was 21 percent lower than in 1953. Clearly, Americans had been sheltered from the real costs of big cars, overheated houses, and energy-wasting appliances for decades.[44] During that notable winter of 1973–74, when oil and gas prices skyrocketed and many waited in long lines for gasoline, Americans were hardly prepared. Daylight Savings Time was introduced, to the chagrin of early risers on dark winter mornings. Government agencies recommended a series of practical, if irksome, household energy conservation measures: adding insulation, washing clothes in warm or cold water; keeping dryers in heated parts of houses, not using outdoor decorative lighting at Christmas, and setting thermostats at 68 degrees in winter. While government felt that these recommendations required no serious change in lifestyle, many Americans wondered, especially when individual savings were relatively slight given the inconvenience. In the wake of the crisis, 55-mile-per-hour speed limits were imposed to save fuel (and lives), to the irritation of speeders everywhere.[45]

This was hardly a propitious moment to wean Americans to an ethic of conservation. Few saw the problem as overconsumption. Instead, Americans blamed American oil companies for "contriving" the crisis and Arab nations for "holding America hostage." Despite higher costs, Americans actually increased their use of electricity by 50 percent in the 1970s. They increased their visits to stores by 39 percent between 1969 and 1983. This trend was due, in good part, to the unimpeded suburbanization of cities like Phoenix and Houston. While most Americans blamed oil interests at first (for example, resisting oil price deregulation), business quite easily shifted responsibility to government regulators and environmentalists. Oil companies expended vast sums on portraying the EPA as tethering the American Gulliver and denying the personal convenience and freedom that defined the American Way.[46]

Energy companies saw the crisis as an opportunity to turn back environmental laws. Rather than foster conservation, President Gerald Ford supported business demands for more nuclear power plants, offshore oil drilling, gas leases, and extended drilling on federal lands as alternatives to growing dependency upon foreign oil. And in 1974 and 1975, business pushed for an end to oil price controls (to encourage domestic drilling) and the relaxation of clean air regulations.[47]

By contrast, Ford's successor, President Jimmy Carter, called for conservation and the reduction of energy consumption growth to 2 percent per year. He embraced an austere policy, demanding that Americans drive

The energy crisis in one of its most upsetting forms — closed gas stations in 1979.
(Library of Congress)

less and accept less comfortable temperatures in their homes during winter and summer. In 1977, he even proposed new gas and oil taxes, penalties
for gas-guzzling cars, and tax credits for the costs of retro-installing insulation, and he deferred construction of breeder reactors. Inevitably, Congress rejected a gas tax (despite its potential for conservation) and passed
only a watered-down environmental bill in 1978. More important, Congress began to give in to the energy industry. In 1977, amendments to the
Clean Air and Water Pollution Acts were delayed. Natural gas and oil
prices began to be deregulated in 1978 and 1979.[48] Carter's moralism
chafed on a country not used to and unwilling to assume austerity. His so-
called "malaise" speech of the summer of 1979, complaining of America's
unwillingness to sacrifice, was widely mocked in the press and only confirmed that Americans would not embrace an ideology of restraint. The
next year, candidate Ronald Reagan refused to acknowledge energy shortages and accused Carter of over-regulation. His own solution was to produce more energy to keep the economic machine humming. For Reagan,
any limit on growth threatened social stability.[49]

The new conservatives understood, as Carter did not, that Americans would not accept the personal costs of full-blown environmentalism. Conservation meant conflict, inconvenience, and narrowed lives. In the 1970s, few Americans embraced car pooling. In the 1980s, when energy prices dropped, so did conservation efforts. Americans accepted unlimited energy as the foundation of an unconstrained individualism. While new houses came with much better insulation, they also got larger. More energy-efficient cars were built, but people drove more. As environmental historian David Nye notes, " 'Thinking green' often meant wanting to live even further from cities."[50] Just as in the 1930s Americans did not adapt to Depression scarcity with an ethic of simplicity, so in the face of the 1970s energy crisis they rejected long-term conservationism. Consuming patterns that freely used energy were too closely associated with freedom itself. Thus the environmental movement was all too easily marginalized.

There remains the legacy of one more challenge to consumerism — the counterculture. Its advocates prided themselves on their all-encompassing rejection of the "system." Although never entirely separate from the other challengers, they went beyond reformism, not merely defending the rational consumer or acknowledging the environmental costs of consumerism in public policy. Their goal was presumably more radical: personal, not interest or issue politics; transforming life, not just belief; and changing consciousness, not just institutions or laws.

Probably the most positive example of these ideas, especially as it applied to consumerism, was the self-provisioning movement. From 1965 to 1970, perhaps 2,000 to 3,500 rural communes formed to feed, clothe, and otherwise provide for the needs of members. The objective was to drop out of the vast corporate network of consumption — eliminating everything from processed foods to fashion. These groups tried to abandon not only the world of hierarchical and "alienating" work but also the culture of the malls and suburban status seeking. Other counterculturalists remained in the cities but shopped and worked at food and craft co-ops. While this movement had roots in an older naturalist tradition (e.g., Euell Gibbons's *Stalking the Wild Asparagus*), it was also deeply influenced by the environmental movement's concerns about the dangers of processed foods and by Gary Snyder's poetics of voluntary simplicity. A few embraced the call in Frances Moore Lappé's *Diet for a Small Planet* (1971) for vegetarianism to reduce the unfair share of world resources used by the meat-eating countries. Some manifestations of this movement were surely extremist (for example, the elaborate rituals and pseudo-Taoist ideas in macrobiotics). The debates about just what from the corporate world one

Merchandisers responded to a new naturalism in African American hair styling in the 1960s. (*Ebony*, June 1967, p. 23)

could use (knives, but not blenders?) and the mystical talk of food with good "vibes" — grown with love and care — amused, if not alienated, most people. Still, this movement made a serious critique of the nutritional value of hyped and processed commercial foods. For some, it offered a way to connect to the nature from which most modern people were alienated due to their reliance on the vast system of corporate provisioning.[51]

While countercultural ideas survived in many guises, countercultural society was largely gone by 1980. It was not crushed by the police or even torn apart by its own fratricidal conflicts. It dissipated mostly because it was a youth movement that, unlike other causes started by the young, was premised on the revolutionary potential of youth *status*. The counterculture failed to be a serious alternative to consumerism because it had so little to say to people farther on in life. It was isolated to a tiny intelligentsia until the 1960s, when the baby boomers hit college campuses in America. Opposition to the Vietnam War and especially to conscription, which had long served to end the carefree lives of young American males, was an important focus. Even though "deferments" protected many male college stu-

"Hippies" in Berkeley, California in 1969 offered an alternative to the corporate food system with organic produce sold directly to consumers.

(Library of Congress)

dents from the military draft in the 1960s, the very possibility of having to go to war created a gnawing anxiety and sensitized young people to the threatened loss of personal freedom. Countercultural youths enjoyed a freedom from adult economic and family responsibilities that often extended into their late twenties or beyond. Perhaps this was only part of a long-term trend of extending the age when careers ended the experimentation and freedom of youth. Psychologist Kenneth Keniston discovered a generation of the "uncommitted" — young males who were insulated from (and fearful of) the professional lives of their fathers and whose mothers nurtured them to value "creativity." According to Keniston, these uncommitted youths resisted the male role of "provider." Similarly, young women rejected the domesticity of their mothers. All this had a great urgency for a while, but obviously, baby boomers grew up, took jobs, and formed families, and thus the values of their youthful rebellion lost relevance.[52]

Another limiting factor was that the counterculture appealed primarily to middle-class youths, self-consciously rebelling against what they took to be a cross-class/mass culture. The youth counterculture was less obviously elitist than earlier intellectual movements critical of popular culture. It appreciated elements of African American art and society and rejected markers of middle-class respectability — "obsession" with personal orderliness, prudence, and respect for authority. Still, the counterculture openly, almost joyously, rejected working-class aspirations as materialistic and culturally repressive.[53] The counterculture of the 1960s was far more individualistic than the gang culture of the working class: gangs were confined to definite spaces in the traditional social environment (bars, streets, or sporting fields) and were constrained by the need to work within the traditional economy. By contrast, middle-class rebels lived in a more mobile and individualistic milieu. They attempted to create alternative institutions (communes, for example) that allowed the children of affluence to "drop out." This neither seriously challenged bourgeois culture nor appealed to disaffected working-class youths.[54]

Counterculturalists alienated both the middle and working classes. They mocked cars, boats, and ranch homes and the values that they represented to the people who possessed or aspired to own them. Their drugs and sexual freedom were an affront to the morality of deferred gratification held by a majority of both the middle and the working class. The youth movement helped to provoke the conservative reaction of the 1970s and 1980s. It certainly made impossible any long-lasting alternative to consumerism because it offered no alternative to anyone but its young creators, and they soon grew up.[55]

Most problematic was the inability of the counterculture to break from the culture of consumption and develop lasting social practices or rituals outside the consumerist system. The counterculture displayed an extraordinary faith in the power of personal objects and physical expressions — torn blue jeans and long, wild hair — that defied middle-class standards and were supposed to serve as substitutes for political action. Unconventional dress, claimed counterculturist Jerry Rubin in 1969, was "revolutionary in a society of passive consumers." Yet those who scorned the consumer trophies of the middle class were simply adopting their own fetishes. The politics of style became just style, another market segment easily integrated into the merchandising system. As radical sociologists Jack Whalen and Richard Flacks later lamented, "By the mid-1970s, most of America was wearing blue jeans . . . [;] instead of waging war on the young, the society and culture were integrating them. But what was remarkable was how little such inclusion changed the central logics of market, bureaucracy, state, and media."[56] Markers of rebellion easily became simply safe symbols of youth or even just informality. As early as April 1967, the hippie "community" of Haight-Ashbury in San Francisco was crowded with bus tours of curious vacationers. Radicals warned repeatedly of the dangers of "co-optation" by the establishment. Still, it is amazing how little the counterculture was armed against this threat. This may be because goods and packaged experiences were so central to the culture. Counterculturalists became rebels through consumption: tie-dyed dresses, *as opposed to* cashmere sweaters and pleated skirts, defined them. The "counter" in the culture was very much within the confines of consumerism. The object was not to create long-lasting communities; the counterculture produced no fraternal or youth-training organizations as had radical movements in previous generations. Reich praised hippies for their "casual uncommittedness and intense communal feeling."[57] However, such people still needed goods to communicate with others and to feel part of a group. Hip consumption was a substitute for new institutions, socially binding rituals, and, of course, serious political action.

It is no surprise that consciousness-altering drugs played such a big role in the counterculture. Reich saw psychedelic chemicals as mind expanding and community building. In fact, they were classic modern consumer products — providing an experience quickly and conveniently without the effort required in contemplation or religious exercise. The hippies' drugs were not their "mother's little helpers," the tranquilizers mocked by the Rolling Stones in a popular song, but they were very much a commodity shortcut. Reich and others warned that it was not enough to buy boots (as opposed to wingtip shoes) to state one's freedom from conformity. For the Consciousness III person, "developing a relationship with them [boots] takes pain, patience, skill."[58] The counterculturalist may have used goods in personal, even creative, ways that seemed to challenge convention and the designs of the corporate producers, but this was hardly creating an alternative to commodity fetishism. Instead, it was confirming the need for goods to define the self and to tell the world who one was.

Christopher Lasch's characterization of the 1960s counterculture as the embodiment of the narcissistic personality with "little capacity for sublimation" may be a little harsh. But the uninhibited quest for personal "authenticity" through freely chosen experiences was surely consistent with an open-ended consumerism. Jerry Rubin was a perfect example. He graduated from radicalism in the late 1960s to hip therapy in the 1970s. As he noted in his autobiography, "In five years, from 1971 to 1975, I directly experienced Est, gestalt therapy, bioenergetics, rolfing, massage, jogging, health foods, tai chi, Esalen, hypnotism, modern dance, meditation, Silva Mind Control, Arica, acupuncture, sex therapy, Reichian therapy and More House — a smorgasbord course in New Consciousness." He explained this strange behavior this way: "I went into therapy for growth. Not fully in touch with my own feelings and needs, I was closed to myself, and therefore closed to others." After years of struggle, he came to the decidedly unradical discovery that "It's O.K. to enjoy the rewards of life that money brings." In the 1960s, Rubin had argued that consumerism makes people passive. Soon he found that it makes people into radical individualists — it makes Jerry Rubins.[59]

The counterculture improved on the consumerism of the 1950s rather than really challenging it. Postwar prosperity had produced anxiety among intellectuals and the elite that high mass consumption meant conformity — most had the "standard" package, and it was difficult to be "exceptional." However, a new style of spending made it possible again to be "true individualists." The self-indulgence of the counterculture helped create and justify that new style. As historian Thomas Frank argues, the "prosperity of a consumer society depends not on the rigid control of people's leisure-time behavior, but exactly its opposite: unrestraint in spending, the willingness to enjoy formerly forbidden pleasures, an abandonment of the values of thrift and the suspicion of leisure that characterized an earlier variety of cap-italism."[60] The counterculture's celebration of uninhibited behavior was more a critique of the domesticated consumerism of the 1950s than a cri-tique of consumerism itself. In fact, the counterculture was part of a broader effort to break free from the 1950s ideology that legitimated spending only if it was "for others" and if it was confined to the roles of male provider and female nurturer. Under the banner of youth, consumption was released from obligations to family. The great irony of those crisis years was that cul-tural rebellion turned individualistic consumption into a mass market. While the serious political movement challenging endless growth was weak-ened, if not defeated, the march of consumerism continued — in a direc-tion pushed along by attitudes reflected in the counterculture.

More Stuff in New Packages

In "Meet Tomorrow's Customer," (1963), *Nation's Business* predicted that Americans would soon be spending more for personal activities — vaca-tions, sports cars, and eating out. Especially among youths, they saw an emerging "rental economy in which the size of the monthly payment rather than the total price really matters." The point was that Americans wanted to enjoy now and pay later. The magazine also saw a declining sense of "class consciousness" in shopping. Not only had the affluent begun to buy in discount stores, but "income brackets" no longer dictated what kind of car or clothing people purchased. Lifestyle and the defiantly personal increasingly determined choice. Consuming became a token of individual validation, no longer primarily a measure of status, an affirma-tion of a family role, or even a marker along the life course.[61]

Naturally, marketing and advertising experts found this less pre-dictable consumer somewhat frustrating. But savvy merchants quickly saw the trend as immensely promising. The expressive consumer was a big buyer. In the mid-1960s while investments dragged, spending pushed growth — with purchases of color TVs, camping equipment, fashionable men's clothing, and even billiard tables. Upscale buying led Federated De-partment Stores to abandon the traditional "bargain basement" in their new locations. And if some conservatives worried about irresponsible con-sumer debt, by the end of the decade banks had learned that it was more profitable to offer credit cards to consumers than to give investors loans. High interest rates protected card issuers from the relatively few defaults.

By the 1970s, not only did Americans spend as much as four times as many hours shopping as did Europeans, but they also devoted far more space to shopping malls and other retail commercial activity.[62]

Part of this seamless growth of consumption in the 1960s and 1970s was simply due to the unimpeded pressures of the market to expand. Nothing really held back the onward march of the adcult. Despite the scandals that linked sponsors to rigged quiz shows in 1958 and the takeover of programming by the networks soon thereafter, ads became more, rather than less, obtrusive. When advertisers began to buy "spots" on programs that sponsors no longer produced, those companies tended to be less troubled by overcommercialization. After all, their products were no longer identified with a particular program. Advertisers also grew more sophisticated about reaching target audiences. For example, cereal, toy, and candy makers began to favor Saturday-morning programming, where cheap cartoons reached a "pure" audience of children, over more expensive but less effective prime-time shows. Hardly anyone noticed the extra 40-second station break added in 1961 for the benefit of local advertising. By 1964, during two late-morning hours of TV watching the viewer sat through 50 promos.[63]

The banning of cigarette ads in 1971 did not mean less commercialized television. Network executives, worrying about the loss of 10 percent of their revenue, scurried to accommodate their other advertising clients. They made it easier for product pushers to buy 30-second spots rather than one-minute ads, often doubling their exposure. Moreover, improved rating services let advertisers know what percentages of a program's audience were made up by seven age groups. An advertiser, for example, could then target the 18–24-year-old age group during a particular time slot. With greater sophistication in delivering markets, the fear of wasted commercials declined and advertising spending rose (from almost $12 billion in 1960 to $54.5 billion by 1980).[64] While idealists in the late 1950s expected "pay TV" to provide an enlightened and commercial-free medium, cable television two decades later offered something very different: a cheaper and more targeted audience for commercials on specialized channels that featured news, sports, popular music, and children's fare. By 1981, cable reached 28 percent of households, and that was only the beginning. By offering more channels, cable TV convinced Americans both to pay for television and to endure ads.[65]

Meanwhile, competition brought retailing into a hitherto questionable zone — Sunday shopping. Discounters, along with drug and food stores, had come to depend on Sunday business (accounting for about 25

percent of sales for the discount store). In the early 1960s, while these outsiders were cutting into sales, department and specialty stores lobbied local
governments to ban Sunday hours or enforce existing "blue laws." Nevertheless, while officially Sears, Roebuck opposed Sunday shopping, individual stores within the chain gave in to night hours. By 1969, Sears had con-
ceded defeat. The retail giant introduced Sunday hours in California even
though it admitted in newspaper ads that it did so "with great regret and
some sense of guilt." Sears even appealed to other retailers to "stop this
Sunday opening" and "give our employees their Sabbath." All to no avail,
as inevitably others followed.[66]

During the Depression, the supermarket had offered cash-strapped
consumers a few pennies off the price of essentials. In the 1960s, this concept broadened in dramatic new directions. Retailing chains, especially the
variety and department stores in town centers that once had been revolutionary, were losing their customers to the suburban shopping strip and to
the discounter. Survival meant joining, even accelerating, change. In 1962,
well-established main-street dime-store chains decided to build entirely
new discount marts in the suburbs, where they could greatly expand floor

The new suburban shopping mall in its late 1960s edition in Virginia.
(Library of Congress)

space, provide free parking, and buy in volume to keep prices low. Woolworth created Woolco and S. S. Kresge, Kmart. Larger department stores also followed suit — Dayton stores built Target discount stores and J. C. Penney created a chain of Treasure Islands. Also in 1962, in the rural town of Rogers, Arkansas, Sam Walton opened his first Wal-Mart, at the time a poor cousin of the large, well-connected chains. The "Wheel of Retailing," a process by which each genre of store appeared and was surpassed, seemed to be turning ever faster, just like the products the stores sold.[67]

The trend toward the superstore did not mean that Americans had turned shopping merely into a pragmatic act of fetching, paying, and carting away. The glamour and quasi-holiness of the temple of consumption in the turn-of-the-century department store was transferred to the shopping mall. In the 1950s, the suburban phenomenon of the department store flanked by strip stores and surrounded by acres of parking was common. By the 1960s, it had evolved into a virtual Emerald City of shopping in the enclosed mall. By 1967, malls offered up to one million square feet of commercial space, sometimes even including hotel, apartment, and office complexes. By 1975, the Woodfield mall near Chicago offered 2.216 million square feet of climate-controlled space for 240 stores. Shopping malls not only were large and convenient, they transformed the nature of the traditional market center. Unlike the old downtown districts, they lacked the mix of public and commercial activities and the serendipity of an old-fashioned book or jewelry store abutting against an ultramodern department store. Giant retailers like Sears controlled which stores were included in malls to prevent, for example, competition with discounters. Adding to this "rationalization" of the shopping experience, the Supreme Court ratified the efforts of mall owners to exclude political pamphleteering. This made malls into privately controlled spaces, retail cities physically related to the wider life of work and home only through freeways or highway junctions. They were essentially artificial places, physically distinct from residential life. Malls were built at the edges of population centers where developers expected "to make the growth follow" them. To be sure, some malls included churches for "convenience" and even experimented with counseling centers. Moreover, people adapted malls to their traditional social needs: teens turned them into hangouts and later elders used them for winter exercise. Still, no one could doubt their purpose — to create an environment where almost everything but the impulse to spend was rigorously excluded. The old temples of consumption had offered a magical world of marble and glass within their doors that gave their wares an aura of wonder. The mall went a step further — even interior walkways had become part of the merchandising magic with "picturesque" fountains and indoor plants. Stores opened onto wide central corridors and multilevel interiors gave the feeling of vast choice as the crowd surveyed the layers of stores from a central atrium. Shopping was no longer confined to a temple but opened out into a garden, so vast, lush, and orderly as to make customers forget that they came from another world where restraint ruled.[68]

It would be easy to see the victory of consumerism as simply the working out of the "laws" of expanding markets. Yet other factors, primarily inflation and slower economic growth, also explain the growth of materialistic attitudes in the 1960s and especially the 1970s. While the spendable real income of a family of four rose 20.4 percent between 1947 and 1957 and increased 13.1 percent in the next ten years, it actually declined by 1.7 percent between 1969 and 1979. Inflation explained much of this. That which cost a dollar in 1967 cost $2.46 in 1980. The decline of American dominance of world markets and stagnant productivity were also important. The 1970s amounted to a reversal of two decades of growth and expectation of endless material progress. It was a crisis of a scale and duration that had not been known since the Great Depression. Yet, unlike the Depression, it produced more division than unity and led to a disenchantment with public solutions to personal economic problems. The Depression brought into being government programs that benefited diverse and often conflicting groups (big business, labor, farmers, the poor, and the elderly). By contrast, the stagflation of the 1970s seemed to require mutual restraint (on profits, wages, price supports, welfare benefits, and pension payments, for example). Collective discipline was far more difficult to impose than acceptance of mutual benefits. Moreover, a democratic government was a poor vehicle for creating consensus around sacrifice, especially without a unifying threat. President Nixon's wage and price controls, introduced in 1973, caused antagonisms between labor and business and seemed to be an inefficient use of resources. Later, President Carter, unwilling to break from his political base in labor, refused to attack inflation by restricting growth and thus increasing unemployment. Instead, he made a lame attempt at voluntary price and wage guidelines. In sum, government had made promises that it could not keep, and with no compromise between interest groups in the offing, Americans pursued their own personal advantage.[69]

There were many ways in which the "me" decade of the 1970s was manifested. An obvious and oft-noted change was the apparent decline in the idealism of college youths. By 1975, there was a dramatic shift away

173

from liberal arts, education, and social work majors and toward fields that promised high-paying jobs upon graduation (especially business, medical services, journalism, and law). In two years, the number of economics majors doubled at the University of Chicago. The percentage of college students rating "developing a meaningful life philosophy" as very important among their goals declined from 80 percent in 1968 to 40 percent by 1986. Those rating "being very well-off financially" as important rose from 40 percent in 1968 to 74 percent by 1986. While high-minded college presidents and prestigious panels complained that schools were turning out "Highly Skilled Barbarians," educators became extraordinarily solicitous of students. As a result, language and history courses were dropped from the list of requirements, and liberal arts classes were watered down to compete for enrollment.[70]

The self-regarding tone of the 1970s even affected the consumer rights movement. Note the approach of David Horowitz in his *Fight Back! and Don't Get Ripped Off*. Instead of calling for new legislation or regulatory powers to protect the public from the predatory manufacturer or professional, he asked, "How often do you allow yourself to be shoved around on an average day?" His tone was militant but individualistic, and even paranoid. The enemy was as much the lazy and self-serving bureaucrat as the con man and faceless big business. The solution was to "wise up" and not be on anyone's suckers list. Horowitz offered practical information about how to maximize personal advantage in getting loans and professional services. David Hapgood in his *The Screwing of the Average Man* went even further. For him, the bigger-pie-for-all economy had ended. The 1970s was a time when everyone "screws" everyone else, but the rich and well-connected benefited by a lower level of "net screwing." Average Americans (not the poor, who didn't count because they were "excluded from the system") were exploited by the expertise of doctors, lawyers, and insurance salespeople upon whom they depended. Government mostly protected these experts. Instead of the Greening of America, Hapgood saw the "Souring of America."[71]

Much of this turn inward was defensive and negative, especially given the increasingly common view that government was impotent. Economic insecurity and inflation reinforced a long-developing identification of the personal with spending. As social critic Christopher Lasch noted, "In an age of diminishing expectations, the Protestant virtues no longer excite enthusiasm. Inflation erodes investments and savings. Advertising undermines the horror of indebtedness, exhorting the consumer to buy now and pay later. As the future becomes menacing and uncertain, only fools put off until tomorrow the fun they can have today."[72]

This attitude was made mundane and even rational by the extraordinary development of the consumer credit card. Unlike earlier forms of borrowing, the credit card did not require references, collateral, or bank officer approval. Neither did it mean the humiliation of signing a note with a finance company or worse, borrowing from a criminal loan shark. The credit card both eased and democratized consumer credit. The revolution came in 1959, when the nation's biggest bank, the Bank of America, "dropped" massive numbers of unsolicited credit cards on thousands of residences in selected towns. This practice encouraged consumers to use the card and thus persuaded retailers to participate. Using the BankAmericard (later Visa) proved to be a convenient way to shop; indeed, it encouraged people to spend more than they would if they had to part with cold cash. It was also an unobtrusive and respectable way to borrow (by paying the monthly minimum rather than the full amount spent). The consumer decided when to "borrow" and, within limits, for how long. By 1966, rival banks set up Master Charge and competition between the two credit networks led to a blizzard of card "drops." Over a million were in use by 1968. Even though the government banned unsolicited card mailings in 1970, paying with plastic became normal, as did carrying a balance — despite the high annual interest rates. After all, in the 1970s, with inflation running in double digits, the consumer paid back with cheaper money.[73]

Americans looked for new ways of making it when salary raises, pension checks, and tiny interest payments from passbook savings accounts did not keep up with inflation. It was no surprise that they legalized lotteries in the 1970s.[74] Dreams of easy money were also fueled by the "democratization" of investment thanks to the growth of low-cost stock brokerages (Merrill Lynch and Charles Schwab, for example). Speculation on real estate became a virtual national pastime when housing prices rose dramatically in the 1970s (59 percent in constant dollars and 217 percent in current dollars).[75] Inflation fueled aggressive patterns of getting and spending and probably made people less altruistic.

Radical Individuality and a New Consumerism

Business trends and the economic crises of the 1970s added momentum to a strong consumerist ethic in the United States. The environmental and consumer rights movements rowed against these very powerful currents. Ironically, however, the counterculture opened new channels for that stream to flow into. The counterculturalist attack on conformity and celebration of expressive individualism did less to undermine the economic and social order than to provide a vocabulary for a distinct personal style of consumerism. The issues that obsessed Vance Packard and his followers — manipulative advertising, middle-class emulation, and even waste-making car manufacturers — were beginning to disappear soon after their books appeared. In their place emerged a consumerism based on anticonformity.

Part of the change was due to the widespread acceptance of the critique of conformity and 1950s consumerism — including advertisers and product developers. In the 1960s, ad makers learned to be less overtly manipulative. Bill Bernbach's campaign for the Volkswagen Beetle, for example, attacked planned obsolescence while praising the relatively unchanging and functional "ugly little bug." Plain photos of the Beetle made no appeals to fashion (like the 1959 Chevrolet's claim to be "All new all over again"), nor did it try to associate itself with the sexy theme of the space race (as did the 1958 Oldsmobile's promise of a "rocket action" engine). The VW Bus was for the independent person, even if she played traditional roles — the wife who could serve 13 when she has table settings for 12, order escargots, or "Live another year without furniture and take a trip to Europe instead." A single career woman was featured in a 1977 ad with the off-color caption "I bought a [VW Dasher] wagon out of wedlock." A 1974 ad for a Cadillac featured a young black male doctor saying, "I don't drive the car for the prestige. I drive it for my own feelings of satisfaction."[76]

Gradually ads adapted the youth culture's language of "cool" to sell cars and clothes. Note the Dodge Rebellions, "Youngmobiles," and the casual and slightly outrageous look of the "Peacock Revolution" in men's shirts and ties of the late 1960s and early 1970s. These trends were more than a "co-optation" of the counterculture. They appealed to shared convictions of ad writer and reader — "staying one step ahead of the consuming crowd." These shoppers were no longer Marcuse's happy slaves, but happy rebels realizing themselves in spending. Even if "flower power" was ephemeral and Bernbach's sardonic ads lost their appeal by the mid-1970s, expressive individualism in spending remained.[77]

In fact, the new style of consumption went way beyond "cool." It showed in a broader informality — for example, the disappearance of the male felt hat and fancy woman's gloves and headgear in the mid-1960s. These fashion accessories had long been traditional symbols of privilege

The rebellious 1960s also produced a "rebellious" consumerism — not a small, boring car, but "more go, show, spice for the same price."

(*Saturday Evening Post*, Oct. 23, 1965, p. 2)

(freedom from physical work) and prestige (raising the person above the crowd so that by doffing their hats, inferiors lowered themselves before the rich and important). The elimination of the hat (or its replacement by billed caps) was a dramatic sign of sartorial democracy.[78] Ostentatious cars and clothes, noted one market researcher, no longer attracted the refined, but rather "the man who had come up the hard way," maybe the "gravel-pit operator or an owner of a successful pizzeria." By the 1960s, according to literary historian John Brooks, "parody display" had become "the new and rising form of American competitive boasting." The objective was to show sophistication by sending mixed messages and showing "style" rather than "naked wealth." The rich attempted to blend into the crowd so as to avoid ridicule. Extravagant banquets, for example, were no longer in fashion. The well-off dressed down by adapting the working-class blue jeans for casual wear.[79]

None of this meant that America had become a classless society. A middling standard was achieved for a majority, but the affluent continued to display their success in ever larger houses, exotic vacations, expensive restaurants, and private schools. A more mobile and impersonal society produced less physical interaction between the rich and poor and thus less need to mark differences in clothing and physical appearance. Mostly, however, increasing affluence created a series of minute grades of status, defined in widely different ways.[80] More important still, status was increasingly hidden as lifestyle. Distinction remained as significant as ever but increasingly took the form of "individuality." This was more than a surface compromise with the sensibilities of a democratic age. It was also a way of standing apart in an era of mass-produced affluence. Superiority could still be asserted, but at a personal rather than class level, and this meant more varied patterns of spending. A *Business Week* writer hit the mark in a 1961 article: "the problem of finding goods that are scarce becomes much greater in a society in which most people have incomes to support a standard of living well above a bare survival level, and in which chemistry can synthesize excellent substitutes for the scarcest materials." In response, the elite strove not for more and bigger but more individual and more distinct goods.[81]

By the early 1960s, consumer surveys showed that Americans wanted a more varied basket than the standard package of car, house, and furnishings that they desired in the late 1940s. George Katona's studies revealed that only among the aged and poor did many Americans lack wants (43 percent), while few among the most affluent had no desires unfulfilled (25 percent). The irony of this is easy to explain. Many wants were conceivable only from the vantage of other needs being met: one had to have a car in order to desire a vacation home or speed boat. So when the share of household budgets for cars dropped from 6.2 percent to 4.6 percent between 1955 and 1960, the spending shifted to recreation and travel. The "annual model changes seem to be losing their appeal," noted a Harvard business professor, because most Americans had cars and thus they were no longer status symbols. The new status item was the vacation home. In 1960, there were already two million families with two or more houses. With the coming of commercial jet flight in the 1960s, the number of overseas travelers rose sharply (from 1.6 million in 1960 to 8.16 million in 1980). Likewise, boating had become the favorite sport of 40 million by 1960, twice the number in 1950, and boat ownership rose from 8 to 11.8 million in the two decades after 1960. New adult toys like snowmobiles (reaching 405,000 in sales by 1970) attracted discretionary dollars. To most, this expansion of

The well-equipped vacationing family is promised fun and an escape from boredom. (*Holiday*, May 1957, p. 192)

desire appeared not as new forms of status seeking but manifestations of "lifestyle choice" and individual expression. All this meant ever greater spending. In constant dollars, personal consumption rose by 82 percent in the 1960s and still by 40 percent in the "stagnant" 1970s.[82]

Reflecting these trends was a new kind of consumer research that focused on "values and lifestyle" rather than income levels in targeting potential markets for products. A pioneer in this research, Arnold Mitchell, found nine lifestyles based on age cohorts and education as well as income. The bottom two thirds of the population were the poor Needs-Driven and lower middle-class Outer-Directed shoppers (subdivided into Belongers, Emulators, and Achievers). The top third were Inner-Directed consumers, consisting of an interesting mix of young rebels from affluent families (the "I Am Mes"), the slightly older "Experientials," the small "Societally Conscious," the older "Combined Outer- and Inner-Directed," and the mature "Integrated" lifestyle groups. Mitchell made no claim to original social theory (he borrowed heavily from David Riesman's terms in the *Lonely Crowd*). Instead, he advised business how to target products. "Belongers," he argued, would buy station wagons while "Experientials" and "Emulators" would favor sporty cars. Advertisers needed to know that different lifestyle groups might buy the same goods for very dissimilar reasons. Moreover, the "I Am Mes" would buy different cars as they got older, and marketers should learn to follow their life courses. Indeed, in the late 1970s, merchandisers welcomed baby boomers to middle age by advertising Oil of Olay anti-aging cream and oversized 38-inch-waist jeans for those men who wanted to hold on to the uniform of their youth but still have "comfort." Pepsico expanded its definition of the Pepsi Generation from the 15–25-year-old set to the 15–75-year-old category of the "young at heart."[83]

Another way of segmenting markets was to appeal to black consumers. White-controlled merchandisers of products as diverse as films, cosmetics, insurance, cigarettes, and alcoholic beverages worked closely with black consultants and media moguls like John H. Johnson of *Ebony* and *Jet Magazine* to target blacks. For example, high-end beauty products appeared in ads appealing to the upwardly mobile black woman, newly introduced to office and middle-class service jobs. So-called "blaxploitation" films like *Shaft*, though produced by whites, featured macho black outlaws who knew how to get "whitey" and sexy women. As historian Robert Weems noted, "the sense of racial unity generated by the Civil Rights Movement gave way to the 'rugged individualism' of such movie characters as . . .

Shaft. Furthermore, the films stimulated conspicuous consumption as young black males sought to emulate the lifestyles of these dubious film icons."[84]

The individualism of the well-educated portion of the baby boomers very much influenced lifestyle and values research. Marketers paid special attention to the relatively late nesting of this cohort into the family home of the suburbs.[85] At the same time, childbearing dropped off sharply in the 1970s (decreasing from 23.7 births per thousand Americans in 1960 to a low of 14.6 in 1976, never to rise above 16.7 for the rest of the century).[86] A common stereotype was the counterculturalist couple who aged into the Young Upwardly Mobile Urban Professional (yuppie) or Double Income No Kids (dink). These were small groups, but they got attention when they demanded more urbane night life, specialty shops, and personal services. The yuppies/dinks "gentrified" charming neighborhoods in the cities or bought new luxury condominiums and townhouses. Reformers criticized these upscale urban cultural neighborhoods for their tendency to displace poor and elderly residents and for their isolation from and indifference to deteriorating areas that surrounded them. The high culture of the performing arts and museums remained the preserve of the affluent and well-educated,[87] yet still provided a new kind of consumption style that appealed to individuals more than families and consumed experiences more than goods.

The expressive individualism of the 1960s and 1970s was more than a style or even a rejection of suburbia. It was a culmination of a trend toward goods, rather than relationships, defining self. A common image of the American way of life in the 1950s had been a family of four happily seated in their comfortable car with a proud dad at the wheel. Advertisers repeatedly portrayed products as gifts of the breadwinner to a grateful family to sell TVs, cars, and the suburban house itself. Possessions linked people in shared meanings, sent messages of love and lessons from older to younger generations, and established roles and power. At the same time, they let people be "themselves" and allowed family members to avoid conflicts and compromises. This essential ambiguity of consumer goods was and is fundamental to their meaning and continued appeal. It helps explain why consumerism is the "ism" that won the century. But the balance between society and the individual tipped sharply toward the self in the 1960s and 1970s.

Personalized consumption was not new to the 1960s, of course; it was at the core of the mass marketing revolution, and we have seen many examples from the 1900s on. Even in the "togetherness decade" of the 1950s, appliance makers saw a trend toward "two refrigerators in every home" and the plumbing fixtures industries promoted the "privazone" house — providing each member of the family with a personal toilet. Radio makers led the way with cheaper but more plentiful transistor radios (three per home by the late 1950s). Entertainer Dinah Shore lamented the poor families who were victims of "one-car captivity," and by 1960, one in six families already were freed of this misery with two or more vehicles.[88]

Thereafter, however, this trend accelerated. During the 1960s, the percentage of two- or more-car families had nearly doubled (reaching 29 percent by 1970). Car companies essentially abandoned the strategy of planned obsolescence based on the expensive and risky idea of the annual model change and ever more outlandish styling innovations. Instead, they found that they could sell more cars to a segmented market, designed for different ages, sexes, and lifestyles. Households continued to buy "family cars," often in the form of station wagons and vans used by parents with children to haul. Increasingly, however, single people, married men, and others purchased a second or third car essentially built around their own "personalities."

The evolution of the compact car is revealing. When the Big Three introduced their small, "stripped down" Falcons, Corvairs, and Valiants in 1959, the marketing idea was to divert American consumers from the economical foreign car market (especially the Volkswagen Beetle). But this appeal to the anti-Sloanist consumer was only halfhearted. The compacts did not stay simple and small for long. While the first compacts were two feet shorter and equipped with one third less horsepower than the standard car of 1960, the Ford Falcon increased in weight from 2,400 pounds to 3,000 pounds within three years. There was a great reluctance in the auto industry to downsize, even in the wake of the energy crisis of 1973 and the invasion of the Japanese imports in the late 1960s and 1970s. The 1974 Ford Granada got only 14 miles per gallon of gas in the city. Americans, insisted Ed Cole of General Motors during the energy crisis in 1973, would not sacrifice comfort for economy. "Downsizing" came in earnest only in 1978, after Japanese car imports had already won millions of American customers.[89]

Rather than ushering in an age of practical vehicles, the compacts simply added to the range of cars available. In fact, the Chevrolet Corvair as "basic transportation" quickly was restyled into a far more flashy model with bucket seats and a floor shift that had the look and feel of a sports car.

Ford's Mustang of 1964 completed this transformation of small into sporty. The souped-up engines in the standard production Pontiac (GTO), also introduced in 1964, offered adults a commercial version of the dragsters raced on Detroit streets. Like the Mustang, these "muscle" cars promised an image of youth, power, and sexuality for men and women still in their first jobs and as yet free from mortgage payments and the costs of baby furniture. They appealed to a variety of tastes in hardtop, convertible, and fastback models and even came with optional racing stripes to complete the image. In 1968, *Hot Rod* editor Ray Brock noted, "The high-performance buff can now literally 'build' his own individualized machine right on the showroom floor" with a wide variety of options in style. Mustang ads appealed to the liberated childless individual: one magazine ad featured the caption, "Six [cylinders] and the single girl"; another included "a newspaper headline" that read PROMINENT EXECUTIVE DISAPPEARS LAST SEEN LEAVING A FORD DEALERSHIP WITH NEW MUSTANG and a picture of a middle-aged businessman at the beach with his Mustang. A somewhat different "lifestyle" choice was embodied in the "Jeepster," a remake of the army utility vehicle. For those suburbanites who liked to think of themselves as free as the wilderness (at least on weekends), the Jeep had a rugged but powerful image and ride. And like the other new models, it came in a variety of shapes — station wagon, roadster, and pickup truck. Americans embraced multiple and more individualized cars. It is no surprise that spending on cars rose by 95 percent in the 1960s and 41 percent more in the 1970s.[90]

The power of the automobile to project a "personal" image — of youth, power, sexuality, and ruggedness — as well as to induce feelings of exhilaration and comfort hid a far more important meaning of the car — its *auto*-mobility. From the beginning, the car gave individuals the choice of when and where to go. With the coming of the multiple-car household, that individualism rose a notch — fights over keys and the misery of being "stranded" waiting for a ride were over. Teenagers could avoid having to make humiliating dates with friends in the family station wagon. There were 3.74 Americans for every car in 1950; that figure dropped to 2.9 in 1960 and 1.86 by 1980.[91]

A similar process occurred in the transformation of the television. In the 1950s, ads featured the TV as an "electronic hearth," a provider's gift to the family of an exciting world in the shared space of the living room. By the mid-1960s, however, the TV had become a movable personal entertainer. Small-screen portable Sony TVs were set in the kitchen, and ads even featured a "Tummy TV" so a man could watch his favorite show at night without bothering his sleeping wife. As cultural historian Cecelia Tichi noted, the new personal TVs meant that "the family's contentment comes from not having to gather to watch the same thing. Technology lets them escape the tyranny of the hearth."[92]

The idea that everyone should have their own stuff quite naturally extended to meals. A 1976 study sponsored by General Mills found a new breed of parent who tolerated family members eating different foods at dinner and ordering individually and unconventionally at restaurants. Processed food makers responded with everything from single-serving canned puddings to personal gourmet frozen dinners. Dinner increasingly lost its social character, the sharing from the soup ladle or taking a slice cut from the roast or loaf of bread.[93]

The shift from domestic to personal goods took still other forms. Note the coming of Atari and the video game. The electronic game appeared first in 1972 in hotels, bars, and bowling alleys as a variation of the pinball machine in the "penny arcade." By 1975, Atari, Magnanox, and Coleco were producing home video game devices adaptable to TVs, and soon hand-held models appeared. While the first games (Pong and Pac Man) attracted college students and older youths, video games rapidly replaced toys on the must-have lists of children for Christmas. These games and their much more sophisticated successors from Nintendo and Sega were not always played in individual isolation. Still, the point was to "beat" the machine, not to relate to, share with, or compromise with other people. In important ways, Americans were enveloping themselves in goods that freed them from interacting with each other.[94]

Gender, Generation, and the New Consumerism

Where did this new individualism come from? In some ways, it flowed from the logic of the consumer economy that personalized needs and their fulfillment through commodities. In the long run, this process dissolved surviving social rituals necessary in an earlier age of mutual dependency. But there were more specific changes that brought a new consumerism. New divisions between men and women and between young and old led to a more individualistic society, which marketers tapped into and exaggerated. Put bluntly, the 1950s ideal of familial solidarity did not work very well. Social critic Barbara Ehrenreich argues that the radical individualism of the 1960s was rooted in men's frustration with their circumscribed role as providers. This went far beyond the rebellions of the Beats or counterculturalists. According to 1950s convention, the man of 30, unmarried and without the responsibilities of supporting family and the nest, was immature, perhaps even of doubtful heterosexuality. The secret of the success of Hugh Hefner's *Playboy* was its rejection of the linkage between manhood and the provider. This "girlie" magazine glorified male sexuality without obligation and unashamedly promoted self-centered consumption. Some "burdened" married men certainly shared this fantasy even if they hid their *Playboy*s in an unused desk drawer. The rebellion against the provider role may explain why the popular press was so often fascinated by the beatniks, and it even makes sense of the obsession with the TV western hero (who never seemed to have a wife and children). It should be no surprise that some men found "vicarious consumption" through their families to be a poor substitute for the real thing. In a decade when personal growth was so widely touted by popular psychology, some men quite naturally concluded that living for and through others was unfulfilling.[95]

This longing for liberation was not the secret desire of men alone. The "Playboy philosophy" of 1953 found its parallel a decade later in Helen Gurley Brown's *Cosmopolitan*, which celebrated female sexual and material gratification. Even Betty Friedan in her famous feminist manifesto, *The Feminine Mystique* (1963), agreed that rising divorce rates showed "the growing aversion and hostility that men have for the feminine millstones hanging around their necks." She hoped for an American family where no adult was dependent upon another. For Friedan, dignity and meaning came from public accomplishment and personal income.[96] Men might have to give up some of their privileges (in employment, education, and even honor) as the self-sacrificing sole breadwinners. But, as Ehrenreich noted, the trade-off was the right to abandon "self-denial, repression and unsatisfied appetites."[97]

Of course, few recognized any of this in the 1960s. Men often saw feminism as a threat, not an opportunity. In the 1970s, things became clearer. Caroline Bird's popular analysis of the two-paycheck marriage made the point bluntly:

> Men are beginning to recognize that they no longer need to work all their lives at jobs they don't like to support wives and children.

> Women are beginning to question the way in which women have adapted their careers to childbearing and some are questioning whether to have children at all.

Of course, few couples were so calculating, self-regarding, or quick to discard traditional sex roles. In the early 1970s, young wives often took jobs "to help out" before children arrived and before husbands' careers took off. Gradually, inflation made meeting house and car payments impossible without a permanent second income. Feminists like Bird knew that many wives working outside the home did not get much help from their husbands with housework and child care. Still, Bird was optimistic that a new age of confident working women with supportive husbands was emerging. Stress from work and ironing and cooking waiting at home could be overcome with smaller families, "quality" time with children, and more reasonable standards of household order: "messy closets worry no one but the woman who feels responsible for them."[98]

This view surely denigrated the value of the unpaid homemaker, and it inadvertently led to still more consumer markets — for fast food, child care, and housecleaning services when necessary domestic jobs did not get done. Still, one could hardly blame the feminists for the declining status of women's work outside the market. In the new consumerism, what counted was what a person could buy, not the work and service she could provide in the home. Ironically, the domestic consumerism of the 1950s was at the root of this change; it had, in the words of historian Lynn Spigel, the "paradoxical effect of sending married women into the labor force in order to obtain the money necessary to live up to the ideal."[99] Moreover, the economic stresses of the 1970s produced a very different response than did the Depression of the 1930s. Instead of reinforcing sex roles (men providing income spent by women for the family), the inflation of the 1970s brought women into the market to get things for themselves and to keep up an ever rising standard of consumption for their families.[100] A culture that could not rein in the desire to consume and instead glorified it in new forms of personal expressiveness and freedom required more and more people to get jobs. The irony of this was that well-appointed homes were left empty and sports cars unused while their owners scurried off to work to earn the wherewithall to buy these things. Many missed the irony, for they had their independence and their own stuff.

Consumerism and individualism interacted to change gender roles. A similar process worked to redefine concepts of youth and age. Consider the

way in which the new consumerism shaped the meaning of old age and retirement. Few over 65 years old could have imagined retirement as a "permanent vacation" before the postwar era. Housing developments and
trailer parks for the retired had existed from the 1920s and 1930s, but until
the 1960s, marketing specialists were wary of elder consumers, fearful of
insulting them by calling them aged. In any case, these were poor consumers, requiring little and having little time to enjoy what they did buy.
The solution to this dilemma was to redefine retirement as a time of freedom from obligations to community, family, and work, a permanent paid
vacation. In many ways, it was a democratic version of the "retirements"
of the traditional aristocracy to their health resorts and country manors.
Increased longevity and improved health in late life, along with pensions,
made retirement possible for the majority and a luxurious unending holiday for a few.[101] Along with Social Security, increasingly generous pension
plans — most notable of which was the "30 (years service) and out"
scheme won by the United Auto Workers union in 1971 — greatly eased
the financial worries of older people.[102] Groups like the American Association of Retired Persons (founded in 1955) propagated the idea of an
independent, informed, and leisurely retirement. It was not to be a relatively brief period of inactivity before death, but a new life stage of fulfillment and compensation for work, unfettered by geographical or time
constraints.[103]

By 1960, businesspeople began to recognize that elders could be
grouped into cohesive markets — no longer isolated and scattered in families, but gathered at golf courses, pleasure cruises, and retirement communities. Of course, most of the elderly continued to live in their old
neighborhoods and near their children. Yet a minority, mostly affluent and
healthy, began to migrate to warmer (and sometimes less expensive) regions far from their old jobs and families. Among them were the "snow-
birds" — seasonal visitors to the trailer parks, apartments, homes, and
condos of Florida or the Southwest, who also spent less inclement months
near family. The appeal of improved climate and freedom from the problems of the industrial environment is obvious. With no economic responsibilities tying them to the Frost Belt or city, they were free to pursue a
more comfortable climate. But the apparent abandonment of family by the
elderly was rather harder to explain, given traditional roles of grandparents. One answer was the physical and cultural separation of generations
that began much earlier when the young, middle-aged, and old began to
peel off into distinct peer cultures around their own music, leisure activi-

Sun City has it all for the permanent vacation of retirement.
(Sun Cities Area Historical Society; courtesy of John Findlay)

ties, and "lifestyles." Moreover, many retirees felt that they were living in an "empty nest" when adult children moved far from home. Smaller and delayed families also meant that elders had fewer opportunities to play the role of grandparent. Finally, pensions and Medicare reduced the need of children to care for aging parents. In the United States, the proportion of the elderly who lived with children declined from 60 percent in 1900 to 16 percent in 1950 to scarcely 9 percent in 1970.[104]

Del Webb's Sun City (1960) fully expressed the idea of retirement as permanent vacation. This planned suburb in the southwestern desert promised maintenance-free housing as well as a community rich in golf courses, recreation centers, imported entertainment, churches, and shopping centers, with easy access to the boom city of Phoenix. With eleven golf courses available by 1979 and recreation centers with dozens of clubs, Sun City was a Organization Man and Woman's utopia. As one resident said, "They offer so many outlets. No one has to say, 'What am I going to do for the rest of my life.'" One observer rather uncharitably labeled Sun City "a resident Disneyland for old folks." By prohibiting permanent residence to anyone under the age of 50, Sun City became a community of shared values. It created an elder peer culture consisting of people who had devoted their younger years to raising families in affluent suburbs. In fact, Sun City was a suburban paradise — minus the sometimes hell of kids and jobs. Webb's sales staff offered incentives to buyers who encouraged neighbors or friends "back home" to join them. What brought people to Sun City was not only a status house but a "hometown" feeling. It was in bad taste to talk about former career successes, and all wore informal clothing. Municipal restrictions also liberated residents of Sun City from industrial blight and school taxes. Not only did they avoid sharing the responsibilities of urban life (like many conventional suburbanites) but they also evaded the problems of the younger generation. Few residents had difficulty justifying this because they had already paid their "dues" to society.[105] They hoped to enjoy an endless weekend, like the best ones recalled back home in Lake Forest or Westchester.

It was easy to criticize these retirees as selfish and escapist, rejecting their responsibility to share their experience, wisdom, and time with grandchildren and struggling, overworked communities. But as Charles Monaghan, editor of *Retirement Living*, noted, the duty of the generations was not to bond together but to live the high American ideal of "political liberty," to allow individuals to exercise their right to choose how to live.[106] In any case, these geriatric ghettos were really no different than the new apartment complexes that catered to singles or young married couples but excluded families with teenagers. They were part of the larger cultural trend — splitting into amiable, like-minded cohorts.

Just as the life stage of the aged increasingly became commercialized and isolated from younger people, so childhood became itself a consumerist lifestyle, separate from adults and their concerns. Long before the 1960s, of course, children had been targeted consumers of candy, movies, toys, and sports equipment. Beginning in 1944, Eugene Gilbert surveyed the youth market and worked to convince businesses that kids had both money to spend and influence on parental spending. Since 1945, cereal makers had found new profits in sugared cereals designed for the childish sweet tooth, and package designers learned to make shampoo and other containers in the shapes of cartoon characters to attract the child's eye. The pace, however, accelerated in the late 1950s, thanks to the discovery that TV was a potential pipeline into the child's imagination. Research found that children responded to TV ads by the age of three because the unique combination of image and simple message could reach preschoolers in ways that print ads could not. Children's television separated the parents' consumer culture from the child's.[107]

Ironically, advertisers were slow to exploit the full potential of kids' TV. Early children's programs featured adult authority figures (Miss Frances, Pinky Lee, and Hopalong Cassidy), and advertisers assumed that parents, not children, controlled the choice of toys and other products advertised. However, with the debut of the *Mickey Mouse Club* in 1955, this began to change. In ads appealing to the five- to twelve-year-old boy, the "Cheerio Kid" again and again saved the girl after being fortified with the essential breakfast food. Mattel Toys risked all to purchase three commercials every weekday for a year, pushing its Burp Gun directly to the imagination of the child; four years later, ad dramas featured girls and their Barbie dolls.[108] Increasingly, TV commercials seen by children did the selling. This made the toy warehouse store Toys 'R' Us successful when it first opened its doors in 1957. Such stores relied on low-wage staff with little training or knowledge of toys while TV ads brought in the customers. By 1980, 47 percent of the dollar value of toys were sold in discount or toy warehouse stores.[109]

Advertising-induced buying and warehouse shopping for children's goods paralleled trends in adult consumption. Still, the growing juvenile consumer culture accelerated a still more important trend — a new autonomous world of the young. Until the 1960s and 1970s, toys had usually conveyed messages between adults and children (while electric trains introduced boys to the world of male technology, baby dolls taught girls nurturing). Because toys had changed relatively slowly (for example, board games or Lincoln Logs), they could evoke parental memories; for example, they even allowed fathers and sons to share "their" train sets. By the 1960s, however, toys and games increasingly were becoming props of a purely children's fantasy world.

Consider the Barbie doll.[110] Mattel's Barbie (1959) clearly broke with the values and memories of mothers. She was neither the traditional companion nor the baby doll; she did not teach girls to be mothers or caring friends. Instead, she was a dress-up doll, a fashion model, inviting the child to fantasize about being a free and free-spending young woman. Barbie was the opposite of the child's mother (a homemaker or perhaps a harried wage earner) and an escape from the fetters of childhood. In fact, mothers at first hated Barbie — not just because of her mature and exaggerated body, but because she was so different from their dolls as children and thus seemed to separate them from their daughters. Barbie's world of fashion and friends changed rapidly, requiring each child to have her own personal set of Barbie gear. Fewer and fewer playthings were passed down to the next child. The ever-changing toy box was the child's first experience with a new kind of consumption — of goods that separated and personalized. The more things one owned, the more free and individual one was.

In the 1960s and 1970s, consumerism was challenged and transformed. In reaction to manipulative advertising, wasteful consumption, and conformist spending, the cultural of constraint saw a rebirth and new creativity. The consumer rights movement insisted that consumers had rights beyond the freedom to buy, even that some corners of life, like childhood, should be protected from the incessant pressure to spend. The environmental movement challenged Americans to balance the obvious joys of cars, expansive suburban lawns, and ever-changing products with their costs in pollution, scarred landscapes, and lost resources. Despite lasting successes, by the end of the 1970s these movements had been pushed to the margins, setting the stage for an unfettered growth of market culture in the 1980s.

In the 1960s and 1970s, consumption society proved to be extraordinarily fluid. Ultimately it depended neither on an egalitarian economics of growth nor on the contained and conformist domesticity of the 1950s to prevail. It did not require status seeking or the waste-driven excess of planned obsolescence. Consumerism was adaptable to the green and the hip; it became an expression of a profoundly fragmenting individualism that was fostered in part by the countercultural movement. American consumer society moved in a new direction after the 1960s, both less constrained and less social than the consumer culture that had emerged at the beginning of the century. The twenty-first century would inherit a new consumerist world.

CHAPTER 6

Markets Triumphant, 1980–2000

R onald Reagan's election in 1980 marked the beginning of a new conservative era in the United States. In 2000, the end of this era was not yet in sight. In some ways, the Reagan Right attempted to restrain boundless consumption. Like their Prohibitionist forbears, this new generation of conservatives saw the danger of addictive desire in kicks-seeking drug users and sex-obsessed youths; the 1960s had unleashed a self-destructive indulgence, symbolized by the murderous cult of Charles Manson and the anarchic Altamont rock festival. The liberation of the libido from work and family responsibility, as preached by countercultural radicals, seemed to upset the critical balance of discipline and freedom that made capitalism succeed. The Right accused liberals of promising access to the American bounty to people who had contributed too little to prosperity and blamed the Left for raising impossible expectations of a bottomless cornucopia. These new conservatives saw the need to preserve family from the panderers of pleasure, yet they also encouraged materialism by denying the collective rights of consumers and tearing down the walls that held back the market from seeping into every corner of the American psyche and society. The result was a consumerism that moved even farther away from social cohesion and reality and toward an enveloping personal fantasy. If the culture of the 1960s generation contributed to a new, fragmenting, individualistic consumption, the unfettered market ideology of the Reagan generation only furthered that trend.

The New Right attempted to rein in consumerist desire, but only when it had to be satisfied by an "entitlement" or was expressed outside the "traditional family" and morality. Thus welfare queens, drug dealers, abortionists, self-indulgent yuppies, and atheists attacking public displays of traditional religiosity were all threats to family and morality. These diverse social types shared a common permissive culture, and government made things worse with aid programs that pampered the unsuccessful and lawbreakers. At the same time, the Right saw government as a drag on profitable enterprise and the free enjoyment of its fruits. There was a logic to this seeming contradiction of control and freedom. While liberal government both indulged an ever-demanding citizenry and fettered enterprise, the market combined discipline with freedom and created growth that was the heart of true democracy. The New Right promised to restore personal responsibility and limited government, the hallmarks of traditional conservatism. At the same time, it also undermined that heritage by abandoning the Victorian ideals of market restraint and social obligation.

Two Faces of Conservatism

The New Right combined an intense longing to control impulse at some levels with a celebration of desire at others. To make sense of this ambiguity, a good place to start is Daniel Bell's *The Cultural Contradictions of Capitalism* (1976). Bell, a leftist in youth and with long-standing ties to the center, came to a pessimistic conclusion: America had reached the "end of the bourgeois era," that tenuous balance of structural constraint and cultural freedom. Work, bureaucracy, and market discipline combined to form an extraordinarily productive society. The secret of the bourgeois success, however, was its celebration of comfort, imagination, and self-expression, which assured continuous innovation. The problem now was that affluence had tipped the balance toward hedonism and away from discipline. It had made consumers more important than producers. With its need for limitless spending to sustain growth, capitalism undermined the very discipline that created prosperity. For Bell, the 1960s' revolt against conformity was only a late stage in a troubling trend. A romantic quest for true selfhood produced people incapable of working in the real world or submitting to structure. In the 1960s, the Bohemian indulgence that had once been confined to the children of the rich and marginal had become a mass movement.[1]

These cultural contradictions of capitalism might have led Bell to a really new analysis (or to despair). But he slipped back into a comforting conventional interpretation. The democratization of personal desire had led to a "revolution of rising entitlements." Bell had an predictable solution: the "establishment" should impose structure, direction, and discipline by restraining government promises of largesse in order to assure growth. Bell's insight about the cultural contradictions of capitalism was lost in the classical notion that the elite as the embodiment of reason must contain the "appetite" of the masses. Bell understood but in the end made little of the fact that the market, far more than politicians, created mass hedonism. Market competition might have leashed individuals to the wheel of work and discipline, but capitalism also requires that people desire goods. The purpose of much of modern work was to make consumption a greater and greater part of life away from work. The most effective panderers of self-expression were not the Bohemians, hippies, or drug dealers, but corporate executives. Bell failed to see that restraint in government entitlements, a return to traditional authority, or even the discipline of the market would not restore balance. They only accelerated a trend toward inequality and guaranteed a more exquisite hedonism of the enriched elite.[2]

Bell was only one of many thinkers who shifted the problem of boundless consumption to government. The thoroughly right-wing Irving Kristol's *Two Cheers for Capitalism* (1978) was even more optimistic about the ability of the market to create social discipline. Economic exchange alone could bring normal, selfish people into crude concord. The countercultural dream of a "community of mutual love" was nonsense. Only an unfettered market society could provide that wonderful balance of discipline and freedom. Kristol admitted that "our spiritual inability to cope with affluence" was the central problem of the age. He believed that Americans somehow must restore the idea of "bourgeois virtue" and the "moral authority of tradition," though he was vague about how this could be achieved. He doubted that Christian fundamentalism was capable of expanding beyond partisanship and negativity or of escaping from the hedonism that surrounded it. Nevertheless, Kristol insisted that "prerationalist" values somehow must be restored to hem in the intemperance of modern individualism.[3]

Concern about cultural restraint, however, was a relatively minor point in Kristol's analysis. He saved his enthusiasm for the unfettered market as the only way of balancing freedom and discipline. Even more than for Bell, the problem was not that advertisers or product developers undermined self-control but that the "new class" of "scientists, lawyers, city planners, social workers, educators, criminologists, sociologists, public health doctors, etc." attempted to restrain the market. In Kristol's view, this new class of public-sector activists was carrying out the "anticapitalist aspirations of the Left." In their efforts to artificially redistribute wealth and restrict enterprise, they threatened to kill the goose that laid golden eggs. So-called consumer rights activists had replaced the old liberal idea of growth with a presumptuous usurpation of the consumer's sovereignty. According to Kristol, the EPA was full of zealots protecting clean air *from* Americans.[4] Kristol's book reaffirmed the growth culture of unrestrained capitalism, even if it also promoted a culturally destructive hedonism.

Bell and especially Kristol were only a small part of a vast neoconservative upsurge that preceded Reagan's victory and challenged the "corporate liberal" establishment that dominated both parties. The New Right mobilized alienated grassroots voters as well as wealthy foundations with calls for restraining entitlements and unleashing enterprise. This was a diverse group, including the establishment easterner William Simon of the Olin Foundation and the upstart Colorado beer man Joseph Coors, founder of the Heritage Foundation. It ranged from Milton Friedman's monetarists, who reduced government economic policy to regulating the money supply, to Jude Wanniski's supply-side economics that found economic salvation in investment encouraged by lower taxes. Not a few were old leftists who felt personally victimized by the counterculture of the 1960s and neglected by the Democrats in the 1970s. Almost all saw big government as the problem, the legacy of New Deal intellectuals, a group of impractical and closet socialists. Virtue and constraint would somehow reappear if government left the stage, and the old balance of discipline and freedom would be restored in the market.[5]

This new conservatism tapped into a broad and growing concern that many Americans consumed but did not work. Great Society antipoverty programs were supposed to raise the uncompetitive and impulsive poor to the status of the hard-working, gratification-deferring middle class. It was easy for supporters to abandon these programs when they did not seem to make the poor adopt the middle-class work ethic. This was the central rationale for restricting welfare: such aid presumably "made" the poor dependent and irresponsible — consumers without labor.[6]

As big a concern was youths whose freedom from work and competition had lengthened in proportion to the affluence of their parents. That postponement of responsibility for middle-class children seemed to undermine values of work and self-discipline. Even worse, these youths, who were supposed to become the leaders of bourgeois society, were exposed to the "pollution" of the music, dance, and sexuality of working-class and minority teenagers. These young people appeared increasingly unprepared for market work and the responsible, domestic consumerism of their parents. According to anxious critics like Lewis Feuer, Bruno Bettelheim, and Midge Decter, parents no longer passed their formula for success on to their offspring. Instead of fostering "strength of character," Decter complained, liberal parents in the 1950s had allowed "no spark of their children's curiosity" to go untended. This coddling produced premature sexual activity, drug obsession, unfocused education, and unpreparedness for the real world. The problem was not the lure of consumption as such, but the lack of willingness to forego gratification and to contain desire within the boundaries of home and family.[7]

Reaction to the "permissiveness" of the 1960s culture was reflected also in the resurgence of traditional religion. Conservative evangelicals insisted that they were the true champions of the family against the threat of unrestraint "out there." While in 1900 that danger came from the uninhibited street crowd, by the 1970s it came from the mass media. Through his boards of volunteer monitors, the Rev. Donald Wildmon called for boycotts of companies that advertised on shows featuring sexual themes or foul language. Television, Wildmon insisted, should support, not undermine, traditional morality. It should not invade the home with the behavior or language of the gutter.[8] Anxiety about commercial culture was very limited, however. Although some evangelists opposed violent children's TV and toys and video games that promoted aggressive play, most opposition to permissiveness was at base a defense of orthodox religion against a secular society.[9]

This religious reaction had much in common with the wider conservative backlash. The Evangelical Right saw public officials as "new class" enemies. After all, the judicial system had banned school prayer in 1962 and had legalized abortion in 1973. By 1986, a group of religious conservatives claimed that secular humanism taught in the schools (for example, the theory of evolution and history without positive treatment of Christianity) was the "establishment" of a state religion and contrary to the Constitution. Tim LaHaye's *The Battle for the Mind* (1980) claimed that the moral relativism that led to abortion, high divorce rates, and drug use was rooted in a common denial of supernatural truths and authority. Preacher Jerry Falwell used radio and TV programs and the Moral Majority, founded in 1979, to fight pornography and sex education in the schools. Pat Robinson combined TV and his 700 Club to advance a conservative religious agenda across old denominational lines.[10]

This effort to extend orthodox religious values beyond the church is understandable, especially when consumer gratification seemed to be replacing the ultimate delayed gratification of faith. Still, it is surprising how little the supernaturalist community questioned commercialization. The religious Right largely limited themselves to opposing the immoral or antireligious content of TV rather than the ads that encouraged lusting after material goods. Turning a blind eye to salesmanship was hardly new to American religion. Hucksterism and revivalism had a long parallel history in the United States. A narrow vision of how the market could subvert personal and family life was also not new. Simply recall the history of Prohibition. The religious Right's compartmentalized thinking seldom questioned the contradictions between calls for moral restraint and toleration of all kinds of commercial freedom.

Anxiety about rampant hedonism surely spurred the popularity of Ronald Reagan's cutbacks of government programs in 1981. The almost gleeful media image of Reagan as the man with an axe suggested that Americans needed a disciplinarian to stop them from their excesses. Sacrifice was required — even if the poor were the main victims when Reagan cut school lunch and food stamp programs. Despite the hardship caused by the recession of 1983, a *Washington Post* editorial noted: "We don't blame you [Reagan] for the recession. We'd gotten too fat, too comfortable, too uncompetitive. Our standards aren't as high as they used to be and there's plenty of blame to go around." The psychohistorian Lloyd DeMause believed that Americans accepted "punishment" as a way to purge themselves of guilt for the indulgences of the 1970s. This, in turn, freed them for a new round of pleasure seeking later in the 1980s.[11]

Politicians' concern about addictive consumption had been highly selective since Prohibition. Not surprisingly, Americans targeted recreational drug use in the 1980s. At a time when experimentation with illegal drugs was actually in decline, especially among the white middle class, efforts to control use increased. In part because drugs could be identified as a minority and urban problem, repression became an alternative to a more positive economic and social policy toward inner cities and disadvantaged minorities. Daryl Gates of the Los Angeles Police Department used armored vehicles and battering rams to break into "crack houses," which the media had identified as centers of open drug use and illicit sex. From his department emerged the DARE (Drug Abuse Resistance Education) Program that involved uniformed officers' teaching schoolchildren the evils of drugs. By 1986, the Reagan administration won legislation permitting the military to gather intelligence on the drug trade and dramatically increasing penalties for users and dealers. Partly as a result, the rate of incarceration more than doubled in the United States between 1985 and 1995. The "war on drugs" went well beyond efforts to control an illegal market in addictive substances or even to reduce the crime and social degradation resulting from the drug plague. It was also a symbolic effort to counteract what conservatives like William Bennett saw as the 1960s revolution against self-control and decency.[12]

Cutbacks and the attack on excess was only one side of the New Right's strategy. More important to its victorious campaign in 1980 was its optimistic promise of a boundless future with massive tax cuts, an increase in defense spending by $750 billion, and a balanced budget in three years. It hardly mattered that this proved to be impossible — tax increases followed within a year of the major cuts of 1981 and deficits ballooned for fifteen years thereafter. The attraction was Reagan's unswerving commitment to limitless economic opportunity. Supply-side advocate Arthur Laffer became famous for his curve claiming to show that lower tax rates meant higher investment and growth (and thus higher tax collection in the long run). Proponents of supply-side economics had an extraordinary faith that only high upper-bracket tax rates stood in the way of a great economic boom. This reversed the argument that had justified dramatic increases in the progressivity of the income tax from the late 1930s. The older "demand-side theory" presumed that the rich were over-savers and that high tax rates on them would produce revenue that when transferred to the poor and elderly, would enable them to spend and thus stimulate the economy. By contrast, said new breed supply-siders like Jude Wanniski and George Gilder, if tax rates were reduced, high-income Americans would invest more and thus increase the supply of goods. Reduced rates were necessary because inflation had shifted the middle class into higher tax brackets designed originally for the rich. More important still, when fifty cents of each additional dollar earned went to income tax, the hard-working saver had less incentive to strive. Only lower taxes would stimulate investment and effort among the critical class of achievers. The other side of this argument was tough love for the less affluent: the poor needed to be liberated from the "welfare plantation" that made them dependent and failed to teach them to compete. Gilder took this argument still further, insisting that breadwinning males would again have an incentive to work hard if the crutch of their wives' income were removed.[13]

In the 1980s, economists and even law school professors embraced a radical faith in the virtue of markets over government. A central doctrine emerged: "De Gustibus Non Est Disputandum" — there is no questioning the taste of Americans for goods and services, even those that might be harmful or embraced only after intense and manipulative advertising. The market always was right because it "revealed preference" in the consumer's purchases. Government should not second-guess such choices with laws that regulated packaging, advertising, or sale of harmful products. The law and economics school advocated that "commercial speech" be protected just as religious and political speech were. The costs as well as the benefits of regulation should enter into court decisions. Awards in liability suits should be limited because open-ended awards were often "inefficient" in their economic impact (disproportionally punishing companies for dangerous products, for example). Some even argued that when consumers bought unsafe products at low prices they were in effect "self-insuring" themselves. This radical approach revealed a basic contradiction in the Reagan Right. As economic critic Robert Kuttner noted, "Either material incentives and rational self-interest are a core principle of the conservative creed, or there are greater goods that transcend calculating egoism. One cannot have it both ways." But conservatives certainly tried. For them, transcendental truths of religion and morality constrained "bad" freedom. At the same time, the immanent logic of a free economy released desire into its appropriate channel — honest enterprise and enjoyment of its fruits in the bosom of the family.[14]

This approach was hardly alien to the American tradition. It was based on a long-standing political consensus that the job of government was to encourage economic growth. After World War II, that idea overcame financial caution among conservative Republicans and commitment to income redistribution among the ranks of left-wing Democrats. In the generation after 1945, growth politics had meant consensus around government's deepening intervention in the economy. However, regulated growth had begun to fail by the mid-1960s, when lower American productivity and renewed global competition made steady expansion much harder to manage. In response, the economic elite increasingly challenged business regulation and "tax and spend" policies. However, this did not mean abandoning the ideal of limitless growth. Jimmy Carter made a haphazard attempt to fashion a "post-growth" policy by cutting the military, trying to tax energy, and supporting lower growth of consumption. But, as he found to his sorrow, there was little political support for real austerity. Reagan's innovation was in promising growth in a new way — not by taxing and spending (at least outside of the military) but by borrowing and deregulating.[15]

Tax cutting may have been a new, more conservative way of claiming the mantle of growth, but it also appealed to the immediate self-interest of Americans. In 1978, Proposition 13 of California dramatically reduced property taxes at a time when rates had increased sharply along with property values. It was hard not to believe that higher property taxes were unfair when incomes did not go up as fast as the nominal value of heavily mortgaged houses. However, the line between appeals to tax fairness and selfishness was hard to find. Land inflation made many homeowners relatively rich in the late 1970s and early 1980s, especially on the two coasts. The more wealthy Americans became, the less willing they seemed to be taxed for services they used less often.[16]

It was clear during Reagan's inauguration in January 1981 that the rich would no longer hide their achievements. The Indiana delegation arrived in style, riding the railroad car of Gilded Age tycoon J. P. Morgan. That year, a cover of *U.S. News and World Report* trumpeted, FLAUNTING WEALTH: IT'S BACK IN STYLE. An advertising journalist could say after the reelection of Reagan in 1984 that Americans "are tired of making sacrifices." No wonder the Democratic Party challenger, Walter Mondale, won only one state. He promised to raise taxes.[17] In their fashion houses and museums, the rich once again embraced the style and taste of the old European aristocracy just as had industrialists during America's Gilded Age. Yet the nouveaux riches of the late twentieth century differed from those a hundred years earlier. Their acquisition of highbrow art and style reflected little of the desire to preserve past civilization that had inspired the likes of Andrew Carnegie. Instead, they drew selectively from an aristocratic aesthetic to assert their membership in the celebrity culture. These images of power, status, and taste were closer to the commercial world of entertainment and fashion than to the world of the court and king. Nancy Reagan cultivated such an image in her ball dresses, but, unlike Jackie Kennedy, she did not see her mission as preserving the heritage of the White House.[18]

Did the 1980s come down to nothing more than a decade of greed, aptly symbolized by the televangelist and stock trader scandals in 1987? The fraudulent promotion of a "Christian" amusement and resort complex by the Rev. Jim and Tammy Bakker neatly paralleled Ivan Boskey's perversion of productive investment with his illegal trade in "junk bonds." The preacher and the investor had proven to be neither morally uplifting nor productive. But it is unfair to characterize the 1980s by merely hypocrisy, free market fantasy, or selfishness. The Right of the 1980s and 1990s had searched for boundaries to desire just as had the Left in the 1960s and 1970s. When conservatives called for less consumption from the poor or marginal while advocating that the middle class and rich have more to spend, they saw no contradiction. The spending of the affluent seemed to be the reward for work and was usually contained within the family, while the poor had not learned market or family responsibility. Eliminating perverse government support and protection for the uncompetitive and undisciplined allowed the logic of the market to prevail. The winners through their work and spending guaranteed growth and preserved the freedom to have more. Government coercion should be restricted to those beyond the gate of respectable desire, who had succumbed to drugs and similar addictions. In many ways the effort to reconcile these conflicting understandings of desire was merely a revival of Victorian attempts to create both pure homes and pure markets. But much of the old *noblesse oblige* and bourgeois devotion to public culture and quiet private life cherished in that Victorian world no longer existed. Instead, conservatives opened up the floodgates to a wider commercialization, in effect the new consumerism that they claimed to oppose, and thus undermined still more the hallowed values of family and faith.

Opening Markets

The year 1981 was a long way from the 1920s, when Republican Herbert Hoover warned broadcasters against turning the uplifting potential of the radio into mere "commercial chatter." Gone was the guilty conscience of 1930s radio executives who deferred to parental concerns about "blood and thunder" programming and "cleaned up" children's radio. Long ago, the "sanctuary" of the home and childhood had been violated by the money changers. In the 1960s and 1970s, the FCC and FTC had promoted a public interest beyond the market, but they suffered major setbacks during the Carter administration. The Reagan era sharply accelerated this trend. The new president appointed officials to regulate the environment, mass media, and advertising who had been critics of the agencies they were to lead and of the laws they were to enforce. In the 1970s, an antagonistic relationship between government agencies and business had been frustrating on both sides and increased the costs of production. Reagan's solution was not to compromise and seek cooperation between the two sides, but to transform the regulators into deregulators and to turn the public interest over to the market.[19]

James Watt, Reagan's first Secretary of the Interior, was an ideologue. His qualification for office was his experience as a lawyer fighting environmental advocates for western oil, power, and mining companies. He had also served as head of a legal foundation supported by the anti-environmentalist Joseph Coors and had gained a following as champion of the "sagebrush rebellion" of prodevelopment westerners. In his view, scriptures "call upon us to occupy the land until Jesus returns." Rather than building a new policy with Congress, Watt used his administrative power to fill positions with antiregulation zealots, cut back on enforcement personnel (justified by substantial reductions in congressional funding), and open public lands to commercial interests. Similarly, Anne Gorsuch, appointed to run the Environmental Protection Agency, loosened rules on disposal of pollutants. Though Watt was forced to resign in 1983 because of an insensitive racial remark, the environmental movement remained on the defensive.[20]

In 1981, Reagan selected another conservative activist, Mark Fowler, to chair the FCC. While working as a radio announcer in college, Fowler resented doing public service messages. Later he became a lawyer, specializing in defending broadcasters against FCC regulations. His motto was, "Let the public's interest determine the public interest," and he denied that there was any difference between listener/viewer selection of existing programming and the public's best interests. He rejected a sixty-year-old principle that broadcasters had a duty to serve the public as well as advertisers because the airwaves were public property. By 1983, Fowler had abandoned the FCC policy that radio and TV stations provide public service and news programming and limit advertising. He also eased restrictions on the number of TV stations a company could purchase. In the name of free markets, Fowler casually ended the traditional expectation that the mass media offer more than commercial entertainment and avoid monopoly control. He insisted that broadcasters should be treated as businesspeople and not be expected to serve as trustees of culture.[21] In particular, Fowler suggested that public TV could take over the role of providing quality children's programming if the advertising market would not pay for it. He wanted to "end government by raised eyebrow" and even suggested that moralists who feared that TV violence was a threat to the innocence and ethical development of the young "underestimate the role of religion" in children's lives. Fowler added: "those parents who abdicate responsibility to television as their electronic babysitter should not expect TV or government to right their wrong." The result of his action was a sharp reduction in children's educational programming (down from a weekly average of 11.3 hours in 1979 to 4.4 hours by 1983).[22]

At the same time as the FCC was relaxing rules governing the commercial networks, Congress cut back the funding of public broadcasting. By 1983, "noncommercial" TV was reduced to selling 15-second ad spots euphemistically called "enhanced underwriting." In 1985, only 7 percent of the budget of a key public TV station, WNET, still came from federal revenues. "High-class" commercials and commercial-like appeals for viewer donations filled the gap. This was a long way from the saturation ads on commercial TV, but it was advertising's foot in the door of public-television culture. The declining difference between the two TV systems, especially with the coming of documentary channels on cable, made many doubt that public television still had any distinctive role to play in American life.[23]

The aggressive government attack on manipulative ads also ended with James Miller's accession to the FTC. Like Fowler, this conservative economist viewed himself as a servant of efficient markets rather than a guarantor of public rights and responsibilities. He embraced a narrow definition of deceptive ads (although Congress rejected it for making the "deception doctrine" unenforceable) and insisted that cost-benefit analysis guide which cases to pursue in court. Miller ended the requirement that admakers back their claims with research and left big companies alone while focusing his diminished resources on small firms "selling offbeat products."[24]

Despite some efforts at reversing Fowler's and Miller's policies after Reagan's departure in 1988, little changed. The Children's Television Act of 1990 limited ads on kid's TV shows to 12 minutes per hour on weekdays and 10.5 minutes per hour on weekends. It also required that the networks provide at least 7 hours of children's programming per week.[25] But stations were creative about counting educational shows (including cartoon programs like *The Flintstones* in the category).[26] By opening a nominally public stage to unrestrained market actors, Reagan tore down the tattered curtain that had preserved a common understanding of the difference.

The supply-siders' deliberate call for a less progressive income tax was a none-too-subtle appeal for greater economic inequality. The intent may have been to increase investment and economic freedom; however, the plan also contributed to a more commercialized society when the new rich indulged themselves in luxuries and racheted up consumer expectations. The tax cut of 1981 was more than an attempt to spur the economy. It attacked the fiscal capacity of government by attempting to end the increases in federal government revenue (which had risen from about 6 percent of GNP in the late 1940s to 9.5 percent in 1979). This increase was largely due to "bracket creep" because inflation forced more middle-class incomes into the tax bracket that was originally designed for the rich. The tax law of 1981 reduced the maximum tax rate to 50 percent, cut 25 percent across the board for the middle class, and indexed brackets so that, as one conservative writer put it, "No longer did the welfare state gain new revenues from the middle class by debasing the currency." As often noted by tax cutters, high-income groups paid more taxes even after rate cuts, although this was because they earned far more.[27] Still, the total impact of tax changes was greater income inequality.[28] Later increases in the 1980s fell disproportionally on the less affluent. Higher levies on alcohol and gas sales, increased rates for the regressive social security tax, and greater reliance on state lotteries recovered some of the revenue lost by lower tax rates on the rich while adding to the burden of the less affluent. Compounding the effects of the tax policy was a trend toward greater salary inequality. While in 1979, the top 5 percent earned 10 times more than the bottom 5 percent, in 1993 the difference was 25-fold. Over half of the additional income generated in the United States from 1977 to 1989 went to people in the top one percent income category.[29]

As the populist conservative, Kevin Phillips, has pointed out, one of the effects of tax cuts was a reduction in and privatization of public services. By 1991, one third of public libraries even in relatively liberal Massachusetts reported reduced service at a time when malls were expanding relentlessly. Spending for private security was double that for public police protection. The hope that reduced public welfare programs would be made up by voluntary charity was not realized. With lower tax rates came less need to shelter income by claiming charitable deductions. The drop in the percentage of income paid by the top tax bracket, from 70 percent in 1980 to 28 percent by 1988, meant that millionaires decreased their giving from an average of $207,089 to $72,784. Moreover, deregulators were not friends of the average consumer, for they allowed higher bank fees, cable TV rates, insurance premiums, and child care and health costs.[30]

This policy of expanding the marketplace via deregulation and tax and program cuts reinforced a still more profound trend — the emergence of what economists Robert Frank and Philip Cook called a "winner-take-all society." The pattern was deceptively simple: modern media and communications meant more people had access to the "best" talent and products. Because highly regarded goods and celebrities were funneled through increasingly narrow media and corporate channels, there was a tendency for a very few products or talents to become "superstars." The time constraints of consumers and limited space in stores and theaters further narrowed the choices. Those lucky enough to become superstars and those slightly more talented than others gained a vastly disproportionate income advantage. This explained the obscene salaries of CEOs like Disney's Michael Eisner and of top professional athletes. Aided by television revenues and new rules (especially free agency), men with skills at playing boys' games earned 50 times the average American wage in 1992, compared to only 8 times that salary in 1976. The top one percent of the richest Americans' pretax income went up 107 percent between 1977 and 1989, while median income increased merely 7 percent.[31]

A lot of that wealth squeezed to the top was invested (one reason for the extraordinary growth in stock market prices and the investment industry in the 1980s and 1990s). But the inequality in income also spurred consumerism. The tax cuts touched off a spending spree and the rich fueled a consumer-driven economic expansion. Deregulation of the FTC and FCC greatly weakened the very concept of consumer protection. Together, these changes broke the boundaries of spending — and greatly intensified consumerism.

Breaking of Boundaries: Home and Children

Early twentieth-century Americans had insisted that there were certain places and times of life into which the intrusion of the market must be strictly prevented. The home, school, and church were some of these places and childhood was one of those times; commerce, with its appeals to personal advantage, excitement of wants, and intensification of the pace of life, seemed inconsistent with their functions. The home was supposed to be a realm of intimacy and quiet, defined as a balanced opposite to the public and dynamic world of the market. Of course, this was merely an ideal that had been compromised long before 1980. Long before Reagan, commercial radio and TV had "invaded" the home and brought domestic life in line with the pace and individualism of the modern commercial world, and the "innocent" child had been transformed into the consuming child. Still, Americans had continued to resist this process and had preserved barriers to keep these worlds apart. The 1980s saw many of those walls fall, with a dramatic commercialization of "sacred" spaces and times. The difference between entertainment and advertising narrowed. Children's play was transformed into accumulating toys. Classrooms became sites for selling stuff to kids.

Given Reagan's media policy, it is no surprise that TV became dramatically more commercialized and the home became more like a shop. By the mid-1990s, there were about 6,000 commercials aired per week, up 50 percent from 1983. This was roughly 15 minutes of ads per hour with an estimated 50 percent more spent per capita on advertising in the United States than in any other country. Ad clutter, long a frustration to admakers' efforts to get their messages across, became an even greater problem. Viewers naturally fought back with their remote controls (which became nearly universal in the 1980s). One ad agency claimed that there was a 30 percent decrease in viewing TV commercials because of the zapper. Men changed channels once every 47 seconds of viewing, according to one study. Clutter and response to clutter led to still more clutter when advertisers responded with shorter (often 15-second) commercials to catch viewers before they had a chance to switch. One study found up to 58 ads in one hour of prime network time.[32]

Other attempted solutions to this self-imposed dilemma only escalated the ad race. Marketers increasingly used public relations firms to get the word out about their products. These companies would, for example, attempt to disguise their promotions as news on consumer and health segments of morning TV shows. Their press releases were vital aids for lazy or understaffed programmers and reporters. New pressure to get ad messages across revived that old trick of paying actors to smoke cigarettes and display labeled products on their TV shows and in movies. Ever resourceful, Ted Turner tried to sell retailers his "Check Out Channel" to show ads to customers caught in lines waiting for cashiers. It failed, but reflected a trend to meet the jaded consumer at every turn with still more ad messages. Turner was more successful with his ad-saturated programming shown on monitors to bored audiences in airport waiting areas.[33] While promoters tried to find new ways of sneaking ads into entertainment and daily life, they also made the commercial into the entertainment itself. In

the 1980s, admakers found that some Americans would endure entire programs that were nothing but commercials. The "advertainment" offered
by the Home Shopping Network made TV into a video sales catalog — a
store in the living room that linked the viewer to must-have gadgets or
fashion via a free 800 telephone number. Created by Lowell Paxson in
1981, the Home Shopping Network reached 64 million cable households
24 hours a day by 1990. Shoppers could buy everything from cubic zirco-
nia diamonds and tacky knick-knacks to women's clothing and home computers. Those with little control over impulse buying no longer had the
"brake" of having to find a stamp and envelope to cool their need to
spend. All they had to do was pick up the phone. By 1993, home shopping
industry revenues reached $2.2 billion.[34]

The distinction between TV programming and ads lessened in other
ways. The 1981 creation of MTV introduced viewers to videos of music performers who, in effect, sold their songs 24 hours a day. By 1988, a study
found teens spent 2 hours per day watching MTV.[35] Even more dramatic
was the transformation of the religious service into an advertising pitch. As
early as 1960, a ruling allowed *paid* religious broadcasts to "count" as public service programming for local stations. This opened the doors to a dramatic change in TV religion. Independent evangelists, who had long
chafed at the dominance of mainline churches on TV, developed a new way
of getting their message and themselves on the air with direct appeals for
money to fund their programs. In 1959, 53 percent of religious broadcasts
were paid "advertisements." By 1977, 92 percent fit this category. Since the
1950s, evangelists like Billy Graham had worked with local churches to organize and finance revivals that were also telecast. The trend in the 1980s
was radically different. The new televangelists identified niche markets and
designed programs meeting the distinct moral, aesthetic, and religious sensibilities of their diverse audiences. Louisiana preacher Jimmy Swaggert
strutted and sweated across the screen, delivering emotionally drenched
sermons that appealed to rural and small-town Americans still close to the
old revivalist tradition. By contrast, Robert Schuller's positive-thinking,
California-style service, set in the modern but dignified Crystal Cathedral,
attracted the comfortable middle class. Schuller's telegenic cathedral, built
in 1979, was a big step up from his earlier "church," an old drive-in movie
theater where worshippers sat in their cars. Many of the techniques used
by televangelists were as old as the frontier revivals. Still, the new TV religion removed the believer from the traditional essentials of a church — interaction with the congregation and accountability of the minister. Tammy

and Jim Bakker's "PTL" program was more like a celebrity talk show than a religious service. The Bakkers were so successful at raising money through on-air "ads" that they grew un-Christianly rich. Enemies reveled in exposés about their six homes and air-conditioned doghouse for their pet. When the Bakkers turned to hyping "Heritage USA," a resort and amusement park for believers, and promised an unlimited annual three nights of lodging for a mere $1,000, they crossed the line. This too-good-to-be-true offer turned out to be just that. After Jim Bakker was exposed as an adulterer with a church secretary, the Bakker empire collapsed in 1987. This case was extreme, but it revealed how blurred the line between religious TV programming and advertising had become.[36]

Of course, commercial TV was not alone responsible for the deepening commercialization of the domestic sanctuary. Telemarketing, or soliciting by phone, had become increasingly common and ever more intrusive in the 1980s. Special software allowed telemarketers to identify the age and income of household heads. Telemarketers even tried to pass on the costs of long distance by persuading consumers to dial up 900 toll numbers. Irate citizens won state laws that allowed people to have their numbers removed from telemarketers' lists. A FCC ruling in 1992 prohibited faxing ads and regulated the use of automatic dialers and artificial voice messages. Nevertheless, telephone selling continued to grow throughout the early 1990s, with revenue increasing by 30 percent each year. The old sign at the edge of many small towns prohibiting solicitations had once warded off the Fuller Brush Man knocking on doors. In the 1990s, little could protect the dinner hour from the telemarketer's phone call except letting the answering machine record all calls.[37] No matter how much Americans wanted to avoid TV ads and evade telemarketers, few would abandon their TVs or telephones. And the advent of the Internet in the mid-1990s only extended the commercial invasion of the home onto still another media platform, the personal computer.

Deregulation also helped to turn children into another market. Deregulation of children's TV allowed merchandisers to transform kids' programs into ads. Cartoon shows created to promote lines of action figure toys became common in the 1980s. These program-length commercials (PLCs) kept the toy line regularly in front of the child. No longer did an entertaining cartoon figure like Mickey Mouse become a licensed toy or doll only after achieving "fame." The point of the new-style program was to advertise a product line and only secondarily to entertain. In the 1983 – 84 season, there were already 14 PLCs selling, among others, toy figures of He-Man, G.I. Joe, Care Bear, and Strawberry Shortcake. By the fall of 1985, cartoons featured all ten top-selling toys.[38]

This was more than a manipulative sales practice. The PLC and other media-generation productions made play into a kind of "additive" consumption. PLC toys were props for the reenactment of stories seen on TV or in the movies. Just one or even a few G.I. Joe figures would not do, and over time, TV and movie characters changed, requiring still more purchases to keep up with the evolving fantasy. Collecting and trading the figures often became more important than play itself. The toy became just one link in a chain of consumption based on a "licensed" image — a Strawberry Shortcake figure, for example — that led to the purchase of matching sheets, backpacks, lunch pails, and, of course, videos and movie tickets.

Childhood became locked in a vast interconnected industry that encompassed movies, TV shows, videos, and other media forms along with toys, clothing, and accessories, all in the business of selling fantasy. About 60 percent of toys sold in the United States by 1987 were based on licensed characters (up from roughly 10 percent in 1980). Long lines of managed fads were carefully doled out to the public to optimize exposure. Fantasy impresarios skillfully directed the display of these wares, creating a "synergy" between them to maximize demand. Toys sold fast-food meals and vice versa. The best example is the *Star Wars* phenomenon. No American parent or child missed George Lucas's trilogy of *Star Wars* films between 1977 and 1983 or the merchandising mania that accompanied it. By 1987, some 94 figures and 60 accessories had been manufactured by Kenner. While the first two *Star Wars* movies earned $870 million at the box office, by 1983 licensed products had pulled in $2 billion.[39] The lessons learned through *Star Wars* were used again and again in highly orchestrated commercial festivals built around PLCs and Disney movies in the 1980s and 1990s.[40]

Children's goods became part of a new era of fast capitalism — the increasingly rapid shift from one product line to another on virtually a global scale. Toys and other children's products functioned less as vehicles connecting generations or linking past and future in the way that parental gifts once had done. Increasingly, kids' stuff was part of a separate fantasy world that children and the merchandisers alone understood and that was designed to stimulate unending desire for more.

Video games were another example of fast commercial play. By 1981, the video arcade business took in $7 billion with the allure of excitement, escape, and control. Many adults complained about how video games seemed to encourage aggression and even petty thievery to feed the obsessive habit of pouring quarters into machines. Some communities banned minors unaccompanied by a parent from entering video arcades. Much of this reflected a perennial concern about congregations of teens at play. But video games were really part of a wider phenomenon — an ephemeral consumer culture that took time from developmental activities and isolated kids from reality in a fantasy world of fun. The video craze went through wildly shifting cycles of boom and bust. The industry had peaked by 1983 when kids got tired of the relatively primitive games available and abandoned their Atari electronic consoles and the arcades for MTV or action figures and the cartoon shows that told their toy tales. By the end of the 1980s, video games were back with much more realistic images and more challenging Nintendo cartridges for playing Mario and other games. Video became not only more visually appealing but also more intense and realistic in the violence portrayed. The thrill of "beating" a level of the Mortal Combat or Doom game, or even surviving the unrelenting attacks from alien monsters or "incoming enemy aircraft," made the game compelling and, for some, addictive. Social play (tag or hide and seek) hardly compared with video games for thrills, and the digital gadgets did not require the frustration and risk of relating directly to others. These video games isolated children in fantasy — as many consumer goods did for adults.[41]

Even public children's television played the marketing game in a big way in the 1990s. Though the PBS *Sesame Street* characters were turned into toys only after the series was a hit in the 1970s, merchandising was part of the original plan for *Arthur*, another PBS morning show in the 1990s. Creator Marc Brown was at first wary of mass marketing his characters. He felt that his program was different from the violent fantasy of the *Power Rangers* because it portrayed children's everyday problems. Eventually, however, in order to support his programming costs, he relented, licensing Arthur for 22 products including T-shirts and dolls. The guilty conscience was still there, but the decline of public support for public programming made it short-lived.[42]

In the 1980s and 1990s, commercial interests increasingly invaded another once sacred space of childhood, the classroom. With pressures on school budgets and demands for electronic aids in education, the traditional vaunted barrier between consumerism and the classroom was firmly breached. In 1989, Chris Whittle stepped in to offer Channel One to public schools. Whittle provided a flashy 12-minute information program in

The video arcade drew the young into the solitary challenges displayed on the electronic screen in the late 1970s. (Library of Congress)

classrooms along with loans of up to $50,000 worth of video equipment. The catch was that the program came with 2 minutes of youth-oriented ads. Some educators criticized Channel One for dishing up fluff (at first, 40 percent of programming featured sports). The producers were more interested in surveying teenage consumption patterns to attract advertisers than in providing educational programs. This captive classroom audience was an opportunity for merchandisers to reach a very profitable market. In 1996, American's 22.2 million teenagers spent $7.5 billion during the holiday season alone. That year, 40 percent of American teenagers saw ads for Nintendo video games, soft drinks, and blue jeans in this authoritative classroom environment. Since the 1920s, American companies had used the allure of free educational materials to promote their brand names and products in American schools. But the effort to reach the young was redoubled in the 1980s and 1990s, and all subtlety was dropped. General Mills sent 8,000 teachers a science program entitled *Gushers: Wonders of the Earth* that taught children about volcanos by using Fruit Gushers candy as an illustration. The makers of Prozac passed out promotional material and provided speakers for "depression awareness" programs in high schools. In the mid-1990s, 350 corporations had developed similar blends of commerce and education that reached children 63 million times a year.[43]

The outrage that would have once kept a Channel One out of the classroom survived in consumer response to another marketing scheme. In the early 1990s, TV ads begged children to call 900 numbers to hear Santa stories or the voices of beloved story characters. One study saw near-universal disapproval of this scheme. When children were exposed to PLCs and character licensing, parents were still there to monitor their "urge" to jump into the commercial pool. By contrast, the 900 number played on the ignorance of the child, often when parents were away and learned about the "transaction" only when they got the bill for the call. It took general public outrage and government regulation in 1993 to stop this extraordinary affront to the "innocence" of the child.[44] While Americans had tolerated a massive assault of telemarketers on the sanctity of the home and even the commercialization of the classroom, they drew the line at the 900 number's threat to the authority and pocketbooks of parents. A rare exception.

Breaking Boundaries: Shopping as Leisure

While consumption became play for kids, shopping became entertainment for adults. The contemporary American obsession with buying cheap and fast was hardly new. It had been behind the success of Sears's mail order catalog in the 1900s, the A & P chain grocery store in the 1910s, and "Big Bear, the Price Crusher" in the 1930s. Personal contact with sales staff had been in decline from the days of the first name-brand packages and self-service stores. Still, the obsession with getting much for little has been refined to a fine art since the 1970s.

When Sam Walton opened his Wal-Mart Discount City in rural Arkansas in 1962, he was an unknown in a mass movement of variety and department stores into discounting. While Kmart dominated the suburban shopping centers of the 1960s and 1970s, Wal-Mart earned retail crumbs in rural America. But by offering prices below what small-town hardware and variety stores needed to charge to stay in business, Walton built a chain of 25 stores by 1971. Compared to Kmart's 488 outlets, Wal-Mart was still a bit player. In the 1980s, however, as Kmart stores aged and failed to modernize, Wal-Mart stepped in. By the time Sam Walton died in 1990, he had become America's richest man (family wealth at $23 billion). He combined team enthusiasm among his 380,000 employee "associates," folksy touches like the "Wal-Mart greeters," and "everyday low prices," made possible by high-tech inventory controls and purchasing. By 1990, there were already about 2,000 Walton stores of various kinds, and 160 more were being built each year. Walton's country-style informality disguised his subversion of small town society. Wal-Marts robbed main streets of their previous vitality — not just as commercial centers, but as sites of social and cultural interaction. Some regions, especially in upper New England, kept Wal-Marts out, but most Americans embraced the thrill of endless shelves of stuff sold at low prices.[45]

Warehouse superstores like Price Club and Sam's Club followed the lead of the general discounter. In exchange for an annual membership fee, shoppers gained access to a variety of dry goods and often prepared and frozen foods sold cheaply in austere warehouse-style buildings. In 1989, 72 percent of San Diego shoppers had visited a Price Club. Sprouting on the edges of suburbs were other, nonmembership warehouse stores that specialized in auto parts, office supplies, electronic equipment, and home-improvement products. The Auto Giant chain, for example, offered 60,000 square feet of warehouse-style shopping for the do-it-yourselfer. Even average supermarkets carried about 30,000 different products in 1996, up from 17,500 in 1986 and about 9,000 in the mid-1970s. Variety and quantity as much as price attracted consumers, and the sheer size and range of these superstores encouraged people to buy. Food retailers sometimes complained about the difficulties in keeping track of the 7,000 new items introduced each year in the 1980s, but computerized inventory methods made it possible for them to meet the increasingly diverse and changing wants of American consumers.[46]

Discount warehouse shopping was a radical change from the old social ritual of making the rounds of family-owned stores. But this new-style shopping was about more than getting stuff cheaply; it remained an experience, not just a transaction, even if very different from the personal intimacy of the old town center. In the 1980s and 1990s, shopping centers offered packaged sensations, divided by age and lifestyle. The enclosed shopping mall was a culmination of car-dependent consumption that had begun in the 1920s. The opening of Southdale, the first climate-controlled shopping mall near Minneapolis in 1955, heralded a new era. The shopper could not only escape the weather but also experience a "retail drama," staged in a setting that combined the look of an amusement park, hotel lobby, and elegant train station. In the 1980s, the mall with its carefully orchestrated sensations had completely triumphed over main street shopping. By 1985, 78 percent of Americans went to a large enclosed mall at least once a month. When the Mall of America in suburban Minneapolis opened in 1992, retail experts were skeptical that investors could recoup their billion-dollar investment. After all, this was a facility of 4.2 million square feet of retail floor space, big enough to fit within its walls 34 average-sized American shopping centers. Forty million visitors per year would be required for the Mall of America to make a profit. Many feared that it was too big and bargain hunters would not buy or go often enough to keep the 250 shops and 4 department stores busy.[47]

Soon the doubters were proven wrong. The Mall of America showed that entertainment and shopping could be successfully combined. The interior of the mall was divided into four "streets," each with its own decorative theme (from European-style train station to main street America). The mall even contained two indoor lakes. To meet the entertainment needs of the whole family, it had an amusement park with 23 rides, a giant aquarium (holding 15,000 fish), a Lego Imagination Center (with interactive Lego models of a whimsical, three-level factory), an 18-hole miniature golf course, a 14-screen theater, and numerous nightclubs and restaurants. Developers included ample toilet facilities to prevent early departures. Comfort, convenience, and variety kept people in the mall for hours. "Themed" clubs and eateries were there to create a particular mood or sensation, no matter the season, including America's Original Sports Bar, Knucklehead's Comedy Club, Gatlin Brothers Music City, Gators Dance Club, Hooters Restaurant, Planet Hollywood, Napa Valley Grille, and Rainforest Cafe. Mall operators saw themselves as impresarios of "shoppertainment" or "entertailing." They even addressed the problem of roving youth gangs with a rule that required children under 16 years old to be accompanied by an adult over 21 years of age. The Mall of America combined shopping, entertainment, and a pleasant, unthreatening crowd experience. No wonder it became a tourist spot (with almost 40 percent of visitors living more than 150 miles away in 1995).[48] Shopping had become leisure, even a vacation. The difference between the mall and the museum, collecting artifacts and accumulating consumer goods, had nearly disappeared.[49]

Indeed, the distinction between "ordinary" shopping and "special" vacation touring lessened in the 1980s and 1990s. Central to both was the consumption of experience, simultaneously more common and yet more diverse than ever before. Americans of all ages and most incomes boarded airplanes and regularly flocked to mass tourist centers. American adults took 45 percent more trips at least 100 miles from home in 1995 than they had 10 years earlier. Moreover, of the 544 million airline tickets sold in 1995 (up from 381 million in 1985), 70 percent were for pleasure. Americans crowded into conventional tourist sites in massive numbers. In 1997, Las Vegas, with its must-see casino resorts like Excalibur and Caesar's Palace, attracted 30 million tourists who spent $9.9 billion. Its opposite (but also twin), Walt Disney World of Orlando, Florida, had been in business only since 1971 but had become the greatest single tourist draw in the country by 1990. Its Magic Kingdom amusement park, Epcot Center with futuristic and international exhibits, Animal Kingdom, and MGM movie-based theme park brought in 28.4 million tourists in 1990. The Disney complex was far more than a collection of rides and uplifting exhibits modeled after modern world's fairs. In the 1980s and 1990s, company executives made Disney World an enveloping experience by adding golf courses and other sports facilities. Hotel resorts — from the low-priced "All-Star Movie Resort" with images of characters from *101 Dalmatians* and *Toy Story* for the young family to the upscale fantasy "Polynesian Resort" — kept visitors in Disney's world for nearly a week per visit. Las Vegas and Orlando were artificial tourist sites that offered well-orchestrated and intense play environments with little of the "travail" of traditional travel. Manufactured thrills and sensual delights (of different kinds) were combined with reasonable comfort and predictability in mass tourist sites that were not dependent upon natural or historic beauty. Moreover, they were easily expanded to accommodate increased crowds: Disney had scarcely developed half of its land in the barrens of central Florida, and the desert was no obstacle for Las Vegas, a town that ballooned into a center of 880,000 by 1999.

By contrast, many of the traditional venues of tourism like Hawaii were very much in danger of overdevelopment. Visitors to these tiny island jewels rose from 263,000 in 1973 to a peak of almost 7 million in 1990. Success brought disillusionment: in 1990, only a quarter of American visitors said they would return because of overcrowding. Other must-see sites like Niagara Falls found that jaded tourists no longer were interested in "merely" an amazing view of nature; by 1992, scarcely half of the hotel rooms were filled.[50]

Alternative tourism was one solution for people who had already "been there, done that" and sought a less crowded beach. Some new travel took the form of "eco-tourism" to distant Amazon villages or jungle huts in the Yucatan, far from the beaches and clubs where traditional tourists went. Most alternative tourism was simply sophisticated niche marketing to the well-traveled consumer eager for something new. These tourists visited Mongolia, Bangkok, Antarctica, and even Kansas. Europeans were perhaps more daring (note the German tourists who journeyed to famous sites of ecological disasters in the United States), but Americans who had already been to Notre Dame Cathedral and seen the Grand Canyon also looked harder for new and personalized experiences. A growing market for "soft adventure" touring emerged in the 1990s — combining exertions like whitewater rafting by day with comfortable hotel rooms and gourmet dinners at night. A few opted for the excitement and discomfort of reenacting Civil War battles. Still others ventured into "volunteer vacations," combining pleasure visits to poor but exotic countries with charity work or joining in archaeological digs. More avoided the summer crowds (and the kids) by touring in the autumn. In 1989, 117.7 million such trips were taken in the fall months, compared to 145.5 million in the summer.[51]

Americans increasingly opted for shorter (often weekend) getaways rather than the long annual vacation. They did not enjoy the greater number of holidays that Europeans experienced in the 1960s and 1970s. Americans had an average of only 13 days' vacation per year in the 1990s, as compared to 35 days in Germany and 42 in Italy. In fact, the length of vacation travel decreased in the late 1980s (from 5.7 nights away from home to 4.7). Increasingly tight work schedules made the 1950s family tradition of touring national parks by station wagon impossible. Instead, Americans bought weekend package deals at resorts and city hotels, and took them more frequently. Regular doses of escape and experience were a break from often exhausting weekends of cleaning and shopping, but also so frequent as to make the vacation a part of "everyday life."[52]

New retail and tourism venues surely spurred a spending spree, but so did greater disposable incomes, especially for the rich. Ironically, public policy designed to encourage savings and investing did more to encourage consumption. Despite the expectations of the supply-siders, the personal savings rate dropped from 9 percent of annual income in the mid-1970s to 2.8 percent by 1986. While spending grew in real terms by 21 percent between 1980 and 1986, income increased only 17.6 percent. Rising consumer debt made up the difference. Installment debt payments rose from 7.3 percent of annual disposable income in 1950 to 15.5 percent in 1980, climbing still higher to 18.8 percent in 1987. By 1997, consumer debt — not including mortgages — reached the all-time high of $1.25 trillion.[53]

America's economic leaders showed the way. The winners in the new winner-take-all economy had a strong incentive to keep up with the Michael Milkens. Thrift was hardly encouraged by the federal government under Reagan, which increased the national debt by 1.5 trillion (from a trillion-dollar debt base in 1980). Not even conservative economist Milton Friedman had much to say about saving. Occasionally the *Wall Street Journal* published an old-fashioned condemnation of "national self-indulgence," the borrow-and spend practices of the supply-siders in Washington, but this was little more than a gesture. Even the traditional child's piggy bank disappeared. In the 1980s, shopping had become a seduction. One marketing expert, Dennis Rook, noted the similarity between the urge to buy and the feeling of "falling in love." Shoppers at checkout counters heard "candy bars calling out" to them. Consumers sometimes tried to substitute "bad" purchases with "good," less expensive, less fattening ones. They felt that they had to buy *something* when the impulse struck them. Rook found 80 percent often felt guilty after a buying trip. Spending itself had become an obsession.[54]

By the 1980s, shopping had finally lost its place as a distinct social ritual. Instead, the object became having, and having as much as possible. The exotic experience of purchased events and moods, once isolated to Coney Island or fairs, became as accessible as the local mall. Underlying the compulsion to spend was the need to purge oneself of money. The clearest example of this was the dramatic rise in legal gambling in the late 1970s. After legal gambling had been isolated for decades in the distant deserts of Nevada, New Jersey allowed casino gambling in Atlantic City in 1978. Within a decade, Indian reservations (free from laws governing gambling) opened casinos; by 1994, gambling centers (Indian and otherwise) were operating in 23 states, many near population centers, and their patronage more than doubled between 1990 and 1993. Opportunities to gamble were available in a wide variety of settings — slot machines in rural South Dakota bars, casinos nested in new family resorts in Las Vegas, roadside gaming on Indian reservations in Wisconsin, greyhound races in Illinois, riverboat gambling on the Mississippi River, and church bingo almost everywhere. This shift was encouraged by the often-repeated argument, "if we don't, our neighbors will." Promoters claimed that sick regional economies would be revitalized by this new industry, and revenue that otherwise would be siphoned off by other states and communities would remain at home. The logic of unrestricted markets and competition was fully realized in the gambling boom.

Public authorities joined the business instead of restraining it. Soon after New Hampshire revived its state lottery in 1964, others followed. The neighboring states of Massachusetts and New York offered their own lotteries to avoid the drain of income into New Hampshire. Far from being watchdogs, governments encouraged gambling through massive ad campaigns for their own lotteries. Even when Iowa limited the scope of gambling on riverboats, Mississippi tried to get an edge by eliminating all restrictions. When a game lost its novelty, new ones appeared. Casino operators replaced slow-paced and sociable card games with more intense, individualized, and thus more profitable machine games. The older pattern of isolating gambling to special places and times (as in the vacation spree to Las Vegas) gave way to off-track betting sites and to 24-hour casinos available near every large population center. The ultimate in making gambling immediately accessible to the impulse bettor may be Internet gambling. While antigambling groups were beginning to slow the spread of this industry in the mid-1990s, betting had become a way of life in many communities. Both the private gambling industry and state lottery commissions had become "dream merchants" selling the ultimate consumerist fantasy — effortless wealth.[55]

The conservative 1980s and 1990s were really not so conservative after all. During these years, the vestiges of Victorian constraint nearly disap-

This image of the bank of slot machines so typical of Reno, Nevada in 1964 would spread across the land in the late 1980s. (Library of Congress)

peared. Few cared to separate private life and childhood from the market, make a virtue of simplicity, or even delay gratification. Increasingly, home became a market terminal and child's play and adult leisure were reduced to spending. In such a society, it was easy to sell the notion that legalized gambling was the only alternative to a stagnant economy.

The Self-Regarding Consumer

The 1980s and 1990s saw not only expanded markets and broken boundaries but also greater income inequality and with it a more dynamic, fragmented, and even obsessive consumerism. A personalized form of consumption that had begun to segment gender and generation in the 1960s accelerated in the 1980s. The Reaganites hoped not simply to make the rich richer but to encourage work, investment, and growth via the "supply side." On the face of it, the policy was the opposite of the self-indulgent, "demand-side," Democratic approach of the 1960s and 1970s. Instead, the conservative formula helped to produce both hard workers and hard spenders, so often symbolized by yuppies. *Newsweek* in 1984 proclaimed them as the new wave. However, they were also roundly castigated. The Right condemned them as the latest additions to the "new class," a band of lawyers and hip entrepreneurs who patronized cocaine dealers and had abortions instead of assuming "normal" family obligations. The Left saw them as opportunists, disdainful of the hurts of the Rust Belt and blue-collar workers, liberal on cultural and social issues but as selfish as any tax-evading plutocrat when it came to their bulging pocketbooks. Magazines published dozens of stories about yuppies. These childless couples, some of whom had become millionaires in their twenties through investing other people's money, gloried in their matching 900 Turbo Saabs and BMW motorcycles. With obligations to nothing but meeting their own increasingly exquisite desires, yuppies patronized new trend-setting fashion houses. Ralph Lauren's Polo brand promised a quick fix of prestige for the yuppie nouveaux riches. More solid routes to status were provided by the Vuitton shops that offered the international elite name-brand luxury goods.[56] Demographers pointed out that yuppies were hardly typical members of the baby boom generation (perhaps 4 out of 78 million in the mid-1980s). But this hardly mattered in the public mind. The yuppie was a convenient target of concerns that crossed the ideological divide — worry that American consumer culture had become terminally self-cen-

AT HOME AMONG RICHES Sparkling celebrations! She gives him tradition. Our exclusive, suave smoking jacket from Trylon. In navy cotton velvet, with shawl collar; for S,M,L or XL sizes. 165.00 He gives her pure platinum. Christian Dior's captivating satin jacquard caftan. Full-length, in polyester for petite, small, medium or large sizes, 120.00 The spirit starts at home. The Men's Shop and Loungewear

The ad image from Bonwit Teller of the yuppie — youthful and luxurious.
(*The New Yorker*, Dec. 3, 1984, p. 33)

tered. Their luxury was neither contained to the home nor tempered with charity and community service.[57]

The radical individualist was hardly new, but the yuppie's personal indulgence was justified by endless hard work. No one in this aspiring group admitted to doing just one thing at a time. Yuppies bought expensive pagers, cell phones, laptop computers, audio tapes, and exercise equipment so that there never would be "down time" or minutes wasted on mere leisure. When some counterculturalists had shifted from pot to cocaine, they had also learned to work. Midge Decter could hardly complain about that. Moreover, work not only became a justification for pleasure but was joined with it in "time-saving" luxuries. This was the opposite of the traditional "leisure class" lifestyle of Veblen, in which the elite reveled in time-wasting activities like golf. Yuppies worked out on Nordic Tracs while watching business news. Work no longer served as a check on indulgence, a guarantor of self-control and simplicity. The traditional division between the honest laborer and the idle rich had disappeared. Work and spend, the couplet that made consumer culture run, was refined to a new intensity. In the name of economic and personal freedom, the cultural truces that had slowed down status-seeking spending had largely been abandoned. Steeply graded income taxes disappeared; blue laws and controls over gambling and TV ads were gone. The competitive spirit at work had spread to leisure and consumption.[58]

The dogma of the 1980s was that sharply unequal incomes and national economic growth were Siamese twins. This doctrine justified any level of wealth and led Americans to form unrealistic hopes for personal achievement. Economist Juliet Schor shows how Americans in the 1990s were no longer comparing themselves with neighbors but with people, often celebrities, earning three or four times their income. TV programs like *Lifestyles of the Rich and Famous* contributed, no doubt, to this illusion, as did attempts of fashion designers to extend their market downward. Encouragement to identify with media "friends" rather than real-life associates made the old American myth that common people could have anything more pervasive and ultimately more frustrating. In the 1990s, surveys showed that 27 percent of people earning over $100,000 per year believed that they could not afford the "basics." This confirmed the old theory that wealth produced only more wants. The idea of the "good life" had shifted even within the few years between 1975 and 1991. The number of Americans expressing the need for a happy marriage declined from 84 to 77 percent of people surveyed, while those requiring wealth rose from 38 to 55 percent. As late as 1986, average Americans felt $50,000 was enough to fulfill their dreams. By 1994, it was $102,000, the level of the richest in the middle class. In the 1920s, the terraces on the side of the hill on which Americans found their place as consumers had rounded corners (as Robert Lynd had noted); by the 1990s, however, the view up and down the spending incline was utterly unimpeded.[59]

Part of this change was simply the refinement of an old practice — spending for display. Americans had lost none of their skill in reading the status of others through the clothes they wore and the cars they drove (even if the "vocabulary" became more subtle). Rising standards, especially when accompanied by growing income inequality, only accentuated emulative consumption. As the hierarchy of income became more steep, the anxieties that caused people to spend grew. In turn, consuming both eased and deepened the hurt of a status society. This had been true throughout the century; however, the tensions creating the need to spend were, if anything, greater by the 1980s when keeping up with neighbor Jones was transformed into emulating the millionaire Trump, known only through the media.

At the same time, yuppie trend-setters marched down still another century-old path. By the late 1980s, journalists discovered that boomers were turning into their parents — domesticated "couch potatoes." Magazine ads for cigarettes shifted from luxurious and exotic settings to backdrops featuring casual groups of friends. Marketers pushed domestic luxuries like big-screen TVs, upscale VCRs, and personal computers as well gourmet gardening and home exercise equipment. When many yuppies eventually settled down with children, the "cocooning" trend continued.[60] This was hardly a return to the "golden days" of the 1950s, with shared family TV and barbecue. Of course, the cocooner, yuppie or otherwise, did not exactly live the dream of Hugh Hefner's Playboy Mansion (or Bill Gates's hypergadgeted estate, with its 45,000 square feet of living space). Still, the median size of new homes had increased from 1,385 square feet in 1970 to 2,000 by 1999; nearly half had 2.5 baths or more, compared to only 20 percent in 1978. Increasingly, each member of the family had their own stuff and a room to put it in. Consumer cocooning in the 1990s was another phase in a culture of self-enveloping spending.[61]

Certainly, the greatest consumer innovation to foster this inwardness was the personal computer. Like the radio and TV, it promised to open the world to its users. Until the late 1970s, computers were too large and expensive for more than business or military use. Then the silicon chip replaced the miles of wire and thousands of vacuum tubes once required for digital processing and memory. When Apple Computer and Commodore Business Machines introduced the first effective personal computers (PCs) in 1977 and IBM offered theirs in 1981, they appealed primarily to the hobbyist or home businessperson, offering little obvious value as an everyday home appliance. Three major improvements in the PC changed people's minds. First, when Apple introduced the Macintosh in 1984 and Microsoft followed with its Windows software in 1985 for IBM computers, PCs became much more "user friendly." These new systems replaced complex typed-line commands with the "mouse" allowing users to point and click on screen icons or pictures. Then, an explosion of software introduced new practical and fun uses for computers (from word and data processing and information retrieval to arcade and adventure games). Spending on software rose from $140 million in 1981 to .6 billion in 1984. The possibilities were greatly enhanced with the introduction of data storage devices like hard drives in the mid-1980s and CD-ROM players in the early 1990s. Finally, when the Internet appeared in 1983 to link academic and government computers via phone and satellite, it was far too technical for home use. By the mid-1990s, however, gaining access to the Internet became child's play with easy-to-use graphic interfaces provided by companies like American Online and Netscape. Within a very short time, fast modems made "surfing the net" and sending e-mail messages an obsessive leisure-time activity for millions.[62]

The striking thing about the computer market was its amazingly fast turnover, unlike anything in the history of consumer goods. Fashion did not drive annual purchases of new computers or accessories. Rather, incessant upgrading of one or all components created a constant demand for replacements. The 16-bit "286" processor of 1982 was followed by the 32-bit "386" in 1985, the "486" in 1989, and the Pentium in 1993. Software was routinely updated every 18 months, and new versions would work only on faster processors with more memory and larger-capacity hard drives. The PC created an ever-deepening technological hole into which forward-minded users (or even those simply trying not to be obsolete) poured thousands of dollars in a ceaseless effort to keep "up to standard." Never before has a consumer product become obsolete so fast in so many different ways. Nevertheless, consumers accepted this burden because with each successive purchase they received more bang for their buck, even if many did not understand what exactly they were getting and might have little use for it. The still broader impact of the PC was that it took the inward/outward culture that began with the radio to a new height. The PC user became the supremely isolated participant in an ephemeral global culture. With a home computer attached to the Internet, an individual could "interact" with millions of other users via web pages, chat groups, and e-mail. That the Internet made the consumer less passive and created a whole new meaning for the word "choice," there can be no doubt. That it contributed to the isolation of the individual, like the video game, "Walkman" entertainment unit, and the personal TV, also cannot be denied.[63]

To be fair, consumerism did not fragment American life so much as reinforce a continuing social process. As media scholar Joseph Turow observed, advertisers had once helped overcome cultural differences by pushing mass-market goods like Coca-Cola and jeans. From the 1980s, however, admakers began to "separate audiences into different worlds according to distinctions that ad people feel make the audiences feel secure and comfortable." New lifestyle clusters, more numerous and distinct than the older regional or class categories, suggested the need for more focused ads. Magazines pioneered the techniques of targeting ads by linking readers with special interests like antique cars, fashions, or sports to advertisers selling to people with those enthusiasms. By the 1970s, TV, that bastion of mass marketing, was also beginning to give in to the logic of fragmented markets.[64]

The coming of cable TV was the critical factor. By adding numerous channels to the existing three networks, cable undermined the logic of "broad"casting. When there were only three competing channels, the networks had incentive to seek the maximum proportion of a mass market and offered programming that appealed to the common denominator, not to specialized audiences. With a much greater number of channels, the advantage went to those able to identify specialized viewers (lovers of sports, business news, country music, old movies, etc.) and link them with advertisers seeking narrow markets. For example, from 1981 MTV targeted teenagers and young adults with popular music videos and age-appropriate ads. Beginning in 1984, Nickelodeon focused on children's programs with ads for kids' stuff like toys and sugared breakfast cereals. The Lifetime Channel was supposed to appeal to adult women, while ESPN, a sports channel, went after the beer and fast car crowd. Cable TV offered channels that reached most market fragments and directed Americans through a consumerist life course as their interests changed. This strategy was made far easier by the fact that by 1996 cable reached 67 percent of American homes. Even more important, by 1995, 66 percent of American homes had three TVs, and more than half of teenagers had sets in their own rooms. One reporter found a family with eight TVs, at least one turned on from 6 A.M. to 11 P.M. This household even had a set placed in the room of an infant. Everyone in the family had their own channels, and often could watch them separately. So attractive was "narrowcasting" to cable TV companies that MTV could air *Beavis and Butt-Head*, a program featuring two obnoxious cartoon characters who greatly annoyed parents while delighting rebellious teenagers, with the expectation that the show would drive away unwanted age and cultural groups.[65]

Cable marketing techniques, in turn, shaped the full commercialization of the Internet in the late 1990s. Special interest sites attracted highly specialized advertising. Businesses attempted to create a loyal corps of customers with their own web pages. The most personal preferences and desires were fulfilled in online auction services like E-Bay and Onsale. Search engines like Yahoo peppered the computer screen with ads tailored to the desires of each user. Internet service providers like American Online offered shopping channels that led, click by click, to electronic sites that fit the most discriminating of tastes.[66]

Fragmented culture and targeted advertising reinforced each other. It is hard not to agree with Turow that this narrowcast advertising and programming "will allow, even encourage, individuals to live in their own personally constructed worlds, separated from people and issues that they don't care about or don't want to be bothered with." Even though this made selling easier, it encouraged personal cocooning and did little to create a sense of a common culture. Individual access to personal video, audio, and computer devices increasingly meant that each family member had their world of entertainment and corresponding room full of goods.[67]

Of course, the new media and advertising strategies by themselves did not create a fragmented society and family. Cultural and political divisions dating from the 1960s echoed down the decades. In the 1990s, the conservative religious and moral messages of the Family Channel were just a click away from the youthful and self-indulgent rebellion of MTV. The 1960s had encouraged a "democratization of personhood," with groups like gays, the elderly, and nature lovers all wanting their own "cultural space" and gratification of their desires. These identities were at first expressed in political or social terms, but gradually they became consumer markets. Once again, goods met needs more easily and more directly than did ideas or a physically real community.[68]

Markets were especially fragmented along the lines of choices women made regarding marriage, family, and career. By 1985, advertisers divided women into eight consumer clusters, up from four in the early 1980s. They found some forty lifestyle groups, often identified by zip codes. Direct marketers, long associated with patent medicines and real estate schemes, gained respect in business as they became more efficient in designing target lists. The frequent flyer promotion (first appearing in 1981) linked free airline tickets for loyal customers to related services like car rentals, telephone service, and hotel rooms. Marketing professionals used surveys and purchase records to track customer preferences. Even the ordinary supermarket developed sophisticated methods of accommodating specialized regional tastes and adapting to changing needs with new services like deli food sections, gourmet coffee beans, and vegetarian and "natural" specialties. By the late 1980s, experts advised managers to abandon coupons and loss-leading sales for specialized mini-markets within the supermarket.[69]

Marketing specialists found also that consumers shifted group identities as they aged and simply changed taste. Women were "moving targets" who had to be identified through sophisticated demographic and marketing analysis. Advertisers recognized that women bought cars and cosmetics for many different reasons, depending upon their work and family situations as well as their views about feminism. Teenage affluence and influence over family continued to be targeted. Thanks to elder Americans' greater life expectancy and increased access to pensions and investment income, *Modern Maturity* and other magazines gained a still larger share of advertisers.[70]

Fragmenting markets may have been just a sign of greater choice and personal freedom in the 1980s and 1990s, merely the logical extension of youth breaking from parents and individuals rebelling against often oppressive ethnic, racial, and class backgrounds. The sometimes deadening conformity of the 1950s had been defeated. Still, it would be incorrect to say that lifestyle spending freed individuals from imitation or status seeking. Americans read others through their goods just as much as before. The old code that defined the status of Chevy owners as "low" and Cadillac owners as "high" had become more complex, but it was still there in the new consumerism.

Most important, the shift from social to individual meanings of goods may have impeded political participation. Active democracy requires cooperation between large groups of people who do not know and may not entirely trust each other. As historian Liz Cohen showed, a common consumer culture may have helped Chicago laborers of differing ethnic groups and even skill levels to communicate with each other and to form effective unions during the New Deal. The fragmented character of the new consumerism, fully developed in the 1980s and 1990s, has made such collaboration much more difficult. It has undermined the coalition building and compromise necessary to formulate clear public policy. Multiple and changing lifestyles may have contributed to political impotence and stalemate.[71]

Late twentieth-century consumerism turned social problems into individual purchasing decisions. For example, the growth of gated communities, especially in southern California and Florida, and homeowners' associations allowed some property owners to secede from the union, or at least local governmental control. These associations, whose power was enforced through property deeds, commonly outlawed trucks in driveways and backyard clotheslines to maintain a "classy" look in the neighborhood. Often they did far more, controlling private security forces and denying outsiders access to parks and natural beauty. Even local governments in Los Angeles suburbs closed public beaches to nonresidents in the 1980s. Americans increasingly bought into packaged environments instead of engaging in the frustrating politics of making viable communities.[72]

The fragmentation of markets changed the meaning of consumerism. In the early decades of the century, goods often placed people in society and marked the flow of time. By century's end, highly individualized com-

A new trend from Florida, the gated suburban community.   (Robert Levine)

modities separated people from the past and future and divided them from each other. Neither the Left with its appeals to expression and difference nor the Right with its celebration of markets and narrow moral concerns really addressed this reality.

The Ironic End of the Suburban Weekend

At the end of the twentieth century, conservatives were still fighting the "cultural war" that the countercultural 1960s had unleashed. In the 1990s, it was not surprising that many were nostalgic for the 1950s family. Through the distorting lens of memories of *Father Knows Best* TV programs, right-wing moralists painted an image of a golden era to criticize permissive child rearing, sex outside of conventional marriage, abortion, and no-fault divorce. Despite all their resources and efforts, the restoration of family values and self-restraint were no closer in 1999 than they had been in 1980.[73] Indeed, these virtues had receded as the consumer society expanded. Ironically, consumption and the work required to get goods invaded the space and time of the family. Despite its evocation of Victorian family values, the new conservatism's commitment to unbounded individualism and markets reinforced this incursion. Thus new conservatives undermined a core idea that grew out of the Victorian culture they hoped to restore — the suburban weekend.

It was in the home set apart from the calculations, distractions, and moral dangers of work and marketplace that children were to be raised to high standards of character and citizenship. A major point of suburban flight in the 1920s and 1950s was to escape to a place where the market was excluded. Moreover, it was in the honoring of the Sabbath that virtuous habits were to grow. The post-1945 idea of the weekend lost much of its religious origins, but it too promised time free from calculation and hurry. In many ways, the 1950s ideal of a suburban house and a two-day weekend during which to enjoy life as a family was a democratization of what the rich had achieved earlier. Affluence would create a family time and place with station wagons, ranch houses with barbecues, and weekends free from wage earning and housecleaning. This ideal survived into the mid-twentieth century even though it was violated and rejected by many.[74]

Economic change and conservative policies, however, undermined the popular suburban weekend in the 1970s and 1980s. Rising housing costs and increasing income inequality were the most important culprits. Home ownership decreased slightly (from 65.6 percent of households in 1980 to 63.8 percent by 1986) and new suburban construction shifted to the upscale market. In order to compensate for rising mortgages and stagnant wages, many American families accepted an increase in working hours.[75] Another and related response to perceived economic pressures was the entry of married women into the labor market. The figures are well known: the participation of married American women in the workforce increased from 25 percent in 1950 to 41 percent in 1970, rising still further to 50 percent by 1980 and 61 percent by 1996.[76] Moonlighting by both men and women increased 20 percent in the 1980s.[77] The dual-income household also meant less weekend time for families to be together because of the need to do housework on Saturdays or even Sundays. Despite much change in the nature of housework, women still did about 70 percent of it in the 1990s.[78] The wall separating men's market work from women's household chores had been only partially breached.

More than economic pressure on families was involved. The logic of uncontrolled suburbanization (and the consumerism that went with it) actually undermined the suburban ideal. In the 1990s, Irvine, California and other increasingly distant suburbs of major cities differed from their postwar predecessors. They were not bedroom communities linked by freeways to cities but knots of mixed commercial/residential sites lining thoroughfares and freeways that once served as conduits to the central business district. The freeways were packed with vehicles in both directions during nearly all waking hours, while suburban streets and houses were empty during the day because few women remained homemakers. Gone was the old rush hour of married men into and out of the city. In its place was the constant flow of shift workers of both sexes who traveled to and from office and retail jobs in mall/business complexes that grew on the freeway exchanges like moss on a tree. Office jobs, once in the city, followed the retailers out to the suburbs. In the decade after 1976, some 1.1 billion square feet of office space (equal to 40 San Francisco city centers) was built in the suburbs. The economic advantages were obvious — low-cost land, free parking for commuters, and easy access to freeways. Even more important, the new office and light industrial parks were located relatively near their employees, saving them the long, often impossible, commute into the city.[79]

The resulting business sprawl, however, made a mockery of the suburban residential utopia. Efforts to control commercial growth were full of contradictions. As Paul Leinberger and Bruce Tucker note: "Many Amer-

icans . . . . continue to want it both ways: They want inexpensive housing *and* a short commute . . . they want to be close to shopping and
recreational facilities *and* to have a great deal of privacy."[80] The contradiction between the ideal of the domestic retreat and easy access to shopping
and work could not be resolved without compromises that few would
make. The conservative faith in private solutions and unlimited markets
impeded any serious discussion of the problem. Open country and leafy
neighborhoods survived, of course, but less as lived-in spaces where kids
roamed and adults traded tips on gardening and child care than as launching pads into the maze of freeway ramps, parking lots, and big box stores.

Increased hours of shopping also threatened the ideal of the suburban
weekend. The extension of shopping hours reflected the logic of modern
consumerism — satisfying the demand for convenience, immediate gratification, and intense experience.[81] Chain discount stores and fast-food outlets used part-time employees to keep their facilities open during nights
and weekends, times once jealously guarded for family and friends. Self-
employed storekeepers unwilling to forego their own social and family life
became increasingly rare and thus less a force for limiting shop hours. The
result of this trend, of course, was a shift toward weekend work by one or
several members of the family. By the mid-1980s, a quarter of American
employees worked Saturday and an eighth on Sunday. One third of American households had members working different shifts. By the 1990s, two
thirds of U.S. workers clocked more than half of their work day outside the
9-to-5, Monday-to-Friday business shift. Many were teenagers or young
adults with few family responsibilities, but others were parents and spouses
with families to care for.[82]

Extending the logic of weekend shopping was the 24-hour store. As
early as 1974, for example, Pathmark, a New Jersey-based grocery chain,
decided to remain open all hours. Given customers' irregular work schedules and shifting lifestyles, this experiment proved profitable. The practice
spread to pharmacies, print shops, and even discount superstores like Wal-
Mart. Kinko's photocopying stores began offering 24-hour service in 1984,
accommodating students and frantic businesspeople needing printing
done at 3:00 A.M. to meet early morning deadlines. Rite Aid pharmacy officials found that their customers were often too busy with work and family to attend to routine purchases until late at night.[83]

The Victorian notion that some time and place should be free from
commerce took decades to die; it had promised a "peaceful refuge" from
the market, forcing Americans to defer desire and, most important, pledge

themselves to a family life beyond the consuming self. Americans continued to lament the eclipse of the suburban weekend, even if they were unwilling to make the sacrifices that restoring it would demand. The answer to the decline of family values could not be found in mere moral exhortation but in a recognition of how consumer culture, unleashed from traditional constraints, had taken over the family in practical space and time.

The last twenty years of the century provided no solution to the cultural contradictions of capitalism. There was no restoration, as Daniel Bell had hoped, of a balance between the expressiveness and discipline of capitalism. Bell's fears that mass hedonism would destroy bourgeois civilization also proved unfounded. Yet the consumer culture continues to undermine the values long demanded by conservatives and others. If the expressive individualism of the 1960s and 1970s made consumerism less social and more selfish, the free-market conservatism of the 1980s and 1990s accelerated that process. The result was a consumerism unbounded, with no consensus about how or whether to find or protect alternative visions of life. Despite the extraordinary machine of growth and the wonderful satisfactions of affluence, Americans were still left with this dilemma as they faced the twenty-first century.

CHAPTER 7

An Ambiguous Legacy

A t the end of the twentieth century, never had Americans taken critiques of consumer culture less seriously, though that culture may never have needed criticism more. Since the 1960s, consumerism has proved to be resilient, rather easily surviving the challenges of the environmental and economic Left. It has prevailed worldwide over other meaning systems for human life — despite the large swaths of the human population still unable to participate. In the late twentieth century, consumerism continued to ease conflicts between generations, the sexes, and classes just as it had early in the century. Fashion products let children break from adults and bond into peer groups. Houses, cars, and thousands of other goods still resolved a myriad of tensions and contradictory longings — blending nostalgia for the past with anticipations of change. Consumers' festivals and fads brought Americans into communion with each other in wave after wave of media-driven crazes. These may have been lonely crowds, but they were often exciting and seldom intimidating. The endless variation of clothing, travel, and entertainment provided opportunity for practically everyone to find a personal niche, no matter their race, age, gender, or class.

That success, however, obscured significant changes in American consumer culture that since the 1960s have disturbed many. To be sure, those years have not produced rampant hedonism. While limits on obsessive desire for sex and gambling were loosened, social pressure and law have restricted tobacco use. Similarly, indulgence in fatty foods and hard drink became less acceptable in health-conscious circles. Americans continued to shape their consumer culture by rejecting some desires while embracing others.[1] Nevertheless, most of the fences that had confined desire have been torn down. The movement for consumer rights has been marginalized as "big government." The consumer has been reduced to the sovereign shopper with the right to select from store shelves and the duty to spend for the "good of the economy." Buying became freer (with night, weekend, 24-hour telephone and online shopping, and easy credit). By 2000, Americans could purchase practically anything, whenever and wherever they wanted. And they wanted more because they saw, smelled, felt, and heard more every day. Few even tried to separate childhood and personal life from the market. The idea of the "simple life," perhaps never more than a daydream, had almost ceased being even a prick to the conscience. Successful and lucky Americans were locked in a seemingly endless upward spiral of emulation, and the less fortunate were frustrated when they could not follow. By 2000, moderately well-off childless couples did not think twice about building for themselves 5,000- or 6,000- square-foot houses.

More important still, since the 1960s the consumer culture has become less social. While earlier forms of consumerism often balanced appeals to individual freedom with the opportunity to join "consumption communities" and thus create social bonds through goods, the new consumerism has tipped the scale toward the self. Lifestyle vacations and play-things for all ages fragmented the mass-consumption society of the 1950s. Personal goods that filled childrens' unshared bedrooms, adults' private studies, and individuals' cars partially replaced communal dinner tables, TVs, and living spaces, at least among America's more affluent families. Christmas gifts less often conveyed meanings between generations and genders; in general, relatively few products unambiguously created or affirmed social relationships. When taken to extremes, things deprived Americans of their capacity to compromise and communicate with each other. Who needed to work with others when they had a Gameboy video toy or a TV remote?

No longer was a particular bundle of goods and purchased experiences symbolic of having "made it," nor was mass achievement of that standard a mark of social equality. Possessions that allowed consumers to situate themselves in place and time — the starter home, the status car, or the vacation of a lifetime — increasingly become just more feathers in the nest, not emblems of personal rites of passage that evoked a meaningful past or anticipated a joyful future. The child's toy box, full of fantastic plastic figures without any obvious reference to past childhoods or the child's future, only exaggerated the adult world's detachment from history. Goods increasingly undermined social life and detached their users from the flow of time.

Is it any surprise that since 1957, the percentage of Americans reporting being "very happy" has actually declined from 35 to 30 despite much greater affluence? Economist Robert Lane has argued that modern consumer society (and especially TV watching) has contributed to the feeling of isolation and depression.[2] While consumer culture may be universal, social critic Todd Gitlin was not alone in labeling it "weightless," offering "no commonality but the lightest, no visions of the future but more fun."[3] The problem was that commodity communion drove out other social interactions — caring for others, sharing in common traditions, making compromises, and cultivating friendships. It denied responsibility to the past and obligation for the future.

Fate of the Jeremiad

Just as consumerism was becoming more problematic, challenges to this life defined by goods began to lose their hold on the American conscience. The overwhelming power of the market's flood broke through almost all dikes, but the critical tradition did not have very thick walls to begin with. Given its origins in a defensive and largely elitist reaction to the mass-consumption revolution, the jeremiad never understood the dynamics of American consumer culture nor offered realistic alternatives.[4] It failed to appreciate how modern affluence transformed the meaning of desire and ultimately the role of individuality in advanced consumer society. Critics defended high culture by attacking immigrants' street life or mocking small-town and later suburban America. Across the decades came a similar message: politicians and advertisers manipulated placid, fickle, and often frustrated crowds. A mass-production economy created individuals with untrained and materialistic desire and groups where conformity and superficiality reigned. The rare person gifted with spiritual values and with the constancy and self-assurance to stand above the crowd was frustrated with a culture corrupted by mass access to the all-important market. For years, middle-class readers of *Brave New World* or *The Status Seekers* learned that mass-consumption society crushed individualism and that the crowds were easily duped by merchandising appeals to pleasure and position.

Again and again, the jeremiad against consumer culture simply misread how spending worked in peoples' lives. As we have seen, far from developing obsessions and addictions or slipping into the confusion of overhelming numbers of choices, ordinary Americans generally reacted with common sense and good humor to the latest display window. Relatively few became either shopaholics or alcoholics. Even when the system did not deliver the goods during the Depression and World War II, the reaction was not massive resentment or revolution, but quiet personal humiliation at being excluded from the feast and a longing to rejoin it when the opportunity came again, as it did after 1945.[5] Consumption often eased, rather than worsened, social tensions.

Until recently, most intellectuals understood materialistic desire in consumerism as primitive, to be surmounted by a higher spiritual culture. They failed to see the ways in which materialism in the twentieth century had become more complex and how the physical and the symbolic were intertwined in goods. In fact, sophisticated children of immigrants did not use their surplus money to consume larger and larger quantities of traditional items like red meat and buttered potatoes or swill gallons upon gallons of beer. Rather, they abandoned the narrow worlds of their families and ethnic neighborhoods with the aid of new items like Hollywood movies and cars. But gluttony was merely transformed, not spiritualized. There was absolutely no reason for sated "basic" needs to be sublimated into the pleasures of the mind and the fellowship of cosmopolitan communities. More easily, affluence led to new manufactured pleasures like packaged sweets or packaged vacations. At the same time, through advertising and the interactions of the modern consuming crowd, products such as candy, clothes, and cars gained symbolic meaning that blended with their functions as chemical stimulants, body coverings, and transportation appliances. They assumed "spiritual" roles, not in the ascetic sense of the Puritan, of course, but in the feelings of quasi-religious joy and contentment that came when consumers were accepted by others (and themselves) through their goods. In some ways, commodities became valued less for their utility (for they were seldom used up or fully consumed) than for their meaning as markers of status, participation, identity, progress, or memory. In the twentieth century, consumerist desire became less materialistic but not more uplifting.[6]

A few early twentieth-century intellectuals like Simon Patten had hoped that affluence would lead "automatically" to a more democratic society. Through emulative spending, the poor and marginal population might become more like the rich, and thus the social distance between the classes could be reduced. Instead, the elite moved on to new "inventions," increasing distance from the masses. When the people had cars, the rich needed vacation homes. Frustration was inevitable and unrelenting even when the majority enjoyed affluence. They could never catch up, and the closer they seemed to get to the prize, the more humiliating was their inability to grasp it. The second half of the twentieth century proved that the role of luxury goods in defining status hardly decreased as basic needs were met.[7] If mass consumption did not unleash wild desire, neither did it create common longings. Little of what critical intellectuals expected came true; more important, whatever continuing influence they have impedes clearer and more accurate understandings of consumer culture. No wonder few young Americans in 2000 took the jeremiads seriously.

The critics also misunderstood the social meaning of consumerism and greatly overemphasized the capacity of individuals to find alternatives. The view that the consuming crowd was passive was essentially wrong. The masses may not have included heroic individualists like those glorified by writers Ernest Hemingway and Ayn Rand, but they were hardly a faceless throng. Even seemingly conformist suburban bungalows and ranch houses were transformed into personal statements when their owners decorated and remodeled their "little boxes." Far from reducing life to bland uniformity, consumer culture gave shape to life transitions. The very fact that goods changed with each stage made them excellent ways for people to express their longings for new ways of growing up, setting up homes, coping with age, and even remembering a past long gone. None of these responses may have impressed those expecting individual pristine creativity, a goal available to only a few, mostly male intellectuals free from the pressure of family obligations and routine jobs. But they did show that the motive to consume derived from more than just the manipulations of merchandisers or even the need to emulate others.

As we have seen, critics of mass consumer culture often set up an illusory contrast between the grasping and impulsive consumption of the street crowd and the sober and uplifting cultivation of self and family in the home. The twentieth century has shown, however, that crowd pleasures were not nearly so self-destructive and home and individual "integrity" were not nearly so free of the allures of the pleasure market. At the very moment when early twentieth-century critics were fixated on crowds gathering at sporting events, amusement parks, and central business districts, the consuming throng was beginning to disperse into living rooms and cars. Members of the new crowd were separated from each other but simultaneously listening to the same radio and, later, TV programs. The masses adopted the home and family ethic of the bourgeois Progressivists almost as soon as they could afford to do so. The automobile also broke up the street throngs by decentralizing the old urban nexuses of commerce and entertainment. By the 1920s, the central shopping district and resort boardwalk were beginning to give way to highway strip stores and family car trips to Yellowstone. Even talking motion pictures silenced the crowd, making audiences into private persons oblivious to each other as they intently listened and watched their stars. None of these changes ended mass culture, of course; they merely isolated its participants from each other. However, the new culture left the individualistic critique of the consuming crowd in confusion. What sort of "mass" absorbed its obsessions in the living room from radio or TV? What kind of mob longed for privacy and personal choice?

Running through the criticism of consumer culture had been the naive but deeply rooted faith that private family life and the child were fixed seats of constraint and innocence. The simple, spontaneous life, based in a domestic world of personal relationships and freed from the bustle of the marketplace, would prepare the young to withstand the temptations of pleasures "out there." Instead, the home became perhaps the most profitable venue for the merchandiser. The domestic nest, nurtured by the Victorian bourgeoisie, became very well feathered in the twentieth century. Affluence brought larger homes that never seemed large enough to contain their increasing contents. Perhaps empty lives were being filled with full garages. Certainly, affluence hardly encouraged introspection and self-cultivation. Instead, Americans found themselves in and through their personal stuff. While home furnishings promised stability in the wider world of change, appliances heralded innovation. In countless ways, goods shaped and eased relationships between family members. Despite efforts of adults to shelter children from the market, the young had even more reason to join the consumer culture than their elders. Youths found in spending a way of gaining autonomy and identity and of overcoming their insecurities. Even their parents collaborated in the selling of childhood with endlessly frustrating efforts to buy their children's affections. There was no private retreat from the world of consumption.

In the final analysis, the problem of consumer culture was not that it threatened the cultivated individual. This essential assumption of the jeremiad from Veblen to Packard was wrong. Rather, the dilemma was that consumerism worked so well in meeting immediate needs that Americans found it difficult to want or even to conceive of ultimately more satisfying options. Critics had no realistic alternative that balanced the personal and the social as well as did early twentieth-century consumerism. Moreover, their stress on individualism provided no real challenge to the more socially fragmenting commercial culture that emerged later in the century. In a word, the jeremiad offered no functional equivalent to consumerism. Advocates of simplicity and cultivation were far less successful in overcoming the humiliations and divisions of class than was the consumer culture. Too often, the jeremiad defended bourgeois or petty bourgeois culture and disdained the "common" and "chaotic" culture of the street. A cultivated life or a community of shared values and long-lasting commitments might well have been a better choice than consumerism, but how many Americans had the psychological or social resources to pursue them? How could they, in a society still built on class and its humiliations? Why would wage earners ever embrace this middle-class vision when it continuously mocked their taste and ignored their psychological needs? It is not surprising then that the jeremiad against consumer society gradually lost its intellectual and moral force.

In its place emerged a form of democratic capitalism that simply equated expanding desire with higher culture and rejected as elitist and authoritarian any attempt to impose a standard for evaluating affluence. Ironically, the cultural Left in the 1960s and the Right in the 1980s, each in their own way critical of consumer culture, actually helped to tear down the remaining barriers to its penetration into every corner of American society. Some counterculturalists turned into eccentric shoppers. American businesspeople and their press lost their bad consciences and rejected the nanny state. The yuppie symbolized to the Right disdain for personal and family duty and to the Left the abandonment of social responsibility. Both sides hit the mark.

The net effect was a near obliteration of the culture of constraint. By the end of the 1970s, appeals to sacrifice for the sake of the environment or even economic stability were soundly defeated. According to the winners in the 1980 election, only growth without limits was consistent with American optimism and political pragmatism. Jobs depended upon it. The key political question became: "Are you better off today than you were four years ago?" Constraint was only for the poor and marginal, who contributed little to growth. The unquestioned dogma was that unlimited desire guaranteed progress because it induced people to work and innovate. In any case, what else was there?

At the same time, it became fashionable for some academics to rationalize, if not celebrate, these trends. The ascetic, romantic, and elitist naysayers of consumerism made easy targets for ridicule, an all too simplistic response. Celebrants of consumption rejected the very idea of manipulated desire and tossed out the entire culture of constraint, thus abandoning the possibility of reform beyond the market. More important, they ignored or mocked what most Americans believed to be true — that the consumer culture was out of control. Instead of seeking new and more satisfactory ways of addressing that problem, the academic critique of consumerist conformity had turned into a celebration of choice, identity in and through goods. Commercial products no longer promoted passivity and commonness but helped individualists escape the crowd. Even oppressed groups used popular music and fashion to create their own communities and protest the power of the hegemonic classes.[8] In its most extreme form, almost any self-defining pattern of spending was good. This approach merely turned the old anticonsumerist individualism into a consumerist individualism.[9] The problem at the end of the century, however, was not that consumerism suppressed (or fulfilled) the individual but that it denied the social. The new celebration was no more a solution than was the old criticism.

Legacies of Culture Wars

The jeremiad tradition may have failed, but that hardly meant that a cogent critique of and workable alternatives to consumerism were impossible. One problem was the deep divisions between groups still willing to challenge consumer culture, which had long roots in the ideological divisions of the 1960s and 1970s. Time and again critics divided between secular relativists and religious absolutists, between those who stressed socioeconomic reform and those who emphasized personal transformation. At the end of the century, Americans continued to see the problem from two distinct perspectives with origins in the Left-leaning movements of the 1960s and the Rightward causes of the 1980s. Despite some interesting signs of a revived anticonsumerism, these divisions severely limited the effectiveness of any reform.

Inheritors of the 1960s Left continued to defend the environment, consumer rights, and individual expression against a system of unrestrained commercialization. In 1992, for example, Alan Durning of the World Watch Institute reminded Americans that the global environment could not sustain indefinitely the consumption style of its 1.1 billion affluent inhabitants, much less of the 5.5 billion souls trying to imitate that behavior. While growth in per capita use of natural resources and energy had plateaued by the 1990s, the spread of global consumerism threatened to swamp the benefits of greater efficiency. The developed countries had started on a course that would be very difficult to reverse in the future (especially land use built around the automobile). Durning returned to the 1970s idea of limiting growth. He warned that the failure to tax energy to pay social and environmental costs would be criminally imprudent and promised that environmentally sound economies could create jobs and profit. The environmentalists of the 1960s and 1970s may have been too pessimistic about how fast consumerism would deplete resources, but (from the vantage of the 1990s) they stood on firmer ground with their claim that unrestrained consumption would degrade the environment. For Durning, there was one unavoidable question: "How much is enough?" Americans had no understanding of limits or the costs of their failure to set them. His solution was solidly in the earlier environmental tradition — "shifting to high-quality, low-input durable goods" and "seeking fulfillment through leisure, human relationships, and other nonmaterial avenues."[10]

Earlier appeals to consumer rights also returned in the 1990s. Groups like the Center for the Study of Commercialism (CSC), Commercial Alert, and The Center for a New American Dream called for legal and voluntary restraints on the commercialization of American life. Suggested reforms included eliminating tax deductions for advertising, making schools into ad-free zones, and limiting telemarketing to certain hours. Like Michael Pertschuk twenty years earlier, the CSC and Commercial Alert attacked ads directed toward children. Michael Jacobson, founder of the CSC, had come to Washington in 1970 as a volunteer for Ralph Nader and had long led the Center for Science in the Public Interest to promote better nutrition. Commercial Alert was headed by Gary Ruskin, also a latter-day Nader Raider. According to Ruskin,

> the advertising and marketing industries are totally out of control and need to be put back into their place. There are millions of people across the country worried about the elevating of base mercantile values — like marketing, money-grubbing, greed and profits — above more traditional values like home, family, civic duties and religion. So this is an effort to place these low commercial values back into their inferior place among the constellation of more important values.[11]

Despite similarities with the consumer rights movement of the 1960s and 1970s, these organizations were far less influential. Even Ruskin's obvious appeal to social conservatives with the call for restoring family values did not get significant airing in the mass media. Still, these groups voiced a common discontent with consumer culture. They promoted downshifting, a voluntary reduction of spending as a personal response to the previous "decade of excess." Amy Saltzman found a group of ex-yuppies who rejected the idea that individual freedom meant unlimited achievement, power, and wealth. Instead, they embraced the notion that liberty meant "setting limits" and time free from job obligations and haste.[12]

A number of simple-living groups, books, magazines, and websites emerged in the 1990s. Amy Dacyczyn's *Tightwad Gazette*, for example, offered practical advice about living comfortably with old clothes and self-prepared foods. In 1998, PBS producer John de Graaf brought to national public television the documentaries *Affluenza* and *Escape from Affluenza*, chronicling American obsession with consumption and suggesting ways to escape its hold. This series (and its website) appealed to reason and common sense:

> Before you buy, ask yourself: Do I need it? Do I want to dust (dry-clean or otherwise maintain) it? Could I borrow it from a friend, neighbor or family member? Is there anything I already own that I could substitute for it? Are the resources that went into it renewable, or non-renewable? How many hours will I have to work to pay for it?

Instead of going to the mall, *Affluenza* advised, go hiking or volunteer for a school or community group.[13]

It is easy to dismiss these movements as impractical, powerless, or even elitist. For the comfortably well-off to downscale from the security of an affluent past is easier than for the poor to give up material aspirations for their future. And, like their simple living forbearers, advocates of downscaling all too readily ignored the deep psychological and cultural meanings of goods. Durning, for example, insisted that "people do not want cars as such; they buy them to gain ready access to a variety of facilities and locations." But is that true? As we have seen, automobiles met far more than practical needs of transportation. Of course, educating Americans to be wary of the manipulative techniques of advertisers could make them more skeptical shoppers and teach them the environmental costs of unconstrained consumption. Moreover, these movements offered not asceticism but attractive activities like conversation, music, sports, education, and nature hikes to fill the psychological void for those abandoning consumerism. Who could challenge the wisdom of restoring "a culture of permanence — a way of life that can endure through countless generations?" However, this approach may not really answer the question of why most Americans chose malls over museums in the first place.[14] The anticonsumerism of the 1960s had matured in many ways by the 1990s, abandoning the excessiveness of its early expressive individualism and disdain for

An appeal to resistance by an anticonsumerist organization: a call to buy nothing on the traditionally "busiest shopping day of the year," the Friday after Thanksgiving, 1999. (Adbusters)

243

middle-class values, but it had not yet solved the riddle of the culture of consumption.

A still deeper problem remained in 2000. No one really believed that they could challenge the powerful ideologies of growth as progress and unregulated markets as freedom. Advocates of limited growth remembered the fate of Jimmy Carter in 1980 and proponents of "new taxes" recalled what happened to Walter Mondale in 1984. They lost. President Clinton's sex scandal, not the attempt to regulate tobacco sales, dominated the news in 1998.

The dilemma of the Left may be even more profound than political impotence. According to economist Robert Frank, the conspicuous spending of the "winners" during the 1990s was not reducible to greed or spiritual malaise. It was an intelligible, even biologically induced competition for rank. In a society that had sacrificed the rituals of social stability for the commodities of personal mobility, it made sense for the individual to compete through goods. Still, as Frank noted, self-interest did not lead necessarily to the general welfare. Conspicuous consumption racheted up the price and standard of luxury. It forced the sacrifice of *in*conspicuous consumption (like free personal time and public education and services) and added to environmental deficits. Emulative spending meant increased personal indebtedness at the price of savings and only provided short-term happiness. Few, however, would abandon status goods for the long-term advantage of constraint, so the dropout from the emulation game would often be the loser. Personal exhortations would not work. They never had. Instead, Frank proposed a progressive consumption tax. This levy would provide a disincentive to spend on luxury (especially among the rich) and avoid the punitive and often presumptuous policy behind "sin" or other luxury taxes targeted at "bad consumption." This seems sane and conciliatory, utterly different from the posturing and confrontational demands of the 1960s. Yet as Frank admitted, given the political climate of the 1990s, "this tax will prove difficult even to *talk* about publicly, much less to advocate."[15] The anticommercialism of the 1960s Left had survived into the 1990s, but with a sober understanding of its marginal status.

By contrast, followers of the 1980s cultural Right continued to demand self-discipline and defend the sanctity of the family, attacking the aspects of consumer culture that seemed to threaten these values. Despite considerable success in controlling the legislative agenda to prevent a reversal of the Reagan Revolution, conservatives in the 1990s believed that the radical values of the 1960s had won the day. They still understood unbound desire in terms of excessive expectations in government services and payments, as was expressed again in Robert Samuelson's *The Good Life and Its Discontents* (1995): Americans remained dissatisfied despite a steady rise in standard of living because government and big business had so long told them to expect endless economic progress. Like Daniel Bell, who had made a similar argument almost twenty years earlier, Samuelson saw the source of undiscipline in government's pandering to popular demands, not unrestrained markets and a decline of alternatives to consumerism.[16]

At the end of the century, conservatives also defended the innocence of the child and the sanctity of the family. Media critic Michael Medved, for example, believed that sex, violence, vulgarity, and disrespect for adults and religion pervaded commercial entertainment. This was evidence not of degraded taste but of Hollywood executives' perverse desire to challenge traditional morality and sensibilities. The entertainment industry had been taken over by purveyors of the permissive and cynical culture of the 1960s, and Hollywood was unwilling to listen to a public that would buy tickets to more PG-rated films if only more were offered.[17] Despite the general victory of conservative politics, the cultural right continued to feel haunted by the 1960s counterculture. In *The Assault on Parenthood: How Our Culture Undermines the Family* (1996), Dana Mack argued that public school teachers undermined parental authority with sex education classes and psychologists falsely accused parents of abuse when they disciplined their children. Her solution was to withdraw from public institutions and to home school to ensure that parents' religious and moral values shaped their children's minds and emotions. For both Medved and Mack, an elite of cultural subversives worked through the private and public sectors to undermine family values.[18]

Many, but not all, conservatives ignored the deep economic and social causes and consequences of consumerism. Instead, they focused on those parts of the consumer society that directly challenged moral absolutes and religious belief. "Life centered on consumption . . . devoid of meaning," declared conservative jurist Robert Bork, was the "end stage of unconfined individualism," no longer constrained by "religion, morality and law." Writing in 1996, Bork spoke for many on the Right when he claimed "the Sixties may be seen in the universities as a Mini-French Revolution that seemed to fail, but ultimately did not." Kristol's "New Class" of the late 1970s had become the "tenured radicals" of the 1990s. This wily secret society of leftists continued to destroy American culture with their denial of limits. This view of modern consumerism as a conspiracy of indulgent liberals, surely sidestepped deeper causes — especially the responsibility of conservatives for opening once-sheltered portions of life to the market.[19]

A conservative focus on secular subversion had deep roots in American history, but it also reflected relatively new divisions over questions of family, art, religion, and morality. Even more, it was an aggressive assertion of traditionalist values in politics and intellectual life. A culture war pitting "absolute truth" against relativism, tradition against bias for change, supernaturalist belief against science and humanism prevented compromise and cooperation between liberals and conservatives over shared concerns. The movements of the 1960s and the 1980s continued to have their supporters — liberals sought to restrain greed and guarantee a healthy environment, conservatives to control self-indulgent drug use and sex and to protect "family values." As a result, no consensus emerged as to which of these moralities should be enforced or how.[20]

This was not to say that the Left and Right shared no common ground over the question of consumerism. In his book, *Saving Childhood*, Michael Medved argued that precocious exposure to the adult world of consumption deprived children of the opportunity to develop into fully rational human beings. This view had much in common with the writings of Neil Postman and others on the Left side of the ideological spectrum. Both the cultural Right and Left shared the Enlightenment idea that adults must protect children from the adult world of limitless choice in order to prepare them to enter it with self-restraint. Medved's solution was to re-create a quiet, nurturing place in the home where innocence survived in optimism, wonder, and security.[21] Similarly, Dana Mack agreed with liberals like Arlie Hochschild, Sylvia Hewlett, and Cornel West that families needed help to avoid the pressures of consumerism and the overwork that a spending culture necessitated. Both sides supported tax and legal reforms that would encourage parents to reserve more time at home with their children.[22] One might be skeptical that this program for restoring innocence and family life would work. After all, it had been recommended for a century (and more) and had been repeatedly defeated by the consumer market's invasion of the home. Still, no time or place can be free from the market unless the right to innocence and privacy is affirmed.

Other signs that the walls between secular and religious America were not impenetrable could be found in the widening criticism of consumerism in conservative religious circles. Pope John Paul II repeatedly attacked the modern culture devoted to "instant gratification and consumerism." In the 1990s, Rodney Clapp of the conservative Protestant weekly, *Christian-*

ity Today, claimed that market values threatened the mission of the church when religion was sold like breath mints. Modernity's threat to faith came not just from the state but also from the market. The language of consumption "militates against the Christian virtues of patience, contentedness, self-denial, and generosity." Unrestrained consumer desire undermined fidelity in marriage and duty to community. Most significantly, Clapp attacked the old doctrine that material comforts were acceptable if embraced with an "inner detachment from goods." This he saw as nothing but a "complete capitulation to consumerism." Christians needed to abandon the notion that their economic lives were entirely private and instead return to stewardship — taking care of God's good creation and replacing consumer festivals with Christian fasts and thanksgiving.[23] If elements within the Left (like Ruskin above) had begun to acknowledge personal responsibility and family as antidotes to consumerism, so portions of the Right began to see the problem of consumerism as systemic, not merely personal.

Still, as the United States finished the twentieth century, challengers to the consumer culture remained largely stalemated and politically marginal. Americans who learned from birth to identify with an endless parade of goods would not easily appreciate quiet walks in the woods, the pleasures of lifelong friendships, or the deep gestures of acknowledging the grief and joys of others. As important, political and intellectual options in conceiving of (much less finding practical solutions to) the frustrations of consumerism have narrowed dramatically since the 1970s.

Thoughts About the Future

What have we learned about the victory of consumerism in the twentieth century that can inform our choices as we enter the twenty-first century? Most historians dismiss this sort of query as beyond their competence. However, this question rises naturally out of this book and should not be avoided. My musings about the future are not really predictions but thoughts about possibilities and calls for responsible action.

To begin, barring an economic or environmental catastrophe, most Americans are not likely to abandon their consumerist course. They held to it tenaciously during two major crises of the twentieth century — the Great Depression and the inflation/energy crisis of the 1970s. Indeed, Americans became even more attached to goods during those two periods.

This response went far beyond mere materialism. Consumer culture has been above all a response to the world Americans experienced — an environment where social mobility coincided with divisions of class, race, and gender. Just as the privileged used commodities to distance themselves from and to humiliate their inferiors, so the humiliated used them to imitate others and salve their wounds. The opportunity for the majority to participate allowed the spiral to rise ever higher. Consumer culture could not eradicate these divisions and constant strivings. It only provided ever more ways to express them. Without a serious effort to confront and reduce social divisions, consumerism will remain the most important (and probably the most peaceful) way of coping with inequality and division. Indeed, most people will take alternatives to consumption seriously only if these alternatives overcome their reactive and cultic pasts and build social and psychological ties between the middle class and wage earners as well as the different races, genders, and generations. Only then will Americans see that the "solutions" provided by consumerism are insufficient and false. None of this seems very likely to happen.

Moreover, no one has found a more effective way than consumerism to help individuals face change and uncertainty. When people display themselves through their goods, they are not required to reveal fragile egos and awkward manners to strangers, very important in a world of lonely crowds. Americans can clothe themselves in fashions and gadgets. Consumerism does not demand self-denial for the individual to be a part of the group, and it allows people to distinguish themselves without denying the rights or existence of others (as have many political or even religious movements). Consumerism filled a need during the twentieth century for freedom and belonging that only very secure individuals and very accepting and supporting social groups could match. Without changes to achieve that security (again unlikely), any alternative would circumscribe personal freedom, replacing consumerism with a more regulated and ritualized private and public life that few would tolerate. No utopia of communal or personal freedom from consumption is probably possible, nor is it desirable.

These are pessimistic conclusions, perhaps to be expected at the end of such a tumultuous and in some ways disappointing hundred years. Yet despite the cushion of affluence that has lulled so many fin-de-siècle Americans into smug cynicism, we cannot afford to march into the new century with a shrug of the shoulders. The simple fact is that we can and must renew efforts to establish boundaries to consumer markets. Americans do not have to choose either unfettered consumerism or a theocratic/nanny state. A key intellectual and moral mistake of the last two decades of the century was to pose the question in terms of such stark contrasts.[24] Contemporary conservatives may need to rethink their free market dogmas and the Left its radical free speech doctrines to reestablish a balance. To adapt past traditions to the twenty-first century, everyone must learn from the failures of the culture of constraint but also try to recover its still useful ideas and practices. While Prohibition and later repressions of "addictive" behaviors were (and are) excessive and socially biased, the need to manage desire in an economy that continuously manufactures wants cannot be denied. Calls for restraining obsessive consumption will come from many directions in the future and will include efforts not just to control drug, alcohol, and tobacco use but also to foster programs for managing compulsive spending and gambling. Inevitably, these proposals will be especially directed toward children, who are inexperienced in dealing with pushers — whether street sellers of drugs or "legitimate" advertisers of tobacco or even playthings. The late 1990s already produced new controls over tobacco sales and advertising to children.[25] Given the rights of "commercial free speech," an attempt to "save the children" will remain one of the main avenues for controlling compulsive consumption. This will be the easiest course because it conforms with long-held American values, but proposals will have to be more measured, less hypocritical, and more willing to recognize that the problem of managing desire cannot be reduced to criminalizing a few "immoral" behaviors. Moderating need is a problem that extends far into respectable society and will be a central question in child rearing, community planning, and personal life decisions in the future.

Past movements for simple living and cultural uplift may be discredited in 2000, but the idea of developing character and community less dependent upon goods continues to appeal to Americans well beyond the ivory tower. As Jackson Lears notes, abundance should mean more than a plentitude of commodities.[26] In the future, American families and communities will try to preserve and restore civic and religious organizations that deliberately exclude consumerist values. There are already plenty around in the descendants of those voluntary organizations that de Tocqueville observed 165 years ago. Group life is not easy — ask anyone who has ever participated in the PTA or a political organization. It is not just lack of time that explains Americans' unwillingness to work on committees. Sartre's exasperating saying, "people are hell," has never been truer, especially when we can have the "heaven" of entertainment and products

249

and when the skills of negotiation and the rituals of civility appear to have declined. Still, such organizations can help Americans to preserve a capacity to conceive of a self and community beyond goods.

Americans particularly must begin to reassess the unacknowledged decision to build a consumer culture around personal products. The history of consumerism may have been a gradual shift of goods from the community (for example, churches and festivals) to family (console TVs) and finally to the individual (Walkman radios). But this socioeconomic trajectory need not dominate the entire culture. Despite the convenience and personal liberty that products have brought, Americans still want balance between the individual and the social and will seek to find it in new rituals of sharing and cross-generational activities. There is nothing wrong with these being essentially rituals — occasional Sunday dinners or family reunions, church services or simple acts of charity. We have seen to what extent spending is a ritual. Counterspending gestures are inevitable ways to adjust the balance and to remind people that there is life beyond the mall. Couples may even transcend parity in income and spending to seek gender equality in a more fair division of child care, housework, and other non-market personal activities.

While for twenty years Americans have heard the constant theme that government is the problem, not the solution, public policy alone can control market behavior that most, as consumers, abhor. The lessons of the "tragedy of the commons" will be continually learned as Americans pursue happiness and privacy in the same places. Only rules imposed on the competitive consumer society as a whole can save them from the excess of their individualism. The consumer rights movements of the 1930s and 1960s–1970s failed to create a consensus around regulating ads, much less make consumers' practical interests equal to the rights of producers. In the 1930s the overwhelming appeal of economic recovery and in the 1970s concern about the costs of regulation prevailed. The political climate in 2000 certainly is not right for another round of consumer rights activism, though legal and regulatory pressures on tobacco interests suggest that this impulse is far from dead. A long period of economic growth will probably give impetus to this movement, just as it did in the 1960s when Americans shifted from personal income to quality-of-life issues.

Despite their legendary commercialism, Americans have long demanded that certain places and times be market-free. The sanctity of the home in the Victorian sense of a place free from business is certainly a thing of the past, and no one really expects Wal-Mart to close on Labor Day, much less on Sundays. But the incessant invasion of commerce into the once-quiet corners of American life will continue to produce defensive reactions — more restrictions on telemarketing, the Internet, and the placement of new shopping malls as well as greater pressure on toy and video game makers to filter or remove products from the market that threaten the innocence of children. This is inevitable, even if the outcome is not so certain. While consumerism has prevailed, it continues to create its opposite — calls for regulation.

Only an unprecedented collapse of the market or environment may produce a thoroughgoing reformation, and it will not be a gentle call for "living simply so others can simply live." It may well be authoritarian and self-righteous and riddled with contradictions. Still, history teaches us that we have choices and may be able to avoid catastrophe if we think ahead. Much can be done at the margins of consumer society by setting rational limits to a system that naturally has no limits. Why should we do a better job with technology and management of resources in the twenty-first century than we have done in the twentieth? The only optimistic answer is that we might learn from the past.

Americans have to bear a terrible responsibility for perfecting twentieth-century consumerism. It has solved many social and psychological problems by giving meaning and satisfaction in extraordinarily diverse ways. Consumer culture has provided contemporary affluent societies with peaceful alternatives to tribalism and class war, and it has been part of a unique formula for economic growth. Yet there is no good reason to think that it will work for another century. The environmental impact of a global "American standard" alone is a frightening prospect. Moreover, there are social and personal costs of an increasingly self-isolating and fantastic culture of consumption. A society that reduces everything to a market inevitably divides those who can buy from those who cannot, undermining any sense of collective responsibility and with it, democracy. Americans must seek a realistic compromise about the need for constraint that will bridge ideological divisions. They must find ways of recovering those ideas and practices from the culture of constraint that remain viable. There is no single analysis or answer, but a challenge of the twenty-first century will be to find ways to control the overpowering success of our past all-consuming century.

NOTES

1. THE IRONY OF THE CENTURY

1. Note, for example, Pierre Bourdieu, *Distinction: A Social Critique of the Judgment of Taste* (Cambridge: Harvard University Press, 1984); John Fiske, *Understanding Popular Culture* (Boston: Unwin Hyman, 1989); Paul Willis, *Common Culture: Symbolic Work at Play in the Everyday Cultures of the Young* (Milton Keynes, England: Open University Press, 1990).

2. I develop this theme in *Time and Money: The Making of Consumer Culture* (London: Routledge, 1993), ch. 5.

3. Jean Baudrillard, *America* (New York: Verso, 1988).

4. "Work, Work and More Work," *Washington Post*, September 11, 1999, A15.

5. Note, for example, Ellen Furlough, "Making Mass Vacations: Tourism and Consumer Culture in France, 1930s to 1970s," *Comparative Studies in Society & History* 40(2)(April 1998): 247–286; Victoria De Grazia, "Changing Consumption Regimes in Europe, 1930–1970," in Susan Strasser, Charles McGovern, and Matthias Judt, eds., *Getting and Spending: European and American Consumer Societies in the Twentieth Century* (Washington, D.C.: Cambridge University Press, 1998), 59–84.

6. In very different ways, they all adapted to twentieth-century society by broadening their appeals. Revisionist socialism abandoned a doctrine narrowly based upon class to include a state that reconciled diverse interests. Even portions of the Right supported social welfare for citizens and promised dignity to many, if not all, members of the nation. And many liberals rejected rigid doctrines of laissez-faire for the public regulation of market excesses and guarantees of minimum labor and living standards. See, for example, James Kloppenberg, *Uncertain Vic-*

tory: Social Democracy and Progressivism in European and American Thought, 1870–1920 (New York: Oxford University Press, 1986), chs. 5, 7, 8.

7. Francis Fukuyama, *The End of History and the Last Man* (New York: Free Press, 1991), 129–139, 178–179.

8. Alvin Toffler, *Power Shift: Knowledge, Wealth and Violence at the Edge of the Twenty-first Century* (New York: Bantam, 1990), 372–379 especially.

9. In 1989, on the eve of the fall of the Berlin Wall, the American historian Robert Darnton noted the curious fact that East Germans did not take their money seriously. The East German Mark seemed meaningless when it bought so little and prices were so artificial. The people knew that personal connections, not money (or entitlements), got them the things they wanted. When the Berlin Wall came down in November 1989, East Berliners flooded into the West for their "greeting money" of 100 West German Marks. There they could get bananas (always scarce in the East) and other "luxuries" without having to depend on ties to insiders or the powerful. This was liberating in many ways, for it made possible the freedom to be unique, even if it only meant easy access to make-up and blue jeans. After that, the rush to unification could not be stopped. As one East German noted, "We voted for the deutsch Mark." Robert Darnton, *Berlin Journal* (New York: Norton, 1991), 3, 297–309; Slavenka Drakulic, *How We Survived Communism and Even Laughed* (New York: Norton, 1991), 23; Jan Adam, *Why Did the Socialist System Collapse in Central and Eastern European Countries?* (New York: St. Martin's, 1996), especially part 4.

10. In the early 1990s, some European socialists and environmentalists still hoped that the collapse of communism would make possible the blooming of a civil society, a plethora of political and social institutions and movements that would counteract the forces of money and power and protect egalitarian and environmental values. The liberal West German Ralf Dahrendorf argued in 1991 that the fall of the Berlin Wall culminated a historic progression toward an open society. He was still hopeful that Europe was entering a liberal era. Robin Blackburn, ed., *After the Fall: The Failure of Communism and the Future of Socialism* (New York: Verso, 1991), 30–42; Ralf Dahrendorf, *Reflections on the Revolution in Europe* (New York: Times Books, 1990), 41, 81, 111.

11. Todd Gitlin, *The Twilight of Common Dreams: Why America Is Wracked by Culture Wars* (New York: Metropolitan Books, 1995), 80, 87–88, 103, ch. 3.

12. Amitai Etzioni, *The New Golden Rule: Community and Morality in a Democratic Society* (New York: Basic, 1996), xviii, 92, 101–106.

13. William Greider, *Who Will Tell the People: The Betrayal of American Democracy* (New York: Simon and Schuster, 1992), 21 especially; Robert Putnam, "Bowling Alone: America's Declining Social Capital," *Journal of Democracy* 6(1)(Jan.

1995): 65–78; Charles Maier, "Democracy and Its Discontents," *Foreign Affairs* 73(4)(July 1995): 48–64.

14. C. B. McPherson, *Political Theory of Possessive Individualism* (Oxford: Clarendon Press, 1962).

15. Juliet Schor, *The Overworked American* (New York: Basic, 1991); Staffen Linder, *The Harried Society* (New York: Columbia University Press, 1970).

16. Fred Hirsch, *The Social Limits of Growth* (Cambridge: Harvard University Press, 1976); Tibor Scitovsky, *The Joyless Economy* (New York: Oxford University Press, 1986); "The Joyless Economy After Twenty Years," *Critical Review* 10 (Fall 1996)(special issue).

17. Robert Lane, "The Road Not Taken: Friendship, Consumerism, and Happiness," *Critical Review* 8 (Fall 1994): 521–554.

18. Marshall Berman, *All That Is Solid Melts Into Air* (New York: Penguin, 1982), 24. See also chapter 4 of this volume.

19. Among the many books that develop this theme is Andrew Ross, *No Respect: Intellectuals and Popular Culture* (London: Routledge, 1989), chs. 1, 2, and 4 especially. Also, I consider it in *Time and Money*, chs. 3–4.

20. Stanley Lebergott, *Pursuing Happiness* (Princeton: Princeton University Press, 1993), ch. 1 and page 60. For interesting commentary on the classic economist's understanding of consumer desire, see Neva Goodwin, Frank Ackerman, and David Kiron, *The Consumer Society* (Washington, D.C.: Island Press, 1997), 1–11, 149–158, 189–200.

21. Mary Douglas and Baron Isherwood, *The World of Goods: Towards an Anthropology of Consumption* (New York: Basic, 1979). Note also Robert Venturi, S. Scott-Brown, and S. Izenour, *Learning from Las Vegas* (Cambridge: Harvard University Press, 1972); Grant McCracken, *Culture and Consumption: New Approaches to the Symbolic Character of Consumer Goods and Activities* (Bloomington: Indiana University Press, 1988); James Twitchell, *Lead Us Into Temptation: The Triumph of American Materialism* (New York: Columbia University Press, 1999); John Fiske, *Understanding Popular Culture* (Boston: Unwin Hyman, 1989); Jean Baudrillard, *Illusion of the End* (Stanford: Stanford University Press, 1994). Critical discussions of this broad approach are found in Fredric Jameson, *Postmodernism, or, The Cultural Logic of Late Capitalism* (Durham: Duke University Press, 1991), ch. 1 and David Harvey, *The Condition of Postmodernity* (Oxford: Blackwell, 1989), ch. 22.

23. See Robert Lane, *The Market Experience* (New York: Cambridge University Press, 1993); Amartya Sen and M. Nussbaum, eds., *The Quality of Life* (Oxford: Clarendon Press, 1996).

24. Hirsch, *The Social Limits of Growth*, 104; Juliet Schor, "Consumption,

Global Stewardship and the Good Life," address given October 2, 1994, University of Maryland, in Neva Goodwin et al., eds., *The Consumer Society*, 33.

2. SETTING THE COURSE, 1900–1930

1. Werner Sombart, *Why There Is No Socialism in America* (White Plains, N.Y.: International Arts and Sciences Press, 1976 [1906]). See also David Wrobel, *The End of American Exceptionalism: Frontier Anxiety from the Old West to the New Deal* (Lawrence: University Press of Kansas, 1993), ch. 8.

2. In fact, mean real wages rose by 40 percent between 1910 and 1929, and even when unemployment losses were deducted, purchasing power grew by 27 percent during the 1920s. This made possible the decrease in the proportion of the wage earner's family income going to food, from 43 percent in the first decade of the century to 32.8 percent by the early 1930s. Committee on Recent Economic Change, *Recent Economic Changes in the United States* (New York: National Bureau of Economic Research 1929), I:625–626; II:104; Don Lescohier, *History of Labor in the United States, 1896–1933*, John R. Commons, ed., vol. III (New York: Macmillan, 1935), 60, 76–85; Lance Davis et al., *American Economic Growth* (New York: Harper and Row, 1972), 213; National Industrial Conference Board, *Conference Board Studies in Enterprise and Social Progress* (New York: National Industrial Conference Board, 1939), 153. See also Winifred Wandersee, *Women's Work and Family Values, 1920–1940* (Cambridge: Harvard University Press, 1981), ch. 1.

3. U.S. Bureau of the Census, *Historical Statistics of the United States* (Stamford, Conn.: Fairfield, 1965), 91.

4. Jackson Lears, *Fables of Abundance: A Cultural History of Advertising in America* (New York: Basic, 1994), 4.

5. Naomi Lamoreaux, *The Great Merger Movement in American Business, 1895–1904* (Cambridge: Harvard University Press, 1985), chs. 2–4. U.S. Bureau of the Census, *Historical Statistics*, 72, 74.

6. Gwendolyne Mink, *Old Labor and New Immigrants in American Political Development* (Ithaca: Cornell University Press, 1986), 48, 51. Peter Shergold, *Working-Class Life: The "American Standard" in Comparative Perspective 1899–1913* (Pittsburgh: University of Pittsburgh Press, 1982), ch. 10. See also David Montgomery, *The Fall of the House of Labor* (New York: Cambridge University Press, 1987), ch. 2.

7. U.S. Bureau of the Census, *Historical Statistics*, 56–57; Leonard Dinnerstein and David Reimers, *Ethnic Americans: A History of Immigration and Assimilation*, 4th ed. (New York: Columbia University Press, 1999), ch. 3; Leonard Dinnerstein, Roger Nichols, and David Reimers, *Natives and Strangers: A Multicultural History of Americans* (New York: Oxford University Press, 1996), ch. 6; Steven Ross,

Working-Class Hollywood: Silent Film and the Shaping of Class in America (Princeton: Princeton University Press, 1998), ch. 7.

8. David Potter, *People of Plenty* (Chicago: University of Chicago Press, 1954), 155, 165.

9. John Cell, *The Highest Stage of White Supremacy: The Origins of Segregation in South Africa and the American South* (Cambridge: Cambridge University Press, 1982); Stan Greenberg, *Race and State in Capitalist Development: Comparative Perspectives* (New Haven: Yale University Press, 1980).

10. Michael McGerr, *The Decline of Popular Politics* (New York: Oxford University Press, 1986), 184–187; Charles McGovern, "Sold American: Inventing the Consumer, 1890–1940," Ph.D. diss., Harvard University, 1993, 60–70; Mink, *Old Labor and New Immigrants*, ch. 4; Gary Marks, *Unions in Politics* (Princeton: Princeton University Press, 1989), 92–99. Note especially the famous article by Walter D. Burnham, "The System of 1896," in Paul Kleppner, ed., *The Evolution of American Electoral Systems* (Westport, Conn.: Greenwood Press, 1981).

11. Robert Wiebe, *Businessmen and Reform* (Chicago: Quadrangle Press, 1968), chs. 6–8; Gabriel Kolko, *The Triumph of Conservatism* (Chicago: University of Chicago Press, 1967), chs. 6, 7, 9; Harold Vatter, *Drive to Industrial Maturity: The U.S. Economy, 1860–1914* (Westport, Conn.: Greenwood Press, 1975), ch. 8 make these points. A definitive treatment is J. Martin Sklar, *The Corporate Reconstruction of American Capitalism, 1890–1916* (Cambridge: Cambridge University Press, 1988), chs. 4 and 6 especially.

12. Frederick W. Taylor, *The Principles of Scientific Management* (New York: Norton, 1967 [1912]), 19–24; Montgomery, *Fall of the House of Labor*, ch. 5.

13. Jeffrey Lustig, *Corporate Liberalism: The Birth of American Political Theory, 1890–1920* (Berkeley: University of California Press, 1982), ch. 5, 103–104; Kolko, *Triumph of Conservatism*, chs. 7–9; John Kendrick, *Productivity Trends in the United States* (Princeton: Princeton University Press, 1961), 328–329.

14. Daniel Boorstin, "Welcome to the Consumption Community," *Fortune* (Sept. 1967):118; Daniel Boorstin, *The Americans: The Democratic Experience* (New York: Vintage, 1973), 89–117, 145–164.

15. Paul Fussel, *Class: A Guide Through the American Status System* (New York: Summit, 1983), 19 for quotation.

16. Richard Sennett and Jonathan Cobb, *The Hidden Injuries of Class* (New York: Vintage, 1972).

17. Loren Baritz, *The Good Life: The Meaning of Success for the American Middle Class* (New York: Knopf, 1989), 8–9; Kerby Miller, *Emigrants and Exiles* (New York: Oxford University Press, 1985), 569. See also Richard Bushman, *Refinement of America: Persons, Houses and Cities* (New York: Knopf, 1992).

18. Thorstein Veblen, *The Theory of the Leisure Class* (New York: New American Library, 1953 [1899]), especially 70–71, chs. 2, 13, and 14; Thorstein Veblen, *Instinct of Workmanship* (New York: Norton, 1964 [1914]), 318–320. See also Daniel Horowitz, "Consumption and Its Discontents," *Journal of American History* (Sept. 1980):307–310.

19. Robert and Helen Lynd, *Middletown* (New York: Harcourt, 1929), 83.

20. John Brooks, *Showing Off in America* (Boston: Little, Brown, 1981), 17–19.

21. Potter, *People of Plenty*, 105, 110 and Fussel, *Class*, 20.

22. Richard Ohmann, *Selling Culture: Magazines, Markets, and Class at the Turn of the Century* (London: Verso, 1996), 57; William Leach, *Land of Desire: Merchants, Power and the Rise of a New American Culture* (New York: Vintage, 1993), 5–7, ch. 9; William Catchings and William Foster, *The Road to Plenty* (Boston: Houghton Mifflin, 1928), 173.

23. Susan Benson, "Living on the Margin: Working-Class Marriages and Family Survival Strategies in the United States, 1919–1941," in Victoria De Grazia and Ellen Furlough, eds., *The Sex of Things* (Berkeley: University of California Press, 1996), 212–214; Roland Marchand, *Advertising the American Dream* (Berkeley: University of California Press, 1988), 64; Lizabeth Cohen, *Making a New Deal* (New York: Cambridge University Press, 1990), 101–104.

24. E. H. Phelps Brown, *A Century of Pay* (London: Routledge, 1968), 258. European infatuation with American productivity was evident in Bertram Austin and W. F. Lloyd, *The Secret of High Wages* (London: Unwin, 1926) and Hyacinthe Dubreuil, *Standards* (translated as *Robots or Men?*) (Paris, 1929; New York: B. Grassett, 1929), 192.

25. C. F. Carter, "Automobiles for Average Incomes," *Outing Magazine* (Jan. 1910):410–419; "The Farmer and the Auto," *Independent* (Nov. 7, 1912):1091; H. W. Perry, "The Automobile and the Full Dinner Pail," *Collier's Magazine* (Jan. 6, 1912):50; James Madison, "How I Made My Car Pay for Itself," *Outing Magazine* (Jan. 1910):439–442; David Gartman, *Auto Opium: A Social History of American Automobile Design* (London: Routledge, 1994), 33–38.

26. Ibid., 43–53; Reynold Wik, *Henry Ford and Grassroots America* (Ann Arbor: University of Michigan Press, 1972), 233; James Flink, *The Automobile Age* (Cambridge: MIT Press, 1993), 131–133.

27. Davis et al., *American Economic Growth*, 259; Ruth Cowan, *More Work for Mother* (New York: Pantheon, 1983); Fred Schroeder, "More 'Small Things Forgotten': Domestic Electrical Plugs and Receptacles, 1881–1931," *Technology and Culture* (1986); Susan Strasser, *Never Done: A History of Housework* (New York: Pantheon, 1981).

28. A good primer is George Basalla, *The Evolution of Technology* (Cambridge: Cambridge University Press, 1988). Also note Gary Cross and Rick Szostak, *Technology in American Society: A History* (Englewood Cliffs, N.J.: Prentice-Hall, 1995). Other useful books include: Martin Melosi, *Thomas A. Edison and the Modernization of America* (Glenview, Ill.: HarperCollins, 1990); Hugh Aitken, *The Continuous Wave* (Princeton: Princeton University Press, 1989); Roger Bilstein, *Flight in America 1900–1983* (Baltimore: Johns Hopkins University Press, 1985).

29. William Leuchtenburg, *Perils of Prosperity* (Chicago: University of Chicago Press, 1958), ch. 9; Stanley Lebergott, *Pursuing Happiness* (Princeton: Princeton University Press, 1993), ch. 6.

30. Derived from ibid., 148–151.

31. M. S. Rukeyser, "Revolution in Retailing," *American Review of Reviews* (Nov. 1928):523–527; Richard Tedlow, *New and Improved: The Story of Mass Marketing in America* (New York: Basic, 1990), 264–267, 290–299; Boris Emmet and John Jeuck, *Catalogues and Counters: A History of Sears, Roebuck, and Company* (Chicago: University of Chicago Press, 1950), chs. 2, 7, 12, 14, 21; Boorstin, *The Americans*, 120–122 especially; John Winkler, *Five and Ten: The Fabulous Life of F. W. Woolworth* (New York: R. M. McBride, 1940), 175.

32. Edward Woolley, "Secrets for Business Success, Filene Merchandizing," *World's Work* (March 1914):548–553; Leach, *Land of Desire*, 22, 44–45; Robert Hendrickson, *The Grand Emporiums: The Illustrated History of America's Great Department Stores* (New York: Stein and Day, 1979), ch. 4; Susan Benson, *Counter Cultures: Saleswomen, Managers, and Customers in American Department Stores, 1890–1940* (Urbana: University of Illinois Press, 1986), 15–25.

33. Martha Olney, *Buy Now, Pay Later: Advertising, Credit, and Consumer Demand in the 1920s* (Chapel Hill: University of North Carolina Press, 1991), 25, 32, 90, 103; Lendol Calder, *Financing the American Dream: A Cultural History of Consumer Credit* (Princeton: Princeton University Press, 1999), 30, 184, 206, 207.

34. Leach, *Land of Desire*, 5, 9, 39–150.

35. Harvey Levenstein, *Revolution at the Table: The Transformation of the American Diet* (New York: Oxford University Press, 1988), 30–44; Scott Bruce and Bill Crawford, *Cerealizing America: The Unsweetened Story of American Breakfast Cereal* (Boston: Faber and Faber, 1995), ch. 5; Susan Strasser, *Satisfaction Guaranteed: The Making of the American Mass Market* (New York: Pantheon, 1989), 95–100; Thomas Hine, *The Total Package: The Evolution and Secret Meanings of Boxes, Bottles, Cans, and Tubes* (Boston: Little, Brown, 1995), 110; Ray Broekel, *The Great American Candy Bar Book* (Boston: Houghton Mifflin, 1982), 70–73; Michael Schudson, *Advertising: The Uneasy Persuasion* (New York: Basic, 1984), 198–200.

36. Tedlow, *New and Improved*, 19.

37. Hine, *The Total Package*, 86–89.

38. Ibid., 76; Strasser, *Satisfaction Guaranteed*, ch. 1; Hendrickson, *The Grand Emporiums*, ch. 6 especially; M. M. Manning, *Slave in a Box: The Strange Career of Aunt Jemima* (Charlottesville: University Press of Virginia, 1998), ch. 4; for ads, see Edgar Jones, ed., *Those Were the Good Old Days* (New York: Simon and Schuster, 1979), 183.

39. Hine, *The Total Package*, 129–34, 136–37, 79, 80; Strasser, *Satisfaction Guaranteed*, 195, 248–49.

40. Cited in Hine, *The Total Package*, 122. See also David Hogan, *Selling 'Em by the Sack: White Castle and the Creation of American Food* (New York: New York University Press, 1997).

41. Frank Presbrey, *The History and Development of Advertising* (Garden City, N.Y.: Doubleday, 1929), 374–413, 419–420; Olney, *Buy Now, Pay Later*, 137, 140–141; Daniel Pope, *The Making of Modern Advertising* (New York: Basic, 1983), 6; Lears, *Fables of Abundance*, 201; Vincent Vinikas, *Soft Soap, Hard Sell: American Hygiene in an Age of Advertisement* (Ames: Iowa State University Press, 1992), 15.

42. See for example Stuart Chase, *The Tragedy of Waste* (New York: Macmillan, 1925), ch. 7; James Rorty, *Our Master's Voice: Advertising* (New York: John Day, 1934), 16–17. More recent versions of this thesis are in James Duesenberry, *Income, Saving, and the Theory of Consumer Behavior* (Cambridge: Harvard University Press, 1949), 28–41; John Galbraith, *The New Industrial State* (Boston: Houghton Mifflin, 1967); Michel Aglietta, *A Theory of Capitalist Regulation* (London: Verso, 1979), 52–61; Pope, *The Making of Modern Advertising*, chs. 1, 2.

43. Presbrey, *The History and Development of Advertising*, 446–489; Strasser, *Satisfaction Guaranteed*, ch. 4.

44. Earnest Calkins, *Modern Advertising* (New York: Appleton, 1905), 3–4; Walter Dill Scott, *The Psychology of Advertising* (Boston: Small, Maynard, 1912), 82–92; F. H. Allport, *Social Psychology* (Boston: Houghton Mifflin, 1924), 52–56; Christine Frederick, *Selling Mrs. Consumer* (New York: The Business Bourse, 1929), 11, 13, 16, ch. 5. See also Stuart Ewen, *Captains of Consciousness* (New York: Pantheon, 1978), part III; Loren Baritz, *The Servants of Power: A History of the Use of Social Science in American Industry* (Middletown, Conn.: Wesleyan University Press, 1960), 21–28.

45. Marchand, *Advertising the American Dream*, ch. 2; Stuart Ewen, *All Consuming Images* (New York: Basic, 1988), 20, 28–29, 32, 51.

46. Olney, *Buy Now, Pay Later*, ch. 5; Marchand, *Advertising the American Dream*, 67; William Ogburn, "The Family and Its Functions," in The President's

Research Committee on Social Trends, *Recent Social Trends in the United States* (New York: McGraw-Hill, 1933), II:661–708.

47. Robert Lynd, "The People as Consumers," in President's Research Committee on Social Trends, *Recent Social Trends*, II:868–871 and 866.

48. Robert Lynd, *Knowledge for What?* (Princeton: Princeton University Press, 1939), 105; Richard Pells, *Radical Visions and American Dreams: Culture and Social Thought in the Depression Years* (New York: Harper and Row, 1973), 319–329; Richard Wightman Fox, "Epitaph for Middletown: Robert S. Lynd and the Analysis of Consumer Culture," in R. W. Fox and Jackson Lears, eds., *Culture of Consumption* (New York: Pantheon, 1983), 103–141.

49. Listerine ads, *Better Homes and Gardens* (Aug. 1927):29; *Collier's* (Aug. 23, 1930):2; Vinikas, *Soft Soap, Hard Sell*, ch. 2.

50. *Book of Etiquette* ad, *Time* (Dec. 17, 1923):21; Lynd, *Middletown*, 81.

51. Majestic stove ad, *Collier's* (March 26, 1904):26; Pond's ad, *New Yorker* (July 1929):31; Jane and Michael Stern, *Auto Ads* (New York: Random House, 1978), 21.

52. Marchand, *Advertising the American Dream*, xviii, 95–200, 210, 213–214, 220, 267; Carl Crow, *The Great American Consumer* (New York: Harper and Row, 1943), 115; and McGovern, "Sold American," 115, 126, 150–152.

53. Marchand, *Advertising the American Dream*, ch 10, 230–232, 359–360.

54. Gilbert ad, *St. Nicholas* (July 1915):45; A. C. Gilbert, *The Man Who Lives in Paradise* (New York: Rhinehart, 1953), 126, 131, 136, 156.

55. Baritz, *The Good Life*, 40–41, 44–45. Alienation between immigrant parents and their American-born offspring also contributed to the problem of a rebellious "Street Corner Society" that William Whyte found among second-generation Italian Americans in the 1930s. William Whyte, *Street Corner Society* (Chicago: University of Chicago Press, 1943).

56. Andrew Heinze, *Adapting to Abundance: Jewish Immigrants, Mass Consumption, and the Search for American Identity* (New York: Columbia University Press, 1990), 4–5.

57. See Jane Addams, *The Spirit of Youth and the City Streets* (Chicago: University of Chicago Press, 1909); Richard H. Edwards, *Popular Amusements* (New York: Association Press, 1915); Paul Cressey, *The Taxi-Dance Hall: A Sociological Study in Commercialized Recreation and City Life* (Chicago: University of Chicago Press, 1932).

58. David Nasaw, *Going Out: The Rise and Fall of Public Amusements* (New York: Basic, 1993), 45; Kathy Peiss, *Cheap Amusements: Working Women and Leisure in Turn-of-the-Century New York* (Philadelphia: Temple University Press, 1986), 121, 125, 130–134; G. Edward White, *Creating the National Pastime: Baseball*

Transforms Itself 1903–1953 (Princeton: Princeton University Press, 1996), chs. 1, 2; John Kasson, *Amusing the Million: Coney Island at the Turn of the Century* (New York: Hill and Wang, 1978), 50.

59. Peiss, *Cheap Amusements*, 5, 95, 102, 148.

60. Only 6.1 percent of 17-year-olds graduated from high school in 1901, but 28.8 percent did so by 1930. While only 2.3 percent of the 24-year-old population attended college in 1900, some 7.2 percent enrolled in 1930. Ben Wattenberg, ed., *The Statistical History of the United States* (New York: Basic, 1976), 379, 383. See also Paula Fass, *The Damned and the Beautiful: American Youth in the 1920s* (New York: Oxford University Press, 1977), ch. 2, 134.

61. Ibid., 23. Influential contemporary sources include George Coe, *What Ails Our Youth* (New York: Scribner's, 1923) and Floyd Dell, *Love in the Machine Age* (New York: Farrar & Rinehart, 1930).

62. Fass, *The Damned and the Beautiful*, 182–199.

63. Lynd, *Middletown*, ch. 9, 95–96, 99, 134–142; George Lundberg and Mirra Komarovsky, *Leisure: A Suburban Study* (New York: Columbia University Press), 175, 182–183.

64. Jane Addams, cited in Stuart Ewen, *Channels of Desire* (New York: McGraw Hill, 1982), 214; Harvey Green, *Uncertainties of Everyday Life* (New York: HarperCollins, 1992), 176; Kathy Peiss, "Making Up, Making Over," in De Grazia and Furlough, eds., *The Sex of Things*, 311–37; Kathy Peiss, *Hope in a Jar: The Making of America's Beauty Culture* (New York: Metropolitan Books, 1998); Joan Jacobs Blumberg, *The Body Project: An Intimate History of American Girls* (New York: Random House, 1997), ch. 3; Lynd, "The People as Consumers," II:898–900; Abraham Cahan, *The Rise of David Levinsky* (New York: Harper and Row, 1960 [1917]), 101; G. Stanley Hall, "Flapper Americana Novissima," *Atlantic Monthly* (June 1922):771–780. See also Lois Banner, *American Beauty* (New York: Knopf, 1983), ch. 3.

65. "Report of the Vice Commission of Minneapolis to His Honor, James C. Haynes, Mayor, 1911," *The Prostitute and the Social Reformer: Commercial Vice in the Progressive Era* (New York: Arno Press, 1974 [1913]), 77.

66. John Burnham, *Bad Habits: Drinking, Smoking, Taking Drugs, Gambling, Sexual Misbehavior, and Swearing in American History* (New York: New York University Press, 1993), 150–156; Francis Couvares, *The Remaking of Pittsburgh: Class and Culture in an Industrializing City, 1877–1919* (Albany: SUNY Press, 1984), 50, 123–124.

67. Ellen Rothman, *Hands and Hearts: A History of Courtship in America* (New York: Basic, 1984), 265; Lewis Erenberg, *Steppin' Out: New York Nightlife and the Transformation of American Culture, 1890–1930* (Westport, Conn.:

Greenwood Press, 1981), ch. 1; Stanley Coben, *Rebellion Against Victorianism* (New York: Oxford University Press, 1991), 54, 99, 101; Peiss, "Making Up, Making Over," 311; Elizabeth Ewing, *History of Twentieth-Century Fashion* (London: Batsford, 1992), 9, 78–79; and Palmolive ad, *Ladies' Home Journal* (June 12, 1922):12.

68. Mary Whitton, "If I Were That Girl's Mother!" *Parents' Magazine* (Aug. 1932):16–18.

69. Gary Cross, *Kids' Stuff: Toys and the Changing World of American Childhood* (Cambridge: Harvard University Press, 1997), ch. 2; William Waits, *The Modern Christmas in America: A Cultural History of Gift Giving* (New York: New York University Press, 1993), ch. 2; Leigh Schmidt, *Consumer Rites: The Buying and Selling of American Holidays* (Princeton: Princeton University Press, 1996), ch. 3; James Carrier, "Gifts in a World of Commodities: The Ideology of the Perfect Gift in American Society," *Social Analysis* 29(1990): 19–37.

70. Mary Read, *The Childcraft Manual* (Boston: Houghton Mifflin, 1916), ch. 13; White House Conference on Child Health and Protection, *The Home and the Child* (New York: Century Co., 1931), 5, 23–24, 39, 46–47; Rose Alschuler and Christine Heinig, *Play: The Child's Response to Life* (Boston: Houghton Mifflin, 1936), ch. 4. Piano ads, *Vanity Fair* (April 1925):93 and *Better Homes and Gardens* (March 1927):73; Cine-Kodak ad, *Time* (Feb. 20, 1928):41; Lisa Jacobson, "Raising Consumers: Children, Childrearing, and the American Mass Market, 1890–1940," Ph.D. diss., UCLA, 1997, 7.

71. Sidonie Gruenberg, *Your Child Today and Tomorrow* (New York: Lippincott, 1910), 42–46; "Editorial," *Toys and Novelties* (June 1913):70; Lawrence Greenfield, "Toys, Children, and the Toy Industry in a Culture of Consumption, 1890–1991," Ph.D. diss., Ohio State University, 1991, 102–104, 112–126.

72. Daniel Cook, "On the Commoditization of Childhood: Personhood, the Children's Wear Industry, and the Moral Dimensions of Consumption, 1917–1967," Ph.D. diss., University of Chicago, 1998, ch. 1; Jacobson, "Raising Consumers," ch. 2; Cross, *Kids' Stuff*, ch. 3; Lionel Trains ad, *American Boy* (Oct. 1918):45; "Lionel Electric Train Catalogue" (1932), Warshaw Collection, Smithsonian Institution, Toys, Box 3, File 12.

73. Children's food ads in *Parents' Magazine* (July 1929):41, (March 1932):54, (Oct. 1932):41; Playskool Institute ad, *Parents' Magazine* (March 1929):59.

74. Thomas Edison, "The Woman of the Future," cited in Robert Atwan, Donald McQuade, and John Wright, *Edsels, Luckies, and Frigidaires: Advertising the American Way* (New York: Delta, 1979), 132.

75. Refrigerator ad, *Vanity Fair* (Aug. 1928):94; Radiator ad, *Vanity Fair* (March 1924):45; Cowan, *More Work for Mother*, chs. 6, 7; Glenna Matthews, *"Just*

a Housewife": The Rise and Fall of Domesticity in America (New York: Oxford, 1987), ch. 7; Jeffrey Meikle, *Twentieth-Century Limited: Industrial Design in America, 1925–1939* (Philadelphia: Temple University Press, 1979), 101–110; Adrian Forty, *Objects of Desire* (New York: Pantheon, 1986), 208–216.

76. Emily Post, *The Personality of a House* (New York: Funk & Wangnalls, 1930), 3. Examples of this literature are Alice Van Leer Carrick, *The Next-to-Nothing House* (Boston: Atlantic Monthly Press, 1922) and the Stanley Rule and Level Plant publication, *How to Work with Tools and Wood: For the Home Workshop* (New Britain, Conn.: Stanley, 1927).

77. See, for example, Marcia Mead, *Homes of Character* (New York: Dodd, Mead, 1926) and *American Home*, a popular magazine reflecting the builder's perspective. Margaret Marsh, *Suburban Lives* (New Brunswick: Rutgers University Press, 1990), 140–142; John Stilgoe, *Borderland: Origin of the American Suburb* (New Haven: Yale University Press, 1988), 290–300.

78. F. Lloyd Warner and Paul Lunt, *The Social Life of a Modern Community* (New Haven: Yale University Press, 1941), 81–91, 105–109, 141–144, 200, 287–300; F. Lloyd Warner, *The Living and the Dead: A Study of the Symbolic Life of Americans* (New Haven: Yale University Press, 1959), 45–50. Note also Mihaly Csikszentmihalyi and Eugene Rochberg-Halton, *The Meaning of Things: Domestic Symbols of the Self* (New York: Cambridge University Press, 1981) and Eugene Rochberg-Halton, *Meaning and Modernity: Social Theory in Pragmatic Attitude* (Chicago: University of Chicago Press, 1986), 155–188.

79. Katherine Grier, *Culture and Comfort: Parlor Making and Middle-Class Identity, 1850–1930* (Washington, D.C.: Smithsonian Institution Press, 1988), ch. 1, 213, 215.

80. Craig Roell, *The Piano in America, 1890–1940* (Chapel Hill: University of North Carolina Press, 1989), xv, 151, 200, 215, 247, 265.

81. Herbert Blumer, "Fashion: From Class Differentiation to Collective Selection," *Sociological Quarterly* 10(Summer 1969): 287–290 especially; George Simmel, *Philosophy of Money* (London: Routledge, 1990 [1900]), 448; George Simmel, "Fashion," *International Quarterly* (1904); reprint, *American Journal of Sociology* 62(1957): 541–558.

82. Fred Davis, *Fashion, Culture, and Identity* (Chicago: University of Chicago Press, 1992), 242, 139; Valerie Steele, *Fashion and Eroticism: Ideals of Feminine Beauty from the Victorian Era to the Jazz Age* (London: Oxford University Press, 1985), 19–20; Claudia Kidwell and Valerie Steele, *Men and Women: Dressing the Part* (Washington, D.C.: Smithsonian Institution Press, 1989), 6–22 especially.

83. Brooks, *Showing Off in America*, 25–27; Baritz, *The Good Life*, 90; Ewing,

History of Twentieth-Century Fashion, chs. 1 and 4; Jones, *Those Were the Good Old Days*, 217.

84. Cross, *Kids' Stuff*, 87–88.

85. Parker Brothers, *75 Years of Fun: The Story of Parker Brothers, Inc.* (Salem, Mass.: Parker Brothers, 1958), 20–24; Joseph Schroeder, *The Wonderful World of Toys, Games, and Dolls, 1860–1930* (Chicago: Follett, 1971), 78; Parker Brothers, *Games* (Salem, Mass.: Parker Brothers, 1891), 5.

86. Cross, *Kids' Stuff*, ch. 3.

87. Robert Rydell, *All the World's a Fair* (Chicago: University of Chicago Press, 1984); Robert Rydell, *World of Fairs: The Century-of-Progress Expositions* (Chicago: University of Chicago Press, 1993), chs. 1, 4, 5.

88. Gartman, *Auto Opium*, 21–33; *Horseless Age* (May 3, 1899) cited in Paul Wilson, *Chrome Dreams: Automobile Styling Since 1893* (Radnor, Penn.: Chilton, 1976), 8; R. M. Cleveland, "How Many Automobiles Can America Buy?" *The World's Work* (April 1914):680–682.

89. Tedlow, *New and Improved*, 155–159; Alfred Sloan, *My Years with General Motors* (New York: Macfadden, 1965), 269, 273–274; Meikle, *Twentieth-Century Limited*, 14.

90. Chevrolet ad, *Saturday Evening Post* (Oct. 8, 1927):82.

91. Allan Nevins, *Ford: Expansion and Challenge 1915–1933* (New York: Scribner's, 1957), 455; Gartman, *Auto Opium*, 95.

92. Ibid., chs. 3, 4.

93. Sloan, *My Years with General Motors*, 273–274; James Flink, *The Car Culture* (Cambridge: MIT Press, 1975), ch. 3.

94. Lynd, *Middletown*, 247; Lynd, "The People as Consumers," II:857, 866–67; Ronald Edsford, *Class Conflict and Cultural Consensus: The Making of a Mass Consumer Society in Flint, Michigan* (New Brunswick: Rutgers University Press, 1987), 83, 95–96.

95. Simon Patten, *Consumption of Wealth* (Philadelphia, 1889) cited in Hine, *The Total Package*, 103.

96. Gillette ad, 1910, in Atwan, McQuade, and Wright, *Edsels, Luckies*, 54; soap ad, *Collier's* (Nov. 4, 1911):31; makeup ad, *New Yorker* (Aug. 15, 1936):31; shaving cream ad, *Time* (March 31, 1924):32; Lears, *Fables of Abundance*, ch. 6.

97. As early as the 1820s, toy and confectionery stores in northeastern cities already used folk and religious symbols to promote buying, but only on Christmas Eve. Soon thereafter, other businesses sold decorations and Christmas cards and offered entertainment to seasonal revelers. This was a long process, however. Only slowly between 1837 and 1890 did individual states recognize Christmas as a legal

holiday. Santa Claus became a regular Christmastime fixture in big-city stores only in the mid-1890s. Schmidt, *Consumer Rites*, 126–127, 162; Waits, *The Modern Christmas in America*, ch. 2, 130–133; Penne Restad, *Christmas in America: A History* (New York: Oxford University Press, 1995), 17–41, 91–104; John Pimlott, *The Englishman's Christmas: A Social History*, (Atlantic Heights, N.J.: Humanities Press, 1978), 23–29, 120–124; James Barnett, *The American Christmas: A Study in National Culture* (New York: Macmillan, 1954), ch. 1; Leach, *Land of Desire*, 89–90, 337; John Gillis, *A World of Their Own Making: Myth, Ritual, and the Quest for Family Values* (New York: Basic, 1996), 102–108; Stephen Nissenbaum, *The Battle for Christmas* (New York: Knopf, 1996), ch. 4.

98. Schmidt, *Consumer Rites*, 212, 219.

99. The prettified floral images of Easter in shop windows were anticipated in church decorations, and the extravagant promises of gifts from Santa Clauses in department stores were preceded by Santa's appearance in Sunday school festivities. Schmidt, *Consumer Rites*, ch. 1 especially.

100. Car ads, *Time* (March 15, 1926):1; *New Yorker* (Apr. 26, 1930):34; *Collier's* (Aug. 3, 1929):19. Note also Lears, *Fables of Abundance*, 229; Henry Adams, *The Education of Henry Adams: An Autobiography* (New York: Book League, 1928), 496–497.

101. Kenneth Jackson, *Crabgrass Frontier* (New York: Columbia University Press, 1985), 182, 248–251; John Jakle, *The Tourist* (Lincoln: University of Nebraska Press, 1985), chs. 6 and 7; and Daniel Boorstin, *The Image: A Guide to Pseudo-Events in America* (New York: Knopf, 1972), ch. 5.

102. Phonograph ads, *Collier's* (Apr. 11, 1913):back cover; *Collier's* (Apr. 11, 1914):21.

103. Radio ads, *Time* (Nov. 9, 1925):23; Jones, *Those Were the Good Old Days*, 165, 379.

104. *Harmsworth Self Educator Magazine* (July 1907), n.p. In Warshaw Collection, Beverages, Box 1, Smithsonian Institution, Museum of American History Archives; cited in Lears, *Fables of Abundance*, 159.

105. Life Savers' ad (1922) in Atwan, McQuade, and Wright, *Edsels, Luckies*, 201. For a very interesting analysis of the pleasures of taste, see Lionel Tiger, *The Pursuit of Pleasure* (New York: Little, Brown, 1992), ch. 5.

106. Broekel, *The Great American Candy Bar Book*, 8–19, 54–55; Jones, *Those Were the Good Old Days*, 188.

107. Richard Kluger, *Ashes to Ashes: America's Hundred-Year Cigarette War* (New York: Knopf, 1996), ch. 3; cigarette ads: *Collier's* (Sept. 4, 1937):66; *Time* (Aug. 15, 1927):33; *Time* (July 9, 1934):46. Milk of magnesia ad, *Collier's* (Nov. 21, 1931):44; Wattenberg, *Statistical History*, 689–690.

108. For example, Coke ad, *Saturday Evening Post* (July 7, 1923):76; Mark Schudson, "Women, Cigarettes, and Advertising in the 1920s," in Catherine Covert and John Stevens, eds., *Mass Media Between the Wars* (Syracuse: Syracuse University Press, 1984), 71–83.

109. Note especially J. M. Golby and A. W. Purdue, *The Civilisation of the Crowd: Popular Culture in England, 1750–1900* (London: Alan & Unwin, 1984), ch. 2.

110. Lears, *Fables of Abundance*, 222, 227; Gary Cross, *Time and Money: The Making of Consumer Culture* (London: Routledge, 1993), 39–40.

111. Neil Harris, *Humbug: The Art of P. T. Barnum* (Boston: Little, Brown, 1973), ch. 2; Nasaw, *Going Out*, chs. 2, 3.

112. Ross, *Working-Class Hollywood*, 1–27, 30–33, 182–194; Tino Balio, *The American Film Industry* (Madison: University of Wisconsin Press, 1976), 103–118, 213–228; Larry May, *Screening out the Past* (New York: Oxford University Press, 1980), ch. 14; Joshua Gamson, *Claims to Fame: Celebrity in Contemporary America* (Berkeley: University of California Press, 1994), ch. 1.

113. Beth Bailey, *From Front Porch to Back Seat: Courtship in Twentieth-Century America* (Baltimore: Johns Hopkins University Press, 1988), 13–19; Nasaw, *Going Out*, 111.

114. Nasaw, *Going Out*, 32, ch. 5.

115. Lears, *Fables of Abundance*, 232.

116. Cited in Wik, *Henry Ford and Grassroots America*, 233.

117. "New Types of Suburban Shopping Area Proposed," *American City Magazine* (Aug. 1926):214–216; Lundberg and Komarovsky, *Leisure*, 77–78; Warren Belasco, *Americans on the Road: From Autocamp to Motel, 1910–1945* (Cambridge: MIT Press, 1979); Jackson, *Crabgrass Frontier*, ch. 14.

118. Green, *Uncertainties of Everyday Life*, 94; Baritz, *The Good Life*, 72–73; Anthony King, *The Bungalow* (London: Routledge, 1984), chs. 2–4; "Labor Department Testimony Before Congress, 1901" cited in U.S. Department of Labor, *How American Buying Habits Change* (Washington, D.C.: U.S. Government Printing Office, 1959), 1; Clifford Clark, *The American Family Home, 1800–1960* (Chapel Hill: University of North Carolina Press, 1986), ch. 5; Marsh, *Suburban Lives*, ch. 5.

119. Cross, *Time and Money*, 166–177, 193; Gary Cross and Peter Shergold, "The Family Economy and the Market," *Journal of Family History* 11(3)(1986): 247–249.

120. Stanley Tool ad, *Better Homes and Gardens* (Sept. 1926):3. See also Steven Gelber, *Hobbies: Leisure and the Culture of Work in America* (New York: Columbia University Press, 1999), 204–217.

121. David Lewis and Laurence Goldstein, eds., *The Automobile and American Culture* (Ann Arbor: University of Michigan Press, 1983), 123–133.

122. Lynd, *Middletown*, 251–254.

123. Ewen, *All Consuming Images*, 93.

124. As late as 1932, there were only about 500,000 radios in France, as compared with 5.2 million in Britain and about 17 million in the United States. Mark Pegg, *Broadcasting and Society, 1918–1939* (London: Croom Helm, 1983), 45; Hadley Cantril and Gordon Allport, *The Psychology of Radio* (New York: Harper, 1935), 37.

125. Catherine Covert, " 'We May Hear Too Much': American Sensibility and the Response to Radio, 1919–1924," in Covert and Stevens, eds., *Mass Media Between the Wars*, 199–220; Forty, *Objects of Desire*, 11–12.

126. Lynd, *Middletown*, 269.

127. See, for example, Paul Lazarsfeld, *Radio and the Printed Page* (New York: Duell, Sloan and Pearce, 1940). Good analysis is in Daniel Czitrom, *Media and the American Mind from Morse to McLuhan* (Chapel Hill: University of North Carolina Press, 1982), 80–83 and Cohen, *Making a New Deal*, 327–330.

128. James B. Twitchell, *Carnival Culture* (New York: Columbia University Press, 1992), 40, 52–56; Joanne Finkelstein, *The Fashioned Self* (Cambridge: Polity Press, 1991), 144, 148.

129. Helga Dittmar, *The Social Psychology of Material Possessions: To Have is to Be* (New York: St. Martin's, 1992), 9.

3. PROMISES OF MORE, 1930–1960

1. Ben Wattenberg, ed., *The Statistical History of the United States* (New York: Basic, 1976), 135.

2. "Introduction," Steven Fraser and Gary Gerstle, eds., *The Rise and Fall of the New Deal Order, 1930–1980* (Princeton: Princeton University Press, 1989), xii–xxi.

3. Richard Schickel, *Intimate Strangers: The Cult of Celebrity* (Garden City, N.Y.: Doubleday, 1985), 72–73; Lendol Calder, *Financing the American Dream* (Princeton: Princeton University Press, 1999), 217–230, 271–274; Jesse Steiner, *Research Memorandum on Recreation in the Depression* (New York: Social Science Research Council, 1937), 16, 40, 43, 45–46; National Recreation Association, *The Leisure Hours of 5,000 People* (New York: National Recreation Association, 1934), 15.

4. Dixon Wecter, *The Age of the Great Depression* (New York: Macmillan, 1948), chs. 1, 2; "Walter Pitkin," in Fred Ringel, ed., *America as Americans See It* (New York: Harcourt, Brace, 1932), 203.

5. Roland Vaile, *Research Memorandum on the Social Aspects of Consumption in the Depression* (New York: Social Science Research Council, 1937), 19; Wattenberg, ed., *Statistical History*, 690; Robert and Helen Lynd, *Middletown in Transition* (New York: Harcourt, 1937), 244–246.

6. Vaile, *Research Memorandum on the Social Aspects of Consumption in the Depression*, 23; "Automobile Trailers," *The Index* 17(1937): 63–70; "Auto Firms will Make Trailers," *Business Week* (Oct. 17, 1936):24–25; "200,000 Trailers," *Fortune Magazine* (March 1937):104–111, 214, 220, 222, 224–229; Allen Wallis, *Wheel Estate: The Rise and Decline of Mobile Homes* (New York: Oxford University Press, 1991), chs. 1–2.

7. Rhea Foster Dulles, *A History of Recreation: America Learns to Play* (New York: Appleton-Century, 1965), 333–334; Hadley Cantril and Gordon Allport, *The Psychology of Radio* (New York: Harper, 1935), 14; Vaile, *Research Memorandum on the Social Aspects of Consumption in the Depression*, 19.

8. Don Lescohier, *History of Labor in the United States, 1896–1933*, John R. Commons, ed. (New York: Macmillan, 1935), III:92–93; Calder, *Financing the American Dream*, 266; Wattenberg, ed., *Statistical History*, 139; Vaile, *Research Memorandum on the Social Aspects of Consumption in the Depression*, 15.

9. Glen Elder, *Children of the Great Depression* (Chicago: University of Chicago Press, 1974), 26, 53, 61.

10. I develop this theme in *Time and Money: The Making of Consumer Culture* (New York: Routledge, 1993), ch. 6.

11. Winifred Wandersee, *Women's Work and Family Values, 1920–1940* (Cambridge: Harvard University Press, 1981), 46–54; "How We Live on $2,500 a Year," *Ladies' Home Journal* (Oct. 1930):104.

12. John Findlay, *People of Chance: Gambling in American Society from Jamestown to Las Vegas* (New York: Oxford University Press, 1986), 1–10, 85, 108, 110, 113, 122, 126.

13. Gary Best, *Nickel and Dime Decade* (Westport, Conn.: Praeger, 1993), 26–31; Samuel Lubell, "Ten Billion Nickels," *Saturday Evening Post* (May 13, 1939): 11–12, 38; Wattenberg, ed., *Statistical History*, 401; St. Clair Drake and Horace Cayton, *Black Metropolis* (New York: Oxford University Press, 1962 [1945]), II: 470–494.

14. P. Eisenberg and Paul Lazarsfeld, "The Psychological Effects of Unemployment," *Psychological Bulletin* 35 (1938); John Halliday and Peer Fuller, eds., *The Psychology of Gambling* (New York: Harper and Row, 1974), 128–130; Vincent Lynch and Bill Henkin, *Jukebox, The Golden Age, 1937 Through 1948* (New York: Lancaster-Miller, 1981); Steiner, *Research Memorandum on Recreation in the Depression*, 45–46.

15. Wandersee, *Women's Work and Family Values*, 43; see also Frederic Mishkin, "The Household Balance Sheet and the Great Depression," *Journal of Economic History* 38 (Dec. 1978):918–936; Jesse Steiner, "Recreation and Leisure Time Activities," in President's Research Committee on Social Trends, *Recent Social Trends in the United States* (New York: McGraw-Hill, 1933), II:896.

16. Vaile, *Research Memorandum on the Social Aspects of Consumption in the Depression*, 19, 28; Lewis Mandell, *The Credit Card Industry: A History* (Boston: Twayne, 1990), 157; Robert Lynd, "People as Consumers," in Research Committee on Social Trends, *Recent Social Trends* II:862–863, 892, 896; Lynd, *Middletown in Transition*, 26.

17. E. Wight Bakke, *Citizens Without Work* (New Haven: Yale University Press, 1940), 190; Calder, *Financing the American Dream*, 275; Wandersee, *Women's Work and Family Values*, 26.

18. Bakke, *Citizens Without Work*, 7–8, 11, 192; Mirra Komarovsky, *The Unemployed Man and His Family* (New York: Dryden Press, 1940), 122–128; Steven Gelber, "A Job You Can't Lose: Work and Hobbies in the Great Depression," *Journal of Social History* 24(4)(Summer 1991): 741–766.

19. Gertrude Fish, ed., *The Story of Housing* (New York: Macmillan, 1979), 136, 183–241; *The President's Conference on Home Building and Home Ownership* (Washington, D.C.: U.S. Government Printing Office, 1932); Delores Hayden, *Redesigning the American Dream* (New York: Norton, 1984), 32–34; Kenneth Jackson, *Crabgrass Frontier: The Suburbanization of the United States* (New York: Columbia University Press, 1985), 172–187, 204–218; Mark Foster, *From Streetcar to Superhighway* (Philadelphia: Temple University Press, 1981), 65–70; Margaret Marsh, *Suburban Lives* (New Brunswick: Rutgers University Press, 1990), 146–155.

20. J. Fred MacDonald, *Don't Touch That Dial: Radio Programming in American Life from 1920 to 1960* (Chicago: Nelson-Hall, 1979), chs. 2–5; Alice Marquis, *Hopes and Ashes: The Birth of Modern Times 1929–1939* (New York: Free Press, 1986), 36–37, 40–42; Michele Hilmes, *Radio Voices: American Broadcasting, 1922–1952* (Minneapolis: University of Minnesota Press, 1997), chs. 6–7.

21. Komarovsky, *The Unemployed Man and His Family*, 81–83.

22. Linda Gordon, *Pitied but Not Entitled: Single Mothers and the History of Welfare* (New York: Free Press, 1994), 293–294.

23. Stephanie Coontz, *The Way We Never Were: Families and the Nostalgia Trap* (New York: Basic, 1992) develops this theme.

24. George H. Gallup, *The Gallup Poll* (New York: Random House, 1972), I:148 (interview of March 4–9, 1939); Loren Baritz, *The Good Life: The Meaning of Success for the American Middle Class* (New York: Knopf, 1988), 108.

25. "Ford's V-8 to be Seen," *Business Week* (Feb. 13, 1932):5; David Gartman,

Auto Opium: A Social History of American Automobile Design (London: Routledge, 1994), 105.

26. "Cigarette Strategy," *Business Week* (Jan. 11, 1933):4; Edgar Jones, *Those Were the Good Old Days: American Advertising, 1880–1950* (New York: Simon and Schuster, 1979), 344, 373; Best, *Nickel and Dime Decade*, 36; Jeffrey Meikle, *Twentieth-Century Limited: Industrial Design in America, 1925–1939* (Philadelphia: Temple University Press, 1979), 97; "Platter War," *Business Week* (Nov. 10, 1934):14; G. Edward White, *Creating the National Pastime: Baseball Transforms Itself 1903–1953* (Princeton: Princeton University Press, 1996), ch. 5; Wattenberg, ed., *Statistical History*, 400.

27. "Department Store Branches," *Business Week* (Oct. 1, 1930):10; "Night Shopping," *Business Week* (Nov. 10, 1934):14; "The Cheapy Thrives," *Business Week* (Feb. 8, 1933):11–12.

28. Vincent Vinikas, *Soft Soap, Hard Sell: American Hygiene in an Age of Advertisement* (Ames: Iowa State University Press, 1992), 16; Marquis, *Hopes and Ashes*, 17, 121; Research Committee on Recent Social Trends, *Recent Social Trends*, II:878; Richard Kluger, *Ashes to Ashes* (New York: Knopf, 1996), 93; Wecter, *The Age of the Great Depression*, 26.

29. "An Appraisal of Radio Advertising Today," *Fortune* (Sept. 1932):3; Marquis, *Hopes and Ashes*, 25–40; Charles McGovern, "Sold American: Inventing the Consumer, 1890–1940," Ph.D. diss., Harvard University, 1993, 46, 334–343; Erik Barnouw, *A Tower in Babel* (New York: Oxford University Press, 1966), 109–110, 238; Susan Smulyan, *Selling Radio: The Commercialization of American Broadcasting, 1920–1934* (Washington, D.C.: Smithsonian Institution Press, 1994), 126–132; William Paley, *Radio as a Cultural Force* (New York: CBS, 1934), 104–105, 1 for quotation.

30. Theodore Peterson, *Magazines in the Twentieth Century* (Urbana: University of Illinois Press, 1956), 155; J. S. Lawrence, "Poverty and Plenty," *Review of Reviews* (Oct. 1934):17; Marquis, *Hopes and Ashes*, ch. 3.

31. Gary Cross, *Kids' Stuff: Toys and the Changing World of American Childhood* (Cambridge: Harvard University Press, 1997), ch. 4.

32. Norman Kline, *Seven Minutes: The Life and Death of the American Animated Cartoon* (London: Verso, 1993), 17, 53, 91–95. Note also, among others, Cecil Munsey, *Disneyana: Walt Disney Collectibles* (New York: Abrams, 1974) and Bevis Hillier, *Walt Disney's Mickey Mouse Memorabilia* (New York: Hawthorn, 1986).

33. "An Excellent Season," *Playthings Magazine* (Jan. 1934):34; "Mickey Mouse Looks Forward to 1936," *Playthings Magazine* (Feb. 1936):56–57. Useful sources on the Disney marketing phenomenon include Munsey, *Disneyana*, 32, 39–48, 80–99, 109–100 and Robert Heide and John Gilman, *Cartoon Collectibles:*

50 Years of Dime Store Memorabilia (Garden City, N.Y.: Doubleday, 1983), 101–102, 113–115, 201–213.

34. Richard O'Brien, *Collecting Toys* (Florence, Ala.: Americana Books, 1990), 175–176, 188, 197–210, 229–231; Peter Johnson, *Toy Armies* (Garden City, N.Y.: Doubleday, 1981), 105; Ruth and Larry Freeman, *Cavalcade of Toys* (Watkins Glen, N.Y.: Century House, 1942), 109.

35. E. Evalyn Grumbine, "Juvenile Clubs and Contests," *Printers' Ink Monthly* (May 1936):22, 23, 56, 57; MacDonald, *Don't Touch That Dial*, 42–44. Roland Marchand, "Precocious Consumers and Junior Salesmen: Advertising to Children in the United States to 1940," unpublished paper supplied by the late author.

36. Mike Benton, *The Illustrated Superhero Comics of the Golden Age* (Dallas, Tex.: Taylor Publishing, 1992), 15–30; Marilyn Boemer, *Children's Hour: Radio Programs for Children, 1929–1956* (Metuchen, N.J.: Scarecrow Press, 1989), 49–50.

37. Baritz, *The Good Life*, 154–156; Best, *Nickel and Dime Decade*, 77; Grace Palladino, *Teenagers: An American History* (New York: Basic, 1996), 49–61, quotation on 57.

38. Stephen Bayley, *Taste: The Secret Meaning of Things* (New York: Pantheon, 1991), 27, 169–170; "Modernizing Main Street," *Business Week* (June 8, 1935):12.

39. "Brave New Model World," *Business Week* (Jan. 11, 1933):3–4; "Detroit Gets Ready in Big Style," *Business Week* (Oct. 10, 1936):17–18; "Automatic Transmission — It's Here," *Business Week* (May 22, 1937):18–19; Chrysler ad (1936) in Jones, *Those Were the Good Old Days*, 408; Gartman, *Auto Opium*, ch. 5.

40. Toastmaster ad, *Better Homes and Gardens* (Dec. 1940):34; Wecter, *The Age of the Great Depression*, 225–227; Frederick Lewis, *Since Yesterday: The Nineteen-Thirties in America* (New York: Bantam, 1961), 182.

41. G. Abbott, "Obsolescence and the Passing of High-Pressure Salesmanship," and Ernest Calkins, "The New Consumption Engineer, and the Artist," in George Frederick, ed., *A Philosophy of Production: A Symposium* (New York: The Business Bourse, 1930), 169–171 and 107–129; Ernest Calkins, "What Consumer Engineering Really Is," in Roy Sheldon and Egmont Arens, eds., *Consumer Engineering* (New York: Harper, 1932), 1; Meikle, *Twentieth-Century Limited*, 4, 59, 52–54, 101–110; Adrian Forty, *Objects of Desire* (New York: Pantheon, 1986), 156–160. See also William Lough and Martin Gainsborough, *High-Level Consumption: Its Behavior, Its Consequences* (New York: McGraw-Hill, 1935) and Henry Link, *The New Psychology of Selling and Advertising* (New York: Macmillan, 1932).

42. Robert Rydell, *World of Fairs: The Century-of-Progress Expositions*

(Chicago: University of Chicago Press, 1993), 123–124; Roland Marchand, *Creating the Corporate Soul: The Rise of Public Relations and Corporate Imagery in American Big Business* (Berkeley: University of California Press, 1998), 301–311; Marquis, *Hopes and Ashes*, ch. 5.

43. John Blum, *V Was for Victory* (New York: HBJ, 1976), 99–103.

44. Frank Fox, *Madison Avenue Goes to War: The Strange Military Career of American Advertising 1941–45* (Provo, Utah: Brigham Young University Press, 1975), 46, 56, 70–71; Nash ad, *Time* (Sept. 20, 1943), inside front cover.

45. Blum, *V Was for Victory*, 101; Fox, *Madison Avenue Goes to War*, 74; Stern, *Car Ads*, 61–64; J. Walter Thompson Company, *Fifty Years of Better Ideas: Ford Advertising 1943–1993* (Detroit: J. Walter Thompson Company, 1993), n.p.; Jones, *Those Were the Good Old Days*, 473; Marchand, *Creating the Corporate Soul*, 354–356 especially.

46. Nelson Lichtenstein, "From Corporatism to Collective Bargaining: Organized Labor and the Eclipse of Social Democracy," in Fraser and Gerstle, eds., *The Rise and Fall of the New Deal Order*, 122–152; Ronald Edsforth, "The Transformation of Industrial Unionism," in Ronald Edsforth and Larry Bennett, eds., *Popular Culture and Political Change in Modern America* (Albany: SUNY Press, 1991), 123–124; Meg Jacobs, "The Politics of Purchasing Power: Political Economy, Consumption Politics, and American State-Building," Ph.D. diss., University of Virginia, 1998.

47. Edsforth, "The Transformation of Industrial Unionism," 106–107.

48. David Nye, *Consuming Power* (Cambridge: MIT Press, 1998), 194; Jackson, *Crabgrass Frontier*, 204.

49. Kluger, *Ashes to Ashes*, 19, 185; Wattenberg, ed., *Statistical History*, 690; Thomas Whiteside, *Selling Death: Cigarette Advertising and Public Health* (New York: Liveright, 1971), 21.

50. "Our Backlog for Spending," *U.S. News and World Report* (Aug. 30, 1946):55; Wattenberg, ed., *Statistical History*, 15.

51. "Spending Spree," *Business Week* (Jan. 4, 1947):20; Nye, *Consuming Power*, 187.

52. "People are Changing Their Buying Habits," *U.S. News and World Report* (Jan. 27, 1956):100–102; "Why People Will Spend More," *U.S. News and World Report* (Dec. 10, 1954):21–23; "Marketing," *Business Week* (Nov. 22, 1952):110–118; "The More People Buy, the More They Want," *U.S. News and World Report* (April 15, 1955):77–80; "How Consumers Take to Newness," *Business Week* (Sept. 24, 1955):41–43; George Katona, *The Mass Consumption Society* (New York: McGraw-Hill, 1964), 269.

53. "New Cars: Who Buys Them?" *U.S. News and World Report* (March 14, 1958):84–86; "Cars," *Collier's* (Aug. 21, 1953):18.

54. "Business Will Stay Good," *U.S. News and World Report* (June 11, 1954):44–46.

55. GE ad, *Better Homes and Gardens* (July 1956):111; Kelvinator ad, *Better Homes and Gardens* (Nov. 1946):29; GM ad, *Better Homes and Gardens* (July 1952):92; David Halberstam, *The Fifties* (New York: Villard Books, 1993), 131.

56. Thomas Hine, *Populuxe* (New York: Knopf, 1986), 12, 22, 38, 55, 83–101, 132.

57. Halberstam, *The Fifties*, 184–187, 267; Edward Ward, G. Stokes, and K. Tucker, *Rock of Ages: The Rolling Stone History of Rock & Roll* (New York: Summit, 1986), 231; Katona, *The Mass Consumption Society*, 269.

58. Alfred Sloan, *My Years with General Motors* (New York: Mcfadden, 1965), 265; Gartman, *Auto Opium*, 158.

59. James Flink, *Automobile Age* (Cambridge: MIT Press, 1988), 287; William Whyte, "The Cadillac Phenomenon," *Fortune Magazine* (Feb. 1955):106–109; Sloan, *My Years with General Motors*, 257; Wattenberg, ed., *Statistical History*, 716; "Biggest Year in Auto History," *U.S. News and World Report* (May 13, 1955): 26–28.

60. Ernest Dichter, *Handbook of Consumer Motivations* (New York: McGraw-Hill, 1964), 161, 324, 327; Halberstam, *The Fifties*, 507; Elaine Tyler May, *Homeward Bound: American Families in the Cold War Era* (New York: Basic, 1988), 172; George Lipsitz, "The Meaning of Memory: Family, Class and Ethnicity in Early Network Television Programs," *Cultural Anthropology* 1 (Nov. 1986): 355–387; Nina Leibman, *Living Room Lectures: The Fifties Family in Film and Television* (Austin: University of Texas Press, 1995), 117–173.

61. Findlay, *People of Chance*, 138, 147, 149, 163–164.

62. Bendix ad, *Life Magazine* (Nov. 26, 1945):140; Wattenberg, ed., *Statistical History*, 317–318, 639–640.

63. Harold Wattel, "Levittown: A Suburban Community," in William Dobriner, ed., *The Suburban Community* (New York: Putnam, 1958), 287–313; Barbara Kelly, *Expanding the American Dream: Building and Rebuilding Levittown* (Albany, N.Y.: SUNY Press, 1993), 17, ch. 5; Clifford Clark, *American Family Home* (Chapel Hill: University of North Carolina Press, 1986), 221–224.

64. A good summary is in Clifford Clark, "Ranch-House Suburbia: Ideals and Realities," in Lary May, ed., *Recasting America: Culture and Politics in the Age of Cold War* (Chicago: University of Chicago Press, 1989), 171–189.

65. Elaine May, "Cold War-Warm Hearth: Politics and the Family in Postwar America," in Fraser and Gerstle, eds., *Rise and Fall of the New Deal Order*, 153–181;

May, *Homeward Bound*, 146, 186–187; Herbert Gans, *The Levittowners* (New York: Pantheon, 1967), 278.

66. Sidney Ahlstrom, *A Religious History of the American People* (New Haven: Yale University Press, 1972), 950; David Riesman, *The Lonely Crowd* (New Haven: Yale University Press, 1950), 176–177; William Whyte, *Organization Man* (Garden City, N.Y.: Doubleday, 1956), 284.

67. Dichter, *Handbook of Consumer Motivations*, 117–118.

68. Clark, *American Family Home*, 221.

69. Dichter, *Handbook of Consumer Motivations*, 117–118, 133; Vance Packard, *The Status Seekers* (New York: David McKay, 1959), 65; Lynn Spigel, "From Theater to Space Ship: Metaphors of Suburban Domesticity in Postwar America," in Roger Silverstone, ed., *Visions of Suburbia* (London: Routledge, 1997), 219, 221; Hine, *Populuxe*, 52.

70. Karal Ann Marling, *As Seen on TV: The Visual Culture of Everyday Life in the 1950s* (Cambridge: Harvard University Press, 1994), 54–84, 216, 218; Steven Gelber, "Do-It-Yourself: Construction, Repairing, and Maintaining Domestic Masculinity," *American Quarterly* 49(1)(March 1997): 89–112; Steven Gelber, *Hobbies: Leisure and the Culture of Work in America* (New York: Columbia University Press, 1999), 255–294.

71. Alison Clarke, "Tupperware: Suburbia, Sociality, and Mass Consumption," in Silverstone, *Visions of Suburbia*, 132–160; Alison Clarke, *Tupperware: The Promise of Plastic in 1950s America* (Washington, D.C.: Smithsonian Institution Press, 1999); Hine, *Populuxe*, 36.

72. Virginia Jenkins, *The Lawn: A History of an American Obsession* (Washington, D.C.: Smithsonian Institution Press, 1994), 107, 112, 134.

73. Cobbett Steinberg, *TV Facts* (New York: Facts on File, 1980), 142.

74. Horace Newcomb, *TV: the Most Popular Art* (Garden City, N.Y.: Anchor, 1974), chs. 2, 3; Rolf Meyersohn, "Social Research in Television," and Dwight MacDonald, "A Theory of Mass Culture," in Bernard Rosenberg and David White, eds., *Mass Culture* (Glencoe, Ill.: Free Press 1957), 352, 361; Robert Sklar, *Prime-Time America* (New York: Oxford University Press, 1980), 3.

75. Erik Barnouw, *Tube of Plenty: The Evolution of American Television* (New York: Oxford University Press, 1977), 193–198, 214, 261, 262, 347; Randy Roberts and James Olson, *Winning is the Only Thing: Sports in America Since 1945* (Baltimore: Johns Hopkins University Press, 1989), 95–113; Andrew Hurley, "From Hash House to Family Restaurant: The Transformation of the Diner in Post-World War II Consumer Culture," *Journal of American History* 4(March 1997): 1282–1308.

76. Marling, *As Seen on TV*, ch. 3. See also John Mosley, *Disney's World* (New York: Stein and Day, 1985) and Margaret King, "Disneyland and Walt Disney World: Traditional Values in Futuristic Form," *Journal of Popular Culture* 15 (Summer 1981).

77. Lynn Spigel, *Make Room for TV: Television and the Family Ideal in Postwar America* (Chicago: University of Chicago Press, 1992), 39; Ruth Rosen, "Soap Operas: Search for Yesterday," and Tom Engelhardt, "Children's Television, The Shortcake Strategy," in Todd Gitlin, ed., *Watching Television* (New York: Pantheon, 1986), 42–111; Warren Susman, *Culture as History: The Transformation of American Society in the Twentieth Century* (New York: Pantheon, 1984), 160; Martin Meyer, *About Television* (New York: Harper and Row, 1972), 389–391.

78. Spigel, *Make Room for TV*, 71–74, 102; Cecelia Tichi, *Electronic Hearth: Creating an American Television Culture* (New York: Oxford University Press, 1991), 16, 19, 29, 32.

79. Barnouw, *Tube of Plenty*, 354; J. Fred MacDonald, *One Nation Under Television* (New York: Pantheon, 1990), 113; Hine, *Populuxe*, 1.

80. Max Boas and Steve Chain, *Big Mac* (New York: Mentor, 1976), 15–16, 19; Halberstam, *The Fifties*, 155–157; Nye, *Consuming Power*, 206.

81. Christopher Finch, *Highways to Heaven: The Auto Biography of America* (New York: HarperCollins, 1992), 237–242.

82. Jackson, *Crabgrass Frontier*, 281.

83. Peter Whelihan, "Jack and Jill Fill the Till," *Nation's Business* (Oct. 1948):42–44, 75; Eugene Balsley, "The Hot-Rod Culture," *American Quarterly* 2(1950): 353; Palladino, *Teenagers*, ch. 10.

84. Mark McGee, *Beyond Ballyhoo: Motion Picture Promotion and Gimmicks* (London: McFarland, 1989), ch. 3–4; Carl Belz, *The Story of Rock* (New York: Oxford University Press, 1969), 36, ch. 2.

85. "Teen-Age Market: It's 'Terrif'," *Business Week* (June 8, 1946):72–73; Eugene Gilbert, *Advertising and Marketing to Young People* (Pleasantville, N.Y.: Printers' Ink, 1957); Palladino, *Teenagers*, 100–107, 110, 112, ch. 8.

86. Coke ad, *Better Homes and Gardens* (Oct. 1944):59; Riesman, *The Lonely Crowd*, 100, 102, 120; Cross, *Kids' Stuff*, ch. 6.

87. James Gilbert, *A Cycle of Outrage: America's Reaction to the Juvenile Delinquent in the 1950s* (New York: Oxford University Press, 1986), ch. 6; Fredric Wertham, *The Seduction of the Innocent* (New York: Rinehart, 1954).

88. Palladino, *Teenagers*, ch. 8 and Halberstam, *The Fifties*, 463.

89. George Lipsitz, *Class and Culture in Cold War America* (South Hadley, Mass.: Bergin & Garvey, 1982), 219; Palladino, *Teenagers*, ch. 9; Marling, *As Seen on TV*, ch. 5; Ward, Stokes, and Tucker, *Rock of Ages*, chs. 5, 8, 9; Larry Bennett,

"The Domestication of Rock and Roll," in Edsforth and Bennett, eds., *Popular Culture and Political Change in Modern America*, 137–162.

90. Gilbert, *The Cycle of Outrage*, ch. 12.

91. Coontz, *The Way We Never Were*, ch. 1.

4. COPING WITH ABUNDANCE

1. Note, for example, James Twitchell, *Lead Us Into Temptation: The Triumph of American Materialism* (New York: Columbia University Press, 1999) and Stanley Lebergott, *Pursuing Happiness: American Consumers in the Twentieth Century* (Princeton: Princeton University Press, 1993), ch. 1.

2. Jackson Lears, *Fables of Abundance: A Cultural History of Advertising in America* (New York: Basic, 1994), 139; Joyce Appleby, *Capitalism and a New Social Order: The Republican Vision of the 1790s* (New York: New York University Press, 1984); John E. Crowley, *This Sheba Self: The Conceptualization of Economic Life in Eighteenth-Century America* (Baltimore: Johns Hopkins University Press, 1974); Michael Merrill, "Putting Capitalism in Its Place," *William and Mary Quarterly* 52(3)(1995): 315–326.

3. A good place to start in this huge literature is Philip Greven, *The Protestant Temperament* (New York: Knopf, 1977) and David Shi, *The Simple Life: Plain Living and High Thinking in American Culture* (New York: Oxford University Press, 1985), 50–214.

4. Mark E. Lender and James Martin, *Drinking in America: A History* (New York: Free Press, 1987), 95, 119, 129, 137; J. C. Burnham, "New Perspectives on the Prohibition Experiment of the 1920s," in Erik Monkkonen, ed., *Prostitution, Drugs, Gambling and Organized Crime* (New York: K. G. Saur, 1992), 97–114; and the classic, W. J. Rorabaugh, *The Alcoholic Republic: An American Tradition* (New York: Oxford University Press, 1979).

5. Edward Behr, *Prohibition: Thirteen Years That Changed America* (New York: Arcade, 1996), 26; David Kyvig, "Sober Thoughts: Myth and Realities of National Prohibition After Fifty Years," in David Kyvig, ed., *Law, Alcohol, and Order* (Westport, Conn.: Greenwood Press, 1985), 3–20. For negative assessments of prohibition, see Richard Hofstadter, *The Age of Reform: From Bryant to FDR* (New York: Knopf, 1955), 292; Andrew Sinclair, *Prohibition: The Era of Excess* (New York: Atlantic Monthly Press, 1962); John Rumbarger, *Profits, Power, and Prohibition* (Albany: SUNY Press, 1988). For an interesting update, see Peter Stearns, *The Battleground of Desire: The Struggle for Self-Control in Modern America* (New York: New York University Press, 1999), ch. 9.

6. Kenneth Meier, *The Politics of Sin: Drugs, Alcohol, and Public Policy* (Armonk, N.Y.: M.E. Sharpe, 1994), ch. 5, 48, 65; Richard Kluger, *Ashes to Ashes* (New

York: Knopf, 1996), ch. 6; Robert Proctor, *Cancer Wars* (New York: Basic, 1995), 110–111; Philip Hilt, *Smoke Screen: The Truth Behind the Tobacco Cover-Up* (Reading, Mass.: Addison-Wesley, 1996), chs. 1 and 2.

7. Reuven Brenner, *Gambling and Speculation* (New York: Cambridge University Press, 1990), 82, 88; Roger Munting, *An Economic and Social History of Gambling in Britain and the USA* (Manchester: Manchester University Press), 6–54.

8. Herbert Marx, *Gambling in America* (New York: H. W. Wilson, 1952), 156; Jan McMillen, "Understanding Gambling," in Jan McMillen, ed., *Gambling Cultures: Studies in History and Interpretation* (New York: Routledge, 1996), ch. 2.

9. Hillel Schwartz, *Never Satisfied: A Cultural History of Diets, Fantasies, and Fat* (New York: Anchor, 1986), 5, 11, 83, 86–87, 96, 105, ch. 5; Peter Stearns, *Fat History: Bodies and Beauty in the Modern West* (New York: New York University Press, 1997); chs. 1, 2; Harvey Green, *Fit for America: Health, Fitness, and Sport in American Society* (New York: Pantheon, 1986); David Armstrong and Elizabeth Armstrong, *The Great American Medicine Show* (New York: Prentice-Hall, 1991), chs. 12, 13; Scott Bruce and Bill Crawford, *Cerealizing America: The Unsweetened Story of American Breakfast Cereal* (Boston: Faber and Faber, 1995), 10–62; Harvey Levenstein, *Revolution at the Table: The Transformation of the American Diet* (New York: Oxford University Press, 1988), 165, 194.

10. Susan Benson, *Counter Cultures: Saleswomen, Managers, and Customers in American Department Stores* (Urbana, Ill.: University of Illinois Press, 1986), 90; Martha Olney, *Buy Now, Pay Later* (Chapel Hill: University of North Carolina Press, 1991), 183; Lendol Calder, *Financing the American Dream* (Princeton: Princeton University Press, 1999), 184–186, 217–230.

11. Charles Wagner, *The Simple Life* (New York: Grosset and Dunlap, 1904), 12, 15, 16; Ralph Borsodi, *The Ugly Civilization* (New York: Simon and Schuster, 1929), 15, 16, 18, 89, 113, 341, 350–351.

12. Shi, *The Simple Life*, 50–214, quotation on 160.

13. Emile Durkheim, *Suicide: A Study in Sociology* (New York: Free Press, 1951 [1897]), 246–258; E. Durkheim, *The Division of Labor in Society* (New York: Free Press, 1964 [1893]), 353–373, 173; Rosiland Williams, *Dream Worlds: Mass Consumption in Late Nineteenth-Century France* (Berkeley: University of California Press, 1981), 322–342; Patrick Brantlinger, *Bread and Circuses: Theories of Mass Culture as Social Decay* (Ithaca: Cornell University Press, 1983), ch. 2; José Ortega y Gasset, *Revolt of the Masses* (New York: Norton, 1957 [1932]), 7–8, 10–11, 48–49.

14. Louise More, *Wage-Earners' Budgets: A Study of Standards and Cost of Living in New York City* (New York: Henry Holt, 1907), 170–180; A. Clark and Edith

Wyatt, *Making Both Ends Meet: The Income and Outlay of New York City Working Girls* (New York: Macmillan, 1911), 10; Peter Roberts, "Immigrant Wage-Earners," in Paul Kellogg, ed., *Wage-Earning Pittsburgh* (New York: Survey Associates, 1914), 50.

15. Richard Edwards, *Popular Amusements* (New York: Association Press, 1915), 133, 138–143.

16. Thorstein Veblen, *The Theory of the Leisure Class* (New York: New American Library, 1953 [1899]), 70–71, chs. 2, 13, 14; T. Veblen, *Instinct of Workmanship* (New York: Norton, 1964 [1914]), 318–320. See also Daniel Horowitz, "Consumption and Its Discontents," *Journal of American History* (Sept. 1980):307–310.

17. Veblen, *The Theory of the Leisure Class*, ch. 13 and Daniel Horowitz, *The Morality of Spending: Attitudes Toward the Consumer Society in America, 1875–1940* (Baltimore: Johns Hopkins University Press, 1985), 37–44.

18. Some examples of this impulse from the 1930s include: James Rorty, *Where Life Is Better* (New York: Reynal & Hitchcock, 1936); Sherwood Anderson, *Puzzled America* (New York: Scribners, 1935); Louis Adamic, *My America* (New York: Harper, 1938); Nathan Asch, *The Road: In Search of America* (New York: Harper, 1936); Erskine Caldwell, *Some American People* (New York: McBride, 1935).

19. Walter Pitkin, *The Consumer, His Nature and His Changing Habits* (New York: McGraw-Hill, 1932), 104–105, 352–370, 372; Gary Cross, *Time and Money: The Making of Consumer Culture* (New York: Routledge, 1993), ch. 2; David Nye, *Consuming Power* (Cambridge: MIT Press, 1998), 203.

20. Simon Patten, *New Basis of Civilization* (New York: Macmillan, 1915), 123.

21. Cross, *Time and Money*, ch. 5.

22. John Dewey, *Democracy and Education* (New York: Free Press, 1966 [1916]), ch. 19; Benjamin Hunnicutt, *Work Without End: Abandoning Shorter Hours for the Right to Work* (Philadelphia: Temple University Press, 1988), 116–120; 1923 ad for Colliers' Publishing, in Ernest Jones, *Those Were the Good Old Days: American Advertising, 1880–1950* (New York: Simon and Schuster, 1979), 250; Joan Rubin, *The Making of Middle/Brow Culture* (Chapel Hill: University of North Carolina Press, 1992), chs. 1, 3, 4, 5; Lawrence Levine, *Highbrow/Lowbrow: The Emergence of a Cultural Hierarchy in America* (Cambridge: Harvard University Press, 1988), 23–30; Susan Smulyan, *Selling Radio: The Commercialization of American Broadcasting, 1920–1934* (Washington, D.C.: Smithsonian Institution Press, 1994), 65–66.

23. The number of public museums in the United States increased from 94 in 1910 to 149 in 1930. The number of public park and recreation departments in the United States rose from 146 in 1921 to 428 by 1931. Jesse Steiner, *Americans at Play*

(New York: Harper Brothers, 1933), ch. 3, 169; President's Research Committee on Social Trends, *Recent Social Trends in the United States* (New York: McGraw-Hill, 1933), II:995; Ben Wattenberg, ed., *Statistical History of the United States* (New York: Basic, 1976), 399.

24. Charles Wrenn, *Time on Their Hands* (Washington: American Council on Education, 1941), 52–54, 94–98, 195–198, 222–232; Dorothy Cline, *Training for Recreation* (Chicago: University of Chicago Press, 1939), ch. 2.

25. William Ogburn, *Social Change with Respect to Cultural and Original Nature* (New York: B. W. Huebsch, 1922), 141; Cross, *Time and Money*, ch. 3.

26. These University of Chicago studies include Frederic Thrasher, *The Gang* (1927); Harvey Zorbaugh, *The Gold Coast and the Slum* (1929); Paul Cressey, *Taxi Dance Hall* (1932); and Walter Reckless, *Vice in Chicago* (1933).

27. "Introduction," Research Committee on Social Trends, *Recent Social Trends*, I:liii.

28. Michael Sandel, *Democracy's Discontent: America in Search of Democracy* (Cambridge: Belknap Press, 1996), ch. 1; Frank Fox, *Madison Avenue Goes to War* (Provo, Utah: Brigham Young University Press, 1975), ch. 2; Robert Mayer, *The Consumer Movement: Guardians of the Marketplace* (Boston: Twyane, 1989), 24–25; H. J. Kenner, *The Fight for Truth in Advertising* (New York: Round Table Press, 1936), 27; Helen Sorenson, *Consumer Movement: What It Is and What It Means* (New York: Harper and Brothers, 1941), 12–14.

29. Robert Lynd, "The People as Consumers," in Research Committee on Social Trends, *Recent Social Trends in the United States*, II:910–911.

30. Paul Douglas, *The Coming of a New Party* (New York: McGraw-Hill, 1932); Liz Cohen, "Making Citizen Consumers Through Depression and War: The Rise of the Consumer in a Faltering Economy," Research Seminar Paper #12, The Center for the History of Business, Technology and Society, Hagley Museum, Wilmington, Del., March 1997, 14–18, 25–68 (used with permission).

31. Caroline Ware, *The Consumer Goes to War* (New York: Funk & Wagnalls, 1941), 194–235.

32. Roger Babson and C. N. Stone, *Consumer Protection: How It Can be Secured* (New York: Harper and Brothers, 1938), ch. 12; Charles McGovern, "Sold American: Inventing the Consumer, 1890–1940," Ph.D. diss., Harvard University, 1993, chs. 5 and 6, especially 201–211, 246–281, 272, 289, 307. See also Stuart Chase, *The Tragedy of Waste* (New York: Macmillan, 1925); S. Chase and Frederick Schlink, *Your Money's Worth* (New York: Macmillan, 1927); Arthur Kallet and F. Schlink, *100,000,000 Guinea Pigs: Dangers in Everyday Foods, Drugs, and Cosmetics* (New York: Vanguard, 1933); James Rorty, *Our Master's Voice: Advertising* (New York:

John Day, 1934); F. Schlink, *Eat, Drink, and Be Wary* (New York: Grosset & Dunlap, 1935); Ruth Lamb, *American Chamber of Horrors* (New York: Farrar & Rinehart, 1935).

33. Robert Fishman, *Bourgeois Utopias: The Rise and Fall of Suburbia* (New York: Basic, 1987), 3–17 and 155–181 especially.

34. See Richard Sennett, *The Fall of Public Man* (New York: Knopf, 1977), chs. 1, 7.

35. Shi, *The Simple Life*, 16, chs. 5, 6; Jennifer Scanlon, *Inarticulate Longings: The* Ladies' Home Journal, *Gender and the Promises of Consumer Culture* (New York: Routledge, 1995), 40–41, 52–54.

36. Fishman, *Bourgeois Utopias*, chs. 1, 5; Ellen Richards, *The Cost of Living as Modified by Sanitary Science* (New York: Wiley, 1910), 85, 129; Horowitz, *The Morality of Spending*, 78–84.

37. Viviana Zelizer, *Pricing the Priceless Child: The Changing Social Value of Children* (New York: Basic, 1985), 3–21, 103–112.

38. Smulyan, *Selling Radio*, ch. 1, 41, 44, 65–66; Gleason Archer, *Big Business and Radio* (New York: American Historical Company, 1939), 31.

39. *Printers' Ink* (Feb. 22, 1923):157; Roland Marchand, *Advertising the American Dream* (Berkeley: University of California Press, 1988), 89; Frank Arnold, *Broadcast Advertising: The Fourth Dimension* (New York: Wiley, 1931), 42; Erik Barnouw, *A Tower in Babel: A History of Broadcasting in the United States* (New York: Oxford University Press, 1966), II:177; Otis Pease, *The Responsibilities of American Advertising* (New Haven: Yale University Press, 1958), 34.

40. Smulyan, *Selling Radio*, 61, 71; Marchand, *Advertising the American Dream*, 109–110; Barnouw, *A Tower in Babel*, 237.

41. J. Fred MacDonald, *Don't Touch That Dial: Radio Programming in American Life, 1920–1960* (Chicago: Nelson-Hall, 1979); chs. 1–3; Paul Lazarsfeld and Frank Stanton, eds., *Radio Research 1941* (New York: Arno Press 1979), 110–139, 189; Rubin, *The Making of Middle/Brow Culture*, 270–272; Daniel Czitrom, *Media and The American Mind: From Morse to McLuhan* (Chapel Hill: University of North Carolina Press, 1982), 102–112.

42. Gilbert Seldes, "Heckling the Hucksters," *Saturday Review* (Jan. 30, 1954):28; Newton Minow, *Equal Time: The Private Broadcaster and the Public Interest* (New York: Atheneum, 1964), ch. 1; J. Fred MacDonald, *One Nation Under Television* (New York: Pantheon, 1990), 133.

43. David Macleod, *The Age of the Child: Children in America, 1890–1920* (New York: Twayne, 1998), 111–118; Zelizer, *Pricing the Priceless Child*, 13; Roland Marchand, "Precocious Consumers and Junior Salesmen: Advertising to Children

in the United State to 1940," unpublished paper supplied by the author. Of course, ads in boys' magazines and comic books did give children "hints" as to how to persuade parents to buy electric trains or air rifles.

44. Kathleen McCarthy, "Nickel Vice and Virtue: Movie Censorship in Chicago, 1907–1915," *Journal of Popular Film* 5(1976): 37–55; Robert Fisher, "Film Censorship and Progressive Reform: The National Board of Censorship of Motion Pictures, 1909–1922," *Journal of Popular Film* 4(1975): 143–156; Tino Balio, *The American Film Industry* (Madison: University of Wisconsin Press, 1976), 103–118, 213–228; Mark Fackler, "Moral Guardians of the Movies and Social Responsibility of the Press," in Catherine Covert and John Stevens, eds., *Mass Media Between the Wars* (Syracuse: Syracuse University Press, 1984), 181–197.

45. Lender and Martin, *Drinking in America*, 152–155; Burnham, "New Perspectives on the Prohibition Experiment," 97–114; Meier, *The Politics of Sin*, ch. 5; Kyvig, "Sober Thoughts," 3–20.

46. Alcoholics Anonymous, *The Twelve Steps and Twelve Traditions* (New York: AA Publishers, 1953); Alcoholics Anonymous, *Alcoholics Anonymous Comes of Age* (New York: Harper, 1957).

47. Dom Cavallo, *Muscles and Morals: Organized Playgrounds and Urban Reform, 1880–1920* (Philadelphia: University of Pennsylvania Press, 1981), 46–48.

48. Cross, *Time and Money*, chs. 3, 5.

49. David Riesman, *Thorstein Veblen, A Critical Interpretation* (New York: Scribner, 1953), 170–208 especially; Andrew Ross, *No Respect: Intellectuals and Popular Culture* (London: Routledge, 1989), ch. 1, 45–47, 220.

50. Jeff Bishop and Paul Hoggett, *Organizing Around Enthusiasms: Mutual Aid in Leisure* (London: Comedia, 1986), 55, 122, ch. 3; Cross, *Time and Money*, ch. 5.

51. Simon Patten, *Product and Climax* (New York: Huebsch, 1909), 53; Patten, *New Basis of Civilization*, 11, 85, 117, 137–140; S. Patten, *The Theory of Prosperity* (New York: Macmillan, 1902), 230–231; Horowitz, *The Morality of Spending*, 30–37, 47; Daniel Fox, *The Discovery of Abundance: Simon N. Patten and the Transformation of Social Theory* (Ithaca: Cornell University Press, 1967), 77–79, 100.

52. William Leach, *Land of Desire: Merchants, Power and the Rise of a New American Culture* (New York: Vintage, 1993), 70, 202–210; Lears, *Fables of Abundance*, 139.

53. Fox, *The Discovery of Abundance*, 73–74; Rubin, *The Making of Middle/Brow Culture*, 25, 31, 32.

54. Donald Meyer, *The Positive Thinkers* (New York: Pantheon, 1980), ch. 8;

T. J. Jackson Lears, "From Salvation to Self-Realization," in Richard Fox and Jackson Lears Fox, eds., *The Culture of Consumption* (New York: Pantheon, 1983), 7–25; Jackson Lears, *No Place for Grace: Antimodernism and the Transformation of American Culture, 1880–1920* (New York: Pantheon, 1981), 35–40; Stanley Coben, *Rebellion Against Victorianism: The Impetus for Cultural Change in 1920s America* (New York: Oxford University Press, 1991), ch. 3 especially; Susan Curtis, *A Consuming Faith: The Social Gospel and Modern American Culture* (Baltimore: Johns Hopkins University Press, 1991), 14.

55. Cohen, "Making Citizen Consumers Through Depression and War," 14–18, 25–68.

56. McGovern, "Sold American," 75–77, 101–103, 107.

57. "American Way" ad by GM, *Saturday Evening Post* (Nov. 7, 1936):34–35; Roy Durstine, "Advertising," in Harold Stearns, ed., *America Now, An Inquiry into Civilization in the United States* (New York: Scribner's Sons, 1938), 167, 172, 176, 181.

58. "AFA Meeting," *Printers' Ink* 29(June 1939): 67; "Guinea Pigs, Left March," *Forum* (Oct. 1939):153–154. See also McGovern, "Sold American," 371–372.

59. Hunnicutt, *Work Without End*, chs. 7, 8.

60. William T. Foster and Waddill Catchings, *Business Without a Buyer* (Boston: Houghton Mifflin, 1928), ix–xi, 11, 115–125; W. Foster and W. Catchings, *The Road to Plenty* (Boston: Houghton Mifflin, 1928), iii–iv; Hunnicutt, *Work Without End*, ch. 2; Olivier Zunz, *Why the American Century* (Chicago: University of Chicago Press, 1998), 81–85.

61. Harry Hopkins, *Congressional Digest*, July 1938, 29; M. S. Eccles, "Government Spending is Sound," *Vital Speeches* 5(Jan. 23, 1939): 272; Hunnicutt, *Work Without End*, 201, 205–206.

62. Maurice Leven, Harold Moulton, and Clark Warburton, *America's Capacity to Consume* (Washington: Brookings Institution, 1934); Zunz, *Why the American Century*, 85–88; Alan Brinkley, *End of Reform: New Deal Liberalism in Recession and War* (New York: Knopf, 1995), 65–85; Alan Brinkley, "The New Deal and the Idea of the State," in Steve Fraser and Gary Gerstle, eds., *Rise and Fall of the New Deal Order* (Princeton: Princeton University Press, 1989), 85–121; Alan Sweezy, "The Keynesians and Government Policy, 1933–1939," *American Economic Review* 62(2)(May 1972): 116–124.

63. J. S. Lawrence, "Poverty and Plenty," *Review of Reviews* (Oct. 1934):4–6, 15, 17; Stuart Chase, *Idle Money Idle Men* (New York: Harcourt, Brace, 1940), 86–95; U.S. Bureau of the Census, *Historical Statistics of the United States* (Stamford, Conn.: Fairfield, 1965), 717.

64. "A Minimum Living Wage," *American Federation* (April 1898):8 cited in Lawrence Glickman, *A Living Wage: American Workers and the Making of Consumer Society* (Ithaca: Cornell University Press, 1997), 5; Alice Kessler-Harris, *A Woman's Wage: Historical Meanings and Social Consequences* (Lexington: University Press of Kentucky, 1990), 9; Gary Gerstle, *Working-Class Americanism: The Politics of Labor in a Textile City, 1914–1960* (Princeton: Princeton University Press, 1989), ch. 1.

65. George Gunton, *Wealth and Progress* (New York: Appleton, 1887), 89, 95, 189 (quotation), 323, 380; Horowitz, *The Morality of Spending*, 41–49.

66. Lears, *Fables of Abundance*, 222, 253; Winston White, *Beyond Conformity* (Glencoe, Ill.: Free Press, 1961), 137–138.

67. Chester Bowles, *Tomorrow Without Fear* (New York: Simon and Schuster, 1946), 49; Steven Fraser, *Labor Will Rule: Sidney Hillman and the Rise of American Labor* (New York: Free Press, 1991), 259–269; Nelson Lichtenstein, *The Most Dangerous Man in Detroit: Walter Reuther and the Fate of American Labor* (New York: Basic, 1995), 175–190; Ronald Edforth, "Why Automation Didn't Shorten the Work Week: The Politics of Work Time in the Automobile Industry, 1926–1970," unpublished paper supplied by the author.

68. George Katona, *The Mass Consumption Society* (New York: McGraw-Hill, 1964), 51.

69. Liz Cohen, *A Consumer's Republic: The Politics of Consumption in Postwar America* (New York: Knopf, forthcoming); David Plotke, *Building a Democratic Political Order: Reshaping American Liberalism in the 1930s and 1940s* (New York: Cambridge University Press, 1996), 271–279; Meg Jacobs, "The Politics of Plenty: Consumerism in the Twentieth-Century United States," Material Politics Conference, Cambridge University, Churchill College, September 3–5, 1999 (used with permission).

70. Leigh E. Schmidt, *Consumer Rites: The Buying and Selling of American Holidays* (Princeton: Princeton University Press, 1995); Horowitz, *The Morality of Spending*, ch. 6.

71. Scanlon, *Inarticulate Longings*, ch. 4; Lears, *Fables of Abundance*, ch 6.

72. Barnouw, *A Tower in Babel*, 237–240; Smulyan, *Selling Radio*, ch. 5.

73. Gary Cross, *Kids' Stuff: Toys and the Changing World of American Childhood* (Cambridge: Harvard University Press, 1997), chs. 2, 5.

74. Peter Stearns, *American Cool* (New York: New York University Press, 1994), 214.

75. William Whyte, *Organization Man* (Garden City, N.Y.: Doubleday, 1957), 128, 111; John K. Galbraith, *The Affluent Society* (New York: New American Library, 1958), 155.

5. A NEW CONSUMERISM, 1960–1980

1. Jim Heath, *John F. Kennedy and the Business Community* (Chicago: University of Chicago Press, 1969), 118–120; Richard Barber, "The New Partnership," *New Republic* 23(Aug. 13, 1966): 22.

2. Harold Wilensky, "Mass Culture and Mass Society," *American Sociological Review* 29(April 1964): 173–197; S. M. Lipset, "The End of Ideology," in Chaim Waxman, ed., *The End of Ideology Debate* (New York: Funk & Wagnalls, 1968), 73; Daniel Bell, *End of Ideology: On the Exhaustion of Political Ideas in the Fifties* (Glencoe, Ill.: Free Press, 1960), ch. 1. See Paul Blumberg, *Inequality in an Age of Decline* (New York: Oxford University Press, 1980), ch. 1 for more on the theory of class convergence.

3. George Katona, *The Mass Consumption Society* (New York: McGraw-Hill, 1964), 50–53, 65; Bell, *End of Ideology*, 38. Note also Daniel Horowitz, "The Emigré as Celebrant of American Consumer Culture," in Susan Strasser, ed., *Getting and Spending: European and American Consumer Societies in the Twentieth Century* (Washington, D.C.: Cambridge University Press, 1998), 149–166. John Rae's history of American automobility combines a similar effort to equate democracy with mass ownership of this mobile durable good and to condemn critics for elitism. J. Rae, *The Road and the Car in America* (Cambridge: MIT Press, 1971). Similar views are in Peter Passell and Leonard Ross, *The Retreat from Riches: Affluence and Its Enemies* (New York: Viking, 1973).

4. Katona, *The Mass Consumption Society*, 3, 9; George Katona et al., *Aspiration and Affluence: Comparative Studies in the United States and Western Europe* (New York: McGraw-Hill, 1971), 12, 11, 15.

5. Steuart Britt, *The Spenders: Where and Why Your Money Goes* (New York: McGraw-Hill, 1960), 31, 37–40, 65, 66, 117, 151.

6. Lucy Black Creighton, *Pretenders to the Throne: The Consumer Movement in the United States* (Lexington, Mass.: Lexington Books, 1976), 33; Barbara Murray, *Consumerism: The Eternal Triangle* (Pacific Palisades, Calif.: Goodyear, 1973), 16–55.

7. Warren Magnuson and Jean Carper, *The Dark Side of the Marketplace: The Plight of the American Consumer* (Englewood Cliffs, N.J.: Prentice-Hall, 1968), ix, 59.

8. Vance Packard, *Hidden Persuaders* (New York: David McKay, 1957), 19, 25, 59, 117; Daniel Horowitz, *Vance Packard and American Social Criticism* (Chapel Hill: University of North Carolina Press, 1994), 133.

9. David Vogel, *Fluctuating Fortunes: The Political Power of Business in America* (New York: Basic, 1988), 31.

10. Sidney Margolius, *The Innocent Consumer vs. the Exploiters* (New York: Trident, 1967), 1, 6, 7, 11, 107, 113; S. Margolius, *The Responsible Consumer, Public Affairs Pamphlet* No. 453 (Sept. 1970): 1, 3, 4. See also David Caplovitz, *The Poor Pay More: Consumer Practices of Low-Income Families* (New York: Free Press, 1963) and Hillel Black, *Buy Now, Pay Later* (New York: Morrow, 1961), 6, 105.

11. Ralph Nader, *Unsafe at Any Speed: The Designed-in Dangers in the American Automobile* (New York: Grossman, 1965). See also John Jerome, *Death of the Automobile* (New York: Norton, 1972); Emma Rothchild, *Paradise Lost: The Decline of the Automobile-Industrial Age* (New York: Random House, 1973); David Gartman, *Auto Opium: A Social History of American Automobile Design* (London: Routledge, 1994), ch. 7.

12. Margolius, *The Innocent Consumer vs. the Exploiters*, 113.

13. Ralph Nader, "A Citizens' Guide to the American Economy," in Ralph Nader, ed., *The Consumer and Corporate Accountability* (New York: Harcourt Brace Jovanovich, 1973), 4–18, 51; Ralph Nader, "The Great American Gyp," in Murray, *Consumerism*, 39–51; and Creighton, *Pretenders to the Throne*, ch. 5.

14. Kendall Bailes, *Environmental History: Critical Issues in Comparative Perspective* (Lanham, Md.: University Press of America, 1985); Victor Scheffer, *The Shaping of Environmentalism in America* (Seattle: University of Washington Press, 1991); J. M. Petulla, *American Environmental History* (Columbus, Ohio: Merrill, 1988).

15. Fairfield Osborn, *The Limits of the Earth* (Boston: Little, Brown, 1953), 226.

16. Rachel Carson, *Silent Spring* (New York: Houghton Mifflin, 1962), 19, 16, 17, 161.

17. Paul Ehrlich, *The Population Bomb* (New York: Ballantine, 1968), 20–21, 60, 67, 129, 137, 185–187.

18. Vance Packard, *The Waste Makers* (New York: David McKay, 1960), 36, 69, 85, 93.

19. Donella Meadows, *The Limits to Growth* (New York: Universe Books, 1972), 127. Jeremy Rifkin, *Entropy, A New World View* (New York: Bantam, 1981), 248–254 saw the dissipation of energy as the ultimate meaning of consumer culture.

20. E. F. Schumacher, *Small Is Beautiful: A Study of Economics as if People Mattered* (London: Blond & Briggs, 1973), 19, 29, 55, 166. Note also Gary Snyder's *Turtle Island* (New York: New Directions, 1974), 91–100, which finds mass consumption the source of conflict, envy, and the breakup of community. For Snyder, a spiritual renewal, not government, was necessary to surmount the causes of consumerism.

21. Thomas Frank, *The Conquest of Cool* (Chicago: University of Chicago

Press, 1997), 59, ch. 1; Barbara Ehrenreich, *Fear of Falling: The Inner Life of the Middle Class* (New York: HarperCollins, 1990), 32–36.

22. Packard, *Hidden Persuaders*, 5, 59, 201, 236; V. Packard, *The Status Seekers* (New York: David McKay, 1961), 200, 220, 314, 318. See also Horowitz, *Vance Packard*, ch. 6.

23. Herbert Marcuse, *One-Dimensional Society* (Boston: Beacon, 1964), 84, 57, 72–73; H. Marcuse, *An Essay on Liberation* (Boston: Beacon, 1969), 4, 51; H. Marcuse, *Counterrevolution and Revolt* (Boston: Beacon, 1972), 14.

24. Norman Mailer, "The White Negro: Superficial Reflections on the Hipster," (1957) in his book of essays, *Advertisements for Myself* (New York: Putnam, 1959), 339; David McReynolds, *We Have Been Invaded by the 21st Century* (New York: Praeger, 1970), 94, 98.

25. Charles Reich, *The Greening of America* (New York: Random House, 1970), 192, 194, 196, 222, 152–153; Theodore Roszak, *The Making of a Counter Culture* (Garden City, N.Y.: Doubleday, 1969), 9, 49, 65.

26. Note Michael Harrington's view of the hippie movement as a democratization of Bohemia made into banality. "We Few, We Happy Few, We Bohemians," *Esquire* (Aug. 1972):164; Leonard Wolf, *Voices from the Love Generation* (Boston: Little, Brown, 1968), xxi.

27. Jerry Rubin, *Do It: Scenarios of a Revolution* (New York: Ballantine, 1970), 55; Bruce Pollack, *When Music Mattered: Rock in the 1960s* (New York: Holt, Rinehart, and Winston, 1984), 181–182; Edward Morgan, *The 60s Experience: Hard Lessons About Modern America* (Philadelphia: Temple University Press, 1991), 178–201.

28. Gordon Fish, "Students in Business: What Do They Think About It: Why?" *Vital Issues* (March 1969):1; "The Private World of the Class of '66," *Fortune* (Feb. 1966):130.

29. Reich, *The Greening of America*, 231; Rubin, *Do It*, 87.

30. Especially good on consumer rights is Vogel, *Fluctuating Fortunes*, chs. 1 and 7.

31. Ibid., 29, 39, 40, 93, 106–108. For conservative perspectives, see Paul Weaver, "Regulation, Social Policy and Class Conflict," *Public Interest* (Winter 1978):59; Irving Kristol, *Two Cheers for Capitalism* (New York: Basic, 1978), 27–28.

32. Erik Barnouw, *Tube of Plenty: The Evolution of American Television* (New York: Oxford University Press, 1975), 300–306.

33. "The Great Medicine Show," *Time* (Oct. 22, 1956):87–88; "New Crackdown on Commercials," *Business Week* (Dec. 19, 1959):72–73; "A Code of Ethics for Advertising," *Saturday Review* (June 9, 1962):47–48.

34. "Caveat Pre-emptor," *Saturday Review* (Jan. 9. 1971):37; Scott Ward, "Kid's TV-Marketers on the Hot Seat," *Harvard Business Review* (July 1972):16–28; Joseph Seldin, "The Saturday Morning Massacre," *Progressive* (Sept. 1974):50–52; Evelyn Kay, *The A.C.T. Guide to Children's Television,* rev. ed. (Boston: Beacon, 1979), 221–222; William Moody, *Children's Television: The Economics of Exploitation* (New Haven: Yale University Press, 1973), 83–116; Edward Palmer, *Children in the Cradle of Television* (Lexington, Mass.: Lexington Books, 1987), 32–36; Heather Hendershot, *Saturday Morning Censors: Television Regulation Before the V-Chip* (Durham: Duke University Press, 1998), ch. 3.

35. Robert Choate noted that 25 percent of Americans were overweight, often, he believed, because of bad childhood eating habits encouraged by advertising. He claimed that American children were invited 10 times per hour during kids' programming to eat sugared cereal or candy. Robert Choate, "The Sugar-Coated Children's Hour," *Nation* (Jan. 31, 1972):146–148.

36. Michael Pertschuk, *Revolt Against Regulation* (Berkeley: University of California Press, 1982), 12, 69–70; "The FTC Broadens Its Attack on Ads," *Business Week* (June 20, 1977):27–28.

37. Federal Trade Commission, *FTC Staff Report on Television Advertising to Children* (Washington, D.C.: U.S. Government Printing Office, 1978), 11, 20, 243, 267. See also F. E. Barcus, *Commercial Children's Television* (Newtonville, Mass.: Action for Children's Television, 1977).

38. Robert Weem, *Desegregating the Dollar: African American Consumerism in the Twentieth Century* (New York: New York University Press, 1998), ch. 3, citation on page 69.

39. Vogel, *Fluctuating Fortunes*, ch. 8. See also Thomas Edsall, *The New Politics of Inequality* (New York: Norton, 1984) and Thomas Ferguson and Joel Rogers, *Right Turn: The Decline of the Democrats and the Future of American Politics* (New York: Hill and Wang, 1986) on the resurgence of business in the 1970s.

40. Stephen Fox, *Mirror Makers* (New York: Morrow, 1984), 315–318; Kenneth Mason, "Revamping Saturday Morning Children's Television," *Vital Speeches of the Day* (Jan. 15, 1979):207; Michael Thorn, "Advertising," *Nation's Business* (Oct. 1979):85–88.

41. Gary Cross, *Kids' Stuff: Toys and the Changing World of American Childhood* (Cambridge: Harvard University Press, 1997), 185–186; Dale Kunkel and D. Roberts, "Young Minds and Marketplace Values: Issues in Children's Television Advertising," *Journal of Social Issues* 47(1991): 57–72; Vogel, *Fluctuating Fortunes*, 168.

42. Creighton, *Pretenders to the Throne*, 4–5, 98–104.

43. David Vogel, *National Styles of Regulation: Environmental Policy in Great*

Britain and the United States (Ithaca: Cornell University Press, 1986), 162–163, ch. 4. Note also Scheffer, *The Shaping of Environmentalism in America,* and especially Susan Strasser, *Waste and Want: A Social History of Trash* (New York: Metropolitan, 1999), ch. 7.

44. Lester Sobel, *Energy Crisis, 1969–73* (New York: Facts on File, 1974), 7; L. Sobel, *Energy Crisis, 1974–75* (New York: Facts on File, 1976), 51.

45. "How to Save Fuel at Home," *U.S. News and World Report* (Dec. 17, 1973):19–20; Martin Greenberger, *Caught Unawares: The Energy Decade in Retrospect* (Cambridge, England: Ballinger, 1983), 27.

46. Martin Melosi, *Coping with Abundance: Energy and Environment in Industrial America* (Philadelphia: Temple University Press, 1985), 280–285; David Nye, *Consuming Power* (Cambridge: MIT Press, 1998), 221, 235–238; Joel Darmstadter, Joy Dunkerlay, and Jack Alterman, *How Industrial Societies Use Energy* (Baltimore: Johns Hopkins University Press, 1977), 186.

47. Sobel, *Energy Crisis, 1974–75,* 97.

48. M. Glenn Abernathy, *The Carter Years* (New York: St. Martin's, 1984), 16–18; Melosi, *Coping with Abundance,* 293; Greenberger, *Caught Unawares,* 37–38.

49. Alan Wolfe, *America's Impasse: The Rise and Fall of the Politics of Growth* (New York: Pantheon, 1981), 11, 43, 57; George Will, "Who Put Morality in Politics?" *Newsweek* (Sept. 15, 1980):108.

50. Energy efficiencies due to technology, not conservation or reduced growth in consumption, accounted for an increase in energy use by only 10 percent in the two decades after 1973. Nye, *Consuming Power,* 235–238.

51. Warren Belasco, *Appetite for Change: How the Counterculture Took on the Food Industry, 1966–1988* (New York: Pantheon, 1989), 76, 43, 27, 47, 54, 55, 69; K. Melville, *Communes in the Counter Culture* (New York: Morrow, 1972), ch. 1.

52. Kenneth Keniston, *The Uncommitted: Alienated Youth in American Society* (New York: Harcourt, 1960), 227, 238, 285, 298.

53. Richard Flacks, *Youth and Social Change* (Chicago: University of Chicago Press, 1971), 17.

54. Barbara Ehrenreich, *Hearts of Men: American Dreams and the Flight from Commitment* (Garden City, N.Y.: Doubleday, 1983), chs. 5, 8, 9.

55. Jay Stevens, *Storming Heaven: LSD and the American Dream* (New York: Harper and Row, 1987), 368; Theodore Roszak, *Where the Wasteland Ends: Politics and Transcendence in Postindustrial Society* (Garden City, N.Y.: Doubleday, 1972), 259; Roszak, *The Making of a Counter Culture,* 1.

56. Rubin, *Do It,* 94; Reich, *The Greening of America,* 153; Jack Whalen and Richard Flacks, *Beyond the Barricades: The Sixties Generation Grows Up* (Philadelphia: Temple University Press, 1989), 270.

57. Reich, *The Greening of America*, 251, 357. Note also Todd Gitlin, "1968: The Two Cultures" in Michael Klein, ed., *An American Half-Century* (London: Pluto, 1994), 59–68.

58. Reich, *The Greening of America*, 379.

59. Christopher Lasch, *The Culture of Narcissism: American Life in an Age of Diminishing Expectations* (New York: Norton, 1979), 85; Jerry Rubin, *Growing (Up) at Thirty-Seven* (New York: M. Evans, 1976), 20–21, 116.

60. Frank, *The Conquest of Cool*, 11–20. See also Todd Gitlin, *The Sixties: Years of Hope, Days of Rage* (New York: Bantam, 1987), ch. 1, and Warren Susman, *Culture as History: The Transformation of American Society in the Twentieth Century* (New York: Pantheon, 1984), xxviii, xx.

61. "Meet Tomorrow's Customer," *Nation's Business* (June 1963):102–106.

62. "Powering the Boom: The Urge to Buy," *U.S. News and World Report* (Oct. 24, 1966):63–65; "Piling up More than Lumber," *Business Week* (Jan. 30, 1965):57–58; "Plenty of Credit for the Consumer," *Business Week* (June 21, 1969):23; Juliet Schor, *The Overworked American: The Unexpected Decline of Leisure in America* (New York: Basic, 1991), 107, ch. 5. See also John Robinson, Philip Converse, and Alexander Szalai, "Everyday Life in Twelve Countries," in A. Szalai, ed., *The Use of Time: Daily Activities of Urban and Suburban Populations in Twelve Countries* (The Hague: Mouton, 1972), 114.

63. Free agency, introduced into baseball in 1967, more than doubled average players' salaries in eight years by allowing veterans to offer their services to the highest-bidding team. By 1991, these players earned an average of one million dollars. But TV, not the Players' Association, made professional football players rich as telecast fees rose from $4.65 million in 1962 to $185 million in 1970. Stephen Fox, *Big Leagues* (New York: Morrow, 1994), 422, 424; Barnouw, *Tube of Plenty*, 347, 354; "TV Advertisers Load up on Buckshot," *Business Week* (April 8, 1967): 74–82.

64. "TV Ads: Shorter Pitches at Better Prospects," *Business Week* (Jan. 23, 1971):88–89; "How Will Television Feel After It Gives up Smoking?" *Fortune* (Jan. 1971):86–89; "Admen Suffer from Overkill," *Business Week* (Oct. 17, 1970):132, 137; U.S. Bureau of the Census, *Statistical Abstract of the United States* (Washington, D.C.: U.S. Government Printing Office, 1982), 566.

65. Lawrence Hughes, "Free Choice or Free TV?" *Saturday Review* (Feb. 22, 1958):39–66; "Why Advertisers Are Rushing to Cable TV," *Business Week* (Nov. 2, 1981):96.

66. E. B. Weiss, *Never on Sunday? A Study on Sunday Retailing* (New York: Doyle Dane Bernbach Inc., 1962) 22, 29, 30, 31, 82; "The Turn to Sunday Shopping," *U.S. News and World Report* (Jan. 5, 1970):7.

67. Sondra Vance and Roy Scott, *Wal-Mart: A History of Sam Walton's Retail Phenomenon* (New York: Twayne, 1994), 31–38, 44; William Davidson, "The Retail Life Cycle," *Harvard Business Review* (Nov.-Dec. 1976):89–96.

68. "Shopping Centers Grow into Shopping Cities," *Business Week* (Sept. 4, 1967):34–38; Burney Breckenfeld, "Downtown Has Fled to the Suburbs," *Fortune* (Oct. 1972):80–87, 158, 162; "How Shopping Malls are Changing Life in U.S.," *U.S. News and World Report* (June 18, 1973): 43–46; "Leisure in the Modern Marketplace," *Parks and Recreation* (Dec. 1976):8–11; Lathrop Douglass, "Tomorrow Omnicenters on the Landscape?" *Harvard Business Review* (March-April 1974):8–9.

69. Blumberg, *Inequality in an Age of Decline*, 71, 79; U.S. Bureau of the Census, *Statistical Abstract* (1982), 461.

70. Roger Geiger, "The College Curriculum and the Marketplace," *Change* (Nov./Dec 1980):17–23; "A Bleak Prospect for Colleges and Universities," *Center Magazine* (July-Aug. 1979):9–10; Eric Dye et. al., *The American Freshmen: Twenty-Five-Year Trends* (Los Angeles: UCLA, 1991) cited in Rodney Clapp, ed., *Consuming Passions* (Downers Grove, Ill.: InterVarsity, 1998), 53; "Universities are Turning Out Highly Skilled Barbarians," *U.S. News and World Report* (Nov. 10, 1980):57–58; "Courses That Lead to Jobs are Taking Over Campus," *U.S. News and World Report* (Dec. 15, 1975):50–51; "More Popular Than Dismal," *Time* (Nov. 26, 1973):113–114.

71. David Horowitz, *Fight Back! and Don't Get Ripped Off* (San Francisco: Harper & Row, 1979), 1, 11; David Hapgood, *The Screwing of the Average Man* (Garden City, N.Y.: Doubleday, 1974), 5, 8–11, 196.

72. Lasch, *The Culture of Narcissism*, 107.

73. Joseph Nocera, *A Piece of the Action: How the Middle Class Joined the Money Class* (New York: Simon and Schuster, 1994), 26, 33, 53, 57, 61; Lewis Mandell, *The Credit Card Industry: A History* (Boston: Twayne, 1990), 160, ch. 2.

74. Roger Munting, *An Economic and Social History of Gambling in Britain and the USA* (Manchester: Manchester University Press), 71–73.

75. Nocera, *A Piece of the Action*, 17; U.S. Bureau of the Census, *Statistical Abstract* (1982), 422.

76. Frank, *The Conquest of Cool*, 61, 63–67; VW Bus ad for 1963, VW Dasher ad for 1977, and Cadillac ad for 1974, Jane and Michael Stern, *Auto Ads* (New York: Random House, 1978), n.p.

77. Frank, *The Conquest of Cool*, 136, 131; Paul Leinberger and Bruce Tucker, *The New Individualists: The Generation After the Organization Man* (New York: HarperCollins, 1991), ch. 2; Peter Clecak, *America's Quest for the Ideal Self: Dissent and Self-Fulfillment in the '60s and '70s* (New York: Oxford Univesity Press, 1983),

6, 203; "TV's New Hard Sell," *Newsweek* (Feb. 2, 1976):64–65; Stephen Fox, *Mirror Makers* (New York: Morrow, 1984), 299.

78. Ernest Ditcher, *Handbook for Consumer Motivation* (New York: McGraw-Hill, 1964), 96–99; Frank, *The Conquest of Cool*, ch. 9, 215, 227.

79. David Riesman, *Thorstein Veblen, A Critical Interpretation* (New York: Scribner, 1953), 170–208; Britt, *The Spenders*, 66; John Brooks, *From Conspicuous Consumption to Parody Display* (Boston: Little, Brown, 1979), 25, 33, 68, 102, 215–216. Similarly Paul Fussell, *Class, A Guide Through the American Status System* (New York: Summit, 1983), 172 sees "class sinking"-with the rise in astrology columns in newspapers and a reduction of hops in beer.

80. Brooks, *From Conspicuous Consumption*, 176; Russell Lynes, *Snobs* (New York: Harper and Row, 1950), 17; Ehrenreich, *Fear of Falling*, 24, 26.

81. "When Too Much Is Not Enough," *Business Week* (Sept. 23, 1961):145–146.

82. Katona, *The Mass Consumption Society*, 257, 258; "Big Changes in Buying Habits," *U.S. News and World Report* (Feb. 6, 1961):72–75; U.S. Bureau of the Census, *Statistical Abstract* (1983), 241, 235, 422.

83. Arnold Mitchell, *The Nine American Lifestyles* (New York: Warner, 1983), ch. 1, 165, 169, 199.

84. Weems, *Desegregating the Dollar*, ch. 5, 90.

85. The mean age for first marriages for men rose from 22.2 years in 1960 to 23.3 in 1970 and 24.7 by 1980. The trend continued thereafter, reaching 26.7 years by 1998. For women the average age remained stable in the 1960s (rising from 20.3 to only 20.9). In the 1970s, the age at first marriage increased to 22 years and reached 25 years by 1998. Census Bureau estimates found on http://www.census.gov/population/socdemo/ms-la/tabms-2.txt.

86. U.S. Bureau of the Census, *Statistical Abstract* (1995), 73.

87. Irving Allen, "The Ideology of Dense Neighborhood Redevelopment," and Neil Smith and Michele LeFaivre, "A Class Analysis of Gentrification," in John Palen and Bruce London, eds., *Gentrification, Displacement, and Neighborhood Revitalization* (Albany, N.Y.: SUNY Press, 1984), 27–42, 43–64. See also C. S. Fischer, "Toward a Subcultural Theory of Urbanism," *American Journal of Sociology* 80(1975):1319–1341.

88. Packard, *The Waste Makers*, 31–32.

89. "Are Big Cars Doomed?" *U.S. News and World Report* (Dec. 21, 1973):320–325; "Keeping Cool at the Wheel," *Business Week* (July 13, 1963):32; "Where, Oh Where, Has My Little Car Gone?" *Popular Science* (Nov. 1963):53–54; "The Small Car Blues at General Motors," *Business Week* (March 16, 1974):76–79; "Password for '78: 'Downsize'," *Time* (Aug. 1, 1977):32.

90. Katona, *The Mass Consumption Society*, 24, 253; "Autos," *Time* (May 23,

1969):97; Gartman, *Auto Opium*, 200, 259; "Muscle with Hustle," *Time* (April 5, 1968):62; Leon Mandel, *American Cars* (New York: Stewart, Tabori, and Chang, 1982), 303, 308, 315; 1966 Ford Mustang ads in J. Walter Thompson Company, *Fifty Years of Better Ideas: Ford Advertising 1943–1993* (New York: J. Walter Thompson Company, 1993), n.p.; "The Jeepster Reborn," *Business Week* (Jan. 7, 1967):62–63; "Autos," *Time* (Nov. 11, 1966):98, 101; U.S. Bureau of the Census, *Statistical Abstract* (1982), 422.

91. Ibid., 12, 614.

92. Cecelia Tichi, *The Electronic Hearth: Creating an American Television Culture* (New York: Oxford University Press, 1991), 63, 70, 78.

93. "Hungry Generation Grows up," *Nation's Restaurant News* (Jan. 5, 1976):18 cited in Belasco, *Appetite for Change*, 205.

94. Scott Cohen, *Zap! The Rise and Fall of Atari* (New York: McGraw-Hill, 1984), 1–80; Richard Levy and Ronald Weingartner, *Inside Santa's Workshop* (New York: Holt, 1990), 63–65.

95. Ehrenreich, *Hearts of Men*, 18, 24, 29–32, 42–49, 90–93; Robert Lindner, *Must You Conform?* (New York: Rinehart, 1956).

96. Betty Friedan, *The Feminine Mystique* (New York: Norton, 1963), 255–256.

97. Ibid., chs. 10, 11; Ehrenreich, *Hearts of Men*, 110.

98. Caroline Bird, *The Two-Paycheck Marriage* (New York: Rawson Wade, 1979), xiii, 5, 11, 23–24, 33, 69, 86, 94, 97, 112.

99. Lynn Spigel, *Make Room for TV* (Chicago: University of Chicago Press, 1992), 42.

100. David Wells, "She Works Hard for the Money: Consumerism and the Movement of Housewives into Wage Work," Ph.D. diss., University of Southern California, 1994, 7–8, 120–124, 262.

101. "How the Old Age Market Looks," *Business Week* (Feb. 13, 1960):72–73; William Graebner, *A History of Retirement: The Meaning and Function of an American Institution, 1885–1920* (New Haven: Yale University Press, 1980), chs. 3–4; Henry Sheldon, "The Changing Demographic Profile," in Clark Tibbitts, ed., *Handbook of Social Gerontology* (Chicago: University of Chicago Press, 1960), 38.

102. "The First of the '30 and Outs'," *Business Week* (May 22, 1971):60; "The Early Retirement Time Bomb," *Nation's Business* (Feb. 1971):20–24; "The Growing Trend to Early Retirement," *Business Week* (Oct. 7, 1972):74–78; "The Big Move to Early Retirement," *Dun's Review* (Feb. 1973):37–39.

103. Max Kaplan, "The Uses of Leisure," in Tibbitts, *Handbook of Social Gerontology*, 407–443; Eugene Friedmann, Robert Havighurst, et al., *The Meaning of Work and Retirement* (Chicago: University of Chicago Press, 1954), 32–39, 187–194. See also W. Andrew Achenbaum, *Shades of Gray: Old Age, American Val-*

ues, and Federal Policies Since 1920 (Boston: Little, Brown, 1983), 20, ch. 4; Graebner, *A History of Retirement*, 227–240.

104. Michael Hunt et al., *Retirement Communities: An American Original* (New York: Haworth, 1984), 13–15; Stephen Golant, "Residential Concentrations of Future Elderly," *Gerontologist* 15(Feb. 1975): 16–17; "Choosing a Lifestyle," *U.S. News and World Report* (Feb. 26, 1979):59–61; "Working at a Life of Leisure," *Sports Illustrated* (Feb. 1, 1971):52–63; "New Life in Retirement Communities," *Business Week* (July 8, 1972):70–72; "For the Retired, a World All their Own," *Life* (May 15, 1970):45–54; Charles Longino, "The Comfortably Retired," *American Demographics* (June 1988):24–26; Charles Sargent, *Metro Arizona* (Scottsdale, Ariz.: Biffington Books, 1988), 132–136.

105. Patricia Gober, "The Retirement Community as a Geographical Phenomenon: The Case of Sun City, Arizona," *Journal of Geography* 84(Sept. – Oct. 1985): 190; "Choosing a Lifestyle," *U.S. News and World Report*, 59–61; and especially John Findlay, *Magic Lands: Western Cityscapes and American Culture After 1940* (Berkeley: University of California Press, 1992), ch. 4.

106. Charles Monaghan, "Editorial," *Retirement Living* (Dec. 1972), 4.

107. F. Gonzalez, "The Moppet Market," *The Reporter* (June 18, 1964):40–43; Stephen Kline, *Out of the Garden: Toys and Children's Culture in the Age of TV Marketing* (London: Verso, 1993), 174–208 especially.

108. Jerry Bowles, *Forever Hold Your Banners High* (Garden City, N.J.: Doubleday, 1976), 16–17 especially; Cy Schneider, *Children's Television: The Art, The Business, and How it Works* (New York: NTC Business Books, 1987), 23–37; Ruth Handler, *Dream Doll* (Stamford, Conn.: Longmeadow, 1994), chs. 4–5.

109. Anne Koopman, *Charles Lazarus: The Titan of Toys 'R' Us* (Ada, Okla.: Garret Educational Publications, 1992), 6, 32; Toy Manufacturers of America, *Toy Fact Book, 1986 Edition* (New York: TMA, 1986), 16.

110. Cross, *Kids' Stuff*, ch. 6 for bibliography.

6. MARKETS TRIUMPHANT, 1980–2000

1. Daniel Bell, *The Cultural Contradictions of Capitalism* (New York: Basic, 1976), 7, 21, 44–45, 55, 65, 67, 72, 79, 80.

2. Ibid., 232–236, 244.

3. Irving Kristol, *Two Cheers for Capitalism* (New York: Basic, 1978), x, 64–67, 250–254.

4. Ibid., 15, 16, 18, 35, 36, 46, 60, 61, 62.

5. Sidney Blumenthal, *The Rise of the Counter-Establishment* (New York: Times, 1986), 1–5, 75, 115, 119, 129; Alan Crawford, *Thunder on the Right: The "New Right" and the Politics of Resentment* (New York: Pantheon, 1980), 5–10; Haynes

Johnson, *Sleepwalking Through History: America in the Reagan Years* (New York: Norton, 1991), 221–227.

6. Barbara Ehrenreich, *Fear of Falling* (New York: Harper, 1985), 39, 41, 52–53, 166, 187–188 is insightful on this theme. See also George Gilder, *Sexual Suicide* (New York: Quadrangle, 1973).

7. Midge Decter, *Liberal Parents, Radical Children* (New York: Coward, Mc-Cann & Geoghegan, 1975), 32, 42, 47, 63, 141, 142.

8. "The New Right's TV Hit List," *Newsweek* (June 15, 1981):102–103.

9. Joan Robie, *Turmoil in the Toy Box* (Lancaster, Penn.: Starbruster, 1989), 18; Phil Phillips, *Saturday Morning Mind Control* (Nashville: Oliver-Nelson, 1991), 118–139.

10. Crawford, *Thunder on the Right*, 66, 70, 146–151.

11. *Washington Post*, June 5, 1983, A16, cited in Lloyd DeMause, *Reagan's America* (New York: Creative Roots, 1984), 6–7; Johnson, *Sleepwalking Through History*, 58–60; Rob Schieffer and Gary Gates, *The Acting President* (New York: Dutton, 1989), 68.

12. Philip Jenkins, *Synthetic Panics: The Symbolic Politics of Designer Drugs* (New York: New York University Press, 1999), ch. 5; Lionel Tiger, *The Pursuit of Pleasure* (New York: Little, Brown, 1992), 110–112.

13. Johnson, *Sleepwalking Through History*, 130, 99; Jude Wanniski, *The Way the World Works: How Economies Fail-and Succeed* (New York: Basic, 1978), 106; George Gilder, *Wealth and Poverty* (New York: Basic, 1981), xi, 14, 15, 29; Victor Canto, Douglas Joines, and Arthur Laffer, *Foundations of Supply-Side Economics* (New York: Academic Press, 1983).

14. Robert Kuttner, *Everything for Sale: The Virtues and Limits of Markets* (New York: Knopf, 1997), 44, 51 (for quotation). Note also Arthur Okun, *Equality and Efficiency: The Big Tradeoff* (Washington, D.C.: Brookings Institution, 1975) and the classic, George Stigler and Gary Becker, "De Gustibus Non Est Disputandum," *American Economic Review* 67(March 1977): 76–90.

15. Of course, conservatives continued throughout the 1950s to resist union-driven wage increases and social programs as inflationary. Alan Wolfe, *America's Impasse: The Rise and Fall of the Politics of Growth* (New York: Pantheon, 1981), 11, 19–24, 38, 43, 45, 47; Meg Jacobs, "The Politics of Purchasing Power: Political Economy, Consumption Politics, and American State-Building," Ph.D. diss., University of Virginia, 1998.

16. Robert Kuttner, *Revolt of the Haves: Tax Rebellions and Hard Times* (New York: Simon and Schuster, 1980), ch. 1; Mike Davis, *City of Quartz* (New York: Vintage, 1992), 181.

17. *U.S. News and World Report* (Sept. 21, 1981):cover; Vance Crain, "Reagan

to Keep Ship on Same Course," *Advertising Age* (Nov. 15, 1984):30 cited in Joseph Turow, *Breaking up America: Advertisers and the New Media World* (Chicago: University of Chicago Press, 1998), 40; Davis, *City of Quartz*, 7, 181.

18. Debora Silverman, *Selling Culture: Bloomingdales' Diana Vreeland and the New Aristocracy of Taste in Reagan's America* (New York: Pantheon, 1986), 5, 13, 18, 20, 43.

19. David Vogel, *National Styles of Regulation: Environmental Policy in Great Britain and the United States* (Ithaca: Cornell University Press, 1986), 24–25, 28, 146, 171, 173, 253, 279.

20. Quotation from *Washington Post*, May 24, 1981, L5; Colman McCarthy, "James Watt's 'Relaxing' Policy," *Washington Post*, Aug. 22, 1982, L13; Michael Kraft and Norman Vig, "Environmental Policy in the Reagan Presidency," *Political Science Quarterly* 99(Autumn 1984): 415–439; Schieffer and Gates, *Acting President*, 29, 152–154.

21. "FCC Won't Force Child Programs," *The Boston Globe*, Feb. 12, 1983, 35.

22. "Evangelist of the Marketplace," *Time* (Nov. 1, 1983):58; Dennis Swann, *The Retreat of the State* (Ann Arbor: University of Michigan Press, 1988), 179; "Fowler no Fan of Federal Pre-emption on Children's TV," *Broadcasting* (Feb. 14, 1983):85.

23. Michael Kinsley, "None Dare Call It Commercial," *Harper's* (March 1983):9; "The Commercialization of PBS," *Media and Marketing Decisions* (Oct. 1985):96; "Public TV Under Assault," *Time* (March 30, 1992):58; James Twitchell, *Adcult USA: The Triumph of Advertising in American Culture* (New York: Columbia University Press, 1996), 102.

24. Miller's policy sometimes backfired because it forced complainants to go to the courts and even the Better Business Bureau to seek redress for fraudulent commercial claims. This only increased advertisers' need to fight on multiple fronts. William MacLeod and Robert Rogowsky, "Consumer Protection at the FTC during the Reagan Administration," in Roger Meiners and Bruce Yandle, eds., *Regulation and the Reagan Era* (New York: Holmes & Meier, 1989), 71–88; "Deceptive Ads," *Business Week* (Dec. 2, 1985):136–137.

25. Children's Television Act of 1990, Publication L. No. 101–437, 101st Congress, 1st Sess. U.S. Congress, *Children's Television Hearing*, Subcommittee on Telecommunications and Finance, March 10, 1993, Serial No. 103–27, 10–19. Among the many sources on this theme, see "Pondering the Place of Children's TV," *Broadcasting* (June 22, 1987):40; "More Kidvid Capers," *Fortune* (Nov. 5, 1990):188; and "Marketing to Children," *Across the Board* (Nov. 1992):56–57.

26. "ACT Challenges Children's TV Rules," *Broadcasting* (May 20, 1991):62; "ACT Seeks Reimposition of Ad Guidelines," *Broadcasting* (Aug. 31, 1987):35–36;

Dale Kunkel, "Crafting Media Policy: The Genesis and Implications of the Children's Television Act of 1990," *American Behavioral Scientist* 35(1991): 81–202.

27. Gary Mucciaroni, *Reversals of Fortune: Public Policy and Private Interests* (Washington, D.C.: Brookings Institution, 1995), 33–35; Richard Rahn, "Supply-Side Success," in David Boaz, ed., *Assessing the Reagan Years* (Washington, D.C.: Cato Institute, 1988), 72–73; C. Eugene Steuerle, *The Tax Decade* (Washington, D.C.: Urban Institute Press, 1991), 1–14.

28. Tax adjustments from 1981 to 1984 (after inflation and bracket creep) meant an income tax increase of 28 percent for low-income families (earning under $10,000), a 1.1 percent drop for the group reporting $30–50,000, but a 15.1 percent decline for those earning over $200,000. Robert Lekachman, *Greed Is Not Enough* (New York: Pantheon, 1982), 35, 66.

29. Gary Burtless, "Trends in the Level and Distribution of U.S. Living Standards, 1973–1993," *Eastern Economic Journal* 22 (Summer 1993):271–290; Andrew Hacker, "Who They Are? The Upper Tail," *New York Times Magazine* (Nov. 19, 1995):70–71; Robert Frank, *Luxury Fever: Why Money Fails to Satisfy in an Era of Excess* (New York: Free Press, 1999), 33–34; Kevin Phillips, *Boiling Point: Republicans, Democrats, and the Decline of Middle-Class Prosperity* (New York: Random House, 1993), xix, 25, 28, 33.

30. Ibid., 133, 141, 143, 144.

31. Robert Frank and Philip Cook, *The Winner-Take-All Society* (New York: Free Press, 1995), 3–5, 80; Paul Krugman, "The Right, the Rich, and the Facts," *The American Prospect* 11(Fall 1992): 21.

32. "The New Hucksterism," *Business Week* (July 1, 1996):76–84; Twitchell, *Adcult USA*, 55; "Coping with the Ad Crunch," *Newsweek* (July 21, 1986):28–29; "Why TV Zappers Worry Ad Industry," *U.S. News and World Report* (Nov. 12, 1984):66–67; "In Search of Zap-Proof Commercials," *Fortune* (Jan. 23, 1985):68–70; and "Cramming More Ads into Prime-Time TV," *Business Week* (March 29, 1982):37–38.

33. "The New Hucksterism," 76–78; Twitchell, *Adcult USA*, 61.

34. Ibid., 104–105, 107; Steve McClellan, "Broadcasters, Cable: The Airing of the Green," *Broadcasting and Cable* (Oct. 25, 1993):24; James Woodhuysen, "The End of the Line," *Management Today* (July 1990):33; "HSN's Paxson," *Broadcasting* (Oct. 10, 1988):87; Mark Poirier, "Catalog TV," *Catalog Age* (Feb. 1994):1.

35. Jay Rosen, "Talk Show," *Channels of Communication* (March 1986):8; Johnson, *Sleepwalking Through History*, 155–161.

36. Ibid., 197; Jeffrey Hadden and Anson Shupe, *Televangelism: Power and Politics on God's Frontier* (New York: Holt, 1988), 52, 119, 128, 130, 213, 360.

37. "Commercial Break," *Utne Reader* (Jan./Feb. 1992):53–77; "Companies

Test 900 Numbers in Place of Toll-free Calls," *Direct* (Sept. 1991):28; Sandra Atchison, "Telemarketers Have the Consumer's Number," *Business Week* (June 22, 1987):118; Ian Volner, *Telemarketing* (Nov. 1992):14; "Nobody's Home," *Forbes* (July 22, 1991):304; Tom McNichol, "Dialing for Dollars," *Washington Post Magazine* (June 24, 1990):23.

38. Dale Kunkel, "From a Raised Eyebrow to a Turned Back: The FCC and Children's Product-Related Programming," *Journal of Communications* 38(4) (1988): 91; Nancy Carlsson-Paige and Diane Levin, "Saturday Morning Pushers," *Utne Reader* (Jan. 2, 1992):68–69.

39. " 'Star Wars' Summer Awaits Marketers," *Advertising Age* (April 11, 1983):1.

40. *Toy Fact Book* (New York: Toy Manufacturers of America, 1987), 15; "Licenses No Substitute for Sound Merchandising," *Playthings* (April 1984):62.

41. Carolyn Meinel, "Will Pac-Man Consume Our Nation's Youth?" *Technology Review* (May/June 1983):10–12; Nancy Needham, "The Impact of Video Games on American Youth," *Education Digest* (Feb. 1983):40–42; S. Blotnick, "From Pac-Man to G.I. Joe," *Forbes* (Aug. 13, 1984):138–139; Eugene Provenzo, "Video Games and the Emergence of Interactive Media for Children," in Shirley Steinberg and Joe Kincheloe, eds., *Kinderculture: The Corporate Construction of Childhood* (Bolder, Colo.: Westview, 1997), 102–113.

42. Paul Farhi, "Animation's New Battle Lines," *Washington Post*, Feb. 28, 1998, G1; Constance Hays, "A Star Is Licensed," *New York Times*, Nov. 21, 1997, D1.

43. Chris Goodrich, "Whittle's Classroom Gamble," *Publishers' Weekly* 239(Sept. 28, 1992): 550–553; Elaine Underwood, "Mall-Y Xmas!" *Brankweek* (Sept. 30, 1996):18; David Shenk, "The Pedagogy of Pasta Sauce," *Harper's Magazine* 291(Sept. 1995): 52; Joshua Levine, "TV in the Classroom," *Forbes* (Jan. 27, 1997):98. A thorough analysis is in Alex Molnar, *Giving Kids the Business* (Boulder, Colo.: Westview Press, 1996).

44. Russell Laczniak et al., "Mothers' Attitudes Toward 900-Number Advertising Directed at Children," *Journal of Public Policy and Marketing* 14(Spring 1995): 108–120.

45. Sandra Vance and Roy Scott, *Wal-Mart: A History of Sam Walton's Retail Phenomenon* (New York: Twayne, 1994), 43, 44, 57, 89, ch. 7; Vance Trimble, *Sam Walton* (New York: Dutton, 1990), 92, 102, 209, 216, 249; and Cynthia Time, "Wal-Mart vs. Main Street," *American Demographics* (June 1990):58.

46. "What Makes Price Club Fly?" *Supermarket Business Magazine* (May 1989):24; Twitchell, *Adcult USA*, 99; "Product Proliferation Seen as No. 1 Drag on Productivity," *Supermarket News* (April 16, 1984):1; "In-Store Focus: Auto Giant," *Automotive Marketing* (April 1990):1.

47. William Kowinski, "Endless Summer at the World's Biggest Shopping

Wonderland," *Smithsonian* (Dec. 1986):35–43; "The Mall's Last Hurrah," *Adweek* (June 22, 1992):20–23.

48. Mary Kay McCune, "Celebrating a Milestone at Mall of America," *Shopping Center World* (June 1997):1; "The Wholesale Success of Factory Outlet Malls," *Business Week* (Feb. 3, 1986):92–93; James Gilmore, "Welcome to the Experience Economy," *Harvard Business Review* (July/Aug. 1998):97–99.

49. Russell Belk, *Collecting in a Consumer Society* (New York: Routledge, 1995), ch. 5.

50. Dean MacCannell, *The Tourist: A New Theory of the Leisure Class* (New York: Schocken, 1976) is the classic interpretation. "Who We Are, Where We Go," *St. Petersburg Times*, Sept. 29, 1996, 1E; "Broadening the Mind into the Magic Kingdom," *The Economist* (March 23, 1991):20; "Hawaii Paradise Lost," *The Economist* (April 3, 1993):32; Bryan Farrell, *Hawaii: The Legend That Sells* (Honolulu: University Press of Hawaii, 1982); Valene Smith and William Eadington, eds., *Tourism Alternatives: Potentials and Problems in the Development of Tourism* (New York: Wiley, 1992), chs. 1, 2; "The Fall of Niagara Falls," *Business Week* (Sept. 6, 1993):30.

51. Of course, most American tourists did not travel too far from home. In 1994, out of a total of 53.8 million who traveled outside of the United States, nearly 16 million went to Mexico and 12 million to Canada while only 13 million ventured to Europe and just 4.8 million dared a trip to Asia. "Where We're Going," *Los Angeles Times*, Jan. 1, 1995, L3. "Careful Planning Guides Ecotourism Development in Punta Laguna," *Business Mexico* (Feb. 1993):15; "Seeing America First," *Business Week* (Sept 14, 1992):34; "Tourists Trek to the Icy Continent," *Business Week International* (Dec. 26, 1994):5; "International Travel Is Growing Rapidly," *Boston Globe*, Feb. 19, 1995, B2; "Senior Citizens: Up, Up, and Away," *Christian Science Monitor*, April 16, 1998, 9; "Leaves of Gold," *American Demographics* (Oct. 1990):4.

52. "Just the Facts: Taking Time Off," *Los Angeles Times*, June 14, 1998, L3; "Families Finding Weekend Great for Mini-Vacations," *Plain Dealer*, Jan. 28, 1996, 11G; "The New Vacation: Weekend at a Time," *New York Times*, March 14, 1990, C1.

53. David Tucker, *The Decline of Thrift in America* (Westport, Conn.: Praeger, 1991), 139–145; Frank, *Luxury Fever*, 46.

54. "Fighting the Urge to Splurge," *Time* (Dec. 14, 1987):58–61; Alfred Malabre, *Beyond Our Means: How America's Long Years of Debt, Deficits and Reckless Borrowing Now Threaten to Overwhelm Us* (New York: Random House, 1987), 7, 77; "Do Malls Seduce Shoppers?" *USA Today* (July 1987), 8–9.

55. Robert Goodman, *The Luck Business* (New York: Free Press, 1995), xi, 3, 10,

16, 19, 123, 131, 132; Richard McGowan, *State Lotteries and Legalized Gambling* (Westport, Conn.: Praeger, 1994), 15–16, 84.

56. Anne Rosenfeld, "Yuppie Be, Yuppie Buy," *Psychology Today* (Jan. 1987):16; "Upmarket Philosophy," *The Economist* (Dec. 26, 1992):91.

57. Paul Lyons, *New Left, New Right and the Legacy of the Sixties* (Philadelphia: Temple University Press, 1996), 160–177, 208.

58. Barbara Ehrenreich, *The Worst Years of Our Lives: Irreverent Notes from a Decade of Greed* (New York: Pantheon, 1991), 23–25, 35; Frank and Cook, *The Winner-Take-All Society*, 14–15.

59. Juliet Schor, *The Overspent American* (New York: Basic, 1998), 4, 14–16.

60. Eva Pomice, "Home Is Where the Market Is," *U.S. News and World Report* (Aug. 8, 1988):46; "Now, It's the Stay-at-Home Society," *U.S. News and World Report* (June 28, 1982):64; "A Man's Home Is his Castle," *Time* (May 23, 1988):8.

61. Steve Johnson, "Big Money and Big Houses," *Centre Daily Times*, Jan. 11, 1998, 1C; Susan Harte, "Today's Topic: Residential Real Estate," *Atlantic Journal*, Jan. 31, 1997, G2; Frank, *Luxury Fever*, 21.

62. Martin Campbell-Kelly and William Aspray, *Computer: A History of the Information Machine* (New York: Basic, 1996), 233–247, 253–288; Joel Shurkin, *Engines of the Mind: The Evolution of the Computer from Mainframes to Microprocessors* (New York: Norton, 1996), ch. 11; Randall E. Stross, *The Microsoft Way* (Reading, Mass.: Addison-Wesley, 1996), 63–66, 68–69.

63. Campbell-Kelly and Aspray, *Computer*, 280; "Dell Ships New 486 Lineup," *PC Week* (Dec. 7, 1992):17; "PC Makers Get Crunched," *Time* (April 5, 1999):50.

64. Turow, *Breaking up America*, 2, 6, 65–67; John Tebbel, *The American Magazine* (New York: Hawthorne, 1969), 234.

65. Turow, *Breaking up America*, 4, 106, 111; Marilyn Gardner, "TV Values: Bart's Bad Influence," *Christian Science Monitor*, Feb. 28, 1995, 4; Kathy Boccella, "Many Children Have Their Own TVs, Study Says," *Centre Daily Times*, Feb. 18, 1998, 3A.

66. Brian Caulfield, "Shift in Gears for Shopping Pioneer," *Internet World* (Feb. 2, 1998):1; Bob Tedeschi, "Can Shopping Networks Survive a Crowded Market?" *New York Times* (*Cybertimes*), Jan. 19, 1999, B10.

67. Turow, *Breaking up America*, 7.

68. Peter Clecak, *America's Quest for the Ideal Self: Dissent and Fulfillment in the 60s and 70s* (New York: Oxford University Press, 1983), 6, 17, 26; Paul Leinberger and Bruce Tucker, *The New Individualists: The Generation After the Organization Man* (New York: HarperCollins, 1991), 11, 15.

69. "On the Cutting Edge," *Progressive Grocer* (July 1995):2; Carl Frankel,

"Green Marketing," *American Demographics* (April 1992):34; "Rethinking the Supermarket Business," *Supermarket Business Magazine* (May 1987):45.

70. Rena Bartos, *The Moving Target: What Every Marketer Should Know About Women* (New York: Free Press, 1982), 40, 41, 153, 164–165, 181; Turow, *Breaking up America*, 43, 45, 64, 71. See also these classics: John Naisbitt, *Megatrends 2000* (New York: Morrow, 1990); Douglas Coupland, *Generation X: Tales for an Accelerated Culture* (New York: St. Martin's, 1991).

71. Schor, *The Overspent American*, 33, 38. Other treatments of the growing fragmentation of American culture are Arthur Schlesinger, Jr., *The Disuniting of America* (New York: Norton, 1992); Douglas Massey and Nancy Denton, *American Apartheid: Segregation and the Making of the Underclass* (Cambridge: Harvard University Press, 1993); Michael Lind, *The Next American Nation* (New York: Free Press, 1995); Peter Brimelow, *Alien Nation* (New York: Random House, 1995).

72. Evan McKenzie, *Privatopia: Homeowner Associations and the Rise of Residential Private Government* (New Haven: Yale University Press, 1994); Davis, *City of Quartz*, 223, 227–228, 244–250.

73. See Stephanie Coontz, *They Way We Never Were: American Families and the Nostalgia Trap* (New York: Basic, 1992) for this topic.

74. Of course, all this presumed that men worked outside and women inside the home, that men's earnings were sufficient to support wives and children, and that women devoted themselves to homemaking. But there was no necessary connection between the suburban weekend and any particular family order. For sources and greater detail, see Gary Cross, "The Suburban Weekend," in Roger Silverstone, ed., *Visions of Suburbia* (New York: Routledge, 1997), 108–131 and Witold Rybczynski, *Waiting for the Weekend* (New York: Penguin, 1992).

75. Home ownership returned to pre-1980s levels in the 1990s (reaching 65.7 percent by 1996), but its long rise (beginning in 1940 at 43.4 percent, reaching 62 percent by 1960) appears to have ended. Willem van Vliet, ed., *The Encyclopedia of Housing* (Thousand Oaks, Calif.: Sage, 1998), 428; U.S. Bureau of the Census, *Statistical Abstract of the United States* (1978), 793. Juliet Schor, *The Overworked American: The Unexpected Decline of Leisure in America* (New York: Basic, 1991), ch. 2 calculates that Americans worked an extra 163 hours or one month in 1989, compared to 1969. Schor estimates that women have borne the major brunt of this increase in paid work (305 extra hours) as compared to the 98 hours of men, even though when housework is included the increased burden is almost equal.

76. Susan Christopherson, "Trading Time for Consumption: The Failure of Working-Hours Reduction in the United States," in Karl Hinrichs, William Roche, and Carmen Sirianni, eds., *Working Time in Transition* (Philadelphia: Temple University Press, 1991), 171–187; Paul Flaim, "Work Schedules of Americans," *Monthly*

Labor Review 109(Nov. 1986): 3; Theodore Caplow et al., *Recent Social Trends in the United States, 1960–1990* (Montreal: McGill-Queens University Press, 1991), 127, 133; U.S. Bureau of the Census, *Statistical Abstract* (1997), 403.

77. Helen Presser, "Employment Schedules Among Dual-Earning Spouses," *American Sociological Review* 59(June 1994): 348–364.

78. This literature is discussed in Cynthia Negrey, *Gender, Time and Reduced Work* (Albany, N.Y.: SUNY Press, 1993), ch. 2. Note also Arlie Hochschild, *The Second Shift: Working Parents and the Revolution at Home* (New York: Viking, 1989).

79. Leinberger and Tucker, *The New Individualists*, 4–6, 311, 312.

80. Ibid., 327; Thomas Stanback, *The New Suburbanization: Challenge to the Central City* (Boulder, Colo.: Westview, 1991), ch. 4; Mark Baldassare, *Trouble in Paradise: The Suburban Transformation in America* (New York: Columbia University Press, 1986), 46–101.

81. Staffan Linder, *The Harried Leisure Class* (New York: Columbia University Press, 1970).

82. Presser, "Employment Schedules," 348–364; N. Paulson, "Change in Family Income Position: The Effect of Wife's Labor Force Participation," *Sociological Focus* 15(2)(1982): 77–91.

83. Jane Brooks, "More Businesses Now Staying Open All Night," *Sacramento Bee*, April 12, 1998, E2; Alan Patureau, "Night Owls Are Off on a Lark," *San Diego Union-Tribune*, Aug. 10, 1993, E3; "The 24-Hour Society," *Brand Strategy* (March 20, 1998):1.

7. AN AMBIGUOUS LEGACY

1. Note Philip Rieff, *The Triumph of the Therapeutic: Uses of Faith After Freud* (Chicago: University of Chicago Press, 1987), ch. 1; Peter Stearns, *The Battleground of Desire: The Struggle for Self-Control in Modern America* (New York: New York University Press, 1999), ch. 1.

2. David Myers, "Money and Misery," in Rodney Clapp, *The Consuming Passion: Christianity and the Consumer Culture* (Downers Grove, Ill.: InterVarsity, 1988), 60; Robert Frank, *Luxury Fever: Why Money Fails to Satisfy in an Era of Excess* (New York: Free Press, 1999), ch. 5; Robert Lane, "Friendship or Commodities? The Road Not Taken: Friendship, Consumerism, and Happiness," *Critical Review* 8(4)(1994): 521–554.

3. Todd Gitlin, *The Twilight of Common Dreams: Why America Is Wracked by Culture Wars* (New York: Holt, 1995), 86–87.

4. For a key figure in the cultural jeremiad, see Matthew Arnold, *Culture and Anarchy* (London: Macmillan, 1957), 44–46, 72, 99–107, 204.

5. Warren Susman, *Culture as History* (New York: Pantheon, 1984), 150–210; Henrik de Man, *The Psychology of Socialism* (New York: Holt, 1927), ch. 2.

6. Jackson Lears, *Fables of Abundance: A Cultural History of Advertising in America* (New York: Basic, 1994), 7, 32.

7. Fred Hirsch, *The Social Limits to Growth* (Cambridge: Harvard University Press, 1976), especially 1–11, 84, 91–92, 151–157, 172.

8. Robin Kelley, *Race Rebels: Culture, Politics, and the Black Working Class* (New York: Free Press, 1994), chs. 1, 2, 7, 8 especially. Note also Dick Hebdige, *Subculture: The Meaning of Style* (London: Methuen, 1979) and John Fiske, *Understanding Popular Culture* (Boston: Unwin Hyman, 1989).

9. James Twitchell, *Lead Us Into Temptation: The Triumph of American Materialism* (New York: Columbia University Press, 1999), chs. 1 and 8 especially; Stanley Lebergott, *Pursuing Happiness: American Consumers in the Twentieth Century* (Princeton: Princeton University Press, 1993), ch. 1.

10. Alan Durning, *How Much Is Enough? The Consumer Society and the Future of the Earth* (New York: Norton, 1992), 25, 54, 79, 127, 107. Similarly, Donella Meadows, Dennis Meadows, and Jorgen Randers, *Beyond the Limits* (Post Mills, Vt.: Chelsea Green, 1992) predict global collapse within three generations unless a sustainable global economy emerges. For a different view, see Mark Sagoff, "Do We Consume Too Much?" *Atlantic Monthly* 279(6)(June 1997): 80–96. Good analysis is provided in Neva Goodwin, Frank Ackerman, and David Kiron, eds., *The Consumer Society* (Washington, D.C.: Island Press, 1997), 269–366.

11. Kathy DeSalvo, "Ralph Nader Launches Commercial Alert," *Shoot* (Sept. 25, 1998):7; Adam Snyder, "Know Your Enemy: From Its Washington Base, The Center for the Study of Commercialism Is Plotting the Overthrow of America's Advertising System," *Inside Media* (Aug. 25, 1993):30; www.essential.org/alert; Michael Jacobson and Laurie Mazur, *Marketing Madness* (Boulder, Colo.: Westview, 1995); Corporate Accountability Research Group, *Ralph Nader Presents: Children First, a Parent's Guide to Fight Corporate Predators* (Washington, D.C.: Corporate Accountability Research Group, 1996).

12. Juliet Schor, *The Overspent American* (New York: Basic, 1998), 113; Amy Saltzman, *Downshifting: Reinventing Success on a Slower Track* (New York: Harper-Collins, 1991), 29, 37, 48, 51, 52; Joseph Dominquez and Vicki Robbin, *Your Money or Your Life* (New York: Viking, 1992).

13. "Affluenza" website: http://www.pbs.org/kcts/affluenza/. See also Cecile Andrews, *Circle of Simplicity* (New York: HarperCollins, 1997); Paul Wachtel, *The Poverty of Affluence* (Philadelphia: New Society, 1989); Thomas Naylor, William Willimon, and Magdalena Naylor, *The Search for Meaning* (Nashville:

Abingdon, 1994); Frank Levering and Wanda Urbanska, *Simple Living* (New York: Penguin, 1992). Websites of simple living groups include the following: Center for a New American Dream (www.newdream.org/index.html); Context Institute (www.context.org); The Simple Living Network (www.simpleliving.net); Overcoming Consumerism (www.hooked.net/users/verdant/index.htm); and Worldwatch Institute (www.worldwatch.org).

14. Durning, *How Much Is Enough?*, 108, 138.

15. We should add too that the decision of the "losers" to buy sports utility vehicles and 32-inch TVs went beyond commercial manipulation and escapism-and thus was far more difficult to root out than the Left ever had thought. Average wage earners also competed for position and often had fewer social contacts and educational resources than the rich with which to resist the emulation game. (And, of course, they had still other, more positive, reasons for wanting these things). Frank, *Luxury Fever*, 88, 279.

16. Robert Samuelson, *The Good Life and Its Discontents* (New York: Random House, 1995), xvii, 48, 50, 51, 142–145.

17. Michael Medved, *Hollywood vs. America* (New York: HarperCollins, 1992), 22, 31, 70, 154, 282, 287. Challenging Medved's view was the conservative media critic William Roanowski, who rejected Medved's "faith in the dynamics of the market" to restore family values. His more pessimistic and challenging message to a conservative religious audience was that consumer culture has shaped those family values and that a more active challenge to that culture is needed: "Family, schools and faith communities need to assert their presence in the cultural discourse about entertainment," and to do so in an informed and sophisticated manner. William Roanowski, *Pop Culture Wars* (Downers Grove, Ill.: InterVarsity, 1996), 309, 311, 337, 338.

18. Dana Mack, *The Assault on Parenthood: How Our Culture Undermines the Family* (New York: Simon and Schuster, 1997), 17, 19, 20, 24, 111. For examples of the "new class" presumably attacking parental rights, see Susan Forward and Craig Buck, *Toxic Parents* (New York: Bantam, 1990) and Alice Miller, *For Your Own Good: Hidden Cruelty in Child-Rearing and the Roots of Violence* (New York: Farrar, Straus, & Giroux, 1983).

19. Robert Bork, *Slouching Towards Gomorrah* (New York: Regan, 1996), 7, 13, 95, 126.

20. James Hunter, "The American Culture War," in Peter Berger, ed., *The Limits of Social Cohesion* (Boulder, Colo.: Westview, 1998), 1–29; James Hunter, *Culture War: The Struggle to Define America* (New York: Basic, 1991), 42–44; Roger Kimbal, *Tenured Radicals: How Politics Has Corrupted Our Higher Education* (New York: Harper and Row, 1990); William Bennett, *To Reclaim a Legacy: A*

Report on the Humanities in Higher Education (Washington, D.C.: National Endowment for the Humanities, 1984).

21. Michael Medved, *Saving Childhood: Protecting Our Children from the National Assault on Innocence* (New York: HarperCollins, 1998), 51, 53; Neil Postman, *The Disappearance of the Child* (New York: Dell, 1982), 46, 89–90. Note also Ron Goulardt, *The Assault on Childhood* (Los Angeles: Sherbourne, 1969), 1, 3, 15, 28–29; Marie Winn, *The Plug-In Drug* (New York: Penguin, 1978); David Elkin, *The Hurried Child* (Reading, Mass.: Addison-Wesley, 1988).

22. Mack, *The Assault on Parenthood*, 197, 198, 201; A. Hochschild, *The Second Shift* (New York: Viking, 1989); Sylvia Ann Hewlett and Cornel West, *The War Against Parents: What We Can Do for America's Beleaguered Moms and Dads* (Boston: Houghton Mifflin, 1998), chs. 3 and 5 especially.

23. William D. Montalbano, "Pope Warns of Global Ecological Crisis," *Los Angeles Times*, Dec. 6, 1989, A6; Rodney Clapp, "Why the Devil Takes Visa," *Christianity Today* (Oct. 7, 1996):18; Clapp, *The Consuming Passion*, 7, 13–14, 171–204. See also R. Laurence Moore, *Selling God: American Religion and the Marketplace of Culture* (New York: Oxford University Press, 1994).

24. Robert Kuttner, *Everything for Sale: Virtues and Limits of Markets* (New York: Knopf, 1997), 47, 351–356.

25. In 1995, the Food and Drug Administration (FDA) introduced new regulations that would ban cigarette vending machines (except in areas where minors were excluded), require that tobacco ads in magazines with a 15 percent under-18-year-old readership be in "black and white text only format," outlaw tobacco billboards within 1000 feet of a playground or school, and prevent cigarette logos from being used to publicize sponsorship of sporting or other cultural events. The point was to restrict children's access to tobacco and advertising exploitation of youths. A 1998 settlement between the tobacco companies and the states was costly even though that year a tough antitobacco tax failed in Congress. FDA, "Regulations Restricting the Sale and Distribution of Cigarettes and Smokeless Tobacco Products to Protect Children and Adolescents," *Federal Register*, Aug. 11, 1995, 41314–316 and 41351; Susan Nielsen, "Though It Coughs up Bucks, Big Tobacco Gets Last Yuks," *Seattle Times*, Nov. 6, 1998, B4; Michael Murphy, "Tobacco Accord Signed," *Arizona Republic*, Nov. 21, 1998, A1; "The Tobacco Bill," *New York Times*, June 18, 1998, A1.

26. Jackson Lears, "Reconsidering Abundance: A Plea for Ambiguity," in Susan Strasser, Charles McGovern, and Matthias Judt, eds., *Getting and Spending: European and American Consumer Societies in the Twentieth Century* (New York: Cambridge University Press, 1998), 449–466.